PENGUIN CLASSICS

THE PROMISED LAND

MARY ANTIN was born on June 13, 1881, in Polotzk, Russia, the daughter of Israel and Esther Weltman Antin. Her father emigrated to the United States in 1891, and three years later the mother followed with the four children, arriving in Boston on the *Polynesia* on May 8, 1894. The Antin family eventually settled on Arlington Street in Chelsea, where Mary and the younger siblings started to go to public school; her older sister had to work as a seamstress. Mary Antin's teacher brought about her first published work, the composition "Snow," in the journal *Primary Education.*

Shortly after the transatlantic voyage, Mary wrote a long and detailed account of it in Yiddish for her uncle. Later, the philanthropist Hattie Hecht introduced Antin to Philip Cowen and Israel Zangwill, and the result was the publication of an English adaptation of the letter in the *American Hebrew.* In 1899, it appeared as a book that misspelled the name of her hometown, *From Plotzk to Boston,* with a glowing introduction by Zangwill. The essayist Josephine Lazarus—Emma Lazarus's sister—reviewed the volume for the *Critic* and became friends with Antin, who had been admitted to the prestigious Boston Latin School for Girls. The family now lived in the Dover Street slum, and Mary associated with the South End Settlement House of Edward Everett Hale. She sat as a model for his daughter Ellen Day Hale, and became a member of the Natural History Club. There she met Amadeus William Grabau (1870–1946), who was finishing his doctoral work in geology and paleontology at Harvard. They were married in Boston on October 5, 1901, and soon took up residence in New York, where Grabau became a professor at Columbia University. Antin never finished Latin School, and therefore could only take a few college courses as a special student. Their daughter, Josephine Esther Grabau, Antin's only child, was born on November 21, 1907. Antin published short stories, essays, and her books *The Promised Land* (1912) and *They Who Knock at Our Gates* (1914), which together sold more than one hundred thousand copies. After some successful years as a writer and Progressive lecturer, Antin suffered a nervous breakdown, and she and Grabau separated. She lived in poor circumstances in later years, publishing little, and died on May 15, 1949. She is buried at Mount Pleasant Cemetery in Hawthorne, New York.

WERNER SOLLORS is Henry B. and Anne M. Cabot Professor of English and African American Studies at Harvard University. Recently he published *Ethnic Modernism* and co-edited with Greil Marcus *A New Literary History of America* (both with Harvard University Press).

MARY ANTIN, 1914

MARY ANTIN

The Promised Land

Introduction and Notes by
WERNER SOLLORS

PENGUIN BOOKS

PENGUIN BOOKS
Published by the Penguin Group
Penguin Group (USA) Inc., 375 Hudson Street, New York, New York 10014, U.S.A.
Penguin Group (Canada), 90 Eglinton Avenue East, Suite 700, Toronto,
Ontario, Canada M4P 2Y3 (a division of Pearson Penguin Canada Inc.)
Penguin Books Ltd, 80 Strand, London WC2R 0RL, England
Penguin Ireland, 25 St Stephen's Green, Dublin 2, Ireland (a division of Penguin Books Ltd)
Penguin Group (Australia), 250 Camberwell Road, Camberwell,
Victoria 3124, Australia (a division of Pearson Australia Group Pty Ltd)
Penguin Books India Pvt Ltd, 11 Community Centre, Panchsheel Park, New Delhi – 110 017, India
Penguin Group (NZ), 67 Apollo Drive, Rosedale, Auckland 0632,
New Zealand (a division of Pearson New Zealand Ltd)
Penguin Books (South Africa) (Pty) Ltd, 24 Sturdee Avenue,
Rosebank, Johannesburg 2196, South Africa

Penguin Books Ltd, Registered Offices:
80 Strand, London WC2R 0RL, England

First published in the United States of America by Houghton Mifflin Company 1912
Published with an introduction and notes by Werner Sollors in Penguin Books 1997
This edition with the addition of "Malinke's Atonement" and "The Lie" published 2012

1 3 5 7 9 10 8 6 4 2

Introduction and notes copyright © Werner Sollors, 1997
All rights reserved

LIBRARY OF CONGRESS CATALOGING IN PUBLICATION DATA
Antin, Mary, 1881–1949.
The promised land / Mary Antin ; introduction and notes by Werner Sollors.
p. cm.—(Penguin classics)
Includes bibliographical references.
ISBN 978-0-14-310677-7
1. Antin, Mary, 1881–1949.   2. Jews—United States—Biography.
3. Jews—Belarus—Polotsk—Biography.   4. Immigrants—United States—Biography.
I. Sollors, Werner.   II. Title.
E184.37.A58A3 2012
973'.04924—dc23   2012011363

Printed in the United States of America

CONTENTS

ILLUSTRATIONS

INTRODUCTION

After all everybody, that is everybody who writes is interested in living inside themselves in order to tell what is inside themselves. That is why writers have to have two countries, the one where they belong and the one in which they live really. The second one is romantic, it is separate from themselves, it is not real but it is really there.... Of course sometimes people discover their own country as if it were the other.

—Gertrude Stein

Among the many immigrant tales I've come across, there is one for which I feel a particular affection. This story was written at the beginning of the century, by a young woman named Mary Antin, and in certain details it so closely resembles my own, that its author seems to be some amusing poltergeist, come to show me that whatever belief in my own singularity I may possess is nothing more than a comical vanity. But this ancestress also makes me see how much, even in my maladaptations, I am a creature of my time—as she, in her adaptations, was a creature of hers.

—Eva Hoffman

REMEMBERING THE DEEP-RED DAHLIAS in a little garden behind her grandfather's house in Polotzk, Mary Antin confronts the cold fact that she has meanwhile been told that they were "not dahlias at all but poppies." This prompts her only to comment that she must insist on her dahlias if she wants to preserve the memory of the garden: "I have so long believed in them, that if I try to see *poppies* in those red masses over the wall, the whole garden crumbles away, and leaves me a gray blank. I have nothing against poppies. It is only that my illusion is more real to me than reality. And so do we often build our world on an error, and cry out that the universe is falling to pieces, if any one but lift a finger to replace the error by truth." *The Promised Land* is the self-conscious, and self-consciously literary, attempt to give aesthetic shape, in remarkably subtle language, to what remain recognizable as fragile memories, wrested from the threatening gray blank of oblivion and cold facts. Memories may fail to return when she invokes them, as the excellent American cherries she eats in a concentrated effort to bring back the taste of Russia cannot evoke in her the fragrant sweet remembrance of things past. She recognizes that this is not just a matter of the contrast between the two countries of her life: "And if I should return to Polotzk, and buy me a measure of cherries at a market stall, and pay for it with a Russian groschen, would the market woman be generous enough to throw in that haunting flavor? I fear I should find that the old species of cherry is extinct in Polotzk." On the other hand, memories may suddenly erupt, as when eating "ripe, red, American strawberries," she is shocked to experience, in breathless amazement, the "very flavor and aroma of some strawberries" she ate twenty years earlier. "I became a child again, and I positively ached with the pain of being so suddenly compressed to that small being. I wandered about Polotzk once more, with large questioning eyes; I rode the Atlantic in an emigrant ship; I took possession of the new world, my ears growing accustomed to a new language."

I. A CONFESSION THAT SPEAKS FOR THOUSANDS

"I was born, I have lived, and I have been made over. Is it not time to write my life's story? I am just as much out of the way as if I were dead, for I am absolutely other than the person whose story I have to tell. . . . My second birth was no less a birth because there was no distinct incarnation." Antin's memoir may have been inspired by St. Augustine's and Rousseau's confessions; and it has its Proustian moments. Yet it is not only the psychological chronicle of the spiritual development of a religious child who, propelled by her profound inquisitiveness, becomes a freethinking student of nature and a mature transcendentalist in examining her own growth for insights into the ways in which "Life Universal" may make itself manifest in "a little body." *The Promised Land* is also the sociological account of the transformation of an East European Jewish immigrant into an American citizen that blends introspective analysis and philosophical self-questioning with political commentary, biographical with historical narrative, and a sense of unusual individuality with a repeatedly staked claim of social representativeness.

Antin asks herself and the reader: "Should I be sitting here, chattering of my infantile adventures, if I did not know that I was speaking for thousands? Should you be sitting there, attending to my chatter, while the world's work waits, if you did not know that I spoke also for you? I might say 'you' or 'he' instead of 'I.'" Her metaphysical quest for a Life Universal beyond all pronouns, and for a unity of such apparent opposites as writer and reader, is made possible by her self-understanding as "typical." In her own terms, her spiritual "transfiguration" is also a sociological "transmutation," making her history "typical of many," and her life "a concrete illustration of a multitude of statistical facts." However unusual she may be, she feels that she can also speak for many who did not, or could not, write their own stories.

The central event that makes Antin's life "typical" is the fact that she is an immigrant who was "transplanted to the new soil" at a most impressionable age. As a good writer, she runs the whole gamut of metaphors that have been applied to the immigration experience: "All the processes of uprooting, transportation, replanting, acclimatization, and development took place in my own soul." She highlights how her "thoughts and conduct" were "typical of the attitude of the intelligent immigrant child toward American institutions." She stresses her young age at the time of emigration; her father's weak class position; the fact that she was a girl; her confrontation with a Gentile host society; and the disorganizing effect of immigration upon the family unit in which various men and women, parents and children, adjusted at different speeds: "The price that all of us paid for this disorganization of our family life has been levied on every immigrant Jewish household where the first generation clings to the traditions of the Old World, while the second generation leads the life of the New." She deplores the chaos in the family in which the old standards of conduct based on parental authority did not survive, and children were given "boundless liberty" as parents knew only that they desired them to "be like American children." "The result was that laxity of domestic organization, that inversion of normal relations which makes for friction, and which sometimes ends in breaking up a family that was formerly united and happy. This sad process of disintegration of home life may be observed in almost any immigrant family of our class and with our traditions and aspirations." Antin's spiritual journey is thus embedded in a set of social and historical circumstances.

Because of her psychological bent and introspective abilities, the exploration of her soul promises to produce an understanding of what one could call *the* immigrant psyche. "Thus everything impressed itself on my memory, and with double associations; for I was constantly referring my new world to the old for comparison, and the old to the new for elucidation." If she at times dissolves the distance between writer and reader, she may also locate in this emigrant doubleness the possibility of viewing herself as separate from the subject of her autobiography: "I could speak in the third person and not feel that I was masquerading. I can analyze my subject; I can reveal everything; for *she*, and not *I*, is my real heroine." If reader and writer can be described by the same pronouns, writer and "heroine" need different ones. Antin even proposed in a letter of July 19, 1911, to the editor of the *Atlantic Monthly*, Ellery Sedgwick, that she would use her own name only on the title page, but a "different name—Esther Altmann, as I have it—in the text" (MHS).* No wonder some modern readers (for example, Buelens and Zaborowska) have looked at Antin's autobiography as if it were a novel.

The writing of a novelistic autobiography (in which the narrator insists on dahlias even though they may have been poppies) and of a typical narrative that speaks for thousands had to be, to some extent, different projects—one separating "author" from "heroine," the other dissolving pronouns; one offering confessions of past individual transgressions, betrayals, and fears, and the other making pronouncements on collective processes; one summoning a specific riverbank on the Polota, a set of topographically precise train tracks in Boston, and such sites as the Chelsea school or the Boston Public Library, and the other speaking with the generalizing voice

* Abbreviations refer to the sources of Antin's unpublished materials and letters listed in "Suggestions for Further Reading," p. xlix.

of someone who gives the reader historical backgrounds, sociological rules, and even prophesies on the future—in short, who pronounces a "moral." One spoke with a voice that could yearn with
love and longing for any stage of the past, be it Russian or American; the other viewed life as a progressive saga transforming the
"heroine" into the "author" and an "alien" into a "citizen." She may
be speaking for thousands in one sense, but in another sense, her
story does not even resemble that of her own sister, a fact that is
highlighted by Antin in the text and in the frontispiece, a Russian
childhood photograph of herself ("Mashke") and her sister
("Fetchke") that is all the more remarkable since none of the eighteen photographs that illustrate the book (and that are reproduced
here together with three new illustrations) portrays the author cen-
trally (Bergland, 55).

One purpose of *The Promised Land* was to merge the different
narratives in order to offset a growing sense of American nativist
hostility to immigration by presenting the inwardness of a consciousness that underwent the transformation from foreign immigrant to American citizen successfully. Yet, as some readers have
noticed, the narratives did remain somewhat at odds despite all
efforts undertaken to fuse them, and at times the social rules we are
given do not seem to be supported by the evidence of the life (Buelens, 93–95).

Most significant is the way in which the autobiography struc-
tured a life in order to suggest individual growth along a progres-
sively conceived historical grid from the "mediæval" Pale of
settlement to the "modern" East Coast of the United States, making tyrannical Russia the problem and democratic America the
solution, patriarchal and rule-governed Judaism the question and a
form of flexible "Hebrew-Christian" universalism, open to men
and women, the fulfillment—in a quest that would be more fully
convincing if the same principle of skepticism with which Antin
approaches the Old World were also applied to the New. Had the
"heroine" of *The Promised Land*, indeed, been called "Esther
Altmann"—the first name evocative of the biblical figure, the surname meaning "old man" but also close to Antin's mother's maiden
name Weltman—this strategy would have further dramatized the
difference between the remembered subject and the remembering
author "Mary Antin." In any event, the contradictions between the

two narratives may have made it necessary for Antin to remember more dahlias than poppies.

Mary Antin's memoir movingly evokes the specific tastes of the past, recognizes that it takes history to make a Polotzk cheesecake, and concedes that the fragrance of childhood cherries may be lost even in the Russia of the author's later years. Thus it is all the more remarkable that even though her faith in America is expressed in such metaphors as "manna," no delight in foodways brightens the memories of her American years. She describes her father's American welcoming meal for the family, "ready to eat, without any cooking, from little tin cans that had printing all over them"; she praises Mr. Wilner's "thirst-producing, lemonade-selling, nickel-bringing potato chips" at the Revere Beach stand; and she mentions chewing candy and taking undetailed and sad "meals in the kitchen" of the gloomy Wheeler Street slum apartment. By far the most detailed American eating scene is the time when her Chelsea schoolteacher Miss Mary S. Dillingham invites her to tea, to Antin's "first entrance into a genuine American household," where she carefully follows others in the use of silverware only to get into unsuspected trouble when she realizes that the strange kind of meat she is offered is ham, the "unjewish," the forbidden food. Angry at her "inner man" for being afraid, she forces herself to eat more of the "pink piece of pig's flesh" than anyone else, but suffers such an agony that she is reminded of the story of the Spartan boy who let a stolen fox "consume his vitals" rather than let it be detected in his bosom. "Polotzk is not America," indeed, and perhaps eating does reveal more than talking. Mary Antin experienced her yearning for a merger of her two worlds not only as promise and bliss, but also as a deep threat. Taking "possession" (as she repeatedly puts it) of the New World was also like swallowing down undesirable food, in defense of principles but over the protests of her "inner man"; and what she took possession of was perceived by her also like a beast that would devour her entrails while she exerted heroic self-control. And what is all the more disturbing about this scene of suffering is that it takes place in the house of the very teacher who brought about Antin's first publication of the school composition "Snow" in the journal *Primary Education*, a "tattered copy" of which lies in Antin's lap as she is writing the chapter "Initiation." Is the stilling of her "hunger" for reading and writing, of which she repeatedly speaks, in any way connected with this painful, traumatic scene of kin betrayal and self-destruction?

The Promised Land is a text *between* worlds, in which Antin mediates one world to another; and though this mediation is undertaken in English, its sensitivity to the issues of switching languages and of translating one into another can be measured by the shrewd pronouncement near the end of the book: "I learned at least to think in English without an accent." It is also a text that shows, and to some extent idealizes, a developmental movement *from* one world *to* another; thus Antin writes: "That I who was born in the prison of the Pale should roam at will in the land of freedom was a marvel that it did me good to realize." And it is a book in which the conflict between worlds is experienced as an inner tension within one person, who may, at various times, regard different aspects of her self as the outer garment or the inner kernel; thus, in the introduction, she thinks of the "past" as "a heavy garment that clings to your limbs when you would run," whereas the ham-eating ritual had made her think of the "inner man" as a specifically Jewish conscience. This makes the book far more complicated than it might appear at first, far more than a pure progress narrative. As one perceptive reader put it, had Antin truly "abandoned her religious and cultural past without a trace of remorse, the book would not read as it does" (Rubin, 41). In fact, some of Antin's best writing is set in Polotzk rather than in the United States.

II. Lost in Translation?

Her first published short story, "Malinke's Atonement," included in this edition, is a case in point. It marked Antin's literary breakthrough that the *Atlantic Monthly* accepted her tale for publication in the September 1911 issue. The story recognizably belongs to Antin's "matter of Polotzk." At the center is a young girl whose name, Malinke, is closer to Antin's Russian nickname, Mashinke, than was her American name to Esther Altmann. (Formally named "Maryashe" after an aunt, Antin was called "Mashinke" or "Mashke" before becoming "Mary" in the United States.) Like the protagonist of *The Promised Land*, young Malinke has religious doubts. When Reb' Nossen rules that the miserable chicken in which the poor family had found a piece of wire was *tref*, so they would have to go hungry, Malinke reasons that the rav should not rob her of the chicken and tells her mother, Breine Henne, the lie that the verdict had been that the chicken was *kosher*. Yet, during the meal, she swallows a bone, sees this as a sign of God's judgment, sacrifices her best Sabbath outfit to God in the Dvina, and confesses everything—only to be taken on by Reb' Nossen as his first female student. At the end, she is looking forward to a great career as a scholar, proving to her and the reader that her brother Yösele was wrong in not believing that she could understand "the same as a boy" (327).

What is at issue in "Malinke's Atonement" is the reconciliation of precociousness, religious doubt, and rebellion with recognition and favoring by God and by the rav as father figures. (It is interesting that there is no father in the story, whereas in *The Promised Land*, Antin's father finds out that he "was not born to be a rav.") There is a fairy-tale quality in the wish to question and defy authority only to be more intimately accepted by it at the end. Meanwhile, Malinke also becomes a celebrity by "committing the sin of religious innovation" (319). The story combines two tones—social comedy of poverty that tends to thin out human beings just like chickens (Breine *Henne*) and religious seeking for meaning that has to overcome poverty and the typecasting of women as "ignorant." It is a story of "chutzpah rewarded," and the reader feels good about this because of the nerve of the young woman who has to overcome significant obstacles—and is always ready to bear the consequences of her actions. The moment at which she questions the rav's authority, "How did he know?" (311), is Malinke's "no, in thunder." Her problem and her salvation is "that tongue of hers" (327).

Connections with *The Promised Land* are manifold. The setting is Polotzk—where the Dvina is the site of a religious sacrifice based on a transcendental or antinomian encounter between Malinke and God—though the Polotzk rabbi also comes to resemble Antin's Boston mentor Edward Everett Hale in his warm paternal sponsoring of the poor young girl. The rav's character is not very clear as the result of his mysterious transformation from a bad, hasty judge to a great benefactor and educator who cares about the welfare of young girls. The theme of doubleness also resembles aspects of *The*

Promised Land. Thus Malinke feels very much beside herself: "The sense of guilt once more overwhelmed her. It seemed to her that she was not herself, but somebody else,—a monstrous, unclean creature, from whom the real Malinke shrank in horror" (318). And after her river sacrifice, she goes home in a state of exaltation: "She heard herself, in a voice not her own, communicate the great news to her mother: that she had atoned, by prayer and sacrifice, and all was well" (320). This sense of heightened self-consciousness to the extent of being outside oneself is developed more fully in the autobiography in which Antin famously declaims that she has been "made over." This is also the phrase Malinke's mother uses—only she refers to the problematic hen: "I can't make the creature over now" (302).

"Malinke's Atonement" brought about Antin's English-language strategies for representing a world that lived and thought in other linguistic media. Antin's choices became clear in an extensive exchange of letters with the famed editor Ellery Sedgwick that accompanied the process of taking the story through the editing and printing stages, in the course of which Sedgwick suggested cuts and "the elimination of Russian [sic] terms" (Sedgwick to Antin, June 6, 1911, MHS), prompting Antin to reduce the number but to insist on the continued presence of Yiddish and Hebrew words and to add some explanations in brackets—"*heder* [Hebrew school]"—or a footnote that annotates "*mikweh*" as "the ritual bath." This use of language was to become one of Antin's trademarks, growing into the shape of a full glossary in *The Promised Land*, inspired perhaps by Israel Zangwill. But as was also to be the case in her autobiography, some terms remain unexplained: thus, in "Malinke's Atonement," neither *Humesh* nor *Gemara* are translated.

Whereas her first book, *From Plotzk to Boston* (1899), had originated in a long Yiddish letter describing to her maternal uncle Moshe Hayyim Weltman her transatlantic voyage, and had been adapted and translated into English (with some editorial assistance) for a Jewish-American audience, writing for the *Atlantic Monthly* meant for Antin that she had to imagine an English-speaking Gentile reader and develop a new voice of linguistic and cultural mediation. It is obvious that in her first publication in the *Atlantic Monthly*, her implied reader is an American Christian, while the story is set in Jewish Russia.

That this language shift marked a corresponding reorientation from a readership that was imagined Jewish to an audience perceived to be Gentile is suggested in the small but telling detail of Herr Schidorsky, who helped the Antins when they needed to cross the Russian-German border en route from Polotzk to Boston. In the 1899 book that was translated from the Yiddish letter, Antin writes:

> I was aware of something like the sweet presence of angels in the persons of good Schidorsky and his family. Oh, that some knowledge of that gratitude might reach those for whom we felt it so keenly! We all felt it. But the deepest emotions are so hard to express. I thought of this as I lay awake a little while, and said to myself, thinking of our benefactor, that he was a Jew, a true "Son of Mercy."

Yet when Antin came to "summarize" her letter in English, in the "Exodus" chapter of *The Promised Land*, the message read somewhat differently: "The Schidorsky brothers were Jews, but it is not on that account that their name has been lovingly remembered for fifteen years in my family." It sounds as if the new self were talking back to her old self. Antin's change of language went along with a corresponding change in orientation; and by 1914, in the book *They Who Knock at Our Gates*, she could start an American sentence with the phrase "If we took our mission seriously,—as seriously, say, as the Jews take theirs ..."

Sedgwick's supportive advice was important for Antin's development of her voice of mediation; thanking him for his flattering praise, she specifically told him:

> I can never know just what my Malinke or my [Y]ösele looks like in your eyes, no matter how fully you express yourself; but what you and others have said does give me some idea of the figures my poor Jewish people make when standing detached from their overwhelming history, in the sight of a world that knows them but little. Malinke, to me, is Malinke with a thousand years of Jewish sorrows behind her, and a thousand years of empty hope. It is when I hear from my critics that I realize how little has been recorded of those centuries upon centuries. I must by all means bear in mind the fact that not all things are in the reader's mind which are in the author's. (Antin to Sedgwick, June 1, 1911, MHS)

Sedgwick directly reacted to the Polotzk materials in her autobiography when he wrote Antin on August 2, 1911, that he had "no doubt that Isaac (I mean Isaac of *Ivanhoe*) brought up Rebecca in much the same surroundings" (MHS), a reader response that suggests affinities between the protagonist of *The Promised Land* and a Jewish daughter's identity as portrayed in the prototypical Anglo-Saxon historical novel.

In *The Promised Land*, Antin at times imagines a more hostile Gentile reader (Wardlaw, 76, and Wasson, 55–56), whom she addresses as "my American friend" and tries to convince of her point:

> "The Jew peddler!" you say, and dismiss him from your premises and from your thoughts, never dreaming that the sordid drama of his days may have a moral that concerns you. . . . What if the cross-legged tailor is supporting a boy in college who is one day going to mend your state constitution for you? What if the ragpicker's daughters are hastening over the ocean to teach your children in the public schools?

This strategy of sometimes addressing, but almost always implying, a reader from the outside would have to have certain effects on the writing of such a text: the in-group reader would feel more excluded, and the role of the author as mediator would be strengthened. Yet in order to sustain this authority, the author, though striving for a "common language" that unites immigrant and American, also must keep a certain sense of language difference alive, which results in the inclusion of many non-English terms and of the glossary that legitimate the author as a translator of cultures.

The glossary appended to *The Promised Land* is an exceptionally detailed instance of a widespread strategy in ethnic writing. It establishes Antin as an authority who gives to the English-speaking non-Jewish reader a minimal vocabulary that replicates at least a small part of the semantic environment of her past. Yet even a casual glance at the glossary in relation to the text reveals that this is not a systematic instrument, but rather a professional documentation of Antin's proficiency in mediation. "Yiddish" is defined, but "Hebrew" is not; "earlocks" are entered into the glossary, but not "skull-cap" (which appears in the text on pages 59, 91). "Pale" (5) is not explained, nor is Tchistopol (54), nor "Vall" (68, 74) nor "Korpus" (66, 68), "Pentateuch" (92) or "*lehrer*" (94). The modern reader may also notice that the expected word "shtetl" appears neither in Antin's text nor in her glossary. Some expressions are not entered in the glossary but are explained only in the text: for example, "*zu refueh*" is followed by a parenthesis with the translation "to your good health" (79), "*wohl gelehrent*" with "well educated" (90), and "*'S gehert a kasse?*" with "Ever hear such a question?" (92)—but none of them makes it into the glossary. Other terms are overexplained in *The Promised Land*: e.g., "*mezuzah*" appears (93) with a footnote that is identical with the text of the glossary; or words are defined briefly in the text, but have longer accounts in the glossary.

Antin the mediator may also strike a completely different pose and explicitly and intentionally *refuse* to give a translation. Thus she used Yiddish phrases in book inscriptions she wrote into copies of *The Promised Land*, informing the American reader "that the first Jewish rag-and-bottle man who disturbs your afternoon nap may be called in as an interpreter" (Antin to Maud Howe Elliott, December 12, 1912, BUL). And in the published text she writes:

> My uncle Berl, for example, gave me the name of "Zukrochene Flum," which I am not going to translate because it is uncomplimentary.

Here, for a change, the Yiddish speaker has the advantage and is rewarded for having had to read many English doublings, explanations of familiar words. Associating Uncle Berl with an untranslated phrase may have all the more poignancy for Antin since he was also the man whom she credited with having preserved the original Yiddish letter of her transatlantic crossing that was the basis of Antin's first book. Antin had destroyed her own copy of the "oily, smelly" letter when the English version was published, finding, as she put it, her "chief satisfaction in tearing up the oil-stained (Yiddish) original, a sheet at a time"; but when she visited Vilna in 1910, Uncle Berl returned the letter to her, and she had it bound by her brother-in-law John F. Grabau as a souvenir of the twentieth anniversary of the Antins' landing in America (*Ms. Am. 178, BPL) (see page xxi).

The complexity of the language issue is compounded by Antin's own development from a Yiddish speaker and writer to the completely Anglophone author of *Atlantic Monthly* publications. One

PAGE FROM MARY ANTIN'S 1894 LETTER TO HER UNCLE
MOSHE HAYYIM WELTMAN, LATER TRANSLATED FREELY AS
FROM PLOTZK TO BOSTON (BPL MS. AM. 178)

biased account of the Antin household included the observation that Antin had to put her own daughter to sleep because the five-year-old child did not understand the Yiddish-speaking maids—Antin's cousins: "I asked 'Doesn't the child understand any Yiddish?' and she seemed shocked I should intimate such a thing. 'Oh! no—not a word'" (Pinzer, 165). Yet in a letter to Horace Kallen of December 6, 1916, she invited him to Scarsdale with the offer that her sister would make Hanukkah pancakes for him and added, in Hebrew lettering, "'latkes' to be exact" (Horace M. Kallen Papers, AJA, Cincinnati). On the other hand, she asked Ellery Sedgwick, of all people, to please check the correct plural of the word "Rav," for "Ravs" did not sound right (Antin to Sedgwick, July 19, 1911, MHS).

III. The Making of an American

Good editor that he was, Sedgwick inquired about publishing projects after "Malinke's Atonement," and Antin was fortunate in having recently finished a draft of her autobiography. For whatever it was that set free a remarkable welling up of her creative energies—whether it was the death of Josephine Lazarus in 1910, who had urged Antin to write an autobiography, had read the first chapters in manuscript, and to whom *The Promised Land* was ultimately dedicated; the passing away of Edward Everett Hale in the year before; the fact that Antin's daughter had turned two, and that Antin herself was approaching thirty and beginning to settle down in New York and Scarsdale; the experience of a memory-enhancing European trip that she was able to take in 1910 and that included a visit to her birthplace; or whether it was simply, as she put it, "the fullness of time"—the first half or so of the 1910s were Antin's truly golden years of literature. She finished her autobiography in a long-hand draft on Sunday, April 10, 1910, at 6 A.M.; it was divided into ten long chapters (five Russian and five American), and ended, as she states in the published introduction to *The Promised Land*, with the bold inscription "FINIS"—next to the hour and date of completion. In large stretches, the manuscript is close to the published version, but Antin also was to make some significant additions and excisions (see page xxiii).

He could count on every member
of the family to support him in this, because
for me. But who could foresee what
dire need might compel him, what bitter
distress, that would leave him no choice
but to send me to work at the soon as
I reached the legal age?

Here my father had an inspiration.
The legal age must be deferred in my
case! A simple matter, simply carried
out. When he filled out our school
certificates, he gave my age as eleven,
instead of thirteen. The blessed law of
compulsory education should protect
his darling for two years more.

Where is the stickler for concrete truth
who will call this act a fraud? "I will
tie my own hands," my father said; "I will
invoke the law against myself, that I
shall be prevented from spoiling the
promise that is within this child,
by any failure or weakness of mine."

This chapter is damaging confessions.
One more can make but little difference.
I want to state that I acquiesced in this
pious fraud without the least shrinking,
and used to give my age, I
told my lie without flinching. I understood my father's motives, and was willing
to benefit by his design. What was more.

Antin sent Sedgwick the manuscript of her as yet untitled autobiography, and Sedgwick read it within a month. He responded with enthusiasm, viewed it "without unfriendly reservation of any sort" as "more interesting and more significant than any description I know of Americans in the making," and proposed a series of five magazine installments from it for the *Atlantic Monthly*, and a subsequent book publication by his "friends and neighbors, Houghton, Mifflin Company . . . because the imprint of this company is on the whole the best in the United States" (Sedgwick to Antin, July 17, 1911, MHS). Antin accepted the offer, and a hectic revising process ensued, in the course of which Antin prepared the shortened excerpts for the magazine and the expanded book manuscript that ultimately rearranged materials so as to contain twenty rather than the original ten chapters. Sedgwick's careful reading called Antin's attention to divergent spellings—"Is it *cheder* or *heder*? . . . In your copy the word varies"—and often returned to the problem of proper names (Sedgwick to Antin, August 17, 1911, MHS). In the discussion of the headings of the various installments, the question of the title of the book also emerged. Antin noted that "Americans in the making" was a phrase that had come of itself to Sedgwick's pen, but that Jacob Riis's autobiography, *The Making of an American* (1901), had made such a title impossible for her (though it did not for Gertrude Stein, who published her novel *The Making of Americans* in 1925). Antin mentioned that she had always called the book "The Heir of the Ages"—a biblically inspired phrase, drawn from John Fiske, Tennyson, and Henry James (Kramer, 140–42), that she uses at the end of *The Promised Land*—but had been told that this "has not a challenging sound" (Antin to Sedgwick, July 30, 1911, MHS), and Sedgwick agreed, as he found that the phrase had "something of the taint of religiosity" (Sedgwick to Antin, August 2, 1911, MHS). She also related Alonzo Rothschild's opinion that the autobiography should concentrate only on the American years and be called, in quotation marks, "My Country"; though she liked that title, reminiscent as it was of Dr. Hale's novella "The Man Without a Country" (1863), she felt that leaving out the Russian part would "leave *me* out of the book" (Antin to Sedgwick, July 31, 1911, MHS). The title ultimately chosen seems to have come from one of the installment headings Antin suggested. The dust jacket carried the subtitle "The Autobiography of a Russian Immigrant."

The effect of the installments was that *Atlantic Monthly* readers—and readers of a "large number of Jewish periodicals" to whom Sedgwick sent copies together with the permission to reprint up to one third of each article—were not likely to forget the name Mary Antin from the time "Malinke's Atonement" appeared (and was, to Antin's delight, featured prominently) to the all-important event of the publication of *The Promised Land* on April 20, 1912.

The *New York Times Book Review* invited Antin to contribute an essay, and her interesting account "How I Wrote *The Promised Land*" is reprinted here. Antin may have written the first manuscript version of her autobiography spontaneously and by associations proceeding from certain clusters, as she states, but she definitely revised that first draft for publication, at times dramatically, and there are recorded instances of such revisions that throw a new light on the published text. There is in *The Promised Land* a recurrent theme of truth-telling—from Washington's famous quality in this respect to her comment: "The noble reader who never told a lie, or never confessed one, will be shocked at these revelations of my childish depravity." There is also the theme of Antin's complicated relationship toward her sister, for it was Fetchke's sacrifice that made Mashke's success possible. In the 1910 manuscript of the autobiography, these two strands were still intertwined and focused on a traumatic moment. Registering his children for school in Chelsea in 1894, Israel Antin realized that Fetchke, just fourteen, would have to work, Mashke, at thirteen, would have one year of compulsory school, and only the younger siblings would have more years to look forward to. Especially protective of Mashke, the father decided that "that should not be."

> If she only had three years, two years, it would give her time to show what was in her; and then—who knows? Brilliant pupils in the public schools attracted attention. Some way is found for them— scholarships, all sorts of openings. If she only had a chance!

Fortunately for Antin, the father had an inspiration:

> When he filled out our school certificates, he gave my age as eleven, instead of thirteen. The blessed law of compulsory education should protect his darling for two years more. (Ms. of autobiography, pp. 211 and 212, *Ms.H.6.3, BPL; see McGinity, 290–94)

The result of the lie was that Antin—who was small of stature—
had to pretend to be two years younger than she really was for
many years to come, but, unlike her sister, she did benefit from an
additional seven years of education.* And it is in this context that
she exonerates the father's action to someone addressed as "you,
noble reader" who "have probably never told a lie." The statement
published in *The Promised Land*, "My father has nothing to answer
for," probably makes fuller sense if one remembers the excised episode that may also account for the disparities concerning Antin's
age around the publication of *From Plotzk to Boston* (Zangwill, and
Lazarus, 317). It was an event important enough for Antin to go
back to it after cutting it out of *The Promised Land*. She wrote and
published in the *Atlantic Monthly* the short story "The Lie" (1913;
included in this edition), in which the American teacher, Miss
Ralston, finds out about the lie concerning the age of the sensitive
Russian immigrant child—here, however, turned into the *boy* David
Rudinsky, who comes down with a fever after lying about his age
when he tries on a Washington costume for a school pageant; he
confesses to the teacher in a letter: "I can't be George Washington
any more because I have lied to you. I must not tell you about what,
because you would blame somebody who did n't do wrong" (341).
This problem throws into question the whole project of assimilation if it is based on a lie, though in the story, the crisis gets resolved
through the teacher's benevolence that helps to bridge the two
worlds by the recognition of the heroism in the father's action. As
Antin wrote Randolph Bourne on August 11, 1913, *"Everything* I
write is autobiography" (CU). Her story does not completely
answer the gnawing question—the same question that emerges in
Henry Roth's *Call It Sleep*—what is the meaning of "my fathers" to
the immigrant child. Singing "Land where my fathers [or "our fod-
ders" in *Call It Sleep*] died" raises the issue of who the "father" is.
Can the "founding fathers" be the "fathers" of children whose real
fathers are visible reminders of their own foreignness, as they retain
exotic accents, fail in understanding, and conforming to, American codes, live in the worst neighborhoods, but ardently believe in

---

* In his biography of Antin and Grabau, Allan Mazur suggests that since Antin's rec-
ords before 1910 indicate 1883 as her year of birth, the story of her father's falsifying
her age may be a fiction.

America as something to which they can never belong, though their children or children's children might?

The Promised Land is an autobiography of twoness, of divisions, and of ways to overcome them. One half of the book is set in Russia and one half in America, and while Russia is divided into oppressed Jews and Russians, America is separated into immigrants and citizens. Tellingly, the first chapter opens with the sentence: "When I was a little girl, the world was divided into two parts." It is an autobiography of sites, external places that correspond to an inner topography according to which the world is divided. Jew is not Gentile, Polotzk is not America, Yiddish is not English, woman is not man, Dover Street is not Beacon Hill, and so forth. Hence there is also what she calls a "dual consciousness" and a juggling of differences within an individual soul that has "double associations."

Yet the world is also united, and *The Promised Land* explores and hovers on the images that suggest unity and that come from the realms of nature and scientific technology. Among these images are unifying rivers and bodies of water, from the Polota to the Atlantic, that hold special meaning for Antin as the "pilot on the seas of memory"; the Russian railroad tracks that went on and on like the Dvina, transcended boundaries, and made her wonder about the railway train—"Where did it come from, and whither did it fly, and how did it feel to be one of the faces at the windows?"; and the South Boston Bridge with its urban sublime of the "dim tangle of the railroad tracks below" that gave Antin a sense of the difficulty of finding her own "proper track." These images of connectedness also correspond to a sense of the self so that she can write of herself and those other immigrants she represents: "We are the strands of the cable that binds the Old World to the New." This mental topography leads to a sacralization of places as sites of mental contemplation: there are spaces of division ("Within the Pale"), and places of openness (the Boston Public Library), the closed slum and the open sky, or the mental enclosure of superstition and the openness of scholarship, education, and especially the science of naturalism. By and large, however, the "prison" of "Russia" remains associated with division, whereas "America" becomes for Antin the symbolic area of unity.

The book's sense of space is related to its sense of time: Polotzk is Antin's past, hence *the* past, the "middle ages," as opposed to

America's modernism; and having lived from "mediæval" Russian times to the "modern" period of America, Antin also takes on an ancient quality far beyond her own years, and it is no coincidence that she alludes to the Ancient Mariner and to the Wandering Jew in the introduction. As an imagined transatlantic cable, the immigrant Antin links worlds; as heir of the ages, she spans centuries— creating the effect of a modern epic self that is larger than life. Sedgwick appears to have been particularly intrigued by Antin's self-representation as a time traveler, and in his 1915 *American Magazine* portrait writes that "Mary Antin was twelve years old when she stepped out of the Old Testament into the new world."

This general frame does not prevent her from making many fresh and startling observations: thus she comments hauntingly on the fears of death the emigrants experienced when they were compelled to undergo disinfection in Germany, on their way to America; or she mentions "the American machine of perpetual motion," the rocking chair. And she distinguishes the horrifying crowd description of the Russian pogrom—"They attacked them with knives and clubs and scythes and axes, killed them or tortured them, and burned their houses"—from the elating and freeing crowd experience of the aspiring flaneur (or is it flaneuse?) in Chelsea: "A million threads of life and love and sorrow was the common street; and whether we would or not, we entangled ourselves in a common maze, without paying homage of a second glance to those who would some day master us; too dull to pick that face from out the crowd which one day would bend over us in love or pity or remorse."

The text offers numerous oppositionally presented parallels between the Old and the New Worlds. For example, the "red, and blue, and white" (the white literally torn from a poor man's shirt) symbolizes the hated Russian flag of tyranny that "must be shown from every house" or the owner faces arrest and fining; it was a source of shame to Jews, and even children hated it, for "as we had no country, so we had no flag to love." In America, however, a senator and an obscure child from the slums may "seal a democratic friendship based on the love of a common flag." Shouts like "Three cheers for the Red, White, and Blue!" are only to be expected in a country in which a Jewish immigrant schoolgirl can recite poems addressed to Washington. The nationalistic phrase appears at another

time in what may be the most troubling, though little-noticed episode in *The Promised Land*, meant to show the superiority of the
American system of justice. Antin's father has a "great, hulky colored boy" who had bullied Mary arrested and brought to court,
and Antin rejoices in the fairness of the process that pitted
"bearded" against "woolheaded Arlington Street." "The evil-doer
was actually punished, and not the victim, as might very easily happen in a similar case in Russia. 'Liberty and justice for all.' Three
cheers for the Red, White, and Blue!" It is remarkable that Antin
did not stop here to imagine any possible analogies between the
roles of Jews in the Pale and of blacks in turn-of-the-century America. Even though two of her photographs include blacks, and despite her description of the warm welcome the Antins received by
Boston blacks, this account may be marred by myopia.

In her analysis of assimilation, however, the book is remarkable,
not only in the detailed psychological observations that she makes
about her own development, but also in such less frequently noted
comments as the following about those Jews who, escaped from the
Pale, wished to "rid themselves, by one impatient effort, of every
strand of their ancient bonds" and though they had completely succeeded in their transformation they saw suddenly that in their
"inmost souls," there was still the image of their father's God. The
careful reader may be surprised by several such assessments in *The
Promised Land*. Whatever comment on the book's themes one may
propose, it is its literary *form* that has helped Antin find so many
readers. The book's stylistic range is impressive, from lyrical-
mystical to historical-descriptive, from analytical to evocative,
from understated to emphatic passages, and from somber notes to
the humor of sudden punch lines.

IV. Public Success and a Last Story of Polotzk

Antin's autobiography was exceptional among Jewish immigrant
writing in the United States by becoming a big popular success.
Reviews were often enthusiastic, and the book's welcoming reception in public libraries and educational institutions was especially
remarkable: Sedgwick had already noticed the interest of librarians
who are "in contact with a large number of foreign-born" when the

section "'My Country'" was published in the *Atlantic Monthly*, but in the summer of 1912, the *New York Sun* reported "the name of the books most called-for at the various libraries; and Mary Antin's name 'led all the rest'" (Pinzer, 149). *The Promised Land* was also published in special educational editions with teacher's manuals and student questions, and it was used as a public school civics class text "as late as 1949" (Yans, 23). It has been taken, together with Abraham Cahan's fiction, as the beginning of Jewish literature in America not only in scholarly works (Guttmann), but also in polemical essays that were sharply critical of Antin (Lewisohn); and it has inspired the writing of autobiographies by immigrants to the United States from many countries (Hoffman). The editors of the *Outlook* hardly overstated the case when they observed: "Few recent American books have made as strong an impression on the reading public as 'The Promised Land'"; and later that year, the editors cited some blurbs in their commentary:

> That book has made a great impression. Louis D. Brandeis says of it that "it teaches anew the blessings of freedom, and will enkindle the latent patriotism in many a native American." Rabbi Stephen S. Wise calls it "a human document of deep impressiveness."

The Dial reviewed it with a special focus on Antin's linguistic and aesthetic accomplishments: "She had to learn our language at an age when the acquisition of a new tongue is not exactly like the imbibing of mother's milk; and yet note the idiomatic raciness of her style." The reviewer also noted the photographs and the glossary. Arthur Guiterman was literally rhapsodic in *Life*: he wrote a rhymed review. Other newspapers and periodicals praised Antin's patriotism and compared her with Benjamin Franklin, Jacob Riis, Carl Schurz, Booker T. Washington, W. E. B. Du Bois, and James Weldon Johnson. Reviewers also accentuated the two aspects of the autobiography; for example, whereas the *Yale Review* criticized Antin's "programme of the extreme individualist" endangering her "to swing off into a hard and ruthless egoism," the *Literary Digest* viewed the book as "a treatise on sociology, of which education is the dominant feature." The *American Hebrew*, which had earlier published *From Plotzk to Boston*, found in Antin's new book "an orgy of egotism" and was repelled by the "I-I-I's" that, as Rudyard Kipling once said, "run throughout its paragraphs . . . like the telegraph poles on the side of a moving train." The *New York Times* stressed the "typical" quality of the narrative, deemed the American section too roseate but found that the Russian half of the book explained the reasons for it well. Many newspapers and periodicals from the Kansas City *Star* to the London *Daily Express*, and from *Hearst's Magazine* to the French *L'Écho Sioniste* printed long excerpts from *The Promised Land*. The scrapbook that Grabau kept for his wife ultimately included nearly two hundred press clippings from 1912 and 1913. A German translation appeared under the title *Vom Ghetto ins Land der Verheißung* (1914). With the success of her autobiography, Antin's career seemed made. When the manuscript of the autobiography had been completed, Sedgwick inquired about the prospect of Antin's returning to fiction, and she sent him other short fiction, including "The Amulet."

"The Amulet" is a fascinating story, perhaps Antin's best, and it is, again, set in Polotzk. Yankel falls in love with his second wife, Sorke (his first wife had died childless), and "among the pious Jews of their time romantic love was unknown, being constantly anticipated by a marriage-broker" (34). Yankel is often absent, and they both yearn for a child. During one of his business trips, he ends up at a rotten shanty of an inn where he meets the idiot child of the old woman who is the innkeeper. The child cannot speak, but wears an amulet, and when the woman tries to grab him, she ends up with his amulet in her hand and gives it to Yankel: it came from her sister and was a charm of a famous rabbi meant to cure childlessness. Yankel is happy and takes it to his "Sorcle," who sometime later becomes pregnant. Yankel is worried that he has not given the old woman enough money for the amulet; and he finds her waiting for him and asking him about the amulet. The old woman is worried because she forgot to tell Yankel the warning:

> "The Rebbe said that if it was twins, one of them would die," the woman said, chanting the words like a text of scripture; "if it was a boy, all would go well; if it was a girl, the mother might not live to nurse her." (38)

His love for Sorke is desperate, overshadowed by his new worry. "Sorele, you are more to me than the child I hope to have," he says

(39). The suspense is taken to the highest pitch, but the story ends happily when the Christian maid reports from the delivery: "Master, O master! it's a little boy, and the mistress will be well."

"The Amulet" showed Antin's literary talent at its peak, as the protosurrealist atmosphere is created and sustained with a sure hand. Such sentences as the following suggest her mastery: "The words came whistling out of her toothless mouth like the wind through a keyhole." This story, written by an author who was a near contemporary of Franz Kafka, raised high hopes for Antin's further production of metaphysically inspired, somewhat magical tales of Eastern Europe, following Sholem Aleichem and anticipating Isaac Bashevis Singer; yet while there is mention of an unpublished novella titled "The Apostate," too long for a short story, too short for a novel (Houghton Mifflin to Antin, March 18, 1920, HLHU), there is no evidence that Antin pursued her wish to tell her "untold" and beloved stories of Polotzk—even though Sedgwick had written her encouragingly that he was looking forward "with confidence" to her "returning to fiction" now that her autobiography would "pave the way for a better understanding of [her] tales of Jewish life." And she had responded: "My head is full of Polotzk. Can you feed your readers more Polotzk?" (Sedgwick to Antin, September 27, 1911, and Antin to Sedgwick, October 5, 1911, MHS).

V. "My Country," "Our Forefathers," and "Real Americans"

In a letter to Mary Austin (with whom she was sometimes confused), Antin explained that through a series of coincidences, she embarked upon the time-consuming career of a lecturer in 1913 and spoke on behalf of Progressive causes and in favor of immigrants (Antin to Austin, March 11, 1925, HHL). But judging by the pre-election essay, programmatically entitled, "A Woman to her Fellow Citizens," that she published in the preceding year, she was already fully engaged in a political career by November of 1912. There Antin sounds a strongly Progressive note but also shows a moderate feminist side, claiming her right as "woman" and as "immigrant" to speak as a "citizen":

I am not a suffragist, but I wish I had a vote just this once, I am very jealous for the reputation of these States. I want America to be the leading nation of this age in respect to justice and humanity. All I have of reason and instinct tells me that the first step towards putting this country in advance of other nations is to send a Progressive President to the White House. That is why I wish I had a vote. . . . If Jane Addams says that Roosevelt stands for righteousness, I know that he stands for righteousness. . . . Recently my fellow-citizens . . . have paid me the compliment of listening to what I had to say concerning America as I found it, when I came here an alien, eighteen years ago. If in these exciting days they can recall what my story was about, they will admit that I am not unqualified to form an opinion on the immigrant problem. . . . It is possible to send the immigrant where additional population would be welcome. It is possible to spare him some of the sufferings of transition that undermine his mental and moral strength, and so lessen his value as a citizen. It is possible to hasten his assimilation, for his own and for the country's good. The restrictionists could afford to hold their peace while the Government tries out a logical method of dealing with the immigrant. It is hardly fair to call immigration a burden before a consistent National effort has been made to turn it into a resource. I call the attention of all naturalized citizens to the fact that the Progressive party is the only one that has any idea of what is due to the immigrant. (485–86)

It is obvious how closely related these feelings were to her autobiographic writings, yet despite her use of Emerson ("That false prudence which dotes on health and wealth is the butt and merriment of heroism") in the course of the essay (as well as her quoting of Hale), the psychological and literary side of her was now being subjugated to that of the political activist.

Though never of sturdy health, she traveled extensively, and lectured on such topics as "The Responsibility of American Citizenship," "The Civic Education of the Immigrant," "The Public School as a Test of American Faith," "Jewish Life in the Pale: A Lesson for Americans," or "The Zionist Movement." Traveling under the management of the Boston agency The Players was quite remunerative — as she stated, she made "from six to ten thousand dollars a season" — but it was also exhausting (Antin to Thomas A. Watson, September 7, 1917, *Ms.D.1.3 v. 12 [46], BPL). Rabbi Abraham Cronbach remembered meeting Antin in 1915, when she was "the most talked-of writer — if not the most talked-of woman — in America. At the height of her celebrity she traveled from city to city, addressing large and enraptured audiences" (Cronbach, 40). In a retrospective essay, "House of the One Father," Antin states that she always worked from a few note cards rather than reading from finished manuscripts ("I always spoke *ex tempore* from the barest captions"), which can be particularly tiring and stressful for lecturers.

However, she did also write down her political sentiments and publish them in such journals as *Outlook*, in which her rather disappointing vignette, "First Aid to the Alien," had appeared, and *American Magazine*, in which Sedgwick had chosen to portray her and to which she then contributed a series of essays that became her last book, *They Who Knock at Our Gates: A Complete Gospel of Immigration*, again published by Houghton Mifflin Company in 1914. Illustrated by Joseph Stella—the Italian immigrant of the stage before he took the modernist turn toward his famous Brooklyn Bridge images—the book presents Mary Antin the Progressive who makes her plea for the immigrant and against immigration restriction and articulates what Orm Øverland has called a "home-making myth," in her case, the wish for a double descent line that would merge her two worlds into one: she stresses that American democracy "is derived from Hebrew sources, as the Psalm-singing founders of New England would be the first to acknowledge," she imagines modern refugees as reenacting, and even surpassing, the history "of the Mayflower troop," and she teased (and probably shocked) some American patriots by claiming that the "Minutemen at Concord Bridge defied a bully; the rioters at St. Petersburg challenged a tiger." Antin, who supported Emma Lazarus's reading of the Statue of Liberty as a symbol of welcome to immigrants (*The Promised Land* as well as *They Who Knock* featured the Statue on the book covers), also offered a mild correction to the ambiguous phrase "wretched refuse" from Lazarus's poem "The New Colossus," for Antin found "convincing proof that what we get in the steerage is not the refuse but the sinew and bone of all the nations" (62–63), a statement that was particularly emphasized by Stella's heroic immigrant portrait that served as the book's frontispiece: "THE SINEW AND BONE OF ALL THE NATIONS."

Antin's America was "not Polotzk" but also an extension of Polotzk. It is for this reason that "a special note" ran through her patriotic

Washington poem that, as she writes in *The Promised Land*, "only Israel Rubinstein and Beckie Aronovitch," her Jewish classmates, "could have fully understood" (see Zaborowska, 61). Antin's home-making myth thus expounded the dual hypothesis that the United States was both different from, and deeply interconnected with, her country of origin—and therefore also a cosmopolitan model nation.

What Antin argued in her autobiography and her lectures constituted in the eyes of some, of course, an erosion of the word "American." As that word was increasingly claimed, or "usurped," by "aliens," alternative terms were launched such as "native Americans," "100% Americans," "only Americans," "real Americans," or "American-Americans." The New Englander Barrett Wendell, for example, who was among the first professors of English to teach American literature at Harvard University, wrote in a letter of 1917, probably in response to *They Who Knock at Our Gates*, that Antin "has developed an irritating habit of describing herself and her people as Americans, in distinction from such folks as Edith [Wendell's wife] and me, who have been here for three hundred years" (Howe, 282). For Wendell—whose conceit of epic longevity was more sedentary than Antin's—being "American" specifically meant *not* being "Hebrew" or "Ethiopian." Yet Wendell, like Mary Antin, also stressed the connection between Puritans and Jews, a belief he anchored in the Old Testament, and perhaps believed even in an actual kinship.

Wendell's letter furthermore suggests Antin's nerve in coolly addressing Brahmins as if they were insufficiently "American":

> The Antins live in Dorchester now. When I mentioned to Mary that my mother's people once lived there, she was of opinion that their departure had proved them not "really American." Yet she stays honest, genuine, aspiring and, though no longer a prodigy, she is a woman not only of intelligence but of admirable personal quality. (Howe, 282, and Lang, 104–5)

Antin amusingly turned the tables on "real Americans," but she may actually have looked at emigration and relocation as poverty-caused uprootings, and therefore yearned for residential stability—which is why, in *The Promised Land*, she could speak of her "exile from Crescent Beach," or, in a later letter that will be of concern again here, of her "exile from Scarsdale" (Antin to Watson, September 11, 1920, *Ms.D.1.3 v. 12 [46], BPL).

Wendell articulated his opinion of Antin in a personal letter to an English friend. Yet the provocation embodied by Antin's stance also led to a more public debate about the nature of "America" and the question of just *who* was entitled to call it "our country" or to view Pilgrims and Revolutionaries as ancestors. Whereas some native-born liberals praised Antin for her "admiration" of America (Beard, 308), and some immigrant readers found her "gratitude" toward her new country disloyal (Granich), the conservative journalist Agnes Repplier was among those Americans who were troubled by Antin's presumptuousness in calling the Pilgrim fathers "kindly, but confusedly, . . . our forefathers," as well as by her critical attitude. Repplier expressed her wartime fear of a disunited country in which, for example, German-Americans would now fight the battle of Germany in the American ballot, and argued pointedly that no other nation cherishes the melting-pot illusion, for "an Englishman knows that a Russian Jew cannot in five years, or in twenty-five years, become English" (Repplier, 226–27, 213, 202).

It must have been particularly troubling for Antin to find Repplier's sentiment on the pages of "her" *Atlantic Monthly*, edited by "her" editor, Ellery Sedgwick, a man with whom she corresponded as late as 1937. Repplier seemed to resent Antin, and even invoked the pluralist philosopher Horace Kallen (one of Wendell's Jewish students) in order to support her dislike of "Mrs. Amadeus Grabau," alluding publicly to the fact that Antin had married an "American." Kallen, who was one of Antin's correspondents and considered himself her friend, partly adopted Antin's argument and compared Polish immigrants with the Pilgrims when he wrote: "The urge that carries [the Poles] in such numbers to America is not so unlike that which carried the pilgrim fathers"; yet in his antiassimilationist foundation of what he came to call "cultural pluralism," he also criticized Antin for being "intermarried, 'assimilated' even in religion, and more excessively, self-consciously flatteringly American than the Americans" (Kallen, 106, 86). Yet it was assimilation, full American identity, even if adopted unilaterally by declaration of will rather than by birth or easy acceptance from old-stock Americans, that entitled Antin to criticize her adopted "promised land"—or to praise it for something that it would first have to become by fully including people like her.

The radical Columbia University intellectual and culture critic Randolph Bourne saw the paradox, in his famous essay of 1916, programmatically entitled "Trans-National America," that "hard-hearted old Brahmins" could be "virtuously indignant at the spectacle of the immigrant refusing to be melted, while they jeer at patriots like Mary Antin who write about 'our forefathers'" (Bourne, 249). Ellery Sedgwick criticized Bourne and wrote him: "You speak . . . as though the last immigrant should have as great an effect upon the determination of our history as the first band of Englishmen." For Sedgwick, the United States "was created by English instinct and dedicated to the Anglo-Saxon ideal," and Bourne's essay was thus simply a "radical and 'unpatriotic' paper"—though he did publish it in the *Atlantic Monthly* (Sedgwick to Bourne, March 30, 1916, CU, and Bender, 247–48).

In the course of Bourne's essay, he entered a dialogue with Antin, who had let the American teacher tell David Rudinsky in the story "The Lie": "Every ship that brings your people from Russia and other countries where they are ill-treated is a *Mayflower*." Bourne amended Antin and argued that "our foreign-born" did not come upon "other Mayflowers, but upon a 'Maiblume,' a 'Fleur du mai,' a 'Fior di Maggio,' a 'Majblomst.'" Bourne opposed the English orientation in American culture (that Antin had come to love) and the requirement that newcomers shed their cultural, religious, or linguistic pasts, and advocated the new ideal of "dual citizenship," both for immigrants who came to the United States and for the increasing number of internationally oriented individuals who, like American expatriates in France, were born in one country but lived in another.

Yet Bourne's pluralism also alienated radical young intellectuals like him from people—except insofar as they belonged to distinct ethnic groups (Higham, 25–29). Thus he expresses his disdain for assimilation sharply:

> It is not the Jew who sticks proudly to the faith of his fathers and boasts of that venerable culture of his who is dangerous to America, but the Jew who has lost the Jewish fire and become a mere elementary, grasping animal. (Bourne, 254)

Again it must have been hard for Antin to find a friend so insensitive toward the position she had presented. She writes in *The Promised Land*, explicitly alluding to Hale's "Man Without a Country," that in Russia, Jews had been "a people without a country," making the great love of "a little Jewish girl from Polotzk" for "her new country" all the more understandable and genuine. (The allusion to Hale also evokes the possibility of reading "the people without a country" as meaning "apostates to Russia." Did Antin wish to imagine Jews in analogy to Philip Nolan of Hale's novella, who had famously expressed the wish that he "may never hear of the United States again"?) Bourne echoed Antin's phrase when he deplored the emergence of assimilated "hordes of men and women without a spiritual country, cultural outlaws without taste, without standards but those of the mob"—but in the context of a passage that reserves animal imagery for the assimilated and employs the nativist term "hordes" to describe them. Bourne's transnationalism preferred stable ethnic identities based on fixed national origins, a dilemma of many pluralistic models of American culture from the 1920s to the age of "multiculturalism." Antin's adoption of assimilation—anathema to Jewish radicals like Mike Gold or Harry Salpeter—was thus also as controversial to the hostile Repplier on the restrictionist right as to the friendly Bourne on the pluralist left. Neither provided much room for an assimilating immigrant who claimed an American identity and the full rights of a citizen.

Could people who were not born Americans become Americans? (Michaels, 122). This question, that the rising pluralism of the 1920s came to resolve more and more negatively, was boldly and unequivocally answered with a yes by Mary Antin, whose autobiography therefore constituted not only a success story but also a provocation. The patriotism of much of her writing was connected with an egalitarian hope. Yet it was a hope that was to be dashed; and the big crisis for Antin came with World War I.

VI. The Promised Land of Evolution and Exile from Scarsdale

At their house on Cooper Road in Scarsdale, Mary Antin and her husband, Amadeus William Grabau, had a rich social life during her short golden years in literature and in public life that had started with the publication of "Malinke's Atonement." Always a good correspondent who mentioned letter-writing repeatedly in *The Promised Land*, Antin exchanged letters with Theodore Roosevelt, Horace Kallen, and the literary critic Van Wyck Brooks, and wrote especially lengthy and revealing epistles to her friend and legal helper Thomas Augustus Watson and to the writer Mary Austin. Antin entertained such diverse figures as Randolph Bourne (with whom she also corresponded), Rabbi Abraham Cronbach (another correspondent who later published a warm memoir of Antin), and (her profession unknown to Antin) the former prostitute Maimie Pinzer, who wrote an exhaustively detailed, sharp, and somewhat mean-spiritedly cutting account of her visit to Antin's house in a letter to Fanny Howe. The Grabaus' circle included writers, artists, scientists, rabbis and ministers, Christians and Zionists.

Though both Antin and Grabau were very busy professionally, their relationship, a Gentile-Christian marriage of a native American Lutheran of German ancestry and a naturalized American freethinker of East European Jewish origins, seems to have been very harmonious. Thus Antin referred to her husband—who was eleven or, if Mazur is right, thirteen years her senior—as her "counselor and guardian" (Antin to Sedgwick, August 13, 1911, MHS), and wrote that he "followed my public career with the same affectionate pride—a pride almost paternal in its intensity—just as he had watched my literary beginnings. It was he who collected volumes of newspaper clippings about me and my doings" (Antin to Austin, March 11, 1925, HHL). The war made an end to all of that:

> When, in 1914, my lover-husband turned into a dreadful hostile stranger who terrorized the household and scandalized the community (no, I am not exaggerating; these are matters of history) I suffered, through my failure to adjust myself, a nervous break-down. Now commenced my real education, through the discipline of mind and heart in *nine years* of nervous derangement. (Antin to Austin, March 11, 1925, HHL)

The native-born Grabau, who also suffered serious setbacks in health, argued for a neutralist position with some sympathy toward the German side in the war, lost his position at Columbia, accepted an invitation to become director of research for the China Geological

Survey and Professor of Paleontology at the National University in Peking, and ended up spending the rest of his life as an active and prolific scientist in China; Antin, the foreign-born American patriot, supported the Allied cause (Koppelman, 231). Antin felt again that she was typical, only now of the social group of "Wives of German-Americans" as portrayed in the *Atlantic Monthly* of 1917 (Antin to Austin, March 11, 1925, HHL). The marriage broke up, though it was apparently not formally ended in divorce, and Antin suffered a collapse (Antin to Watson, September 7, 1917, BPL). At the same time, her father died, the Scarsdale house was sold at a great loss, and she was destitute when she was released from psychiatric care. She spent many years on Gould Farm in the Berkshires, was connected at some points with Zionism (see her published essay "A Confession of Faith," JTSA, and Antin to Kallen, November 16, 1916, AJA), but also became deeply interested in Christian universalism, the mystic Meher Baba (Antin to Eleanor Brooks, December 28, 1931, UP), and Rudolf Steiner's anthroposophy (Antin to Cronbach, December 20, 1940, AJA).

Antin's relationship with her husband was a difficult matter, and while, on the one hand, the war may not contain all the answers to their breakup, on the other hand, Antin clearly expressed contradictory feelings for him even in much later years. It is thus remarkable that the most detailed accounts—by Rabbi Cronbach and Maimie Pinzer—of visits to the Grabau house in Scarsdale in the good days mention that the husband was not there; and only in Antin's correspondence with Randolph Bourne is there the sense of a person who, perhaps because of his Columbia University connections, knew Grabau as well as he knew Antin.

In *The Promised Land*, written in the tenth year of the marriage, Grabau and their daughter, Josephine, are only a shadowy, hidden, never named though still palpable presence. For example, Antin writes in the manuscript of her autobiography: "If, on a later occasion, when I became aware of two blue eyes of innocence looking into mine, and two rosy lips forming their first words of love, and I began to search my heart, to see if I were worthy to receive them, I found spectres lying long forgotten, goblins, ugly shapes,—that is matter for my private confessions; it does not belong to this history of a person that I have ceased to be" (Ms. of autobiography, p. 216, "Farewell," 50, *Ms.H.6.3, BPL). The printed edition followed the logic of this argument and simply cut the reference; yet several other passages foreshadowing a love story that *The Promised Land* ultimately withheld remain in the text.

When she sees Polotzk at an early mystical and magical morning hour, much like the painter Marc Chagall tended to see his native Vitebsk, as if the houses were creatures—"Some stood up straight, and some leaned, and some looked as if they saw me"—she continues: "In those moments, I think, I could have loved somebody as well as I loved later—somebody who cared to get up secretly, and stand and see the sun get up." And in the chapter "The Burning Bush," she writes similarly: "Robert Louis Stevenson, in one of his delightful essays, credits the lover with a feeling of remorse and shame at the contemplation of that part of his life which he lived without his beloved, content with his barren existence." Yet what follows is *not* the story of her love and marriage, but the account of her immersion into the Natural History Club where she met Grabau—though the book does not mention it. Hence one logic of *The Promised Land* was also a displacement of a personal story by a tale of nature, her love for a scientist by her fascination with science. Thus she continues her reflections on her life before the arrival of the beloved: "It is with just such a feeling of remorse that I look back to my bookworm days, before I began the study of natural history outdoors; and with a feeling of shame akin to the lover's I confess how late in my life nature took the first place in my affections."

The language of the study of nature, inspired by such Grabau works as "Paleontology and Ontogeny" (1910), permeates the book from the way in which Antin traces her genealogical origins on a paleontological time frame (in "Both Their Houses") to the inspiration she gets in the "stupendous panorama which is painted in the literature of Darwinism" and in the "book of cosmogony" to learn about what she calls the "promised land of evolution" (in "The Burning Bush"). There is thus a poetic reason for Antin to include the funny picture of the Natural History Club excursion (in which Grabau and Antin might well be secretly represented) rather than an explicit courtship scene, and to close the book with a romantic photograph of Nahant entitled "The Tide Had Rushed In, Stealing Away Our Seaweed Cushions" rather than with a wedding picture.

After their separation, Grabau did not disappear from Antin's horizon. She covered up for his financial problems, worried about his health, and in 1920 wrote her lawyer and friend Thomas A. Watson protectively in response to the question that she rephrases as "what is Amadeus to me or I to him."

> A woman would not need to ask that question. Amadeus is the man for whom I laid out clean linen as he needed it for fifteen years. Perhaps a man cannot understand that by the performance of these small personal services a woman fetters herself with a sense of responsibility that outlasts less material bonds. I am not a domestic woman; I have incurred enough reproach on that score to be quite convinced of it. Yet in all these dreary years since my exile from Scarsdale, when loneliness has oppressed me and emptiness of heart sapped my very life, it would have been an unspeakable solace if I could have gone secretly unseen by him to the place where he was, to put his rooms in order and mend his socks and dust his books. . . .
>   He to me is the man who brought glory into my life, and chaos. He is the one who cherished me like father and mother and lover and dearest friend in one; he is the one who wounded me and trampled on me and made sport of the sufferings he inflicted. Having him I had heaven and earth for my own; losing him I have had to fight day and night to preserve my mental and spiritual integrity, and physically to be content with a broken life. (Antin to Watson, September 11, 1920, *Ms.D.1.3 v. 12 [46], BPL)

One wonders whether her feeling of loss was intensified by her previous view of the "paternal" Grabau as "father and mother and lover and dearest friend in one." Perhaps no reference to Grabau in Antin's writing is more revealing than the one in this letter to Dr. Watson in which she casts her husband as typifying her adopted country, and associates him in part with a destructive, "vitals"-threatening force that she had similarly described in the ham-eating episode of *The Promised Land*: "He typified to me at one time my country's basic law; at another time, the canker gnawing at her vitals." Yet in a letter to Dr. Charles T. D. Belden of July 22, 1927, Antin explained that she was giving the manuscript of her autobiography to the Boston Public Library since she was not free to burn it, "because it was my husband, Dr. Grabau, who originally saved it and he may call me to account for it when he returns from his extended sojourn in China" (*Ms.H.6.3, BPL). As late as 1937, she announced in a letter to Sedgwick (whose wife had just passed away): "I go to Washington on April 27th as my husband's proxy, to receive a medal awarded to him [the Thompson medal] 'for most important services to geology and paleontology', by the National Academy of Sciences. The flavor of melodrama is in the thing, but I have a deep substantial joy in the event. He has so heroically labored without thought of reward" (Antin to Sedgwick, March 19, 1937, MHS). And in 1940 Grabau dedicated his book *The Rhythm of the Ages* "to my wife Mary Antin, my daughter Josephine, and my granddaughters Margaret and Elizabeth Ross."

VII. A Nice Obituary and the Oneness of Life

After 1917, Antin's correspondence with her publishers raised little hope for new projects and consisted mostly of requests for small advances against royalties or collateral statements for bank loans. In the 1920s, she had become estranged from her past political positions and felt, after the victory of the immigration restrictionists, that *They Who Knock* had become so dated that she wanted Houghton Mifflin to stop selling the book she now contemptuously called "The Knockers" (Antin to Houghton Mifflin, November 4, 1925, and response December 2, 1925; June 27, 1926, and response July 9, 1926; July 13, 1926; bMS Am 1925 [68], HLHU) and described as "an amazing mixture of naiveté and rhapsody" (Antin to Austin, March 11, 1925, HHL).

Antin's disillusionment was stark. As a schoolchild, she had written patriotic poetry on Washington's birthday and fulfilled her dream to see it published in the *Boston Herald*. In *The Promised Land*, Antin (the Antin some reviewers accused of "egotism") wrote up this experience with enthusiasm and mentioned that she dreamed of finding her name "Antin, Mary" in an encyclopedic dictionary, not far from "Alcott, Louisa M." In 1926, however, when she was asked by the publicity department of Houghton Mifflin to contribute something for a portrait gallery of contemporary New Englanders for the *Boston Herald*, she sarcastically commented that it would "soon be time for them to reheat the patriotic hash from The Promised Land which they have served up at shortish intervals, about Washington's Birthday, ever since Houghton Mifflin have been paying me royalties." She suggested using an old picture ("Anything less than ten years back would be anachronistic"), questioned whether she even existed as a contemporary, and bitterly offered the following suggestion to be understood by later readers:

M——A——author of [*blaa, blaa, blaa*—where you tell them what a wonderful book The Promised Land is—started a deluge of immigrant autobiographies etc.—affected legislation etc.—translated etc.] and of [more *blaa, blaa* about The Knockers—that unique document in defense of Americanism at any cost—compared by a reviewer to old Amos—repented of by the author—etc.]. Seldom has an author created so much of a flurry by such a meager literary performance. Just the two volumes named, and a . . . very few short stories [*blaa, blaa*— ask Mr. Sedgwick] lost in what are now back numbers of the Atlantic Monthly. It is about ten years now since her last published story. What has happened to choke the [*blaa, blaa*] literary gift which in the course of a few years' activity won the hearts of such a large reading public? [Statistics of sales etc.] M——A——dropped out of sight during the dark days of the war and has not been heard of since. A nervous breakdown is understood to have accounted for the greater part of this hiatus, but since her recovery? For her friends say that she came out of her valley of shadows in better health than she ever knew before in her life. Still her many admirers [*blaa, blaa*] wait in vain for a sign. One asks, what fatal crippling may have occurred in the process of nervous breakdown? One recalls the theory advanced by some observers of her meteoric career that her genius was seduced in its infancy, and hurt beyond repair, by the exploitation of the lecture platform. Coaxed into public work against her own conviction, by importunate appeals of great public leaders like Theodore Roosevelt and Jane Addams, she was an instant success on the platform [*blaa, blaa*—pages of slush on file at the office of The Players, Boston, my managers—won her way with every type of audience, from grammar school assemblies to university forums—churches, prisons, political mass meetings (where her candidates were invariably defeated), national conventions of educators etc. etc. statistics from The Players]. Opposed to those who saw danger for her in public life, there were many who valued M——A——'s contribution as a publicist no less than her literary achievement. But over both phases of her activity suddenly fell the veil of obscurity, and no one can be found sufficiently informed, or sufficiently prophetic, to read us the riddle of M——A——'s ten years' silence. *Who's Who* gives her address as Gould Farm, in the Berkshires. Shall we hear some day from Gould Farm, or will M——A——'s career be likened finally to a skyrocket? That, as Hamlet would say, is the question. (Antin to Dale Warren, December 17, 1926, Ms.Am.2173 [13], BPL)

Antin called this bitter self-assessment a "nice obituary," and she published only two pieces in the remaining twenty-three years of her life.

"The Soundless Trumpet" (1937), her good-bye to the *Atlantic Monthly*, is the account of a series of visions, at the core of which one may recognize some of Antin's familiar desires and fears: self-division, oneness out of two, or the image of a sister, but also some new sensations. One vision is that of two men on a roof going through trivial motions against a drab November sky: "Then, suddenly, with lances of insight weaving through and through me, I *see* them, I see what they are: they are the one who sits at the window watching! I have been looking at myself, as I might absently look in a mirror and fail to recognize the reflection."

Another vision seems connected to her sister Fetchke; and she speaks of "translating" for the reader what starts like a modernist experiment in automatic writing:

Seamstress at her window—stitching humanity's robe of immortality. And an additional note in pencil, to indicate that it was put down after reflection had played on the original memorandum: *Awake! Awake! Awake, my sister!* In my private vocabulary, these phrases have elaborate and explicit connotations, like a page in an artist's sketchbook. Translating, I find that on that day of flickering clairvoyance the seamstress in her servitude and I in my comparative mastery appeared as interchangeable members of an algebraic equation where X equals the Oneness of life.

The problem of language, and of the relation between "inside" and "outside" that has always been a concern to Antin, can no longer be resolved with a glossary. And she again draws on the all-important separation between sign and interpretation: "It is a pantomime I am writing, a shadow play, requiring an informed interpreter; a smoke signal sent up from a desert height, in the hope that some fellow explorer somewhere may catch the message and reply, or at least be heartened to continue his own quest."

One vision is auditory and brings suddenly—and removes just as rapidly—the sounds of schoolchildren; another is prompted by a piebald alley cat—leading Antin to the perception of a radio concert and remembering that only one octave of wavelength is perceptible to human beings, out of sixty-two known octaves. One image picks up her notion of the past, of memory as a garment, and combines it with describing her visions as a secretly patterned patchwork quilt. All of this is, however, preparatory of things to come, and the piece comes to a dramatic end in the expectation of "the thrill of the soundless trumpet summoning me to cross the barrier of sense" and with the question, "Who shall ascend into the hill of the Lord?" The unity in God that she here sought was also the unity of death. As she wrote Sedgwick in the same year, "In death we are not divided" (Antin to Sedgwick, March 19, 1937, MHS).

In her last published essay, "House of the One Father" (1941), Antin reflects on group affiliation. She opens with a Scarsdale vignette in which she makes a rational plea for tolerance: Why should Mrs. Grabau not support a Catholic priest as she does Jewish rabbis Rosen and Garfinkle who interrogate her? Don't Catholic priests also teach that "all men have one Father, and that's the beginning of Americanism—of democracy"? Upon the rabbis' pressure, Antin gladly pronounces her familiar homemaking myth: "It was the model of the Hebrew Commonwealth they had in mind, the first Americans. They were great students of the Old Testament." The fact that she "'discovered' the Hebrew-Christian basis of American democracy" was "very exciting. And integrating." The two halves of her life, her "Russian-Jewish beginnings" and her "new life as an American," rested on "two philosophical systems, the Hebrew and the American," that "were essentially one."

The rabbis successfully challenge her notion of oneness by reminding Antin of the Christian pogroms, and Antin now remembers how her European tour took her to an uncomfortable moment in a Catholic church in Prague—with its maximum of imagery dramatizing the separation between Christians and Jews. Yet America is different; and here even the church of the Catholics is only "the place where *their* people are reminded of God and brotherhood, and that's at the bottom of Americanism."

Later, Antin is on one of her lecture tours in Vermont and is shocked to realize very late that she, "a fugitive from the Ghetto," is actually about to speak in a Protestant church. She proclaims: "Open your eyes, America, and see a miracle. . . . Centuries of

Jewish history are atoned for in this moment you have created. The dark abyss of separation between Jew and Gentile is closed by my presence in this pulpit." Inspired by the New Testament, she feels no more dividing walls, for in America, many doors (to the school-house, the public library, the playground, the workplace) were opened: "each was a door to the House of the one Father, where differences shrank and sometimes fell away. The God of their fathers was gaining ground in my heart because all doors had been left open for my fathers' God as well."

Antin's essay strikes an ecumenical note that is specifically understood by her to be antifascist. (Antin also made several allusions to the terrifying news from Europe; for example, she wrote Abraham Cronbach on December 5, 1938 [AJA]: "Don't let me make any parenthetical allusions to the situation in Europe. I have moments of poise and hours of raw agony. Forgive me for saying this much.") "House of the One Father" was published just before the full onslaught of the Holocaust reached Vilna and Vitebsk, and the *Einsatzgruppen* massacred seven thousand Jews in Polotzk alone in December 1941 (Gilbert, maps 86, 87, and 96). Contemplating Hitler's "object lesson on the fruits of intolerance," Antin reviews her own attitudes and practices and questions her own "divorcement" from Jewish life:

> Today I find myself pulled by the old forgotten ties, through the violent projection of an immensely magnified Jewish problem. It is one thing to go your separate way, leaving your friends and comrades behind in peace and prosperity; it is another thing to fail to remember them when the world is casting them out.

Yet this act of solidarity does not mean for Antin that it is easy or even possible to return to "her people" or her past.

> I can no more return to the Jewish fold than I can return to my mother's womb [see John 3:4]; neither can I in decency continue to enjoy my accidental personal immunity from the penalties of being a Jew in a time of virulent anti-Semitism. The least I can do, in my need to share the sufferings of my people, is declare that I am as one of them.
>
> Here, in my own case, is a hint of the historic tragedy of the individual Jew whose nature is to lose himself in universal relationships, but who is driven back into some Ghetto without walls by the action

of anti-Semitism. God helping, I shall not let myself be stampeded. . . . In all those places where race lines are drawn, I shall claim the Jewish badge; but in my Father's house of many mansions I shall continue a free spirit.

It is on freedom of thought and of association that she now bases a broader sense of group loyalty:

Humbly, respectful of those who feel called to that bitter labor, I shall no more spend myself in defense of the Jew on sectarian or folk lines, except incidentally, as my knowledge of things Jewish may illumine a given situation. Not to dissociate myself from the Jewish lot, but to establish the more unassailable bond, I here declare that the point where I come to life as a member of modern society, where my fullest sense of responsibility is kindled, is deep below the ache and horror of the Jewish dilemma, at the juncture of social forces where I see the persecution or belittlement of a group—*any* group, whether of race, creed, or color—as an attack on democracy. (41–42)

Antin's wish for responsible, democratic group membership included the individual's right to express solidarity with the persecuted, yet also a freethinking person's entitlement to refuse to be stampeded into some Ghetto without walls. Antin's assertion of bonds was based on past experience with "things Jewish" and a modern sense of democratic humanism and not on what she termed "sectarian and folk lines." This was to be her last published word.

WERNER SOLLORS

SUGGESTIONS FOR FURTHER READING

1. By Mary Antin

a. Books

From Plotzk to Boston. With a foreword by Israel Zangwill. Boston: W. B. Clarke, 1899.

They Who Knock at Our Gates: A Complete Gospel of Immigration. With illustrations by Joseph Stella. Boston and New York: Houghton Mifflin Company, 1914.

b. Contributions to Journals

"Malinke's Atonement," *Atlantic Monthly* 108 (September 1911): 300–19.

"First Aid to the Alien," *Outlook* 101 (June 29, 1912): 481–85.

"How I Wrote *The Promised Land*," *New York Times Book Review* (June 30, 1912): 392.

"A Woman to Her Fellow Citizens," *Outlook* 102 (November 2, 1912): 482–86.

"The Amulet," *Atlantic Monthly* 111 (January 1913): 31–41.

"The Lie," *Atlantic Monthly* 112 (August 1913): 177–90.

"A Confession of Faith," *Boston Jewish Advocate* (February 15, 1917): 5.

"The Soundless Trumpet," *Atlantic* 159 (April 1937): 560–69.

"House of the One Father," *Common Ground* 1 (Spring 1941): 36–42.

c. Unpublished Materials and Letters

AJA—American Jewish Archives (Horace M. Kallen Papers, Abraham Cronbach Correspondence, Max Heller Correspondence).

BPL—Boston Public Library (various letters and manuscripts).

BUL—Brown University Library (Maud Howe Elliott Papers).

CPP—College of Physicians of Philadelphia (Israel Bram Collection).

CU—Columbia University (Randolph Bourne Papers).

HHL—Henry Huntington Library (Mary Austin Papers).

HLHU—Houghton Library, Harvard University (Houghton Mifflin Papers).

JTSA—Jewish Theological Seminary of America (Bernhard G. Richards Correspondence).

LC—Library of Congress (2 letters).

MHS—Massachusetts Historical Society (Ellery Sedgwick Papers).
PUL—Princeton University Libraries (General Manuscripts).
SUL—Syracuse University Library (Anita Weschler Papers).
TU—Temple University Library (John M. Stahl Papers).
UAL—University of Arkansas Libraries (John Gould Fletcher Papers).
UCBL—University of California, Bancroft Library (Simon Lubin Papers).
UP—University of Pennsylvania Libraries (Van Wyck Brooks Papers).

2. ABOUT MARY ANTIN

a. Reviews of *The Promised Land*

Clara A. Alexander, "The Promised Land: A New Book which Proves to be an Extraordinary Human Document," *Presbyterian* (Philadelphia, September 25, 1912).

Annals of the American Academy 43 (September 1912): 327.

Percy F. Bicknell, "How One Immigrant Girl Discovered America," *Dial* 52 (May 1, 1912): 348–50.

Amelia von Ende, "Amerikanischer Brief," *Literarisches Echo* 14 (August 15, 1912): 1593–94.

"Flight from the Pogrom," *Daily Express* (London, September 24, 1912).

"From Russian Tyranny to American Freedom," *Baltimore Sun* (December 15, 1912).

Helen C. Gale, *Mail* (Medford, Oregon, April 12, 1913).

Jeannette L. Gilder, "Russian Prodigy's Autobiography Reviewed," *New York Sun* (April 21, 1912): 6.

Angeline Loesch Graves, "A Russian Immigrant's Story," *The Public* (Chicago, July 5, 1912).

Arthur Guiterman, "Rhymed Reviews: The Promised Land," *Life* (August 29, 1912).

Phillip Hildreth, "Mary Antin in the Promised Land," *Classmate* (Cincinnati, January 23, 1915 (with photographic portrait by Harris & Ewing).

"The Immigrant," *New York Times* (April 14, 1912): 228.

Independent (New York, August 22, 1912).

Joseph Jacobs, "An Orgy of Egotism," *American Hebrew* (May 31, 1912).

"Keeping the Promise of the Promised Land," *Survey* (New York, February 8, 1913): 637–38.

Kurt Kuechler, *Literarisches Echo* 16 (July 1, 1914): 1367–68.

Life and Labor (November 1912).

Frederick Lynch, "How Shall We Look at the Immigrant?," *Christian Work* (New York, July 13, 1912).

"The Making Over of Mary Antin," *Boston Sunday Herald* (April 28, 1912): 29.

"Mary Antin and Her Tale of an Immigrant," *New York Sun* (May 4, 1912).

William H. Maxwell, *Literary Digest* 44 (June 15, 1912): 1261–62.

George Middleton, *The Bookman* 35 (June 1912): 419–21.

Nation 94 (May 23, 1912): 517.

National Magazine (Boston, January 1913).

Outlook 101 (June 29, 1912): 502.

Charles H. Pankhurst, "The Book of the Month," *Hearst's Magazine* (September 1912): 107–12.

"The Rise of an Immigrant," *New York Post* (May 25, 1912).

William E. Sage, "Mary Antin's Call to Our Patriotism," Cleveland, Ohio *Leader* (May 27, 1912).

"She Found the Promised Land," *Boston Globe* (March 16, 1913).

Frederick Boyd Stevenson, "What the Promised Land Did for Mary Antin," *Brooklyn Daily Eagle* (February 16, 1913).

"Tells of Race Characteristics Altered by Residence in America," *Christian Science Monitor* (April 22, 1912).

"This Land of Promise," *Boston Jewish Advocate* (May 17, 1912).

"Das verheißene Land," *Straßburger Post* (February 8, 1914).

Elizabeth Woodbridge, *Yale Review* n.s. 2 (1912): 175–76.

b. Reviews of *From Plotzk to Boston*

"From Russia to America," *New York Times Saturday Review* (May 27, 1899): 341.

Josephine Lazarus, "From Plotzk to Boston," *Critic* 34 (April 1899): 317–18 (with portrait of Antin on p. 295).

c. Reviews of *They Who Knock at Our Gates*

American Review (July 1914): 159–60.

"A Plea for the Poor Immigrant," *Dial* 56 (June 1, 1914): 470–71.

"Sensibility in Economics," *New York Times Book Review* (July 12, 1914): 305.

d. Selected Criticism

Annie E. S. Beard, *Our Foreign-Born Citizens: What They Have Done for America* (New York: Crowell, 1922), 308–16.

Betty Bergland, "Rereading Photographs and Narratives in Ethnic Autobiography: Memory and Subjectivity in Mary Antin's *The Promised Land*," in *Memory, Narrative, and Identity: New Essays in Ethnic American Literatures*, ed. Amritjit Singh, Joseph T. Skerrett, Jr., and Robert E. Hogan (Boston: Northeastern University Press, 1994), 45–88.

Gert Buelens, "The New Man and the Mediator: (Non-)Remembrance in Jewish-American Immigrant Narrative," in *Memory, Narrative, and Identity: New Essays in Ethnic American Literatures*, ed. Amritjit Singh, Joseph T. Skerrett, Jr., and Robert E. Hogan (Boston: Northeastern University Press, 1994), 89–113.

Abraham Cronbach, "Autobiography," *American Jewish Archives* 11.1 (April 1959): 3–81; especially "Memories of Mary Antin," 40–43.

Irwin Granich [a.k.a. Mike Gold], "Surveys of the Promised Land," *Liberator* (July 1918): 32–33.

Allen Guttmann, *The Jewish Writer in America: Assimilation and the Crisis of Identity* (New York: Oxford University Press, 1971), 25–33.

Oscar Handlin, "Antin, Mary," in *Notable American Women 1607–1950: A Biographical Dictionary*, ed. Edward T. James, Janet Wilson James, and Paul S. Boyer (Cambridge, Mass. and London: Harvard University Press, 1971), 57–59.

Steven G. Kellman, "Lost in the Promised Land: Eva Hoffman Revises Mary Antin," *Prooftexts* 18 (1998): 149–59.

Susan Koppelman, "Mary Antin (13 June 1881–15 May 1949)," in *Dictionary of Literary Biography Yearbook: 1984*, ed. Jean W. Ross (Detroit: Gale Research Company, 1984), 225–32.

Michael P. Kramer, "Assimilation in *The Promised Land*: Mary Antin and the Jewish Origins of the American Self," *Prooftexts* 18 (1998): 121–48.

Hans-Joachim Lang, "Mary Antin und das Vermächtnis von Emma Lazarus," in *Women's Studies and Literature: Neun Beitrage aus der Erlanger Amerikanistik*, ed. Fritz Fleischmann and Deborah Lucas Schneider, Erlanger Studien, vol. 73 (Erlangen: Palm & Enke, 1987), 83–130.

Ludwig Lewisohn, "A Panorama of a Half-Century of American Jewish Literature," *Jewish Book Annual* 9/5711 (1950–1951): 3–10.

Allan Mazur, *A Romance in Natural History: The Lives and Works of Amadeus Grabau and Mary Antin* (Syracuse, N.Y.: Garret, 2004).

Keren R. McGinity, "The Real Mary Antin: Woman on a Mission in the Promised Land," *American Jewish History* 86.3 (1998): 285–307.

Pamela S. Nadell, "Introduction," *From Plotzk to Boston* (1899; repr. New York: Markus Wiener, 1986), v–xxi.

Mary R. Parkman, "The Making of a Patriot: Mary Antin," in *Heroines of Service* (New York: Century, 1918), 185–208 (with portrait by Falk opposite p. 200).

[Maimie Pinzer], *The Maimie Papers*, ed. Ruth Rosen and Sue Davidson (Old Westbury, N.Y.: Feminist Press, 1977), 113–14, 128, 134, 144, 149, 158–67, 189.

Steven J. Rubin, "Style and Meaning in Mary Antin's *The Promised Land*: A Reevaluation," *Studies of American Jewish Literature* 5 (1986): 35–43.

Harry Salpeter, "The Jew as Autobiographer," *The Menorah Journal* 5 (June 1919): 175–78.

Evelyn Salz, "The Letters of Mary Antin: A Life Divided," M.A. thesis, Department of English, University of Massachusetts, Amherst, 1995.

Ellery Sedgwick, "Mary Antin," *American Magazine* (March 1914): 65 (with photographic portrait, p. 64).

Barbara Shollar, "Writing Ethnicity/Writing Modernity: Autobiographies by Jewish-American Women," dissertation, City University of New York, 1992.

Mary H. Wade, *Pilgrims of To-day* (Boston: Little, Brown, 1916), 112–41 (with photographic portrait by Harris & Ewing opposite p. 140).

Ruth Wardlaw, "Recastings of the Self: The Interaction of Metaphor and Personal History in American Immigrant Autobiography," dissertation, Emory University, 1976.

Sam Bass Warner, Jr., *Province of Reason* (Cambridge, Mass. and London: Harvard University Press, 1984).

Kirsten-Anna Wasson, "Daughters of Promise, Mothers of Revision: Three Jewish American Immigrant Writers and Cultural Inscriptions of Identity," dissertation, University of Wisconsin, Madison, 1993.

Hana Wirth-Nesher, "'I learned at least to think in English without an accent,' Mary Antin: Linguistic Passing," *Call It English: The Languages of Jewish American Literature* (Princeton and Oxford: Princeton University Press, 2006), 52–75.

Virginia McLaughlin Yans, "Antin, Mary," in *Dictionary of American Biography: Supplement Four, 1946–1950*, ed. John A. Garraty and Edward T. James (New York: Scribner's, 1974), 23–24.

Sunny Yudkoff, "Mary Antin's 1894 Letter to her Uncle Moshe Hayyim Weltman," *Studies in American Jewish Literature* (forthcoming, 2012).

Magdalena J. Zaborowska, *How We Found America: Reading Gender through East-European Immigrant Narratives* (Chapel Hill: University of North Carolina Press, 1995).

Israel Zangwill, "Introduction," *From Plotzk to Boston* (Boston: W. B. Clarke, 1899).

3. RELATED READINGS

Thomas Bender, *New York Intellect: A History of Intellectual Life in New York City, from 1750 to the Beginnings of Our Own Time* (Baltimore: Johns Hopkins University Press, 1987), 247–48.

Randolph S. Bourne, *The Radical Will: Selected Writings, 1911–1918*, ed. and introd. Olaf Hansen (New York: Urizen Press, 1977).

Martin Gilbert, *Atlas of the Holocaust* (London: Michael Joseph, 1982).

A. W. Grabau, "Paleontology and Ontogeny," *Popular Science Monthly* 77.3 (September 1910): 295–98.

Amadeus W. Grabau, *The Rhythm of the Ages: Earth History in the Light of the Pulsation and Polar Control Theories* (Peking: Henry Vetch, 1940).

Amadeus W. Grabau, *The World We Live In: A New Interpretation of Earth History*, intr. V. C. Juan (The Geological Society of China, 1961).

John Higham, "The Redefinition of America, 1910–1930," ms. (1989).

Eva Hoffman, *Lost in Translation: A Life in a New Language* (1988; New York: Penguin, 1990), 162.

M. A. DeWolfe Howe, *Barrett Wendell in His Letters* (Boston: The Atlantic Monthly Press, 1924), 281–82.

Horace M. Kallen, *Culture and Democracy in the United States: Studies in the Group Psychology of the American Peoples* (New York: Boni and Liveright, 1924).

Walter Benn Michaels, *Our America: Nativism, Modernism, and Pluralism* (Durham and London: Duke University Press, 1995).

Orm Øverland, *Immigrant Minds, American Identities: Making the United States Home, 1870–1930* (Urbana: University of Illinois Press, 2000).

Agnes Repplier, "The Modest Immigrant," *Counter-Currents* (Boston: Houghton Mifflin, 1916), 197–232.

Evelyn Salz, ed. *The Selected Letters of Mary Antin* (Syracuse: Syracuse University Press, 2000). Includes 110 of Antin's letters as well as five letters written to her.

A NOTE ON THE TEXT

This edition follows the text of the second printing of the first edition (in which some typographical errors were corrected). The text has been compared in some instances with those sections that appeared in *Atlantic Monthly* and are here reprinted in modern typesetting. The chapter "The Exodus" has been read against Antin's first book, *From Plotzk to Boston* (1899); and Antin's longhand manuscript of "The Promised Land" was consulted in some cases. A few significant variants are given in the textual notes. This edition includes all the photographs that accompanied the first edition together with three new illustrations. Some of these photographs were reportedly taken by Amadeus Grabau. Antin's essay on the writing of *The Promised Land*, which first appeared in 1912 in the *New York Times Book Review*, is appended, as are Antin's short stories, "Malinke's Atonement" (1911) and "The Lie" (1913).

EDITOR'S ACKNOWLEDGMENTS

THIS EDITION COULD NOT HAVE BEEN PREPARED without Breda O'Keeffe's energetic and imaginative research assistance. I am also grateful to Joyce Antler, Sacvan Bercovitch, Alide Cagidemetrio, Jules Chametzky, Thomas J. Ferraro, Oscar Handlin, Susan Koppelman, Michael Kramer, Hans-Joachim Lang, Keren McGinity, Allan Mazur, Evelyn Salz, Jonathan Sarna, and Hana Wirth-Nesher for helpful suggestions, and to the students in the History of American Civilization Colloquium at Harvard University—Adam Biggs, Lan Bui, Camille Forbes, Jennifer Goloboy, Christian Ruettger, and Woden Teachout—for an intense discussion of the text. Nicole Morreale proofread the two short stories against the original *Atlantic Monthly* versions.

Denison Beach kindly guided me through the Houghton Mifflin papers at the Houghton Library of Harvard University, and Virginia Smith at the Massachusetts Historical Society very generously provided copies of Antin's extensive and important correspondence with Ellery Sedgwick within minutes after I requested them. Kevin Proffitt at the American Jewish Archives, Andrea Cantrell at the Research Services Department, Special Collections of the University of Arkansas Libraries, Raymond Stokes and Dr. Bonnie Hardwick at the Bancroft Library of the University of California at Berkeley, Mark Brown at the John Hay Library of Brown University, Kevin Crawford at the Archives of The College of Physicians of Philadelphia, Jean Ashton at the Rare Book and Manuscript Library at Columbia University, Dr. Seth Jerchower, Research Associate at the Special Collections of the Jewish Theological Seminary of America, Sara S. Hodson and Hoang-My Dunkle at the Huntington Library, Mr. Shawcross at the Van Pelt-Dietrich Library Center of the University of Pennsylvania, Margaret Sherry at Princeton University Rare Books and Special Collections, Ruth Copans of the Lucy Scribner Library at Skidmore College, Carolyn Davis at the Department of Special Collections at Syracuse University Library, Thomas W. Whitehead at Special Collections and

George D. Brightbill at Urban Archives of the Temple University Library, as well as the researcher at the YIVO Institute for Jewish Research, New York City, sent copies of Antin letters. Mr. Giuseppe Bisaccia, Curator of Manuscripts at the Boston Public Library, extended his help at the research stage, and Laura V. Monti, Keeper of Rare Books and Manuscripts, Boston Public Library, granted permission to copy selected manuscripts.

Unpublished letters are quoted in the Introduction by permission of the Massachusetts Historical Society (Ellery Sedgwick Papers), of the Houghton Library, Harvard University (bMS Am 1925 [68]), of the Huntington Library (Mary Austin Papers), of the American Jewish Archives (Horace M. Kallen Papers and Abraham Cronbach Correspondence), of the Brown University Library (Maud Howe Elliott Papers), of the Rare Books and Manuscript Library, Columbia University (Randolph Bourne Papers), and by courtesy of the Trustees of the Boston Public Library (various letters and manuscripts by Mary Antin). Special thanks also to Anne Ross for permission to quote from the Antin letters and unpublished materials, for making accessible to me the family scrapbook on the publication and reception of *The Promised Land*, and for her valuable comments on a draft of this introduction.

THE PROMISED LAND

To the Memory of
JOSEPHINE LAZARUS
Who lives in the fulfilment
of her prophecies

Mashke and Fetchke

INTRODUCTION

I WAS BORN, I have lived, and I have been made over. Is it not time to write my life's story? I am just as much out of the way as if I were dead, for I am absolutely other than the person whose story I have to tell. Physical continuity with my earlier self is no disadvantage. I could speak in the third person and not feel that I was masquerading. I can analyze my subject, I can reveal everything; for *she*, and not *I*, is my real heroine. My life I have still to live; her life ended when mine began.

A generation is sometimes a more satisfactory unit for the study of humanity than a lifetime; and spiritual generations are as easy to demark as physical ones. Now I am the spiritual offspring of the marriage within my conscious experience of the Past and the Present. My second birth was no less a birth because there was no distinct incarnation. Surely it has happened before that one body served more than one spiritual organization. Nor am I disowning my father and mother of the flesh, for they were also partners in the generation of my second self; copartners with my entire line of ancestors. They gave me body, so that I have eyes like my father's and hair like my mother's. The spirit also they gave me, so that I reason like my father and endure like my mother. But did they set me down in a sheltered garden, where the sun should warm me, and no winter should hurt, while they fed me from their hands? No; they early let me run in the fields—perhaps because I would not be held—and eat of the wild fruits and drink of the dew. Did they teach me from books, and tell me what to believe? I soon chose my own books, and built me a world of my own.

In these discriminations *I* emerged, a new being, something that had not been before. And when I discovered my own friends, and ran home with them to convert my parents to a belief in their excellence, did I not begin to make my father and mother, as truly as they had ever made me? Did I not become the parent and they the children, in those relations of teacher and learner? And so I can say that there has been more than one birth of myself, and I can regard my earlier self as a separate being, and make it a subject of study.

A proper autobiography is a death-bed confession. A true man finds so much work to do that he has no time to contemplate his yesterdays; for to-day and to-morrow are here, with their impatient tasks. The world is so busy, too, that it cannot afford to study any man's unfinished work; for the end may prove it a failure, and the world needs masterpieces. Still there are circumstances by which a man is justified in pausing in the middle of his life to contemplate the years already passed. One who has completed early in life a distinct task may stop to give an account of it. One who has encountered unusual adventures under vanishing conditions may pause to describe them before passing into the stable world. And perhaps he also might be given an early hearing, who, without having ventured out of the familiar paths, without having achieved any signal triumph, has lived his simple life so intensely, so thoughtfully, as to have discovered in his own experience an interpretation of the universal life.

I am not yet thirty, counting in years, and I am writing my life history. Under which of the above categories do I find my justification? I have not accomplished anything, I have not discovered anything, not even by accident, as Columbus discovered America. My life has been unusual, but by no means unique. And this is the very core of the matter. It is because I understand my history, in its larger outlines, to be typical of many, that I consider it worth recording. My life is a concrete illustration of a multitude of statistical facts. Although I have written a genuine personal memoir, I believe that its chief interest lies in the fact that it is illustrative of scores of unwritten lives. I am only one of many whose fate it has been to live a page of modern history. We are the strands of the cable that binds the Old World to the New. As the ships that brought us link the shores of Europe and America, so our lives span the bitter sea of racial differences and misunderstandings. Before we came, the New World knew not the Old; but since we have begun to come, the Young World has taken the Old by the hand, and the two are learning to march side by side, seeking a common destiny.

Perhaps I have taken needless trouble to furnish an excuse for my autobiography. My age alone, my true age, would be reason enough for my writing. I began life in the Middle Ages, as I shall prove, and here am I still, your contemporary in the twentieth century, thrilling with your latest thought.

Had I no better excuse for writing, I still might be driven to it by my private needs. It is in one sense a matter of my personal salvation. I was at a most impressionable age when I was transplanted to the new soil. I was in that period when even normal children, undisturbed in their customary environment, begin to explore their own hearts, and endeavor to account for themselves and their world. And my zest for self-exploration seems not to have been distracted by the necessity of exploring a new outer universe. I embarked on a double voyage of discovery, and an exciting life it was! I took note of everything. I could no more keep my mind from the shifting, changing landscape than an infant can keep his eyes from the shining candle moved across his field of vision. Thus everything impressed itself on my memory, and with double associations; for I was constantly referring my new world to the old for comparison, and the old to the new for elucidation. I became a student and philosopher by force of circumstances.

Had I been brought to America a few years earlier, I might have written that in such and such a year my father emigrated, just as I would state what he did for a living, as a matter of family history. Happening when it did, the emigration became of the most vital importance to me personally. All the processes of uprooting, transportation, replanting, acclimatization, and development took place in my own soul. I felt the pang, the fear, the wonder, and the joy of it. I can never forget, for I bear the scars. But I want to forget —sometimes I long to forget. I think I have thoroughly assimilated my past—I have done its bidding—I want now to be of to-day. It is painful to be consciously of two worlds. The Wandering Jew in me seeks forgetfulness. I am not afraid to live on and on, if only I do not have to remember too much. A long past vividly remembered is like a heavy garment that clings to your limbs when you would run. And I have thought of a charm that should release me from the folds of my clinging past. I take the hint from the Ancient Mariner, who told his tale in order to be rid of it. I, too, will tell my tale, for once, and never hark back any more. I will write a bold "Finis" at the end, and shut the book with a bang!

CHAPTER I

WITHIN THE PALE

WHEN I WAS A LITTLE GIRL, the world was divided into two parts; namely, Polotzk, the place where I lived, and a strange land called Russia. All the little girls I knew lived in Polotzk, with their fathers and mothers and friends. Russia was the place where one's father went on business. It was so far off, and so many bad things happened there, that one's mother and grandmother and grown-up aunts cried at the railroad station, and one was expected to be sad and quiet for the rest of the day, when the father departed for Russia.

After a while there came to my knowledge the existence of another division, a region intermediate between Polotzk and Russia. It seemed there was a place called Vitebsk, and one called Vilna, and Riga, and some others. From those places came photographs of uncles and cousins one had never seen, and letters, and sometimes the uncles themselves. These uncles were just like people in Polotzk; the people in Russia, one understood, were very different. In answer to one's questions, the visiting uncles said all sorts of silly things, to make everybody laugh; and so one never found out why Vitebsk and Vilna, since they were not Polotzk, were not as sad as Russia. Mother hardly cried at all when the uncles went away.

One time, when I was about eight years old, one of my grown-up cousins went to Vitebsk. Everybody went to see her off, but I did n't. I went with her. I was put on the train, with my best dress tied up in a bandana, and I stayed on the train for hours and hours, and came to Vitebsk. I could not tell, as we rushed along, where the end of Polotzk was. There were a great many places on the way, with strange names, but it was very plain when we got to Vitebsk.

The railroad station was a big place, much bigger than the one in Polotzk. Several trains came in at once, instead of only one. There was an immense buffet, with fruits and confections, and a place where books were sold. My cousin never let go my hand, on

5

account of the crowd. Then we rode in a cab for ever so long, and I saw the most beautiful streets and shops and houses, much bigger and finer than any in Polotzk.

We remained in Vitebsk several days, and I saw many wonderful things, but what gave me my one great surprise was something that was n't new at all. It was the river—the river Dvina. Now the Dvina is in Polotzk. All my life I had seen the Dvina. How, then, could the Dvina be in Vitebsk? My cousin and I had come on the train, but everybody knew that a train could go everywhere, even to Russia. It became clear to me that the Dvina went on and on, like a railroad track, whereas I had always supposed that it stopped where Polotzk stopped. I had never seen the end of Polotzk; I meant to, when I was bigger. But how could there be an end to Polotzk now? Polotzk was everything on both sides of the Dvina, as all my life I had known; and the Dvina, it now turned out, never broke off at all. It was very curious that the Dvina should remain the same, while Polotzk changed into Vitebsk!

The mystery of this transmutation led to much fruitful thinking. The boundary between Polotzk and the rest of the world was not, as I had supposed, a physical barrier, like the fence which divided our garden from the street. The world went like this now: Polotzk—more Polotzk—more Polotzk—Vitebsk! And Vitebsk was not so different, only bigger and brighter and more crowded. And Vitebsk was not the end. The Dvina, and the railroad, went on beyond Vitebsk,—went on to Russia. Then was Russia more Polotzk? Was here also no dividing fence? How I wanted to see Russia! But very few people went there. When people went to Russia it was a sign of trouble; either they could not make a living at home, or they were drafted for the army, or they had a lawsuit. No, nobody went to Russia for pleasure. Why, in Russia lived the Czar, and a great many cruel people; and in Russia were the dreadful prisons from which people never came back.

Polotzk and Vitebsk were now bound together by the continuity of the earth, but between them and Russia a formidable barrier still interposed. I learned, as I grew older, that much as Polotzk disliked to go to Russia, even more did Russia object to letting Polotzk come. People from Polotzk were sometimes turned back before they had finished their business, and often they were cruelly treated on the way. It seemed there were certain places in Russia—St. Petersburg, and Moscow, and Kiev—where my father or my uncle or my neighbor must never come at all, no matter what important things invited them. The police would seize them and send them back to Polotzk, like wicked criminals, although they had never done any wrong.

It was strange enough that my relatives should be treated like this, but at least there was this excuse for sending them back to Polotzk, that they belonged there. For what reason were people driven out of St. Petersburg and Moscow who had their homes in those cities, and had no other place to go to? Ever so many people, men and women and even children, came to Polotzk, where they had no friends, with stories of cruel treatment in Russia; and although they were nobody's relatives, they were taken in, and helped, and set up in business, like unfortunates after a fire.

It was very strange that the Czar and the police should want all Russia for themselves. It was a very big country; it took many days for a letter to reach one's father in Russia. Why might not everybody be there who wanted to?

I do not know when I became old enough to understand. The truth was borne in on me a dozen times a day, from the time I began to distinguish words from empty noises. My grandmother told me about it, when she put me to bed at night. My parents told me about it, when they gave me presents on holidays. My playmates told me, when they drew me back into a corner of the gateway, to let a policeman pass. Vanka, the little white-haired boy, told me all about it, when he ran out of his mother's laundry on purpose to throw mud after me when I happened to pass. I heard about it during prayers, and when women quarrelled in the market place; and sometimes, waking in the night, I heard my parents whisper it in the dark. There was no time in my life when I did not hear and see and feel the truth—the reason why Polotzk was cut off from the rest of Russia. It was the first lesson a little girl in Polotzk had to learn. But for a long while I did not understand. Then there came a time when I knew that Polotzk and Vitebsk and Vilna and some other places were grouped together as the "Pale of Settlement," and within this area the Czar commanded me to stay, with my father and mother and friends, and all other people like us. We must not be found outside the Pale, because we were Jews.

So there was a fence around Polotzk, after all. The world was divided into Jews and Gentiles. This knowledge came so gradually that it could not shock me. It trickled into my consciousness drop by drop. By the time I fully understood that I was a prisoner, the shackles had grown familiar to my flesh.

The first time Vanka threw mud at me, I ran home and complained to my mother, who brushed off my dress and said, quite resignedly, "How can I help you, my poor child? Vanka is a Gentile. The Gentiles do as they like with us Jews." The next time Vanka abused me, I did not cry, but ran for shelter, saying to myself, "Vanka is a Gentile." The third time, when Vanka spat on me, I wiped my face and thought nothing at all. I accepted ill-usage from the Gentiles as one accepts the weather. The world was made in a certain way, and I had to live in it.

Not quite all the Gentiles were like Vanka. Next door to us lived a Gentile family which was very friendly. There was a girl as big as I, who never called me names, and gave me flowers from her father's garden. And there were the Parphens, of whom my grandfather rented his store. They treated us as if we were not Jews at all. On our festival days they visited our house and brought us presents, carefully choosing such things as Jewish children might accept; and they liked to have everything explained to them, about the wine and the fruit and the candles, and they even tried to say the appropriate greetings and blessings in Hebrew. My father used to say that if all the Russians were like the Parphens, there would be no trouble between Gentiles and Jews; and Fedora Pavlovna, the landlady, would reply that the Russian *people* were not to blame. It was the priests, she said, who taught the people to hate the Jews. Of course she knew best, as she was a very pious Christian. She never passed a church without crossing herself.

The Gentiles were always crossing themselves; when they went into a church, and when they came out, when they met a priest, or passed an image in the street. The dirty beggars on the church steps never stopped crossing themselves; and even when they stood on the corner of a Jewish street, and received alms from Jewish people, they crossed themselves and mumbled Christian prayers. In every Gentile house there was what they called an "icon," which was an image or picture of the Christian god, hung up in a corner, with a light always burning before it. In front of the icon the Gentiles said their prayers, on their knees, crossing themselves all the time.

I tried not to look in the corner where the icon was, when I came into a Gentile house. I was afraid of the cross. Everybody was, in Polotzk—all the Jews, I mean. For it was the cross that made the priests, and the priests made our troubles, as even some Christians admitted. The Gentiles said that we had killed their God, which was absurd, as they never had a God—nothing but images. Besides, what they accused us of had happened so long ago; the Gentiles themselves said it was long ago. Everybody had been dead for ages who could have had anything to do with it. Yet they put up crosses everywhere, and wore them on their necks, on purpose to remind themselves of these false things; and they considered it pious to hate and abuse us, insisting that we had killed their God. To worship the cross and to torment a Jew was the same thing to them. That is why we feared the cross.

Another thing the Gentiles said about us was that we used the blood of murdered Christian children at the Passover festival. Of course that was a wicked lie. It made me sick to think of such a thing. I knew everything that was done for Passover, from the time I was a very little girl. The house was made clean and shining and holy, even in the corners where nobody ever looked. Vessels and dishes that were used all the year round were put away in the garret, and special vessels were brought out for the Passover week. I used to help unpack the new dishes, and find my own blue mug. When the fresh curtains were put up, and the white floors were uncovered, and everybody in the house put on new clothes, and I sat down to the feast in my new dress, I felt clean inside and out. And when I asked the Four Questions, about the unleavened bread and the bitter herbs and the other things, and the family, reading from their books, answered me, did I not know all about Passover, and what was on the table, and why? It was wicked of the Gentiles to tell lies about us. The youngest child in the house knew how Passover was kept.

The Passover season, when we celebrated our deliverance from the land of Egypt, and felt so glad and thankful, as if it had only just happened, was the time our Gentile neighbors chose to remind us that Russia was another Egypt. That is what I heard people say, and it was true. It was not so bad in Polotzk, within the Pale; but in Russian cities, and even more in the country districts, where Jewish families lived scattered, by special permission of the police, who were always changing their minds about letting them stay, the Gentiles made the Passover a time of horror for the Jews. Somebody would start up that lie about murdering Christian children, and the stupid peasants would get mad about it, and fill themselves with vodka, and set out to kill the Jews. They attacked them with knives and clubs and scythes and axes, killed them or tortured them, and burned their houses. This was called a "pogrom." Jews who escaped the pogroms came to Polotzk with wounds on them, and horrible, horrible stories, of little babies torn limb from limb before their mothers' eyes. Only to hear these things made one sob and sob and choke with pain. People who saw such things never smiled any more, no matter how long they lived; and sometimes their hair turned white in a day, and some people became insane on the spot.

Often we heard that the pogrom was led by a priest carrying a cross before the mob. Our enemies always held up the cross as the excuse of their cruelty to us. I never was in an actual pogrom, but there were times when it threatened us, even in Polotzk; and in all my fearful imaginings, as I hid in dark corners, thinking of the horrible things the Gentiles were going to do to me, I saw the cross, the cruel cross.

I remember a time when I thought a pogrom had broken out in our street, and I wonder that I did not die of fear. It was some Christian holiday, and we had been warned by the police to keep indoors. Gates were locked; shutters were barred. If a child cried, the nurse threatened to give it to the priest, who would soon be passing by. Fearful and yet curious, we looked through the cracks in the shutters. We saw a procession of peasants and townspeople, led by a number of priests, carrying crosses and banners and images. In the place of honor was carried a casket, containing a relic from the monastery in the outskirts of Polotzk. Once a year the Gentiles paraded with this relic, and on that occasion the streets were considered too holy for Jews to be about; and we lived in fear till the end of the day, knowing that the least disturbance might start a riot, and a riot lead to a pogrom.

On the day when I saw the procession through a crack in the shutter, there were soldiers and police in the street. This was as usual, but I did not know it. I asked the nurse, who was pressing to the crack over my head, what the soldiers were for. Thoughtlessly she answered me, "In case of a pogrom." Yes, there were the crosses and the priests and the mob. The church bells were pealing their loudest. Everything was ready. The Gentiles were going to tear me in pieces, with axes and knives and ropes. They were going to burn me alive. The cross—the cross! What would they do to me first?

There was one thing the Gentiles might do to me worse than burning or rending. It was what was done to unprotected Jewish children who fell into the hands of priests or nuns. They might baptize me. That would be worse than death by torture. Rather would I drown in the Dvina than a drop of the baptismal water should touch my forehead. To be forced to kneel before the hideous images, to kiss the cross,—sooner would I rush out to the mob that was passing, and let them tear my vitals out. To forswear the One God, to bow before idols,—rather would I be seized with the plague, and be eaten up by vermin. I was only a little girl, and not very brave; little pains made me ill, and I cried. But there was no pain that I would not bear—no, none—rather than submit to baptism.

Every Jewish child had that feeling. There were stories by the dozen of Jewish boys who were kidnapped by the Czar's agents and brought up in Gentile families, till they were old enough to enter the army, where they served till forty years of age; and all those years the priests tried, by bribes and daily tortures, to force them to accept baptism, but in vain. This was in the time of Nicholas I, but men who had been through this service were no older than my grandfather, when I was a little girl; and they told their experiences with their own lips, and one knew it was true, and it broke one's heart with pain and pride.

Some of these soldiers of Nicholas, as they were called, were taken as little boys of seven or eight—snatched from their mothers' laps. They were carried to distant villages, where their friends could never trace them, and turned over to some dirty, brutal peasant, who used them like slaves and kept them with the pigs. No two were ever left together; and they were given false names, so that they were entirely cut off from their own world. And then the lonely child was turned over to the priests, and he was flogged and starved and terrified—a little helpless boy who cried for his mother; but still he refused to be baptized. The priests promised him good things to eat, and fine clothes, and freedom from labor; but the boy turned away, and said his prayers secretly—the Hebrew prayers.

As he grew older, severer tortures were invented for him; still he refused baptism. By this time he had forgotten his mother's face, and of his prayers perhaps only the "Shema" remained in his memory; but he was a Jew, and nothing would make him change. After he entered the army, he was bribed with promises of promotions and honors. He remained a private, and endured the cruellest discipline. When he was discharged, at the age of forty, he was a broken man, without a home, without a clue to his origin, and he spent the rest of his life wandering among Jewish settlements, searching for his family; hiding the scars of torture under his rags, begging his way from door to door. If he were one who had broken down under the cruel torments, and allowed himself to be baptized, for the sake of a respite, the Church never let him go again, no matter how loudly he protested that he was still a Jew. If he was caught practicing Jewish rites, he was subjected to the severest punishment.

My father knew of one who was taken as a small boy, who never yielded to the priests under the most hideous tortures. As he was a very bright boy, the priests were particularly eager to convert him. They tried him with bribes that would appeal to his ambition. They promised to make a great man of him—a general, a noble. The boy turned away and said his prayers. Then they tortured him, and threw him into a cell; and when he lay asleep from exhaustion, the priest came and baptized him. When he awoke, they told him he was a Christian, and brought him the crucifix to kiss. He protested, threw the crucifix from him, but they held him to it that he was a baptized Jew, and belonged to the Church; and the rest of his life he spent between the prison and the hospital, always clinging to his faith, saying the Hebrew prayers in defiance of his tormentors, and paying for it with his flesh.

There were men in Polotzk whose faces made you old in a minute. They had served Nicholas I, and come back unbaptized. The white church in the square—how did it look to them? I knew. I cursed the church in my heart every time I had to pass it; and I was afraid—afraid.

On market days, when the peasants came to church, and the bells kept ringing by the hour, my heart was heavy in me, and I could find no rest. Even in my father's house I did not feel safe. The church bell boomed over the roofs of the houses, calling, calling, calling. I closed my eyes, and saw the people passing into the church: peasant women with bright embroidered aprons and glass beads; barefoot little girls with colored kerchiefs on their heads; boys with caps pulled too far down over their flaxen hair; rough men with plaited bast sandals, and a rope around the waist,— crowds of them, moving slowly up the steps, crossing themselves again and again, till they were swallowed by the black doorway, and only the beggars were left squatting on the steps. *Boom, boom!* What are the people doing in the dark, with the waxen images and the horrid crucifixes? *Boom, boom, boom!* They are ringing the bell for me. Is it in the church they will torture me, when I refuse to kiss the cross?

They ought not to have told me those dreadful stories. They were long past; we were living under the blessed "New Régime." Alexander III was no friend of the Jews; still he did not order little boys to be taken from their mothers, to be made into soldiers and Christians. Every man had to serve in the army for four years, and a Jewish recruit was likely to be treated with severity, no matter if his behavior were perfect; but that was little compared to the dreadful conditions of the old régime.

The thing that really mattered was the necessity of breaking the Jewish laws of daily life while in the service. A soldier often had to eat trefah and work on Sabbath. He had to shave his beard and do reverence to Christian things. He could not attend daily services at the synagogue; his private devotions were disturbed by the jeers and insults of his coarse Gentile comrades. He might resort to all sorts of tricks and shams, still he was obliged to violate Jewish law. When he returned home, at the end of his term of service, he could not rid himself of the stigma of those enforced sins. For four years he had led the life of a Gentile.

Piety alone was enough to make the Jews dread military service, but there were other things that made it a serious burden. Most men of twenty-one—the age of conscription—were already married and had children. During their absence their families suffered, their business often was ruined. At the end of their term they were beggars. As beggars, too, they were sent home from their military post. If they happened to have a good uniform at the time of their dismissal, it was stripped from them, and replaced by a shabby one.

They received a free ticket for the return journey, and a few kopecks a day for expenses. In this fashion they were hurried back
into the Pale, like escaped prisoners. The Czar was done with them.
If within a limited time they were found outside the Pale, they
would be seized and sent home in chains.

There were certain exceptions to the rule of compulsory service.
The only son of a family was exempt, and certain others. In the
physical examination preceding conscription, many were rejected
on account of various faults. This gave the people the idea of in-
flicting injuries on themselves, so as to produce temporary deformities on account of which they might be rejected at the
examination. Men would submit to operations on their eyes, ears,
or limbs, which caused them horrible sufferings, in the hope of
escaping the service. If the operation was successful, the patient was
rejected by the examining officers, and in a short time he was well,
and a free man. Often, however, the deformity intended to be temporary proved incurable, so that there were many men in Polotzk
blind of one eye, or hard of hearing, or lame, as a result of these
secret practices; but these things were easier to bear than the memory of four years in the Czar's service.

Sons of rich fathers could escape service without leaving any
marks on their persons. It was always possible to bribe conscription
officers. This was a dangerous practice,—it was not the officers
who suffered most in case the negotiations leaked out,—but no
respectable family would let a son be taken as a recruit till it had
made every effort to save him. My grandfather nearly ruined himself to buy his sons out of service; and my mother tells thrilling
anecdotes of her younger brother's life, who for years lived in hiding, under assumed names and in various disguises, till he had
passed the age of liability for service.

If it were cowardice that made the Jews shrink from military
service they would not inflict on themselves physical tortures
greater than any that threatened them in the army, and which often
left them maimed for life. If it were avarice—the fear of losing the
gains from their business for four years—they would not empty
their pockets and sell their houses and sink into debt, on the chance
of successfully bribing the Czar's agents. The Jewish recruit
dreaded, indeed, brutality and injustice at the hands of officers and
comrades; he feared for his family, which he left, often enough, as

dependents on the charity of relatives; but the fear of an unholy life was greater than all other fears. I know, for I remember my cousin who was taken as a soldier. Everything had been done to save him. Money had been spent freely—my uncle did not stop at his unmarried daughter's portion, when everything else was gone. My cousin had also submitted to some secret treatment,—some devastating drug administered for months before the examination, —but the effects were not pronounced enough, and he was passed. For the first few weeks his company was stationed in Polotzk. I saw my cousin drill on the square, carrying a gun, *on a Sabbath*. I felt unholy, as if I had sinned the sin in my own person. It was easy to understand why mothers of conscript sons fasted and wept and prayed and worried themselves to their graves.

There was a man in our town called David the Substitute, because he had gone as a soldier in another's stead, he himself being exempt. He did it for a sum of money. I suppose his family was starving, and he saw a chance to provide for them for a few years. But it was a sinful thing to do, to go as a soldier and be obliged to live like a Gentile, of his own free will. And David knew how wicked it was, for he was a pious man at heart. When he returned from service, he was aged and broken, bowed down with the sense of his sins. And he set himself a penance, which was to go through the streets every Sabbath morning, calling the people to prayer. Now this was a hard thing to do, because David labored bitterly all the week, exposed to the weather, summer or winter; and on Sabbath morning there was nobody so tired and lame and sore as David. Yet he forced himself to leave his bed before it was yet daylight, and go from street to street, all over Polotzk, calling on the people to wake and go to prayer. Many a Sabbath morning I awoke when David called, and lay listening to his voice as it passed and died out; and it was so sad that it hurt, as beautiful music hurts. I was glad to feel my sister lying beside me, for it was lonely in the gray dawn, with only David and me awake, and God waiting for the people's prayers.

The Gentiles used to wonder at us because we cared so much about religious things,—about food, and Sabbath, and teaching the children Hebrew. They were angry with us for our obstinacy, as they called it, and mocked us and ridiculed the most sacred things. There were wise Gentiles who understood. These were educated people, like Fedora Pavlovna, who made friends with their Jewish neighbors. They were always respectful, and openly admired some of our ways. But most of the Gentiles were ignorant and distrustful and spiteful. They would not believe that there was any good in our religion, and of course we dared not teach them, because we should be accused of trying to convert them, and that would be the end of us.

Oh, if they could only understand! Vanka caught me on the street one day, and pulled my hair, and called me names; and all of a sudden I asked myself *why—why?*—a thing I had stopped asking years before. I was so angry that I could have punished him; for one moment I was not afraid to hit back. But this *why—why?* broke out in my heart, and I forgot to revenge myself. It was so wonderful—Well, there were no words in my head to say it, but it meant that Vanka abused me only because *he did not understand.* If he could feel with my heart, if he could be a little Jewish boy for one day, I thought, he would know—he would know. If he could understand about David the Substitute, now, without being told, as I understood. If he could wake in my place on Sabbath morning, and feel his heart break in him with a strange pain, because a Jew had dishonored the law of Moses, and God was bending down to pardon him. Oh, why could I not make Vanka understand? I was so sorry that my heart hurt me, worse than Vanka's blows. My anger and my courage were gone. Vanka was throwing stones at me now from his mother's doorway, and I continued on my errand, but I did not hurry. The thing that hurt me most I could not run away from.

There was one thing the Gentiles always understood, and that was money. They would take any kind of bribe at any time. Peace cost so much a year in Polotzk. If you did not keep on good terms with your Gentile neighbors, they had a hundred ways of molesting you. If you chased their pigs when they came rooting up your garden, or objected to their children maltreating your children, they might complain against you to the police, stuffing their case with false accusations and false witnesses. If you had not made friends with the police, the case might go to court; and there you lost before the trial was called, unless the judge had reason to befriend you. The cheapest way to live in Polotzk was to pay as you went along. Even a little girl understood that, in Polotzk.

Perhaps your parents were in business,—usually they were, as almost everybody kept store,—and you heard a great deal about the chief of police, and excise officers, and other agents of the Czar. Between the Czar whom you had never seen, and the policeman whom you knew too well, you pictured to yourself a long row of officials of all sorts, all with their palms stretched out to receive your father's money. You knew your father hated them all, but you saw him smile and bend as he filled those greedy palms. You did the same, in your petty way, when you saw Vanka coming toward you on a lonely street, and you held out to him the core of the apple you had been chewing, and forced your unwilling lips into a smile. It hurt, that false smile; it made you feel black inside.

In your father's parlor hung a large colored portrait of Alexander III. The Czar was a cruel tyrant,—oh, it was whispered when doors were locked and shutters tightly barred, at night,—he was a Titus, a Haman, a sworn foe of all Jews,—and yet his portrait was seen in a place of honor in your father's house. You knew why. It looked well when police or government officers came on business.

You went out to play one morning, and saw a little knot of people gathered around a lamp-post. There was a notice on it—a new order from the chief of police. You pushed into the crowd, and stared at the placard, but you could not read. A woman with a ragged shawl looked down upon you, and said, with a bitter kind of smile, "Rejoice, rejoice, little girl! The chief of police bids you rejoice. There shall be a pretty flag flying from every housetop to-day, because it is the Czar's birthday, and we must celebrate. Come and watch the poor people pawn their samovars and candlesticks, to raise money for a pretty flag. It is a holiday, little girl. Rejoice!"

You know the woman is mocking,—you are familiar with the quality of that smile,—but you accept the hint and go and watch the people buy their flags. Your cousin keeps a dry-goods store, where you have a fine view of the proceedings. There is a crowd around the counter, and your cousin and the assistant are busily measuring off lengths of cloth, red, and blue, and white.

"How much does it take?" somebody asks. "May I know no more of sin than I know of flags," another replies. "How is it put together?" "Do you have to have all three colors?" One customer puts down a few kopecks on the counter, saying, "Give me a piece of flag. This is all the money I have. Give me the red and the blue; I'll tear up my shirt for the white."

You know it is no joke. The flag must show from every house, or the owner will be dragged to the police station, to pay a fine of twenty-five rubles. What happened to the old woman who lives in that tumble-down shanty over the way? It was that other time when flags were ordered up, because the Grand Duke was to visit Polotzk. The old woman had no flag, and no money. She hoped the policeman would not notice her miserable hut. But he did, the vigilant one, and he went up and kicked the door open with his great boot, and he took the last pillow from the bed, and sold it, and hoisted a flag above the rotten roof. I knew the old woman well, with her one watery eye and her crumpled hands. I often took a plate of soup to her from our kitchen. There was nothing but rags left on her bed, when the policeman had taken the pillow.

The Czar always got his dues, no matter if it ruined a family. There was a poor locksmith who owed the Czar three hundred rubles, because his brother had escaped from Russia before serving his term in the army. There was no such fine for Gentiles, only for Jews; and the whole family was liable. Now, the locksmith never could have so much money, and he had no valuables to pawn. The police came and attached his household goods, everything he had, including his young bride's trousseau; and the sale of the goods brought thirty-five rubles. After a year's time the police came again, looking for the balance of the Czar's dues. They put their seal on everything they found. The bride was in bed with her first baby, a boy. The circumcision was to be next day. The police did not leave a sheet to wrap the child in when he is handed up for the operation.

Many bitter sayings came to your ears if you were a Jewish little girl in Polotzk. "It is a false world," you heard, and you knew it was so, looking at the Czar's portrait, and at the flags. "Never tell a police officer the truth," was another saying, and you knew it was good advice. That fine of three hundred rubles was a sentence of lifelong slavery for the poor locksmith, unless he freed himself by some trick. As fast as he could collect a few rags and sticks, the police would be after them. He might hide under a false name, if he could get away from Polotzk on a false passport; or he might bribe the proper officials to issue a false certificate of the missing brother's death. Only by false means could he secure peace for himself and his family, as long as the Czar was after his dues.

It was bewildering to hear how many kinds of duties and taxes we owed the Czar. We paid taxes on our houses, and taxes on the rents from the houses, taxes on our business, taxes on our profits. I am not sure whether there were taxes on our losses. The town collected taxes, and the county, and the central government; and the chief of police we had always with us. There were taxes for public works, but rotten pavements went on rotting year after year; and when a bridge was to be built, special taxes were levied. A bridge, by the way, was not always a public highway. A railroad bridge across the Dvina, while open to the military, could be used by the people only by individual permission.

My uncle explained to me all about the excise duties on tobacco. Tobacco being a source of government revenue, there was a heavy tax on it. Cigarettes were taxed at every step of their process. The tobacco was taxed separately, and the paper, and the mouthpiece, and on the finished product an additional tax was put. There was no tax on the smoke. The Czar must have overlooked it.

Business really did not pay when the price of goods was so swollen by taxes that the people could not buy. The only way to make business pay was to cheat—cheat the Government of part of the duties. But playing tricks on the Czar was dangerous, with so many spies watching his interests. People who sold cigarettes without the government seal got more gray hairs than bank notes out of their business. The constant risk, the worry, the dread of a police raid in the night, and the ruinous fines, in case of detection, left very little margin of profit or comfort to the dealer in contraband goods. "But what can one do?" the people said, with the shrug of the shoulders that expresses the helplessness of the Pale. "What can one do? One must live."

It was not easy to live, with such bitter competition as the congestion of population made inevitable. There were ten times as many stores as there should have been, ten times as many tailors, cobblers, barbers, tinsmiths. A Gentile, if he failed in Polotzk, could go elsewhere, where there was less competition. A Jew could make the circle of the Pale, only to find the same conditions as at home. Outside the Pale he could only go to certain designated localities, on payment of prohibitive fees, augmented by a constant stream of bribes; and even then he lived at the mercy of the local chief of police.

Artisans had the right to reside outside the Pale, on fulfilment of certain conditions. This sounded easy to me, when I was a little girl, till I realized how it worked. There was a capmaker who had duly qualified, by passing an examination and paying for his trade papers, to live in a certain city. The chief of police suddenly took it into his head to impeach the genuineness of his papers. The capmaker was obliged to travel to St. Petersburg, where he had qualified in the first place, to repeat the examination. He spent the savings of years in petty bribes, trying to hasten the process, but was detained ten months by bureaucratic red tape. When at length he returned to his home town, he found a new chief of police, installed during his absence, who discovered a new flaw in the papers he had just obtained, and expelled him from the city. If he came to Polotzk, there were then eleven capmakers where only one could make a living.

Merchants fared like the artisans. They, too, could buy the right of residence outside the Pale, permanent or temporary, on conditions that gave them no real security. I was proud to have an uncle who was a merchant of the First Guild, but it was very expensive for my uncle. He had to pay so much a year for the title, and a certain percentage on the profits from his business. This gave him the right to travel on business outside the Pale, twice a year, for not more than six months in all. If he were found outside the Pale after his permit expired, he had to pay a fine that exceeded all he had gained by his journey, perhaps. I used to picture my uncle on his Russian travels, hurrying, hurrying to finish his business in the limited time; while a policeman marched behind him, ticking off the days and counting up the hours. That was a foolish fancy, but some of the things that were done in Russia really were very funny.

There were things in Polotzk that made you laugh with one eye and weep with the other, like a clown. During an epidemic of cholera, the city officials, suddenly becoming energetic, opened stations for the distribution of disinfectants to the people. A quarter of the population was dead when they began, and most of the dead were buried, while some lay decaying in deserted houses. The survivors, some of them crazy from horror, stole through the empty streets, avoiding one another, till they came to the appointed stations, where they pushed and crowded to get their little bottles of carbolic acid. Many died from fear in those horrible days, but some must have died from laughter. For only the Gentiles were allowed to receive the disinfectant. Poor Jews who had nothing but their new-made graves were driven away from the stations.

Perhaps it was wrong of us to think of our Gentile neighbors as a different species of beings from ourselves, but such madness as that did not help to make them more human in our eyes. It was easier to be friends with the beasts in the barn than with some of the Gentiles. The cow and the goat and the cat responded to kindness, and remembered which of the housemaids was generous and which was cross. The Gentiles made no distinctions. A Jew was a Jew, to be hated and spat upon and used spitefully.

The only Gentiles, besides the few of the intelligent kind, who did not habitually look upon us with hate and contempt, were the stupid peasants from the country, who were hardly human themselves. They lived in filthy huts together with their swine, and all they cared for was how to get something to eat. It was not their fault. The land laws made them so poor that they had to sell themselves to fill their bellies. What help was there for us in the good will of such wretched slaves? For a cask of vodka you could buy up a whole village of them. They trembled before the meanest townsman, and at a sign from a long-haired priest they would sharpen their axes against us.

The Gentiles had their excuse for their malice. They said our merchants and money-lenders preyed upon them, and our shop-keepers gave false measure. People who want to defend the Jews ought never to deny this. Yes, I say, we cheated the Gentiles when-ever we dared, because it was the only thing to do. Remember how the Czar was always sending us commands,—you shall not do this and you shall not do that, until there was little left that we might honestly do, except pay tribute and die. There he had us cooped up, thousands of us where only hundreds could live, and every means of living taxed to the utmost. When there are too many wolves in the prairie, they begin to prey upon each other. We starv-ing captives of the Pale—we did as do the hungry brutes. But our humanity showed in our discrimination between our victims. Whenever we could, we spared our own kind, directing against our

THE GRAVE DIGGER OF POLOTZK

racial foes the cunning wiles which our bitter need invented. Is not that the code of war? Encamped in the midst of the enemy, we could practice no other. A Jew could hardly exist in business unless he developed a dual conscience, which allowed him to do to the Gentile what he would call a sin against a fellow Jew. Such spiritual deformities are self-explained in the step-children of the Czar. A glance over the statutes of the Pale leaves you wondering that the Russian Jews have not lost all semblance to humanity.

A favorite complaint against us was that we were greedy for gold. Why could not the Gentiles see the whole truth where they saw half? Greedy for profits we were, eager for bargains, for savings, intent on squeezing the utmost out of every business transaction. But why? Did not the Gentiles know the reason? Did they not know what price we had to pay for the air we breathed? If a Jew and a Gentile kept store side by side, the Gentile could content himself with smaller profits. He did not have to buy permission to travel in the interests of his business. He did not have to pay three hundred rubles fine if his son evaded military service. He was saved the expense of hushing inciters of pogroms. Police favor was retailed at a lower price to him than to the Jew. His nature did not compel him to support schools and charities. It cost nothing to be a Christian; on the contrary, it brought rewards and immunities. To be a Jew was a costly luxury, the price of which was either money or blood. Is it any wonder that we hoarded our pennies? What his shield is to the soldier in battle, that was the ruble to the Jew in the Pale.

The knowledge of such things as I am telling leaves marks upon the flesh and spirit. I remember little children in Polotzk with old, old faces and eyes glazed with secrets. I knew how to dodge and cringe and dissemble before I knew the names of the seasons. And I had plenty of time to ponder on these things, because I was so idle. If they had let me go to school, now—But of course they did n't.

There was no free school for girls, and even if your parents were rich enough to send you to a private school, you could not go very far. At the high school, which was under government control, Jewish children were admitted in limited numbers,—only ten to every hundred,—and even if you were among the lucky ones, you had your troubles. The tutor who prepared you talked all the time about the examinations you would have to pass, till you were scared. You heard on all sides that the brightest Jewish children were turned down if the examining officers did not like the turn of their noses. You went up to be examined with the other Jewish children, your heart heavy about that matter of your nose. There was a special examination for the Jewish candidates, of course; a nine-year-old Jewish child had to answer questions that a thirteen-year-old Gentile was hardly expected to understand. But that did not matter so much. You had been prepared for the thirteen-year-old test; you found the questions quite easy. You wrote your answers triumphantly—and you received a low rating, and there was no appeal.

I used to stand in the doorway of my father's store, munching an apple that did not taste good any more, and watch the pupils going home from school in twos and threes; the girls in neat brown dresses and black aprons and little stiff hats, the boys in trim uniforms with many buttons. They had ever so many books in the satchels on their backs. They would take them out at home, and read and write, and learn all sorts of interesting things. They looked to me like beings from another world than mine. But those whom I envied had their own troubles, as I often heard. Their school life was one struggle against injustice from instructors, spiteful treatment from fellow students, and insults from everybody. Those who, by heroic efforts and transcendent good luck, successfully finished the course, found themselves against a new wall, if they wished to go on. They were turned down at the universities, which admitted them in the ratio of three Jews to a hundred Gentiles, under the same debarring entrance conditions as at the high school,—especially rigorous examinations, dishonest marking, or arbitrary rulings without disguise. No, the Czar did not want us in the schools.

I heard from my mother of a different state of affairs, at the time when her brothers were little boys. The Czar of those days had a bright idea. He said to his ministers: "Let us educate the people. Let us win over those Jews through the public schools, instead of allowing them to persist in their narrow Hebrew learning, which teaches them no love for their monarch. Force has failed with them; the unwilling converts return to their old ways whenever they dare. Let us try education."

Perhaps peaceable conversion of the Jews was not the Czar's only motive when he opened public schools everywhere and compelled parents to send their boys for instruction. Perhaps he just wanted to be good, and really hoped to benefit the country. But to the Jews the public schools appeared as a trap door to the abyss of apostasy. The instructors were always Christians, the teaching was Christian, and the regulations of the schoolroom, as to hours, costume, and manners, were often in opposition to Jewish practices. The public school interrupted the boy's sacred studies in the Hebrew school. Where would you look for pious Jews, after a few generations of boys brought up by Christian teachers? Plainly the Czar was after the souls of the Jewish children. The church door gaped for them at the end of the school course. And all good Jews rose up against the schools, and by every means, fair or foul, kept their boys away. The official appointed to keep the register of boys for school purposes waxed rich on the bribes paid him by anxious parents who kept their sons in hiding.

After a while the wise Czar changed his mind, or he died,— probably he did both,—and the schools were closed, and the Jewish boys perused their Hebrew books in peace, wearing the sacred fringes[1] in plain sight, and never polluting their mouths with a word of Russian.

And then it was the Jews who changed their minds—some of them. They wanted to send their children to school, to learn histories and sciences, because they had discovered that there was good in such things as well as in the Sacred Law. These people were called progressive, but they had no chance to progress. All the czars that came along persisted in the old idea, that for the Jew no door should be opened,—no door out of the Pale, no door out of their mediævalism.

---

[1] A four-cornered cloth with specially prepared fringes is worn by pious males under the outer garments, but with the fringes showing. The latter play a part in the daily ritual.

CHAPTER II

CHILDREN OF THE LAW

As I LOOK BACK TO-DAY I see, within the wall raised around my birthplace by the vigilance of the police, another wall, higher, thicker, more impenetrable. This is the wall which the Czar with all his minions could not shake, the priests with their instruments of torture could not pierce, the mob with their firebrands could not destroy. This wall within the wall is the religious integrity of the Jews, a fortress erected by the prisoners of the Pale, in defiance of their jailers; a stronghold built of the ruins of their pillaged homes, cemented with the blood of their murdered children.

Harassed on every side, thwarted in every normal effort, pent up within narrow limits, all but dehumanized, the Russian Jew fell back upon the only thing that never failed him,—his hereditary faith in God. In the study of the Torah he found the balm for all his wounds; the minute observance of traditional rites became the expression of his spiritual cravings; and in the dream of a restoration to Palestine he forgot the world.

What did it matter to us, on a Sabbath or festival, when our life was centred in the synagogue, what czar sat on the throne, what evil counsellors whispered in his ear? They were concerned with revenues and policies and ephemeral trifles of all sorts, while we were intent on renewing our ancient covenant with God, to the end that His promise to the world should be fulfilled, and His justice overwhelm the nations.

On a Friday afternoon the stores and markets closed early. The clatter of business ceased, the dust of worry was laid, and the Sabbath peace flooded the quiet streets. No hovel so mean but what its easement sent out its consecrated ray, so that a wayfarer passing in the twilight saw the spirit of God brooding over the lowly roof.

Care and fear and shrewishness dropped like a mask from every face. Eyes dimmed with weeping kindled with inmost joy. Wherever a head bent over a sacred page, there rested the halo of God's presence.

Not on festivals alone, but also on the common days of the

week, we lived by the Law that had been given us through our teacher Moses. How to eat, how to bathe, how to work—everything had been written down for us, and we strove to fulfil the Law. The study of the Torah was the most honored of all occupations, and they who engaged in it the most revered of all men.

My memory does not go back to a time when I was too young to know that God had made the world, and had appointed teachers to tell the people how to live in it. First came Moses, and after him the great rabbis, and finally the Rav of Polotzk, who read all day in the sacred books, so that he could tell me and my parents and my friends what to do whenever we were in doubt. If my mother cut up a chicken and found something wrong in it,—some hurt or mark that should not be,—she sent the housemaid with it to the rav, and I ran along, and saw the rav look in his big books; and whatever he decided was right. If he called the chicken "trefah" I must not eat of it; no, not if I had to starve. And the rav knew about everything: about going on a journey, about business, about marrying, about purifying vessels for Passover.

Another great teacher was the dayyan, who heard people's quarrels and settled them according to the Law, so that they should not have to go to the Gentile courts. The Gentiles were false, judges and witnesses and all. They favored the rich man against the poor, the Christian against the Jew. The dayyan always gave true judgments. Nohem Rabinovitch, the richest man in Polotzk, could not win a case against a servant maid, unless he were in the right.

Besides the rav and the dayyan there were other men whose callings were holy,—the shohat, who knew how cattle and fowls should be killed; the hazzan and the other officers of the synagogue; the teachers of Hebrew, and their pupils. It did not matter how poor a man was, he was to be respected and set above other men, if he were learned in the Law.

In the synagogue scores of men sat all day long over the Hebrew books, studying and disputing from early dawn till candles were brought in at night, and then as long as the candles lasted. They could not take time for anything else, if they meant to become great scholars. Most of them were strangers in Polotzk, and had no home except the synagogue. They slept on benches, on tables, on the floor; they picked up their meals wherever they could. They had come from distant cities, so as to be under good teachers in Polotzk; and the townspeople were proud to support them by giving them food and clothing and sometimes money to visit their homes on holidays. But the poor students came in such numbers that there were not enough rich families to provide for all, so that some of them suffered privation. You could pick out a poor student in a crowd, by his pale face and shrunken form.

There was almost always a poor student taking meals at our house. He was assigned a certain day, and on that day my grandmother took care to have something especially good for dinner. It was a very shabby guest who sat down with us at table, but we children watched him with respectful eyes. Grandmother had told us that he was a lamden (scholar), and we saw something holy in the way he ate his cabbage.

Not every man could hope to be a rav, but no Jewish boy was allowed to grow up without at least a rudimentary knowledge of Hebrew. The scantiest income had to be divided so as to provide for the boys' tuition. To leave a boy without a teacher was a disgrace upon the whole family, to the remotest relative. For the children of the destitute there was a free school, supported by the charity of the pious. And so every boy was sent to heder (Hebrew school) almost as soon as he could speak; and usually he continued to study until his confirmation, at thirteen years of age, or as much longer as his talent and ambition carried him. My brother was five years old when he entered on his studies. He was carried to the heder, on the first day, covered over with a praying-shawl, so that nothing unholy should look on him; and he was presented with a bun, on which were traced, in honey, these words: "The Torah left by Moses is the heritage of the children of Jacob."

After a boy entered heder, he was the hero of the family. He was served before the other children at table, and nothing was too good for him. If the family were very poor, all the girls might go barefoot, but the heder boy must have shoes; he must have a plate of hot soup, though the others ate dry bread. When the rebbe (teacher) came on Sabbath afternoon, to examine the boy in the hearing of the family, everybody sat around the table and nodded with satisfaction, if he read his portion well; and he was given a great saucerful of preserves, and was praised, and blessed, and made much of. No wonder he said, in his morning prayer, "I thank Thee,

Lord, for not having created me a female." It was not much to be a girl, you see. Girls could not be scholars and rabbonim.

I went to my brother's heder, sometimes, to bring him his dinner, and saw how the boys studied. They sat on benches around the table, with their hats on, of course, and the sacred fringes hanging beneath their jackets. The rebbe sat at an end of the table, rehearsing two or three of the boys who were studying the same part, pointing out the words with his wooden pointer, so as not to lose the place. Everybody read aloud, the smallest boys repeating the alphabet in a sing-song, while the advanced boys read their portions in a different sing-song; and everybody raised his voice to its loudest so as to drown the other voices. The good boys never took their eyes off their page, except to ask the rebbe a question; but the naughty boys stared around the room, and kicked each other under the table, till the rebbe caught them at it. He had a ruler for striking the bad boys on the knuckles, and in a corner of the room leaned a long birch wand for pupils who would not learn their lessons.

The boys came to heder before nine in the morning, and remained until eight or nine in the evening. Stupid pupils, who could not remember the lesson, sometimes had to stay till ten. There was an hour for dinner and play at noon. Good little boys played quietly in their places, but most of the boys ran out of the house and jumped and yelled and quarrelled.

There was nothing in what the boys did in heder that I could not have done—if I had not been a girl. For a girl it was enough if she could read her prayers in Hebrew, and follow the meaning by the Yiddish translation at the bottom of the page. It did not take long to learn this much,—a couple of terms with a rebbetzin (female teacher),—and after that she was done with books.

A girl's real schoolroom was her mother's kitchen. There she learned to bake and cook and manage, to knit, sew, and embroider; also to spin and weave, in country places. And while her hands were busy, her mother instructed her in the laws regulating a pious Jewish household and in the conduct proper for a Jewish wife; for, of course, every girl hoped to be a wife. A girl was born for no other purpose.

How soon it came, the pious burden of wifehood! One day the girl is playing forfeits with her laughing friends, the next day she is missed from the circle. She has been summoned to a conference with the shadchan (marriage broker), who has been for months past advertising her housewifely talents, her piety, her good looks, and her marriage portion, among families with marriageable sons. Her parents are pleased with the son-in-law proposed by the shadchan, and now, at the last, the girl is brought in, to be examined and appraised by the prospective parents-in-law. If the negotiations go off smoothly, the marriage contract is written, presents are exchanged between the engaged couple, through their respective parents, and all that is left the girl of her maidenhood is a period of busy preparation for the wedding.

If the girl is well-to-do, it is a happy interval, spent in visits to the drapers and tailors, in collecting linens and featherbeds and vessels of copper and brass. The former playmates come to inspect the trousseau, enviously fingering the silks and velvets of the bride-elect. The happy heroine tries on frocks and mantles before her glass, blushing at references to the wedding day; and to the question, "How do you like the bridegroom?" she replies, "How should I know? There was such a crowd at the betrothal that I did n't see him."

Marriage was a sacrament with us Jews in the Pale. To rear a family of children was to serve God. Every Jewish man and woman had a part in the fulfilment of the ancient promise given to Jacob that his seed should be abundantly scattered over the earth. Parenthood, therefore, was the great career. But while men, in addition to begetting, might busy themselves with the study of the Law, woman's only work was motherhood. To be left an old maid became, accordingly, the greatest misfortune that could threaten a girl; and to ward off that calamity the girl and her family, to the most distant relatives, would strain every nerve, whether by contributing to her dowry, or hiding her defects from the marriage broker, or praying and fasting that God might send her a husband.

Not only must all the children of a family be mated, but they must marry in the order of their ages. A younger daughter must on no account marry before an elder. A houseful of daughters might be held up because the eldest failed to find favor in the eyes of prospective mothers-in-law; not one of the others could marry till the eldest was disposed of.

A cousin of mine was guilty of the disloyalty of wishing to

HEDER (HEBREW SCHOOL) FOR BOYS IN POLOTZK

marry before her elder sister, who was unfortunate enough to be rejected by one mother-in-law after another. My uncle feared that the younger daughter, who was of a firm and masterful nature, might carry out her plans, thereby disgracing her unhappy sister. Accordingly he hastened to conclude an alliance with a family far beneath him, and the girl was hastily married to a boy of whom little was known beyond the fact that he was inclined to consumption.

The consumptive tendency was no such horror, in an age when superstition was more in vogue than science. For one patient that went to a physician in Polotzk, there were ten who called in unlicensed practitioners and miracle workers. If my mother had an obstinate toothache that honored household remedies failed to relieve, she went to Dvoshe, the pious woman, who cured by means of a flint and steel, and a secret prayer pronounced as the sparks flew up. During an epidemic of scarlet fever, we protected ourselves by wearing a piece of red woolen tape around the neck. Pepper and salt tied in a corner of the pocket was effective in warding off the evil eye. There were lucky signs, lucky dreams, spirits, and hobgoblins, a grisly collection, gathered by our wandering ancestors from the demonologies of Asia and Europe.

Antiquated as our popular follies was the organization of our small society. It was a caste system with social levels sharply marked off, and families united by clannish ties. The rich looked down on the poor, the merchants looked down on the artisans, and within the ranks of the artisans higher and lower grades were distinguished. A shoemaker's daughter could not hope to marry the son of a shopkeeper, unless she brought an extra large dowry; and she had to make up her mind to be snubbed by the sisters-in-law and cousins-in-law all her life.

One qualification only could raise a man above his social level, and that was scholarship. A boy born in the gutter need not despair of entering the houses of the rich, if he had a good mind and a great appetite for sacred learning. A poor scholar would be preferred in the marriage market to a rich ignoramus. In the phrase of our grandmothers, a boy stuffed with learning was worth more than a girl stuffed with bank notes.

Simple piety unsupported by learning had a parallel value in the eyes of good families. This was especially true among the Hasidim, the sect of enthusiasts who set religious exaltation above rabbinical lore. Ecstasy in prayer and fantastic merriment on days of religious rejoicing, raised a Hasid to a hero among his kind. My father's grandfather, who knew of Hebrew only enough to teach beginners, was famous through a good part of the Pale for his holy life. Israel Kimanyer he was called, from the village of Kimanye where he lived; and people were proud to establish even the most distant relationship with him. Israel was poor to the verge of beggary, but he prayed more than other people, never failed in the slightest observance enjoined on Jews, shared his last crust with every chance beggar, and sat up nights to commune with God. His family connections included country peddlers, starving artisans, and ne'er-do-wells; but Israel was a zaddik—a man of piety—and the fame of his good life redeemed the whole wretched clan. When his grandson, my father, came to marry, he boasted his direct descent from Israel Kimanyer, and picked his bride from the best families.

The little house may still be standing which the pious Jews of Kimanye and the neighboring villages built for my great-grandfather, close on a century ago. He was too poor to build his own house, so the good people who loved him, and who were almost as poor as he, collected a few rubles among themselves, and bought a site, and built the house. Built, let it be known, with their own hands; for they were too poor to hire workmen. They carried the beams and boards on their shoulders, singing and dancing on the way, as they sang and danced at the presentation of a scroll to the synagogue. They hauled and sawed and hammered, till the last nail was driven home; and when they conducted the holy man to his new abode, the rejoicing was greater than at the crowning of a czar.

That little cabin was fit to be preserved as the monument to a species of idealism that has rarely been known outside the Pale. What was the ultimate source of the pious enthusiasm that built my great-grandfather's house? What was the substance behind the show of the Judaism of the Pale? Stripped of its grotesque mask of forms, rites, and mediæval superstitions, the religion of these fanatics was simply the belief that God was, had been, and ever would be, and that they, the children of Jacob, were His chosen messengers to carry His Law to all the nations. Beneath the mountainous volumes of the Talmudists and commentators, the Mosaic

tablets remained intact. Out of the mazes of the Cabala the pure
doctrine of ancient Judaism found its way to the hearts of the faithful. Sects and schools might rise and fall, deafening the ears of the
simple with the clamor of their disputes, still the Jew, retiring
within his own soul, heard the voice of the God of Abraham.
Prophets, messiahs, miracle workers might have their day, still the
Jew was conscious that between himself and God no go-between
was needed; that he, as well as every one of his million brothers,
had his portion of God's work to do. And this close relation to
God was the source of the strength that sustained the Jew through
all the trials of his life in the Pale. Consciously or unconsciously,
the Jew identified himself with the cause of righteousness on earth;
and hence the heroism with which he met the battalions of tyrants.

No empty forms could have impressed the unborn children of
the Pale so deeply that they were prepared for willing martyrdom
almost as soon as they were weaned from their mother's breast.
The flame of the burning bush that had dazzled Moses still lighted
the gloomy prison of the Pale. Behind the mummeries, ceremonials,
and symbolic accessories, the object of the Jew's adoration was the
face of God.

This has been many times proved by those who escaped from
the Pale, and, excited by sudden freedom, thought to rid themselves, by one impatient effort, of every strand of their ancient
bonds. Eager to be merged in the better world in which they found
themselves, the escaped prisoners determined on a change of mind,
a change of heart, a change of manner. They rejoiced in their transformation, thinking that every mark of their former slavery was
obliterated. And then, one day, caught in the vise of some crucial
test, the Jew fixed his alarmed gaze on his inmost soul, and found
there the image of his father's God.

Merrily played the fiddlers at the wedding of my father, who was
the grandson of Israel Kimanyer of sainted memory. The most pious men in Polotzk danced the night through, their earlocks dangling, the tails of their long coats flying in a pious ecstasy. Beggars
swarmed among the bidden guests, sure of an easy harvest where
so many hearts were melted by piety. The wedding jester excelled
himself in apt allusions to the friends and relatives who brought up
their wedding presents at his merry invitation. The sixteen-year-

old bride, suffocated beneath her heavy veil, blushed unseen at the numerous healths drunk to her future sons and daughters. The whole town was a-flutter with joy, because the pious scion of a godly race had found a pious wife, and a young branch of the tree of Judah was about to bear fruit.

When I came to lie on my mother's breast, she sang me lullabies on lofty themes. I heard the names of Rebecca, Rachel, and Leah as early as the names of father, mother, and nurse. My baby soul was enthralled by sad and noble cadences, as my mother sang of my ancient home in Palestine, or mourned over the desolation of Zion. With the first rattle that was placed in my hand a prayer was pronounced over me, a petition that a pious man might take me to wife, and a messiah be among my sons.

I was fed on dreams, instructed by means of prophecies, trained to hear and see mystical things that callous senses could not perceive. I was taught to call myself a princess, in memory of my forefathers who had ruled a nation. Though I went in the disguise of an outcast, I felt a halo resting on my brow. Sat upon by brutal enemies, unjustly hated, annihilated a hundred times, I yet arose and held my head high, sure that I should find my kingdom in the end, although I had lost my way in exile; for He who had brought my ancestors safe through a thousand perils was guiding my feet as well. God needed me and I needed Him, for we two together had a work to do, according to an ancient covenant between Him and my forefathers.

This is the dream to which I was heir, in common with every sad-eyed child of the Pale. This is the living seed which I found among my heirlooms, when I learned how to strip from them the prickly husk in which they were passed down to me. And what is the fruit of such seed as that, and whither lead such dreams? If it is mine to give the answer, let my words be true and brave.

CHAPTER III

BOTH THEIR HOUSES

AMONG THE MEDIÆVAL CUSTOMS which were preserved in the Pale when the rest of the world had long forgotten them was the use of popular sobriquets in place of surnames proper. Family names existed only in official documents, such as passports. For the most part people were known by nicknames, prosaic or picturesque, derived from their occupations, their physical peculiarities, or distinctive achievements. Among my neighbors in Polotzk were Yankel the Wig-maker, Mulye the Blind, Moshe the Six-fingered; and members of their respective families were referred to by these nicknames: as, for example, "Mirele, niece of Moshe the Six-fingered."

Let me spread out my family tree, raise aloft my coat-of-arms, and see what heroes have left a mark by which I may be distinguished. Let me hunt for my name in the chronicles of the Pale.

In the village of Yuchovitch, about sixty versts above Polotzk, the oldest inhabitant still remembered my father's great-grandfather when my father was a boy. Lebe the Innkeeper he was called, and no reproach was coupled with the name. His son Hayyim succeeded to the business, but later he took up the glazier's trade, and developed a knack for all sorts of tinkering, whereby he was able to increase his too scanty earnings.

Hayyim the Glazier is reputed to have been a man of fine countenance, wise in homely counsel, honest in all his dealings. Rachel Leah, his wife, had a reputation for practical wisdom even greater than his. She was the advice giver of the village in every perplexity of life. My father remembers his grandmother as a tall, trim, handsome old woman, active and independent. Satin headbands and lace-trimmed bonnets not having been invented in her day, Rachel Leah wore the stately knupf or turban on her shaven head. On Sabbaths and holidays she went to the synagogue with a long, straight mantle hanging from neck to ankle; and she wore it with an air, on one sleeve only, the other dangling empty from her shoulder.

Hayyim begat Joseph, and Joseph begat Pinchus, my father. It behooves me to consider the stuff I sprang from.

Joseph inherited the trade, good name, and meagre portion of his father, and maintained the family tradition of honesty and poverty unbroken to the day of his death. For that matter, Yuchovitch never heard of any connection of the family, not even a doubtful cousin, who was not steeped to the earlocks in poverty. But that was no distinction in Yuchovitch; the whole village was poor almost to beggary.

Joseph was an indifferent workman, an indifferent scholar, and an indifferent hasid. At one thing only he was strikingly good, and that was at grumbling. Although not unkind, he had a temper that boiled over at small provocation, and even in his most placid mood he took very little satisfaction in the world. He reversed the proverb, looking for the sable lining of every silver cloud. In the conditions of his life he found plenty of food for his pessimism, and merry hearts were very rare among his neighbors. Still a certain amount of gloom appears to have been inherent in the man. And as he distrusted the whole world, so Joseph distrusted himself, which made him shy and awkward in company. My mother tells how, at the wedding of his only son, my father, Joseph sat the whole night through in a corner, never as much as cracking a smile, while the wedding guests danced, laughed, and rejoiced.

It may have been through distrust of the marital state that Joseph remained single till the advanced age of twenty-five. Then he took unto himself an orphan girl as poor as he, namely, Rachel, the daughter of Israel Kimanyer of pious memory.

My grandmother was such a gentle, cheerful soul, when I knew her, that I imagine she must have been a merry bride. I should think my grandfather would have taken great satisfaction in her society, as her attempts to show him the world through rose-hued spectacles would have given him frequent opportunity to parade his grievances and recite his wrongs. But from all reports it appears that he was never satisfied, and if he did not make his wife unhappy it was because he was away from home so much. He was absent the greater part of the time; for a glazier, even if he were a better workman than my grandfather, could not make a living in Yuchovitch. He became a country peddler, trading between Polotzk and Yuchovitch, and taking in all the desolate little hamlets scattered along that route. Fifteen rubles' worth of goods was a big bill to carry out of Polotzk. The stock consisted of cheap pottery, tobacco, matches, boot grease, and axle grease. These he bartered for country produce, including grains in small quantity, bristles, rags, and bones. Money was seldom handled in these transactions.

A rough enough life my grandfather led, on the road at all seasons, in all weathers, knocking about at smoky little inns, glad sometimes of the hospitality of some peasant's hut, where the pigs slept with the family. He was doing well if he got home for the holidays with a little white flour for a cake, and money enough to take his best coat out of pawn. The best coat, and the candlesticks, too, would be repawned promptly on the first workday; for it was not for the like of Joseph of Yuchovitch to live with idle riches around him.

For the credit of Yuchovitch it must be recorded that my grandfather never had to stay away from the synagogue for want of his one decent coat to wear. His neighbor Isaac, the village money lender, never refused to give up the pledged articles on a Sabbath eve, even if the money due was not forthcoming. Many Sabbath coats besides my grandfather's, and many candlesticks besides my grandmother's, passed most of their existence under Isaac's roof, waiting to be redeemed. But on the eve of Sabbath or holiday Isaac delivered them to their respective owners, came they empty-handed or otherwise; and at the expiration of the festival the grateful owners brought them promptly back, for another season of retirement.

While my grandfather was on the road, my grandmother conducted her humble household in a capable, housewifely way. Of her six children, three died young, leaving two daughters and an only son, my father. My grandmother fed and dressed her children the best she could, and taught them to thank God for what they had not as well as for what they had. Piety was about the only positive doctrine she attempted to drill them in, leaving the rest of their education to life and the rebbe.

Promptly when custom prescribed, Pinchus, the petted only son, was sent to heder. My grandfather being on the road at the time, my grandmother herself carried the boy in her arms, as was usual on the first day. My father distinctly remembers that she wept on the way to the heder; partly, I suppose, from joy at starting her son on a holy life, and partly from sadness at being too poor to set forth the wine and honeycake proper to the occasion. For Grandma Rachel, schooled though she was to pious contentment, probably had her moments of human pettiness like the rest of us.

My father distinguished himself for scholarship from the first. Five years old when he entered heder, at eleven he was already a *yeshibah bahur*—a student in the seminary. The rebbe never had occasion to use the birch on him. On the contrary, he held him up as an example to the dull or lazy pupils, praised him in the village, and carried his fame to Polotzk.

My grandmother's cup of pious joy was overfilled. Everything her boy did was pleasant in her sight, for Pinchus was going to be a scholar, a godly man, a credit to the memory of his renowned grandfather, Israel Kimanyer. She let nothing interfere with his schooling. When times were bad, and her husband came home with his goods unsold, she borrowed and begged, till the rebbe's fee was produced. If bad luck continued, she pleaded with the rebbe for time. She pawned not only the candlesticks, but her shawl and Sabbath cap as well, to secure the scant rations that gave the young scholar strength to study. More than once in the bitter winter, as my father remembers, she carried him to heder on her back, because he had no shoes; she herself walking almost barefoot in the cruel snow. No sacrifice was too great for her in the pious cause of her boy's education. And when there was no rebbe in Yuchovitch learned enough to guide him in the advanced studies, my father was sent to Polotzk, where he lived with his poor relations, who were not too poor to help support a future rebbe or rav. In Polotzk he continued to distinguish himself for scholarship, till people began to prophesy that he would live to be famous; and everybody who remembered Israel Kimanyer regarded the promising grandson with double respect.

At the age of fifteen my father was qualified to teach beginners in Hebrew, and he was engaged as instructor in two families living six versts apart in the country. The boy tutor had to make himself useful, after lesson hours, by caring for the horse, hauling water from the frozen pond, and lending a hand at everything. When the little sister of one of his pupils died, in the middle of the winter, it fell to my father's lot to take the body to the nearest Jewish cemetery, through miles of desolate country, no living soul accompanying him.

After one term of this, he tried to go on with his own studies, sometimes in Yuchovitch, sometimes in Polotzk, as opportunity dictated. He made the journey to Polotzk beside his father, jogging along in the springless wagon on the rutty roads. He took a boy's pleasure in the gypsy life, the green wood, and the summer storm; while his father sat moody beside him, seeing nothing but the spavins on the horse's hocks, and the mud in the road ahead.

There is little else to tell of my father's boyhood, as most of his time was spent in the schoolroom. Outside the schoolroom he was conspicuous for high spirits in play, daring in mischief, and independence in everything. But a boy's playtime was so short in Yuchovitch, and his resources so limited, that even a lad of spirit came to the edge of his premature manhood without a regret for his nipped youth. So my father, at the age of sixteen and a half, lent a willing ear to the cooing voice of the marriage broker.

Indeed, it was high time for him to marry. His parents had kept him so far, but they had two daughters to marry off, and not a groschen laid by for their dowries. The cost of my father's schooling, as he advanced, had mounted to seventeen rubles a term, and the poor rebbe was seldom paid in full. Of course my father's scholarship was his fortune—in time it would be his support; but in the meanwhile the burden of feeding and clothing him lay heavy on his parents' shoulders. The time had come to find him a well-to-do father-in-law, who should support him and his wife and children, while he continued to study in the seminary.

After the usual conferences between parents and marriage brokers, my father was betrothed to an undertaker's daughter in Polotzk. The girl was too old,—every day of twenty years,—but three hundred rubles in dowry, with board after marriage, not to mention handsome presents to the bridegroom, easily offset the bride's age. My father's family, to the humblest cousin, felt themselves set up by the match he had made; and the boy was happy enough, displaying a watch and chain for the first time in his life, and a good coat on week days. As for his fiancée, he could have no objection to her, as he had seen her only at a distance, and had never spoken to her.

When it was time for the wedding preparations to begin, news came to Yuchovitch of the death of the bride-elect, and my father's prospects seemed fallen to the ground. But the undertaker had another daughter, a girl of thirteen, and he pressed my father to take her in her sister's place. At the same time the marriage broker proposed another match; and my father's poor cousins bristled with importance once more.

Somehow or other my father succeeded in getting in a word at the family councils that ensued; he even had the temerity to express a strong preference. He did not want any more of the undertaker's daughters; he wanted to consider the rival match. There were no serious objections from the cousins, and my father became engaged to my mother.

This second choice was Hannah Hayye, only daughter of Raphael, called the Russian. She had had a very different bringing-up from Pinchus, the grandson of Israel Kimanyer. She had never known a day of want; had never gone barefoot from necessity. The family had a solid position in Polotzk, her father being the owner of a comfortable home and a good business.

Prosperity is prosaic, so I shall skip briefly over the history of my mother's house.

My grandfather Raphael, early left an orphan, was brought up by an elder brother, in a village at no great distance from Polotzk. The brother dutifully sent him to heder, and at an early age betrothed him to Deborah, daughter of one Solomon, a dealer in grain and cattle. Deborah was not yet in her teens at the time of the betrothal, and so foolish was she that she was afraid of her affianced husband. One day, when she was coming from the store with a bottle of liquid yeast, she suddenly came face to face with her betrothed, which gave her such a fright that she dropped the bottle, spilling the yeast on her pretty dress; and she ran home crying all the way. At thirteen she was married, which had a good effect on her deportment. I hear no more of her running away from her husband.

Among the interesting things belonging to my grandmother, besides her dowry, at the time of the marriage, was her family. Her father was so original that he kept a tutor for his daughters—sons he had none—and allowed them to be instructed in the rudiments of three or four languages and the elements of arithmetic. Even more unconventional was her sister Hode. She had married a fiddler, who travelled constantly, playing at hotels and inns, all through "far Russia." Having no children, she ought to have spent her days in fasting and praying and lamenting. Instead of this, she accompanied her husband on his travels, and even had a heart to enjoy the excitement and variety of their restless life. I should be the last to blame my great-aunt, for the irregularity of her conduct afforded my grandfather the opening for his career, the fruits of which made my childhood so pleasant. For several years my grandfather travelled in Hode's train, in the capacity of shohat providing kosher meat for the little troup in the unholy wilds of "far Russia"; and the grateful couple rewarded him so generously that he soon had a fortune of eighty rubles laid by.

My grandfather thought the time had now come to settle down, but he did not know how to invest his wealth. To resolve his perplexity, he made a pilgrimage to the Rebbe of Kopistch, who advised him to open a store in Polotzk, and gave him a blessed groschen to keep in the money drawer for good luck.

The blessing of the "good Jew" proved fruitful. My grandfather's business prospered, and my grandmother bore him children, several sons and one daughter. The sons were sent to heder, like all respectable boys; and they were taught, in addition, writing and arithmetic, enough for conducting a business. With this my grandfather was content; more than this he considered incompatible with piety. He was one of those who strenuously opposed the influence of the public school, and bribed the government officials to keep their children's names off the register of schoolboys, as we have already seen. When he sent his sons to a private tutor, where they could study Russian with their hats on, he felt, no doubt, that he was giving them all the education necessary to a successful business career, without violating piety too grossly.

If reading and writing were enough for the sons, even less would suffice the daughter. A female teacher was engaged for my mother, at three kopecks a week, to teach her the Hebrew prayers; and my grandmother, herself a better scholar than the teacher, taught her writing in addition. My mother was quick to learn, and expressed an ambition to study Russian. She teased and coaxed, and her mother pleaded for her, till my grandfather was persuaded to send her to a tutor. But the fates were opposed to my mother's education. On the first day at school, a sudden inflammation of the eyes blinded my mother temporarily, and although the distemper vanished as suddenly as it had appeared, it was taken as an omen, and my mother was not allowed to return to her lessons.

Still she did not give up. She saved up every groschen that was given her to buy sweets, and bribed her brother Solomon, who was proud of his scholarship, to give her lessons in secret. The two strove earnestly with book and quill, in their hiding-place under the rafters, till my mother could read and write Russian, and translate a simple passage of Hebrew.

My grandmother, although herself a good housewife, took no pains to teach her only daughter the domestic arts. She only petted and coddled her and sent her out to play. But my mother was as ambitious about housework as about books. She coaxed the housemaid to let her mix the bread. She learned knitting from watching her playmates. She was healthy and active, quick at everything, and restless with unspent energy. Therefore she was quite willing, at the age of ten, to go into her father's business as his chief assistant.

As the years went by she developed a decided talent for business, so that her father could safely leave all his affairs in her hands if he had to go out of town. Her devotion, ability, and tireless energy made her, in time, indispensable. My grandfather was obliged to admit that the little learning she had stolen was turned to good account, when he saw how well she could keep his books, and how smoothly she got along with Russian and Polish customers. Perhaps that was the argument that induced him, after obstinate years, to remove his veto from my mother's petitions and let her take up lessons again. For while piety was my grandfather's chief concern on the godly side, on the worldly side he set success in business above everything.

My mother was fifteen years old when she entered on a career of higher education. For two hours daily she was released from the store, and in that interval she strove with might and main to conquer the world of knowledge. Katrina Petrovna, her teacher, praised and encouraged her; and there was no reason why the promising pupil should not have developed into a young lady of culture, with Madame teaching Russian, German, crocheting, and singing—yes, out of a book, to the accompaniment of a clavier—all for a fee of seventy-five kopecks a week.

Did I say there was no reason? And what about the marriage

The Wood Market, Polotzk

broker? Hannah Hayye, the only daughter of Raphael the Russian, going on sixteen, buxom, bright, capable, and well educated, could not escape the eye of the shadchan. A fine thing it would be to let such a likely girl grow old over a book! To the canopy with her, while she could fetch the highest price in the marriage market!

My mother was very unwilling to think of marriage at this time. She had nothing to gain by marriage, for already she had everything that she desired, especially since she was permitted to study. While her father was rather stern, her mother spoiled and petted her; and she was the idol of her aunt Hode, the fiddler's wife.

Hode had bought a fine estate in Polotzk, after my grandfather settled there, and made it her home whenever she became tired of travelling. She lived in state, with many servants and dependents, wearing silk dresses on week days, and setting silver plate before the meanest guest. The women of Polotzk were breathless over her wardrobe, counting up how many pairs of embroidered boots she had, at fifteen rubles a pair. And Hode's manners were as much a subject of gossip as her clothes, for she had picked up strange ways in her travels. Although she was so pious that she was never tempted to eat trefah, no matter if she had to go hungry, her conduct in other respects was not strictly orthodox. For one thing, she was in the habit of shaking hands with men, looking them straight in the face. She spoke Russian like a Gentile, she kept a poodle, and she had no children.

Nobody meant to blame the rich woman for being childless, because it was well known in Polotzk that Hode the Russian, as she was called, would have given all her wealth for one scrawny baby. But she was to blame for voluntarily exiling herself from Jewish society for years at a time, to live among pork-eaters, and copy the bold ways of Gentile women. And so while they pitied her childlessness, the women of Polotzk regarded her misfortune as perhaps no more than a due punishment.

Hode, poor woman, felt a hungry heart beneath her satin robes. She wanted to adopt one of my grandmother's children, but my grandmother would not hear of it. Hode was particularly taken with my mother, and my grandmother, in compassion, loaned her the child for days at a time; and those were happy days for both aunt and niece. Hode would treat my mother to every delicacy in her sumptuous pantry, tell her wonderful tales of life in distant parts, show her all her beautiful dresses and jewels, and load her with presents.

As my mother developed into girlhood, her aunt grew more and more covetous of her. Following a secret plan, she adopted a boy from the poorhouse, and brought him up with every advantage that money could buy. My mother, on her visits, was thrown a great deal into this boy's society, but she liked him less than the poodle. This grieved her aunt, who cherished in her heart the hope that my mother would marry her adopted son, and so become her daughter after all. And in order to accustom her to think well of the match, Hode dinned the boy's name in my mother's ears day and night, praising him and showing him off. She would open her jewel boxes and take out the flashing diamonds, heavy chains, and tinkling bracelets, dress my mother in them in front of the mirror, telling her that they would all be hers—all her own—when she became the bride of Mulke.

My mother still describes the necklace of pearls and diamonds which her aunt used to clasp around her plump throat, with a light in her eyes that is reminiscent of girlish pleasure. But to all her aunt's teasing references to the future, my mother answered with a giggle and a shake of her black curls, and went on enjoying herself, thinking that the day of judgment was very, very far away. But it swooped down on her sooner than she expected—the momentous hour when she must choose between the pearl necklace with Mulke and a penniless stranger from Yuchovitch who was reputed to be a fine scholar.

Mulke she would not have even if all the pearls in the ocean came with him. The boy was stupid and unteachable, and of unspeakable origin. Picked up from the dirty floor of the poorhouse, his father was identified as the lazy porter who sometimes chopped a cord of wood for my grandmother; and his sisters were slovenly housemaids scattered through Polotzk. No, Mulke was not to be considered. But why consider anybody? Why think of a *hossen* at all, when she was so content? My mother ran away every time the shadchan came, and she begged to be left as she was, and cried, and invoked her mother's support. But her mother, for the first time in her history, refused to take the daughter's part. She joined the enemy—the family and the shadchan—and my mother saw that she was doomed.

Of course she submitted. What else could a dutiful daughter do, in Polotzk? She submitted to being weighed, measured, and appraised before her face, and resigned herself to what was to come.

When that which was to come did come, she did not recognize it. She was all alone in the store one day, when a beardless young man, in top boots that wanted grease, and a coat too thin for the weather, came in for a package of cigarettes. My mother climbed up on the counter, with one foot on a shelf, to reach down the cigarettes. The customer gave her the right change, and went out. And my mother never suspected that that was the proposed hossen, who came to look her over and see if she was likely to last. For my father considered himself a man of experience now, this being his second match, and he was determined to have a hand in this affair himself.

No sooner was the hossen out of the store than his mother, also unknown to the innocent storekeeper, came in for a pound of tallow candles. She offered a torn bill in payment, and my mother accepted it and gave change; showing that she was wise enough in money matters to know that a torn bill was good currency.

After the woman there shuffled in a poor man evidently from the country, who, in a shy and yet challenging manner, asked for a package of cheap tobacco. My mother produced the goods with her usual dispatch, gave the correct change, and stood at attention for more trade.

Parents and son held a council around the corner, the object of their espionage never dreaming that she had been put to a triple test and not found wanting. But in the evening of the same day she was enlightened. She was summoned to her elder brother's house, for a conference on the subject of the proposed match, and there she found the young man who had bought the cigarettes. For my mother's family, if they forced her to marry, were willing to make her path easier by letting her meet the hossen, convinced that she must be won over by his good looks and learned conversation.

It does not really matter how my mother felt, as she sat, with a protecting niece in her lap, at one end of a long table, with the hossen fidgeting at the other end. The marriage contract would be written anyway, no matter what she thought of the hossen. And the contract was duly written, in the presence of the assembled families of both parties, after plenty of open discussion, in which everybody except the prospective bride and groom had a voice.

One voice in particular broke repeatedly into the consultations of the parents and the shadchan, and that was the voice of Henne Rösel, one of my father's numerous poor cousins. Henne Rösel was not unknown to my mother. She often came to the store, to beg, under pretence of borrowing, a little flour or sugar or a stick of cinnamon. On the occasion of the betrothal she had arrived late, dressed in indescribable odds and ends, with an artificial red flower stuck into her frowzy wig. She pushed and elbowed her way to the middle of the table, where the shadchan sat ready with paper and ink to take down the articles of the contract. On every point she had some comment to make, till a dispute arose over a note which my grandfather offered as part of the dowry, the hossen's people insisting on cash. No one insisted so loudly as the cousin with the red flower in her wig; and when the other cousins seemed about to weaken and accept the note, Red-Flower stood up and exhorted them to be firm, lest their flesh and blood be cheated under their noses. The meddlesome cousin was silenced at last, the contract was signed, the happiness of the engaged couple was pledged in wine, the guests dispersed. And all this while my mother had not opened her mouth, and my father had scarcely been heard.

That is the way my fate was sealed. It gives me a shudder of wonder to think what a narrow escape I had; I came so near not being born at all. If the beggarly cousin with the frowzy wig had prevailed upon her family and broken off the match, then my mother would not have married my father, and I should at this moment be an unborn possibility in a philosopher's brain. It is right that I should pick my words most carefully, and meditate over every comma, because I am describing miracles too great for careless utterance. If I had died after my first breath, my history would still be worth recording. For before I could lie on my mother's breast, the earth had to be prepared, and the stars had to take their places; a million races had to die, testing the laws of life; and a boy and girl had to be bound for life to watch together for my coming. I was millions of years on the way, and I came through the seas of chance, over the fiery mountain of law, by the zigzag path of human possibility. Multitudes were pushed back into the abyss of non-existence, that I should have way to creep into being. And at the last, when I stood at the gate of life, a weazen-faced fishwife, who had not wit enough to support herself, came near shutting me out.

Such creatures of accident are we, liable to a thousand deaths before we are born. But once we are here, we may create our own world, if we choose. Since I have stood on my own feet, I have never met my master. For every time I choose a friend I determine my fate anew. I can think of no cataclysm that could have the force to move me from my path. Fire or flood or the envy of men may tear the roof off my house, but my soul would still be at home under the lofty mountain pines that dip their heads in star dust. Even life, that was so difficult to attain, may serve me merely as a wayside inn, if I choose to go on eternally. However I came here, it is mine to be.

CHAPTER IV

DAILY BREAD

MY MOTHER OUGHT TO HAVE been happy in her engagement. Everybody congratulated her on securing such a scholar, her parents loaded her with presents, and her friends envied her. It is true that the hossen's family consisted entirely of poor relations; there was not one solid householder among them. From the worldly point of view my mother made a mésalliance. But as one of my aunts put it, when my mother objected to the association with the undesirable cousins, she could take out the cow and set fire to the barn; meaning that she could rejoice in the hossen and disregard his family.

The hossen, on his part, had reason to rejoice, without any reservations. He was going into a highly respectable family, with a name supported by property and business standing. The promised dowry was considerable, the presents were generous, the trousseau would be liberal, and the bride was fair and capable. The bridegroom would have years before him in which he need do nothing but eat free board, wear his new clothes, and study Torah; and his poor relations could hold up their heads at the market stalls, and in the rear pews in the synagogue.

My mother's trousseau was all that a mother-in-law could wish. The best tailor in Polotzk was engaged to make the cloaks and gowns, and his shop was filled to bursting with ample lengths of velvet and satin and silk. The wedding gown alone cost every kopeck of fifty rubles, as the tailor's wife reported all over Polotzk. The lingerie was of the best, and the seamstress was engaged on it for many weeks. Featherbeds, linen, household goods of every sort—everything was provided in abundance. My mother crocheted many yards of lace to trim the best sheets, and fine silk coverlets adorned the plump beds. Many a marriageable maiden who came to view the trousseau went home to prink and blush and watch for the shadchan.

The wedding was memorable for gayety and splendor. The guests included some of the finest people in Polotzk; for while my grandfather was not quite at the top of the social scale, he had business connections with those that were, and they all turned out for the wedding of his only daughter, the men in silk frock coats, the women in all their jewelry.

The bridegroom's aunts and cousins came in full force. Wedding messengers had been sent to every person who could possibly claim relationship with the hossen. My mother's parents were too generous to slight the lowliest. Instead of burning the barn, they did all they could to garnish it. One or two of the more important of the poor relations came to the wedding in gowns paid for by my rich grandfather. The rest came decked out in borrowed finery, or in undisguised shabbiness. But nobody thought of staying away— except the obstructive cousin who had nearly prevented the match.

When it was time to conduct the bride to the wedding canopy, the bridegroom's mother missed Henne Rösel. The house was searched for her, but in vain. Nobody had seen her. But my grandmother could not bear to have the marriage solemnized in the absence of a first cousin. Such a wedding as this was not likely to be repeated in her family; it would be a great pity if any of the relatives missed it. So she petitioned the principals to delay the ceremony, while she herself went in search of the missing cousin.

Clear over to the farthest end of the town she walked, lifting her gala dress well above her ankles. She found Henne Rösel in her untidy kitchen, sound in every limb but sulky in spirit. My grandmother exclaimed at her conduct, and bade her hurry with her toilet, and accompany her; the wedding guests were waiting; the bride was faint from prolonging her fast. But Henne Rösel flatly refused to go; the bride might remain an old maid, for all she, Henne Rösel, cared about the wedding. My troubled grandmother expostulated, questioned her, till she drew out the root of the cousin's sulkiness. Henne Rösel complained that she had not been properly invited. The wedding messenger had come,—oh, yes!—but she had not addressed her as flatteringly, as respectfully as she had been heard to address the wife of Yohem, the money-lender. And Henne Rösel was n't going to any weddings where she was not wanted. My grandmother had a struggle of it, but she succeeded in soothing the sensitive cousin, who consented at length to don her best dress and go to the wedding.

While my grandmother labored with Henne Rösel, the bride sat in state in her father's house under the hill, the maidens danced, and the matrons fanned themselves, while the fiddlers and *zimblers* scraped and tinkled. But as the hours went by, the matrons became restless and the dancers wearied. The poor relations grew impatient for the feast, and the babies in their laps began to fidget and cry; while the bride grew faint, and the bridegroom's party began to send frequent messengers from the house next door, demanding to know the cause of the delay. Some of the guests at last lost all patience, and begged leave to go home. But before they went they deposited the wedding presents in the bride's satin lap, till she resembled a heathen image hung about with offerings.

My mother, after thirty years of bustling life, retains a lively memory of the embarrassment she suffered while waiting for the arrival of the troublesome cousin. When that important dame at last appeared, with her chin in the air, the artificial flower still stuck belligerently into her dusty wig, and my grandmother beaming behind her, the bride's heart fairly jumped with anger, and the red blood of indignation set her cheeks afire. No wonder that she speaks the name of the Red-Flower with an unloving accent to this day, although she has forgiven the enemies who did her greater wrong. The bride is a princess on her wedding day. To put upon her an indignity is an unpardonable offense.

After the feasting and dancing, which lasted a whole week, the wedding presents were locked up, the bride, with her hair discreetly covered, returned to her father's store, and the groom, with his new praying-shawl, repaired to the synagogue. This was all according to the marriage bargain, which implied that my father was to study and pray and fill the house with the spirit of piety, in return for board and lodging and the devotion of his wife and her entire family.

All the parties concerned had entered into this bargain in good faith, so far as they knew their own minds. But the eighteen-year-old bridegroom, before many months had passed, began to realize that he felt no such hunger for the word of the Law as he was supposed to feel. He felt, rather, a hunger for life that all his studying did not satisfy. He was not trained enough to analyze his own thoughts to any purpose; he was not experienced enough to understand where his thoughts were leading him. He only knew that he felt no call to pray and fast, that the Torah did not inspire him, and his days were blank. The life he was expected to lead grew distasteful to him, and yet he knew no other way to live. He became lax in his attendance at the synagogue, incurring the reproach of the family. It began to be rumored among the studious that the son-in-law of Raphael the Russian was not devoting himself to the sacred books with any degree of enthusiasm. It was well known that he had a good mind, but evidently the spirit was lacking. My grandparents went from surprise to indignation, from exhortation they passed to recrimination. Before my parents had been married half a year, my grandfather's house was divided against itself, and my mother was torn between the two factions. For while she sympathized with her parents, and felt personally cheated by my father's lack of piety, she thought it was her duty to take her husband's part, even against her parents, in their own house. My mother was one of those women who always obey the highest law they know, even though it leads them to their doom.

How did it happen that my father, who from his early boyhood had been pointed out as a scholar in embryo, failed to live up to the expectations of his world? It happened as it happened that his hair curled over his high forehead: he was made that way. If people were disappointed, it was because they had based their expectations on a misconception of his character, for my father had never had any aspirations for extreme piety. Piety was imputed to him by his mother, by his rebbe, by his neighbors, when they saw that he rendered the sacred word more intelligently than his fellow students. It was not his fault that his people confused scholarship with religious ardor. Having a good mind, he was glad to exercise it; and being given only one subject to study, he was bound to make rapid progress in that. If he had ever been offered a choice between a religious and a secular education, his friends would have found out early that he was not born to be a rav. But as he had no mental opening except through the hedder, he went on from year to year winning new distinction in Hebrew scholarship; with the result that witnesses with preconceived ideas began to see the halo of piety playing around his head, and a well-to-do family was misled into making a match with him for the sake of the glory that he was to attain.

When it became evident that the son-in-law was not going to develop into a rav, my grandfather notified him that he would have to assume the support of his own family without delay. My father therefore entered on a series of experiments with paying occupations, for none of which he was qualified, and in none of which he succeeded permanently.

My mother was with my father, as equal partner and laborer, in everything he attempted in Polotzk. They tried keeping a wayside inn, but had to give it up because the life was too rough for my mother, who was expecting her first baby. Returning to Polotzk, they went to storekeeping on their own account, but failed in this also, because my father was inexperienced, and my mother, now with the baby to nurse, was not able to give her best attention to business. Over two years passed in this experiment, and in the interval the second child was born, increasing my parents' need of a home and a reliable income.

It was then decided that my father should seek his fortune elsewhere. He travelled as far east as Tchistopol, on the Volga, and south as far as Odessa, on the Black Sea, trying his luck at various occupations within the usual Jewish restrictions. Finally he reached the position of assistant superintendent in a distillery, with a salary of thirty rubles a month. That was a fair income for those days, and he was planning to have his family join him when my Grandfather Raphael died, leaving my mother heir to a good business. My father thereupon returned to Polotzk, after nearly three years' absence from home.

As my mother had been trained to her business from childhood, while my father had had only a little irregular experience, she naturally remained the leader. She was as successful as her father before her. The people continued to call her Raphael's Hannah Hayye, and under that name she was greatly respected in the business world. Her eldest brother was now a merchant of importance, and my mother's establishment was gradually enlarged; so that, altogether, our family had a solid position in Polotzk, and there were plenty to envy us.

We were almost rich, as Polotzk counted riches in those days; certainly we were considered well-to-do. We moved into a larger house, where there was room for out-of-town customers to stay overnight, with stabling for their horses. We lived as well as any people of our class, and perhaps better, because my father had brought home with him from his travels a taste for a more genial life than Polotzk usually asked for. My mother kept a cook and a nursemaid, and a dvornik, or outdoor man, to take care of the horses, the cow, and the woodpile. All the year round we kept open house, as I remember. Cousins and aunts were always about, and on holidays friends of all degrees gathered in numbers. And coming and going in the wing set apart for business guests were merchants, traders, country peddlers, peasants, soldiers, and minor government officials. It was a full house at all times, and especially so during fairs, and at the season of the military draft.

In the family wing there was also enough going on. There were four of us children, besides father and mother and grandmother, and the parasitic cousins. Fetchke was the eldest; I was the second; the third was my only brother, named Joseph, for my father's father; and the fourth was Deborah, named for my mother's mother.

I suppose I ought to explain my own name also, especially because I am going to emerge as the heroine by and by. Be it therefore known that I was named Maryashe, for a bygone aunt. I was never called by my full name, however. "Maryashe" was too dignified for me. I was always "Mashinke," or else "Mashke," by way of diminutive. A variety of nicknames, mostly suggested by my physical peculiarities, were bestowed on me from time to time by my fond or foolish relatives. My uncle Berl, for example, gave me the name of "Zukrochene Flum," which I am not going to translate, because it is uncomplimentary.

My sister Fetchke was always the good little girl, and when our troubles began she was an important member of the family. What sort of little girl I was will be written by and by. Joseph was the best Jewish boy that ever was born, but he hated to go to heder, so he had to be whipped, of course. Deborah was just a baby, and her principal characteristic was single-mindedness. If she had teething to attend to, she thought of nothing else day or night, and communicated with the family on no other subject. If it was whooping-cough, she whooped most heartily; if it was measles, she had them thick.

It was the normal thing in Polotzk, where the mothers worked as well as the fathers, for the children to be left in the hands of grandmothers and nursemaids. I suffer reminiscent terrors when I recall Deborah's nurse, who never opened her lips except to frighten us children—or else to lie. That girl never told the truth if she could help it. I know it is so because I heard her tell eleven or twelve unnecessary lies every day. In the beginning of her residence with us, I exposed her indignantly every time I caught her lying; but the tenor of her private conversations with me was conducive to a cessation of my activity along the line of volunteer testimony. In shorter words, the nurse terrified me with horrid threats until I did not dare to contradict her even if she lied her head off. The things she promised me in this life and in the life to come could not be executed by a person without imagination. The nurse gave almost her entire attention to us older children, disposing easily of the baby's claims. Deborah, unless she was teething or whoop-coughing, was a quiet baby, and would lie for hours on the nurse's lap, sucking at a "pacifier" made of bread and sugar tied up in a muslin rag, and previously chewed to a pulp by the nurse. And while the baby sucked the nurse told us things—things that we must remember when we went to bed at night.

A favorite subject of her discourse was the Evil One, who lived, so she told us, in our attic, with his wife and brood. A pet amusement of our invisible tenant was the translating of human babies into his lair, leaving one of his own brats in the cradle; the moral of which was that if nurse wanted to loaf in the yard and watch who went out and who came in, we children must mind the baby. The girl was so sly that she carried on all this tyranny without being detected, and we lived in terror till she was discharged for stealing.

In our grandmothers we were very fortunate: They spoiled us to our hearts' content. Grandma Deborah's methods I know only from hearsay, for I was very little when she died. Grandma Rachel I remember distinctly, spare and trim and always busy. I recall her coming in midwinter from the frozen village where she lived. I remember, as if it were but last winter, the immense shawls and wraps which we unwound from about her person, her voluminous brown sack coat in which there was room for three of us at a time, and at last the tight clasp of her long arms, and her fresh, cold cheeks on ours. And when the hugging and kissing were over, Grandma had a treat for us. It was *talakno,* or oat flour, which we mixed with cold water and ate raw, using wooden spoons, just like the peasants, and smacking our lips over it in imaginary enjoyment.

But Grandma Rachel did not come to play. She applied herself energetically to the housekeeping. She kept her bright eye on everything, as if she were in her own trifling establishment in Yuchovitch. Watchful was she as any cat—and harmless as a tame rabbit. If she caught the maids at fault, she found an excuse for them at the same time. If she was quite exasperated with the stupidity of Yakub, the dvornik, she pretended to curse him in a phrase of her own invention, a mixture of Hebrew and Russian, which, translated, said, "Mayst thou have gold and silver in thy bosom"; but to the choreman, who was not a linguist, the mongrel phrase conveyed a sense of his delinquency.

Grandma Rachel meant to be very strict with us children, and accordingly was prompt to discipline us; but we discovered early in our acquaintance with her that the child who got a spanking was sure to get a hot cookie or the jam pot to lick, so we did not stand in great awe of her punishments. Even if it came to a spanking it was only a farce. Grandma generally interposed a pillow between the palm of her hand and the area of moral stimulation.

The real disciplinarian in our family was my father. Present or absent, it was fear of his displeasure that kept us in the straight and narrow path. In the minds of us children he was as much represented, when away from home, by the strap hanging on the wall as by his portrait which stood on a parlor table, in a gorgeous frame adorned with little shells. Almost everybody's father had a strap, but our father's strap was more formidable than the ordinary. For one thing, it was more painful to encounter personally, because it was not a simple strap, but a bunch of fine long strips, clinging as rubber. My father called it noodles; and while his facetiousness was lost on us children, the superior sting of his instrument was entirely effective.

In his leisure, my father found means of instructing us other than by the strap. He took us walking and driving, answered our questions, and taught us many little things that our playmates were not taught. From distant parts of the country he had imported little tricks of speech and conduct, which we learned readily enough; for we were always a teachable lot. Our pretty manners were very much admired, so that we became used to being held up as models to children less polite. Guests at our table praised our deportment, when, at the end of a meal, we kissed the hands of father and

My Father's Portrait

mother and thanked them for food. Envious mothers of rowdy children used to sneer, "Those grandchildren of Raphael the Russian are quite the aristocrats."

And yet, off the stage, we had our little quarrels and tempests, especially I. I really and truly cannot remember a time when Fetchke was naughty, but I was oftener in trouble than out of it. I need not go into details. I only need to recall how often, on going to bed, I used to lie silently rehearsing the day's misdeeds, my sister refraining from talk out of sympathy. As I always came to the conclusion that I wanted to reform, I emerged from my reflections with this solemn formula: "Fetchke, let us be good." And my generosity in including my sister in my plans for salvation was equalled by her magnanimity in assuming part of my degradation. She always replied, in aspiration as eager as mine, "Yes, Mashke, let us be good."

My mother had less to do than any one with our early training, because she was confined to the store. When she came home at night, with her pockets full of goodies for us, she was too hungry for our love to listen to tales against us, too tired from work to discipline us. It was only on Sabbaths and holidays that she had a chance to get acquainted with us, and we all looked forward to these days of enjoined rest.

On Friday afternoons my parents came home early, to wash and dress and remove from their persons every sign of labor. The great keys of the store were put away out of sight; the money bag was hidden in the featherbeds. My father put on his best coat and silk skull-cap; my mother replaced the cotton kerchief by the well-brushed wig. We children bustled around our parents, asking favors in the name of the Sabbath—"Mama, let Fetchke and me wear our new shoes, in honor of Sabbath"; or "Papa, will you take us tomorrow across the bridge? You said you would, on Sabbath." And while we adorned ourselves in our best, my grandmother superintended the sealing of the oven, the maids washed the sweat from their faces, and the dvornik scraped his feet at the door.

My father and brother went to the synagogue, while we women and girls assembled in the living-room for candle prayer. The table gleamed with spotless linen and china. At my father's place lay the Sabbath loaf, covered over with a crocheted doily; and beside it stood the wine flask and *kiddush* cup of gold or silver. At the opposite end of the table was a long row of brass candlesticks, polished to perfection, with the heavy silver candlesticks in a shorter row in front; for my mother and grandmother were very pious, and each used a number of candles; while Fetchke and I and the maids had one apiece.

After the candle prayer the women generally read in some book of devotion, while we children amused ourselves in the quietest manner, till the men returned from synagogue. "Good Sabbath!" my father called, as he entered; and "Good Sabbath! Good Sabbath!" we wished him in return. If he brought with him a Sabbath guest from the synagogue, some poor man without a home, the stranger was welcomed and invited in, and placed in the seat of honor, next to my father.

We all stood around the table while *kiddush,* or the blessing over the wine, was said, and if a child whispered or nudged another my father reproved him with a stern look, and began again from the beginning. But as soon as he had cut the consecrated loaf, and distributed the slices, we were at liberty to talk and ask questions, unless a guest was present, when we maintained a polite silence.

Of one Sabbath guest we were always sure, even if no destitute Jew accompanied my father from the synagogue. Yakub the choreman partook of the festival with us. He slept on a bunk built over the entrance door, and reached by means of a rude flight of steps. There he liked to roll on his straw and rags, whenever he was not busy, or felt especially lazy. On Friday evenings he climbed to his roost very early, before the family assembled for supper, and waited for his cue, which was the breaking-out of table talk after the blessing of the bread. Then Yakub began to clear his throat and kept on working at it until my father called to him to come down and have a glass of vodka. Sometimes my father pretended not to hear him, and we smiled at one another around the table, while Yakub's throat grew worse and worse, and he began to cough and mutter and rustle in his straw. Then my father let him come down, and he shuffled in, and stood clutching his cap with both hands, while my father poured him a brimming glass of whiskey. This Yakub dedicated to all our healths, and tossed off to his own comfort. If he got a slice of boiled fish after his glassful, he gulped it down as a chicken gulps worms, smacked his lips explosively, and wiped his fingers on his unkempt locks. Then, thanking his master and mistress, and scraping and bowing, he backed out of the room and ascended to his roost once more; and in less time than it takes to write his name, the simple fellow was asleep, and snoring the snore of the just.

On Sabbath morning almost everybody went to synagogue, and those who did not, read their prayers and devotions at home. Dinner, at midday, was a pleasant and leisurely meal in our house. Between courses my father led us in singing our favorite songs, sometimes Hebrew, sometimes Yiddish, sometimes Russian, or some of the songs without words for which the Hasidim were famous. In the afternoon we went visiting, or else we took long walks out of town, where the fields sprouted and the orchards waited to bloom. If we stayed at home, we were not without company. Neighbors dropped in for a glass of tea. Uncles and cousins came, and perhaps my brother's rebbe, to examine his pupil in the hearing of the family. And wherever we spent the day, the talk was pleasant, the faces were cheerful, and the joy of Sabbath pervaded everything.

The festivals were observed with all due pomp and circumstance in our house. Passover was beautiful with shining new things all through the house; *Purim* was gay with feasting and presents and the jolly mummers; *Succoth* was a poem lived in a green arbor; New-Year thrilled our hearts with its symbols and promises; and the Day of Atonement moved even the laughing children to a longing for consecration. The year, in our pious house, was an endless song in many cantos of joy, lamentation, aspiration, and rhapsody.

We children, while we regretted the passing of a festival, found plenty to content us in the common days of the week. We had everything we needed, and almost everything we wanted. We were welcomed everywhere, petted and praised, abroad as well as at home. I suppose no little girls with whom we played had a more comfortable sense of being well-off than Fetchke and I. "Raphael the Russian's grandchildren" people called us, as if referring to the quarterings in our shield. It was very pleasant to wear fine clothes, to have kopecks to spend at the fruit stalls, and to be pointed at admiringly. Some of the little girls we went with were richer than we, but after all one's mother can wear only one pair of earrings at a time, and our mother had beautiful gold ones that hung down on her neck.

As we grew older, my parents gave us more than physical comfort and social standing to rejoice in. They gave us, or set out to give us, education, which was less common than gold earrings in Polotzk. For the ideal of a modern education was the priceless ware that my father brought back with him from his travels in distant parts. His travels, indeed, had been the making of my father. He had gone away from Polotzk, in the first place, as a man unfit for the life he led, out of harmony with his surroundings, at odds with his neighbors. Never heartily devoted to the religious ideals of the Hebrew scholar, he was more and more a dissenter as he matured, but he hardly knew what he wanted to embrace in place of the ideals he rejected. The rigid scheme of orthodox Jewish life in the Pale offered no opening to any other mode of life. But in the large cities in the east and south he discovered a new world, and found himself at home in it. The Jews among whom he lived in those parts were faithful to the essence of the religion, but they allowed themselves more latitude in practice and observance than the people in Polotzk. Instead of bribing government officials to relax the law of compulsory education for boys, these people pushed in numbers at every open door of culture and enlightenment. Even the girls were given books in Odessa and Kherson, as the rock to build their lives on, and not as an ornament for idleness. My father's mind was ready for the reception of such ideas, and he was inspired by the new view of the world which they afforded him.

When he returned to Polotzk he knew what had been wrong with his life before, and he proceeded to remedy it. He resolved to live, as far as the conditions of existence in Polotzk permitted, the life of a modern man. And he saw no better place to begin than with the education of the children. Outwardly he must conform to the ways of his neighbors, just as he must pay tribute to the policeman on the beat; for standing room is necessary to all operations, and social ostracism could ruin him as easily as police persecution. His children, if he started them right, would not have to bow to the yoke as low as he; his children's children might even be free men. And education was the one means to redemption.

Fetchke and I were started with a rebbe, in the orthodox way, but we were taught to translate as well as read Hebrew, and we had a secular teacher besides. My sister and I were very diligent pupils, and my father took great satisfaction in our progress and built great plans for our higher education.

My brother, who was five years old when he entered heder, hated to be shut up all day over a printed page that meant nothing to him. He cried and protested, but my father was determined that he should not grow up ignorant, so he used the strap freely to hasten the truant's steps to school. The heder was the only beginning allowable for a boy in Polotzk, and to heder Joseph must go. So the poor boy's life was made a nightmare, and the horror was not lifted until he was ten years old, when he went to a modern school where intelligible things were taught, and it proved that it was not the book he hated, but the blindness of the heder.

For a number of peaceful years after my father's return from "far Russia," we led a wholesome life of comfort, contentment, and faith in to-morrow. Everything prospered, and we children grew in the sun. My mother was one with my father in all his plans for us. Although she had spent her young years in the pursuit of the ruble, it was more to her that our teacher praised us than that she had made a good bargain with a tea merchant. Fetchke and Joseph and I, and Deborah, when she grew up, had some prospects even in Polotzk, with our parents' hearts set on the highest things; but we were destined to seek our fortunes in a world which even my father did not dream of when he settled down to business in Polotzk.

Just when he felt himself safe and strong, a long series of troubles set in to harass us, and in a few years' time we were reduced to a state of helpless poverty, in which there was no room to think of anything but bread. My father became seriously ill, and spent large sums on cures that did not cure him. While he was still an invalid, my mother also became ill and kept her bed for the better part of two years. When she got up, it was only to lapse again. Some of us children also fell ill, so that at one period the house was a hospital. And while my parents were incapacitated, the business was ruined through bad management, until a day came when there was not enough money in the cash drawer to pay the doctor's bills.

For some years after they got upon their feet again, my parents struggled to regain their place in the business world, but failed to do so. My father had another period of experimenting with this or that business, like his earlier experience. But everything went wrong, till at last he made a great resolve to begin life all over again.

And the way to do that was to start on a new soil. My father
determined to emigrate to America.

I have now told who I am, what my people were, how I began
life, and why I was brought to a new home. Up to this point I
have borrowed the recollections of my parents, to piece out my
own fragmentary reminiscences. But from now on I propose to be
my own pilot across the seas of memory; and if I lose myself in
the mists of uncertainty, or run aground on the reefs of speculation,
I still hope to make port at last, and I shall look for welcoming
faces on the shore. For the ship I sail in is history, and facts will
kindle my beacon fires.

CHAPTER V

I REMEMBER

MY FATHER AND MOTHER could tell me much more that I have forgotten, or that I never was aware of; but I want to reconstruct my childhood from those broken recollections only which, recurring to me in after years, filled me with the pain and wonder of remembrance. I want to string together those glimpses of my earliest days that dangle in my mind, like little lanterns in the crooked alleys of the past, and show me an elusive little figure that is myself, and yet so much a stranger to me, that I often ask, Can this be I?

I have not much faith in the reality of my first recollection, but as I can never go back over the past without bringing up at last at this sombre little scene, as at a door beyond which I cannot pass, I must put it down for what it is worth in the scheme of my memories. I see, then, an empty, darkened room. In the middle, on the floor, lies a long Shape, covered with some black stuff. There are candles at the head of the Shape. Dim figures are seated low, against the walls, swaying to and fro. No sound is in the room, except a moan or a sigh from the shadowy figures; but a child is walking softly around and around the Shape on the floor, in quiet curiosity.

The Shape is the body of my grandfather laid out for burial. The child is myself—myself asking questions of Death.

I was four years old when my mother's father died. Do I really remember the little scene? Perhaps I heard it described by some fond relative, as I heard other anecdotes of my infancy, and unconsciously incorporated it with my genuine recollections. It is so suitable a scene for a beginning: the darkness, the mystery, the impenetrability. My share in it, too, is characteristic enough, if I really studied that Shape by the lighted candles, as I have always pretended to myself. So often afterwards I find myself forgetting the conventional meanings of things, in some search for a meaning of my own. It is more likely, however, that I took no intellectual interest in my grandfather's remains at the time, but later on, when I sought for a First Recollection, perhaps, elaborated the scene, and my part in it, to something that satisfied my sense of dramatic fitness. If I really committed such a fraud, I am now well punished, by being obliged, at the very start, to discredit the authenticity of my memoirs.

The abode of our childhood, if not revisited in later years, is apt to loom in our imagination as a vast edifice with immense chambers in which our little self seems lost. Somehow I have failed of this illusion. My grandfather's house, where I was born, stands, in my memory, a small, one-story wooden building, whose chimneys touch the sky at the same level as its neighbors' chimneys. Such as it was, the house stood even with the sidewalk, but the yard was screened from the street by a board fence, outside which I am sure there was a bench. The gate into the yard swung so high from the ground that four-footed visitors did not have to wait till it was opened. Pigs found their way in, and were shown the way out, under the gate; grunting on their arrival, but squealing on their departure.

Of the interior of the house I remember only one room, and not so much the room as the window, which had a blue sash curtain, and beyond the curtain a view of a narrow, walled garden, where deep-red dahlias grew. The garden belonged to the house adjoining my grandfather's, where lived the Gentile girl who was kind to me.

Concerning my dahlias I have been told that they were not dahlias at all, but poppies. As a conscientious historian I am bound to record every rumor, but I retain the right to cling to my own impression. Indeed, I must insist on my dahlias, if I am to preserve the garden at all. I have so long believed in them, that if I try to see *poppies* in those red masses over the wall, the whole garden crumbles away, and leaves me a gray blank. I have nothing against poppies. It is only that my illusion is more real to me than reality. And so do we often build our world on an error, and cry out that the universe is falling to pieces, if any one but lift a finger to replace the error by truth.

Ours was a quiet neighborhood. Across the narrow street was the orderly front of the Korpus, or military academy, with straight rows of unshuttered windows. It was an imposing edifice in the eyes of us all, because it was built of brick, and was several stories high. At one of the windows I pretend I remember seeing a tailor mending the uniforms of the cadets. I knew the uniforms, and I knew, in later years, the man who had been the tailor; but I am not

My Grandfather's House, Where I Was Born

sure that he did not emigrate to America, there to seek his fortune in a candy shop, and his happiness in a family of triplets, twins, and even odds, long before I was old enough to toddle as far as the gate.

Behind my grandfather's house was a low hill, which I do *not* remember as a mountain. Perhaps it was only a hump in the ground. This eminence, of whatever stature, was a part of the Vall, a longer and higher ridge on the top of which was a promenade, and which was said to be the burying-ground of Napoleonic soldiers. This historic rumor meant very little to me, for I never knew what Napoleon was.

It was not my way to accept unchallenged every superstition that came to my ears. Among the wild flowers that grew on the grassy slopes of the Vall, there was a small daisy, popularly called "blind flower," because it was supposed to cause blindness in rash children who picked it. I was rash, if I was awake; and I picked "blind flowers" behind the house, handfuls of them, and enjoyed my eyesight unimpaired. If my faith in nursery lore was shaken by this experience, I kept my discovery to myself, and did not undertake to enlighten my playmates. I find other instances, later on, of the curious fact that I was content with *finding out* for myself. It is curious to me because I am not so reticent now. When I discover anything, if only a new tint in the red sunset, I must publish the fact to all my friends. Is it possible that in my childish reflections I recognized the fact that ours was a secretive atmosphere, where knowledge was for the few, and wisdom was sometimes a capital offence?

In the summer-time I lived outdoors considerably. I found many occasions to visit my mother in the store, which gave me a long walk. If my errand was not pressing—or perhaps even if it was— I made a long stop on the Platz, especially if I had a companion with me. The Platz was a rectangular space in the centre of a roomy square, with a shady promenade around its level lawn. The Korpus faced on the Platz, which was its drill ground. Around the square were grouped the fine residences of the officers of the Korpus, with a great white church occupying one side. These buildings had a fearful interest for me, especially the church, as the dwellings and sanctuary of the enemy; but on the Platz I was not afraid to play and seek adventures. I loved to watch the cadets drill and play ball, or pass them close as they promenaded, two and two, looking so perfect in white trousers and jackets and visored caps. I loved to run with my playmates and lay out all sorts of geometric figures on the four straight sides of the promenade; patterns of infinite variety, traceable only by a pair of tireless feet. If one got so wild with play as to forget all fear, one could swing, until chased away by the guard, on the heavy chain festoons that encircled the monument at one side of the square. This was the only monument in Polotzk, dedicated I never knew to whom or what. It was the monument, as the sky was the sky, and the earth, earth: the only phenomenon of its kind, mysterious, unquestionable.

It was not far from the limits of Polotzk to the fields and woods. My father was fond of taking us children for a long walk on a Sabbath afternoon. I have little pictures in my mind of places where we went, though I doubt if they could be found from my descriptions. I try in vain to conjure up a panoramic view of the neighborhood. Even when I stood on the apex of the Vall, and saw the level country spread in all directions, my inexperienced eyes failed to give me the picture of the whole. I saw the houses in the streets below, all going to market. The highroads wandered out into the country, and disappeared in the sunny distance, where the edge of the earth and the edge of the sky fitted together, like a jewel box with the lid ajar. In these things I saw what a child always sees: the unrelated fragments of a vast, mysterious world. But although my geography may be vague, and the scenes I remember as the pieces of a paper puzzle, still my breath catches as I replace this bit or that, and coax the edges to fit together. I am obstinately positive of some points, and for the rest, you may amend the puzzle if you can. You may make a survey of Polotzk ever so accurate, and show me where I was wrong; still I am the better guide. You may show that my adventureful road led nowhere, but I can prove, by the quickening of my pulse and the throbbing of my rapid recollections, that *things happened to me* there or here; and I shall be believed, not you. And so over the vague canvas of scenes half remembered, half imagined, I draw the brush of recollection, and pick out here a landmark, there a figure, and set my own feet back in the old ways, and live over the old events. It is real enough, as by my beating heart you might know.

Sometimes my father took us out by the Long Road. There is

no road in the neighborhood of Polotzk by that name, but I know very well that the way was long to my little feet; and long are the backward thoughts that creep along it, like a sunbeam travelling with the day.

The first landmark on the sunny, dusty road is the house of a peasant acquaintance where we stopped for rest and a drink. I remember a cool gray interior, a woman with her bosom uncovered pattering barefoot to hand us the hospitable dipper, and a baby smothered in a deep cradle which hung by ropes from the ceiling. Farther on, the empty road gave us shadows of trees and rustlings of long grass. This, at least, is what I imagine over the spaces where no certain object is. Then, I know, we ran and played, and it was father himself who hid in the corn, and we made havoc following after. Laughing, we ramble on, till we hear the long, far whistle of a locomotive. The railroad track is just visible over the field on the *left* of the road; the cornfield, I say, is on the *right*. We stand on tiptoe and wave our hands and shout as the long train rushes by at a terrific speed, leaving its pennon of smoke behind.

The passing of the train thrilled me wonderfully. Where did it come from, and whither did it fly, and how did it feel to be one of the faces at the windows? If ever I dreamed of a world beyond Polotzk, it must have been at those times, though I do not honestly remember.

Somewhere out on that same Long Road is the place where we once attended a wedding. I do not know who were married, or whether they lived happily ever after; but I remember that when the dancers were wearied, and we were all sated with goodies, day was dawning, and several of the young people went out for a stroll in a grove near by. They took me with them—who were they?— and they lost me. At any rate, when they saw me again, I was a stranger. For I had sojourned, for an immeasurable moment, in a world apart from theirs. I had witnessed my first sunrise; I had watched the rosy morning tiptoe in among the silver birches. And that grove stands on the *left* side of the road.

We had another stopping-place out in that direction. It was the place where my mother sent her hundred and more house plants to be cared for one season, because for some reason they could not fare well at home. We children went to visit them once; and the memory of that is red and white and purple.

The Long Road went ever on and on; I remember no turns. But we turned at last, when the sun was set and the breeze of evening blew; and sometimes the first star came in and the Sabbath went out before we reached home and supper.

Another way out of town was by the bridge across the Polota. I recall more than one excursion in that direction. Sometimes we made a large party, annexing a few cousins and aunts for the day. At this moment I feel a movement of affection for these relations who shared our country adventures. I had forgotten what virtue there was in our family; I do like people who can walk. In those days, it is likely enough, I did not always walk on my own legs, for I was very little, and not strong. I do not remember being carried, but if any of my big uncles gave me a lift, I am sure I like them all the more for it.

The Dvina River swallowed the Polota many times a day, yet the lesser stream flooded the universe on one occasion. On the hither bank of that stream, as you go from Polotzk, I should plant a flowering bush, a lilac or a rose, in memory of the life that bloomed in me one day that I was there.

Leisurely we had strolled out of the peaceful town. It was early spring, and the sky and the earth were two warm palms in which all live things nestled. Little green leaves trembled on the trees, and the green, green grass sparkled. We sat us down to rest a little above the bridge; and life flowed in and out of us fully, freely, as the river flowed and parted about the bridge piles.

A market garden lay on the opposite slope, yellow-green with first growth. In the long black furrows yet unsown a peasant pushed his plow. I watched him go up and down, leaving a new black line on the bank for every turn. Suddenly he began to sing, a rude plowman's song. Only the melody reached me, but the meaning sprang up in my heart to fit it—a song of the earth and the hopes of the earth. I sat a long time listening, looking, tense with attention. I felt myself discovering things. Something in me gasped for life, and lay still. I was but a little body, and Life Universal had suddenly burst upon me. For a moment I had my little hand on the Great Pulse, but my fingers slipped, empty. For the space of a wild heartbeat I *knew,* and then I was again a simple child, looking to my earthly senses for life. But the sky had stretched for me, the earth had expanded; a greater life had dawned in me.

We are not born all at once, but by bits. The body first, and the spirit later; and the birth and growth of the spirit, in those who are attentive to their own inner life, are slow and exceedingly painful. Our mothers are racked with the pains of our physical birth; we ourselves suffer the longer pains of our spiritual growth. Our souls are scarred with the struggles of successive births, and the process is recorded also by the wrinkles in our brains, by the lines in our faces. Look at me, and you will see that I have been born many times. And my first self-birth happened, as I have told, that spring day of my early springs. Therefore would I plant a rose on the green bank of the Polota, there to bloom in token of eternal life.

Eternal, divine life. This is a tale of immortal life. Should I be sitting here, chattering of my infantile adventures, if I did not know that I was speaking for thousands? Should you be sitting there, attending to my chatter, while the world's work waits, if you did not know that I spoke also for you? I might say "you" or "he" instead of "I." Or I might be silent, while you spoke for me and the rest, but for the accident that I was born with a pen in my hand, and you without. We love to read the lives of the great, yet what a broken history of mankind they give, unless supplemented by the lives of the humble. But while the great can speak for themselves, or by the tongues of their admirers, the humble are apt to live inarticulate and die unheard. It is well that now and then one is born among the simple with a taste for self-revelation. The man or woman thus endowed must speak, will speak, though there are only the grasses in the field to hear, and none but the wind to carry the tale.

It is fun to run over the bridge, with a clatter of stout little shoes on resounding timbers. We pass a walled orchard on the right, and remind each other of the fruit we enjoyed here last summer. Our next stopping-place is farther on, beyond the wayside inn where lives the idiot boy who gave me such a scare last time. It is a poor enough place, where we stop, but there is an ice house, the only one I know. We are allowed to go in and see the greenish masses of ice gleaming in the half-light, and bring out jars of sweet, black "lager beer," which we drink in the sunny doorway. I shall always remember the flavor of the stuff, and the smell, and the wonder and chill of the ice house.

I vaguely remember something about a convent out in that direction, but I was tired and sleepy after my long walk, and glad to be returning home. I hope they carried me a bit of the way, for I was very tired. There were stars out before we reached home, and the men stopped in the middle of the street to bless the new moon.

It is pleasant to recall how we went bathing in the Polota. On Friday afternoons in summer, when the week's work was done, and the houses of the good housewives stood shining with cleanliness, ready for the Sabbath, parties of women and girls went chattering and laughing down to the river bank. There was a particular spot which belonged to the women. I do not know where the men bathed, but our part of the river was just above Bonderoff's gristmill. I can see the green bank sloping to the water, and the still water sliding down to the sudden swirl and spray of the mill race.

The woods on the bank screened the bathers. Bathing costumes were simply absent, which caused the mermaids no embarrassment, for they were accustomed to see each other naked in the public hot baths. They had little fear of intrusion, for the spot was sacred to them. They splashed about and laughed and played tricks, with streaming hair and free gestures. I do not know when I saw the girls play as they did in the water. It was a pretty picture, but the bathers would have been shocked beyond your understanding if you had suggested that naked women might be put into a picture. If it ever happened, as it happened at least once for me to remember, that their privacy was outraged, the bathers were thrown into a panic as if their very lives were threatened. Screaming, they huddled together, low in the water, some hiding their eyes in their hands, with the instinct of the ostrich. Some ran for their clothes on the bank, and stood shrinking behind some inadequate rag. The more spirited of the naiads threw pebbles at the cowardly intruders, who, safe behind the leafy cover that was meant to shield modesty, threw jeers and mockery in return. But the Gentile boys ran away soon, or ran away punished. A chemise and a petticoat turn a frightened woman into an Amazon in such circumstances; and woe to the impudent wretch who lingered after the avengers plunged into the thicket. Slaps and cuffs at close range were his portion, and curses pursued him in retreat.

Among the liveliest of my memories are those of eating and drinking; and I would sooner give up some of my delightful remembered walks, green trees, cool skies, and all, than to lose my images of suppers eaten on Sabbath evenings at the end of those walks. I make no apology to the spiritually minded, to whom this statement must be a revelation of grossness. I am content to tell the truth as well as I am able. I do not even need to console myself with the reflection that what is dross to the dreamy ascetic may be gold to the psychologist. The fact is that I ate, even as a delicate child, with considerable relish; and I remember eating with a relish still keener. Why, I can dream away a half-hour on the immortal flavor of those thick cheese cakes we used to have on Saturday night. I am no cook, so I cannot tell you how to make such cake. I might borrow the recipe from my mother, but I would rather you should take my word for the excellence of Polotzk cheese cakes. If you should attempt that pastry, I am certain, be you ever so clever a cook, you would be disappointed by the result; and hence you might be led to mistrust my reflections and conclusions. You have nothing in your kitchen cupboard to give the pastry its notable flavor. It takes history to make such a cake. First, you must eat it as a ravenous child, in memorable twilights, before the lighting of the week-day lamp. Then you must have yourself removed from the house of your simple feast, across the oceans, to a land where your cherished pastry is unknown even by name; and where daylight and twilight, work day and fête day, for years rush by you in the unbroken tide of a strange, new, overfull life. You must abstain from the inimitable morsel for a period of years,—I think fifteen is the magic number,—and then suddenly, one day, rub the Aladdin's lamp of memory, and have the renowned tidbit whisked upon your platter, garnished with a hundred sweet herbs of past association.

Do you think all your imported spices, all your scientific blending and manipulating, could produce so fragrant a morsel as that which I have on my tongue as I write? Glad am I that my mother, in her assiduous imitation of everything American, has forgotten the secrets of Polotzk cookery. At any rate, she does not practise it, and I am the richer in memories for her omissions. Polotzk cheese cake, as I now know it, has in it the flavor of daisies and clover picked on the Vall; the sweetness of Dvina water; the richness of newly turned earth which I moulded with bare feet and hands; the ripeness of red cherries bought by the dipperful in the market place; the fragrance of all my childhood's summers.

Abstinence, as I have mentioned, is one of the essential ingredients in the phantom dish. I discovered this through a recent experience. It was cherry time in the country, and the sight of the scarlet fruit suddenly reminded me of a cherry season in Polotzk, I could not say how many years ago. On that earlier occasion my Cousin Shimke, who, like everybody else, was a storekeeper, had set a boy to watch her store, and me to watch the boy, while she went home to make cherry preserves. She gave us a basket of cherries for our trouble, and the boy offered to eat them with the stones if I would give him my share. But I was equal to that feat myself, so we sat down to a cherry-stone contest. Who ate the most stones I could not remember as I stood under the laden trees not long ago, but the transcendent flavor of the historical cherries came back to me, and I needs must enjoy it once more.

I climbed into the lowest boughs and hung there, eating cherries with the stones, my whole mind concentrated on the sense of taste. Alas! the fruit had no such flavor to yield as I sought. Excellent American cherries were these, but not so fragrantly sweet as my cousin's cherries. And if I should return to Polotzk, and buy me a measure of cherries at a market stall, and pay for it with a Russian groschen, would the market woman be generous enough to throw in that haunting flavor? I fear I should find that the old species of cherry is extinct in Polotzk.

Sometimes, when I am not trying to remember at all, I am more fortunate in extracting the flavors of past feasts from my plain American viands. I was eating strawberries the other day, ripe, red American strawberries. Suddenly I experienced the very flavor and aroma of some strawberries I ate perhaps twenty years ago. I started as from a shock, and then sat still for I do not know how long, breathless with amazement. In the brief interval of a gustatory perception I became a child again, and I positively ached with the pain of being so suddenly compressed to that small being. I wandered about Polotzk once more, with large, questioning eyes; I rode the Atlantic in an emigrant ship; I took possession of the New World, my ears growing accustomed to a new language; I sat at the feet of renowned professors, till my eyes contracted in dreaming over what they taught; and there I was again, an American among Americans, suddenly made aware of all that I had been, all that I had become —suddenly illuminated, inspired by a complete vision of myself, a daughter of Israel and a child of the universe, that taught me more of the history of my race than ever my learned teachers could understand.

All this came to me in that instant of tasting, all from the flavor of ripe strawberries on my tongue. Why, then, should I not treasure my memories of childhood feasts? This experience gives me a great respect for my bread and meat. I want to taste of as many viands as possible; for when I sit down to a dish of porridge I am certain of rising again a better animal, and I may rise a wiser man. I want to eat and drink and be instructed. Some day I expect to extract from my pudding the flavor of manna which I ate in the desert, and then I shall write you a contemporaneous commentary on the Exodus. Nor do I despair of remembering yet, over a dish of corn, the time when I fed on worms; and then I may be able to recall how it felt to be made at last into a man. Give me to eat and drink, for I crave wisdom.

My winters, while I was a very little girl, were passed in comparative confinement. On account of my delicate health, my grandmother and aunts deemed it wise to keep me indoors; or if I went out, I was so heavily coated and mittened and shawled that the frost scarcely got a chance at the tip of my nose. I never skated or coasted or built snow houses. If I had any experience of snowballs, it was with those thrown at me by the Gentile boys. The way I dodge a snowball to this day makes me certain that I learned the act in my fearful childhood days, when I learned so many cowardly tricks of bending to a blow. I know that I was proud of myself when, not many years ago, I found I was not afraid to stand up and catch a flying baseball; but the fear of the snowball I have not conquered. When I turn a corner in snowball days, the boys with bulging pockets see a head held high and a step unquickened, but I know that I cringe inwardly; and this private mortification I set down against old Polotzk, in my long score of grievances and shames. Fear is a devil hard to cast out.

Let me make the most of the winter adventures that I recall. First, there was sleighing. We never kept horses of our own, but the horses of our customer-guests were always at our disposal, and many a jolly ride they gave us, with the dvornik at the reins, while their owners haggled with my mother in the store about the price of soap. We had no luxurious sleigh, with cushions and fur robes, no silver bells on our harness. Ours was a bare sledge used for hauling wood, with a padding of straw and burlap, and the reins, as likely as not, were a knotted rope. But the horses did fly, over the river and up the opposite bank if we chose; and whether we had bells or not, the merry, foolish heart of Yakub would sing, and the whip would crack, and we children would laugh; and the sport was as good as when, occasionally, we did ride in a more splendid sleigh, loaned us by one of our prouder guests. We were wholesome as apples to look at when we returned for bread and tea in the dusk; at least I remember my sister, with cheeks as red as a painted doll's under her close-clipped curls; and my little brother, rosy, too, and aristocratic-looking enough, in his little greatcoat tied with a red sash, and little fur cap with earlaps. For myself, I suppose my nose was purple and my cheeks pinched, just as they are now in the cold weather; but I had a good time.

At certain—I mean uncertain—intervals we were bundled up and marched to the public baths. This was so great an undertaking, consuming half a day or so, and involving, in winter, such risk of catching cold, that it is no wonder the ceremony was not practised oftener.

The public baths were situated on the river bank. I always stopped awhile outside, to visit the poor patient horse in the tread-mill, by means of which the water was pumped into the baths. I was not sentimental about animals then. I had not read of "Black Beauty" or any other personified monsters; I had not heard of any societies for the prevention of cruelty to anything. But my pity stirred of its own accord at the sight of that miserable brute in the treadmill. I was used to seeing horses hard-worked and abused. This horse had no load to make him sweat, and I never saw him whipped. Yet I pitied this creature. Round and round his little circle he trod, with head hanging and eyes void of expectation; round and round all day, unthrilled by any touch of rein or bridle, interpreters of a living will; round and round, all solitary, never driven, never checked, never addressed; round and round and round, a walking machine, with eyes that did not flash, with teeth that did not threaten, with hoofs that did not strike; round and round the dull day long. I knew what a horse's life should be, entangled with the life of a master: adventurous, troubled, thrilled; petted and opposed, loved and abused; to-day the ringing city pavement underfoot, and the buzz of beasts and men in the market place; to-morrow the yielding turf under tickled flanks, and the lone whinny of scattered mates. How empty the existence of the treadmill horse beside this! As empty and endless and dull as the life of almost any woman in Polotzk, had I had eyes to see the likeness.

But to my ablutions!

We undress in a room leading directly from the entry, and furnished only with benches around the walls. There is no screen or other protection against the drafts rushing in every time the door is opened. When we enter the bathing-room we are confused by a babel of sounds—shrill voices of women, hoarse voices of attendants, wailing and yelping of children, and rushing of water. At the same time we are smitten by the heat of the room and nearly suffocated by clouds of steam. We find at last an empty bench, and surround ourselves with a semicircle of wooden pails, collected from all around the room. Sometimes two women in search of pails lay hold of the same pail at the same moment, and a wrangle ensues, in the course of which each disputant reminds the other of all her failings, nicknames, and undesirable connections, living, dead, and unborn; until an attendant interferes, with more muscle than argument, punctuating the sentence of justice with newly coined expletives suggested by the occasion. The centre of the room, where the bathers fill their pails at the faucets, is a field of endless battle, especially on a crowded day. The peaceful women seated within earshot stop their violent scrubbing, to the relief of unwilling children, while they attend to the liveliest of the quarrels.

I like to watch the *poll*, that place of torture and heroic endurance. It is a series of steps rising to the ceiling, affording a gradually mounting temperature. The bather who wants to enjoy a violent sweating rests full length for a few minutes on each step, while an attendant administers several hearty strokes of a stinging besom. Sometimes a woman climbs too far, and is brought down in a faint. On the poll, also, the cupping is done. The back of the patient, with the cups in even rows, looks to me like a muffin pan. Of course I never go on the poll: I am not robust enough. My spankings I take at home.

Another centre of interest is the *mikweh*, the name of which it is indelicate to mention in the hearing of men. It is a large pool of standing water, its depth graded by means of a flight of steps. Every married woman must perform here certain ceremonious ablutions at regular intervals. Cleanliness is as strictly enjoined as godliness, and the manner of attaining it is carefully prescribed. The women are prepared by the attendants for entering the pool, the curious children looking on. In the pool they are ducked over their heads the correct number of times. The water in the pool has been standing for days; it does not look nor smell fresh. But we had no germs in Polotzk, so no harm came of it, any more than of the pails used promiscuously by feminine Polotzk. If any were so dainty as to have second thoughts about the use of the common bath, they could enjoy, for a fee of twenty-five kopecks, a private bathtub in another part of the building. For the rich there were luxuries even in Polotzk.

Cleansed, red-skinned, and steaming, we return at last to the dressing-room, to shiver, as we dress, in the cold drafts from the entry door; and then, muffled up to the eyes, we plunge into the refreshing outer air, and hurry home, looking like so many big bundles running away with smaller bundles. If we meet acquaintances on the way we are greeted with *"zu refueh"* ("to your good health"). If the first man we meet is a Gentile, the women who have been to the mikweh have to return and repeat the ceremony of purification. To prevent such a calamity, the kerchief is worn hooded over the eyes, so as to exclude unholy sights. At home we are indulged with extra pieces of cake for tea, and otherwise treated like heroes returned from victory. We narrate anecdotes of our expedition, and my mother complains that my little brother is getting too old to be taken to the women's bath. He will go hereafter with the men.

My winter confinement was not shared by my older sister, who otherwise was my constant companion. She went out more than I, not being so afraid of the cold. She used to fret so when my mother was away in the store that it became a custom for her to accompany my mother from the time she was a mere baby. Muffled and rosy and frost-bitten, the tears of cold rolling unnoticed down her plump cheeks, she ran after my busy mother all day long, or tumbled about behind the counter, or nestled for a nap among the bulging sacks of oats and barley. She warmed her little hands over my mother's pot of glowing charcoal—there was no stove in the store—and even learned to stand astride of it, for further comfort, without setting her clothes on fire.

Fetchke was like a young colt inseparable from the mare. I make this comparison not in disrespectful jest, but in deepest pity. Fetchke kept close to my mother at first for love and protection, but the petting she got became a blind for discipline. She learned early, from my mother's example, that hands and feet and brains were made for labor. She learned to bow to the yoke, to lift burdens, to do more for others than she could ever hope to have done for her in turn. She learned to see sugar plums lie around without asking for her share. When she was only fit to nurse her dolls, she learned how to comfort a weary heart.

And all this while I sat warm and watched over at home, untouched by any discipline save such as I directly incurred by my own sins. I differed from Fetchke a little in age, considerably in health, and enormously in luck. It was my good luck, in the first place, to be born after her, instead of before; in the second place, to inherit, from the family stock, that particular assortment of gifts which was sure to mark me for special attentions, exemptions, and privileges; and as fortune always smiles on good fortune, it has ever been my luck, in the third place, to find something good in my idle hand—whether a sunbeam, or a loving heart, or a congenial task —whenever, on turning a corner, I put out my hand to see what my new world was like; while my sister, dear, devoted creature, had her hands so full of work that the sunbeam slipped, and the loving comrade passed out of hearing before she could straighten from her task, and all she had of the better world was a scented zephyr fanned in her face by the irresistible closing of a door.

Perhaps Esau has been too severely blamed for selling his birthright for a mess of pottage. The lot of the firstborn is not necessarily to be envied. The firstborn of a well-to-do patriarch, like Isaac, or of a Rothschild of to-day, inherits, with his father's flocks and slaves and coffers, a troop of cares and responsibilities; unless he be a man without a sense of duty, in which case we are not sup-

THE MEAT MARKET, POLOTZK

posed to envy him. The firstborn of an indigent father inherits a double measure of the disadvantages of poverty,—a joyless childhood, a guideless youth, and perhaps a mateless manhood, his own life being drained to feed the young of his father's begetting. If we cannot do away with poverty entirely, we ought at least to abolish the institution of primogeniture. Nature invented the individual, and promised him, as a reward for lusty being, comfort and immortality. Comes man with his patented brains and copyrighted notions, and levies a tax on the individual, in the form of enforced coöperation, for the maintenance of his pet institution, the family. Our comfort, in the grip of this tyranny, must lie in the hope that man, who is no bastard child of Mother Nature, may be approaching a more perfect resemblance to her majestic features; that his fitful development will culminate in a spiritual constitution capable of absolute justice.

I think I was telling how I stayed at home in the winter, while my sister helped or hindered my mother in her store-keeping. The days drew themselves out too long sometimes, so that I sat at the window thinking what should happen next. No dolls, no books, no games, and at times no companions. My grandmother taught me knitting, but I never got to the heel of my stocking, because if I discovered a dropped stitch I insisted on unravelling all my work till I picked it up; and grandmother, instead of encouraging me in my love for perfection, lost patience and took away my knitting needles. I still maintain that she was in the wrong, but I have forgiven her, since I have worn many pairs of stockings with dropped stitches, and been grateful for them. And speaking of such everyday things reminds me of my friends, among whom also I find an impressive number with a stitch dropped somewhere in the pattern of their souls. I love these friends so dearly that I begin to think I am at last shedding my intolerance; for I remember the day when I could not love less than perfection. I and my imperfect friends together aspire to cast our blemishes, and I am happier so.

There was not much to see from my window, yet adventures beckoned to me from the empty street. Sometimes the adventure was real, and I went out to act in it, instead of dreaming on my stool. Once, I remember, it was early spring, and the winter's ice, just chopped up by the street cleaners, lay muddy and ragged and high in the streets from curb to curb. So it must lie till there was time to cart it to the Dvina, which had all it could do at this season to carry tons, and heavy tons, of ice and snow and every sort of city rubbish, accumulated during the long closed months. Polotzk had no underground communication with the sea, save such as water naturally makes for itself. The poor old Dvina was hard-worked, serving both as drinking-fountain and sewer, as a bridge in winter, a highway in summer, and a playground at all times. So it served us right if we had to wait weeks and weeks in thawing time for our streets to be cleared; and we deserved all the sprains and bruises we suffered from clambering over the broken ice in the streets while going about our business.

Leah the Short, little and straight and neat, with a basket on one arm and a bundle under the other, stood hesitating on the edge of the curb opposite my window. Her poor old face, framed in its calico kerchief, had a wrinkle of anxiety in it. The tumbled ice heap in the street looked to her like an impassable barrier. Tiny as she was, and loaded, she had reason to hesitate. Perhaps she had eggs in her basket,—I thought of that as I looked at her across the street; and I thought of my old ambition to measure myself, shoulder to shoulder, with Leah, reputedly short. I was small myself, and was constantly reminded of it by a variety of nicknames, lovingly or vengefully invented by my friends and enemies. I was called Mouse and Crumb and Poppy Seed. Should I live to be called, in my old age, Mashke the Short? I longed to measure my stature by Leah's, and here was my chance.

I ran out into the street, my grandmother scolding me for going without a shawl, and I calling back to her to be sure and watch me. I skipped over the ice blocks like a goat, and offered my assistance to Leah the Short. With admirable skill and solicitude I guided her timid steps across the street, at the same time winking to my grandmother at the window, and pointing to my shoulder close to Leah's. Once on the safe sidewalk, the tiny woman thanked me and blessed me and praised me for a thoughtful child; and I watched her toddle away without the least stir of shame at my hypocrisy. She had convinced me that I was a good little girl, and I had convinced myself that I was not so very short. My chin was almost on a level with Leah's shoulder, and I had years ahead in which to elevate it. Grandma at the window was witness, and I was entirely happy. If

I caught cold from going bareheaded, so much the better; mother would give me rock candy for my cough.

For the long winter evenings there was plenty of quiet occupation. I liked to sit with the women at the long bare table picking feathers for new featherbeds. It was pleasant to poke my hand into the soft-heaped mass and set it all in motion. I pretended that I could pick out the feathers of particular hens, formerly my pets. I reflected that they had fed me with eggs and broth, and now were going to make my bed so soft; while I had done nothing for them but throw them a handful of oats now and then, or chase them about, or spoil their nests. I was not ashamed of my part; I knew that if I were a hen I should do as a hen does. I just liked to think about things in my idle way.

Itke, the housemaid, was always the one to break in upon my reflections. She was sure to have a fit of sneezing just when the heap on the table was highest, sending clouds of feathers into the air, like a homemade snowstorm. After that the evening was finished by our picking the feathers from each other's hair.

Sometimes we played cards or checkers, munching frost-bitten apples between moves. Sometimes the women sewed, and we children wound yarn or worsted for grandmother's knitting. If somebody had a story to tell while the rest worked, the evening passed with a pleasant sense of semi-idleness for all.

On a Saturday night, the Sabbath being just departed, ghost stories were particularly in favor. After two or three of the creepy legends we began to move closer together under the lamp. At the end of an hour or so we started and screamed if a spool fell, or a window rattled. At bedtime nobody was willing to make the round of doors and windows, and we were afraid to bring a candle into a dark room.

I was just as much afraid as anybody. I am afraid now to be alone in the house at night. I certainly was afraid that Saturday night when somebody, in bravado, suggested fresh-baked buns, as a charm to dispel the ghosts. The baker who lived next door always baked on Saturday night. Who would go and fetch the buns? Nobody dared to venture outdoors. It had snowed all evening; the frosted windows prevented a preliminary survey of the silent night. *Brr-rr!* Nobody would take the dare.

Nobody but me. Oh, how the creeps ran up and down my back!

and oh! how I loved to distinguish myself! I let them bundle me up till I was nearly smothered. I paused with my mittened hand on the latch. I shivered, though I could have sat the night out with a Polar bear without another shawl. I opened the door, and then turned back, to make a speech.

"I am not afraid," I said, in the noble accents of courage. "I am not afraid to go. God goes with me."

Pride goeth before a fall. On the step outside I slid down into a drift, just on the eve of triumph. They picked me up; they brought me in. They found all of me inside my wrappings. They gave me a piece of sugar and sent me to bed. And I was very glad. I did hate to go all the way next door and all the way back, through the white snow, under the white stars, invisible company keeping step with me.

And I remember my playmates.

There was always a crowd of us girls. We were a mixed set,—rich little girls, well-to-do little girls, and poor little girls,—but not because we were so democratic. Rather it came about, if my sister and I are considered the centre of the ring, because we had suffered the several grades of fortune. In our best days no little girls had to stoop to us; in our humbler days we were not so proud that we had to condescend to our chance neighbors. The granddaughters of Raphael the Russian, in retaining their breeding and manners, retained a few of their more exalted friends, and became a link between them and those whom they later adopted through force of propinquity.

We were human little girls, so our amusements mimicked the life about us. We played house, we played soldiers, we played Gentiles, we celebrated weddings and funerals. We copied the life about us literally. We had not been to a Froebel kindergarten, and learned to impersonate butterflies and stones. Our elders would have laughed at us for such nonsense. I remember once standing on the river bank with a little boy, when a quantity of lumber was floating down on its way to the distant sawmill. A log and a board crowded each other near where we stood. The board slipped by first, but presently it swerved and swung partly around. Then it righted itself with the stream and kept straight on, the lazy log following behind. Said Zalmen to me, interpreting: "The board looks back and says,

'Log, log, you will not go with me? Then I will go on by my-self.' " That boy was called simple, on account of such speeches as this. I wonder in what language he is writing poetry now.

We had very few toys. Neither Fetchke nor I cared much for dolls. A rag baby apiece contented us, and if we had a set of jack-stones we were perfectly happy. Our jackstones, by the way, were not stones but bones. We used the knuckle bones of sheep, dried and scraped; every little girl cherished a set in her pocket.

I did not care much for playing house. I liked soldiers better, but it was not much fun without boys. Boys and girls always played apart.

I was very fond of playing Gentiles. I am afraid I liked every-thing that was a little risky. I particularly enjoyed being the corpse in a Gentile funeral. I was laid across two chairs, and my playmates, in borrowed shawls and long calicoes, with their hair loose and with candlesticks in their hands, marched around me, singing un-earthly songs, and groaning till they scared themselves. As I lay there, covered over with a black cloth, I felt as dead as dead could be; and my playmates were the unholy priests in gorgeous robes of velvet and silk and gold. Their candlesticks were the crosiers that were carried in Christian funeral processions, and their chantings were hideous incantations to the arch enemy, the Christian God of horrible images. As I imagined the bareheaded crowds making way for my funeral to pass, my flesh crept, not because I was about to be buried, but because the people *crossed themselves.* But our pro-cession stopped outside the church, because we did not dare to carry even our make-believe across that accursed threshold. Besides, none of us had ever been inside,—God forbid!—so we did not know what did happen next.

When I arose from my funeral I was indeed a ghost. I felt unreal and lost and hateful. I don't think we girls liked each other much after playing funeral. Anyway, we never played any more on the same day; or if we did, we soon quarrelled. Such was the hold which our hereditary terrors and hatreds had upon our childish minds that if we only mocked a Christian procession in our play, we suffered a mutual revulsion of feeling, as if we had led each other into sin.

We gathered oftener at our house than anywhere else. On Sab-bath days we refrained, of course, from soldiering and the like, but we had just as good a time, going off to promenade, two and two, in our very best dresses; whispering secrets and telling stories. We had a few stories in the circle—I do not know how they came to us—and these were told over and over. Gutke knew the best story of all. She told the story of Aladdin and the Wonderful Lamp, and she told it well. It was her story, and nobody else ever attempted it, though I, for one, soon had it by heart. Gutke's version of the famous tale was unlike any I have since read, but it was essentially the story of Aladdin, so that I was able to identify it later when I found it in a book. Names, incidents, and "local color" were slightly Hebraized, but the supernatural wonders of treasure caves, jewelled gardens, genii, princesses, and all, were not in the least marred or diminished. Gutke would spin the story out for a long afternoon, and we all listened entranced, even at the hundredth rehearsal. We had a few other fairy stories,—I later identified them with stories of Grimm's or of Andersen's,—but for the most part the tales we told were sombre and unimaginative; tales our nurses used to tell to frighten us into good behavior.

Sometimes we spent a whole afternoon in dancing. We made our own music, singing as we danced, or somebody blew on a comb with a bit of paper over its teeth; and comb music is not to be despised when there is no other sort. We knew the polka and the waltz, the mazurka, the quadrille, and the lancers, and several fancy dances. We did not hesitate to invent new steps or figures, and we never stopped till we were out of breath. I was one of the most enthusiastic dancers. I danced till I felt as if I could fly.

Sometimes we sat in a ring and sang all the songs we knew. None of us were trained,—we had never seen a sheet of music—but some of us could sing any tune that was ever heard in Polotzk, and the others followed half a bar behind. I enjoyed these singing-bees. We had Hebrew songs and Jewish and Russian; solemn songs, and jolly songs, and songs unfit for children, but harmless enough on our innocent lips. I enjoyed the play of moods in these songs—I liked to be harrowed one minute and tickled the next. I threw all my heart into the singing, which was only fair, as I had very little voice to throw in.

Although I always joined the crowd when any fun was on foot, I think I had the best times by myself. My sister was fond of housework, but I—I was fond of idleness. While Fetchke pottered in the kitchen beside the maid or trotted all about the house after my grandmother, I wasted time in some window corner, or studied the habits of the cow and the chickens in the yard. I always found something to do that was of no use to anybody. I had no particular fondness for animals; I liked to see what they did, merely because they were curious. The red cow would go to meet my grandmother as she came out of the kitchen with a bucket of bran for her. She drank it up in no time, the greedy creature, in great loud gulps; and then she stood with dripping nostrils over the empty bucket, staring at me on the other side. I teased grandmother to give the cow more, because I enjoyed her enjoyment of it. I wondered, if I ate from a bucket instead of a plate, should I take so much more pleasure in my dinner? That red cow liked everything. She liked going to pasture, and she liked coming back, and she stood still to be milked, as if she liked that too.

The chickens were not all alike. Some of them would not let me catch them, while others stood still till I took them up. There were two that were particularly tame, a white hen and a speckled one. In winter, when they were kept in the house, my sister and I had these two for our pets. They let us handle them by the hour, and stayed just where we put them. The white hen laid her eggs in a linen chest made of bark. We would take the warm egg to grandmother, who rolled it on our eyes, repeating this charm: "As this egg is fresh, so may your eyes be fresh. As this egg is sound, so may your eyes be sound." I still like to touch my eyelids with a fresh-laid egg, whenever I am so happy as to possess one.

On the horses in the barn I bestowed the same calm attention as on the cow, speculative rather than affectionate. I was not a very tender-hearted infant. If I have been a true witness of my own growth, I was slower to love than I was to think. I do not know when the change was wrought, but to-day, if you ask my friends, they will tell you that I know how to love them better than to solve their problems. And if you will call one more witness, and ask me, I shall say that if you set me down before a noble landscape, I feel it long before I begin to see it.

Idle child though I was, the day was not long enough sometimes for my idleness. More than once in the pleasant summer I stole out of bed when even the cow was still drowsing, and went barefoot through the dripping grass and stood at the gate, awaiting the morning. I found a sense of adventure in being conscious when all other people were asleep. There was not much of a prospect from the gateway, but in that early hour everything looked new and large to me, even the little houses that yesterday had been so familiar. The houses, when creatures went in and out of them, were merely conventional objects; in the soft gray morning they were themselves creatures. Some stood up straight, and some leaned, and some looked as if they saw me. And then over the dewy gardens rose the sun, and the light spread and grew over everything, till it shone on my bare feet. And in my heart grew a great wonder, and I was ready to cry, my world was so strange and sweet about me. In those moments, I think, I could have loved somebody as well as I loved later—somebody who cared to get up secretly, and stand and see the sun come up.

Was there not somebody who got up before the sun? Was there not Mishka the shepherd? Aye, that was an early riser; but I knew he was no sun-worshipper. Before the chickens stirred, before the lazy maid let the cow out of the barn, I heard his rousing horn, its distant notes harmonious with the morning. Barn doors creaked in response to Mishka's call, and soft-eyed cattle went willingly out to meet him, and stood in groups in the empty square, licking and nosing each other; till Mishka's little drove was all assembled, and he tramped out of town behind them, in a cloud of dust.

CHAPTER VI

THE TREE OF KNOWLEDGE

HISTORY SHOWS that in all countries where Jews have equal rights with the rest of the people, they lose their fear of secular science, and learn how to take their ancient religion with them from century to awakening century, dropping nothing by the way but what their growing spirit has outgrown. In countries where progress is to be bought only at the price of apostasy, they shut themselves up in their synagogues, and raise the wall of extreme separateness between themselves and their Gentile neighbors. There is never a Jewish community without its scholars, but where Jews may not be both intellectuals and Jews, they prefer to remain Jews.

The survival in Russia of mediæval injustice to Jews was responsible for the narrowness of educational standards in the Polotzk of my time. Jewish scholarship, as we have seen, was confined to a knowledge of the Hebrew language and literature, and even these limited stores of learning were not equally divided between men and women. In the mediæval position of the women of Polotzk education really had no place. A girl was "finished" when she could read her prayers in Hebrew, following the meaning by the aid of the Yiddish translation especially prepared for women. If she could sign her name in Russian, do a little figuring, and write a letter in Yiddish to the parents of her betrothed, she was called *wohl gelehrent*—well educated.

Fortunately for me, my parents' ideals soared beyond all this. My mother, although she had not stirred out of Polotzk, readily adopted the notion of a liberal education imported by my father from cities beyond the Pale. She heartily supported him in all his plans for us girls. Fetchke and I were to learn to translate as well as pronounce Hebrew, the same as our brother. We were to study Russian and German and arithmetic. We were to go to the best *pension* and receive a thorough secular education. My father's ambition, after several years' sojourn in enlightened circles, reached even beyond the *pension;* but that was flying farther than Polotzk could follow him with the naked eye.

I do not remember our first teacher. When our second teacher came we were already able to read continuous passages. Reb' Lebe was no great scholar. Great scholars would not waste their learning on mere girls. Reb' Lebe knew enough to teach girls Hebrew. Tall and lean was the rebbe, with a lean, pointed face and a thin, pointed beard. The beard became pointed from much stroking and pulling downwards. The hands of Reb' Lebe were large, and his beard was not half a handful. The fingers of the rebbe were long, and the nails, I am afraid, were not very clean. The coat of Reb' Lebe was rusty, and so was his skull-cap. Remember, Reb' Lebe was only a girls' teacher, and nobody would pay much for teaching girls. But lean and rusty as he was, the rebbe's pupils regarded him with entire respect, and followed his pointer with earnest eyes across the limp page of the alphabet, or the thumbed page of the prayer-book.

For a short time my sister and I went for our lessons to Reb' Lebe's heder, in the bare room off the women's gallery, up one flight of stairs, in a synagogue. The place was as noisy as a reckless expenditure of lung power could make it. The pupils on the bench shouted their way from *aleph* to *tav*, cheered and prompted by the growl of the rebbe; while the children in the corridor waiting their turn played "puss in the corner" and other noisy games.

Fetchke and I, however, soon began to have our lessons in private, at our own home. We sat one on each side of the rebbe, reading the Hebrew sentences turn and turn about.

When we left off reading by rote and Reb' Lebe began to reveal the mysteries to us, I was so eager to know all that was in my book that the lesson was always too short. I continued reading by the hour, after the rebbe was gone, though I understood about one word in ten. My favorite Hebrew reading was the Psalms. Verse after verse I chanted to the monotonous tune taught by Reb' Lebe, rocking to the rhythm of the chant, just like the rebbe. And so ran the song of David, and so ran the hours by, while I sat by the low window, the world erased from my consciousness.

What I thought I do not remember; I only know that I loved the sound of the words, the full, dense, solid sound of them, to the meditative chant of Reb' Lebe. I pronounced Hebrew very well, and I caught some mechanical trick of accent and emphasis, which was sufficiently like Reb' Lebe's to make my reading sound intelligent. I had a clue to the general mood of the subject from the few Psalms I had actually translated, and drawing on my imagination for details, I was able to read with so much spirit that ignorant listeners were carried away by my performance. My mother tells me, indeed, that people used to stop outside my window to hear me read. Of this I have not the slightest recollection, so I suppose I was an unconscious impostor. Certain I am that I thought no ignoble thoughts as I chanted the sacred words; and who can say that my visions were not as inspiring as David's? He was a shepherd before he became a king. I was an ignorant child in the Ghetto, but I was admitted at last to the society of the best; I was given the freedom of all America. Perhaps the "stuff that dreams are made of" is the same for all dreamers.

When we came to read Genesis I had the great advantage of a complete translation in Yiddish. I faithfully studied the portion assigned in Hebrew, but I need no longer wait for the next lesson to know how the story ends. I could read while daylight lasted, if I chose, in the Yiddish. Well I remember that Pentateuch, a middling thick octavo volume, in a crumbly sort of leather cover; and how the book opened of itself at certain places, where there were pictures. My father tells me that when I was just learning to translate single words, he found me one evening poring over the *humesh* and made fun of me for pretending to read; whereupon I gave him an eager account, he says, of the stories of Jacob, Benjamin, Moses, and others, which I had puzzled out from the pictures, by the help of a word here and there that I was able to translate.

It was inevitable, as we came to Genesis, that I should ask questions.

Rebbe, translating: "In the beginning God created the earth."

Pupil, repeating: "In the beginning—Rebbe, when was the beginning?"

Rebbe, losing the place in amazement: "'*S gehert a kasse?* (Ever hear such a question?) The beginning was—the beginning—the beginning was in the beginning, of course! *Nu! nu!* Go on."

Pupil, resuming: "In the beginning God made the earth.— Rebbe, what did He make it out of?"

Rebbe, dropping his pointer in astonishment: "What did—? What sort of a girl is this, that asks questions? Go on, go on!"

The lesson continues to the end. The book is closed, the pointer put away. The rebbe exchanges his skull-cap for his street cap, is about to go.

Pupil, timidly, but determinedly, detaining him: "Reb' Lebe, *who made God?*"

The rebbe regards the pupil in amazement mixed with anxiety. His emotion is beyond speech. He turns and leaves the room. In his perturbation he even forgets to kiss the *mezuzah*[1] on the doorpost. The pupil feels reproved and yet somehow in the right. Who *did* make God? But if the rebbe will not tell—will not tell? Or, perhaps, he does not know? The rebbe—?

It was some time after this conflict between my curiosity and his obtuseness that I saw my teacher act a ridiculous part in a trifling comedy, and then I remember no more of him.

Reb' Lebe lingered one day after the lesson. A guest who was about to depart, wishing to fortify himself for his journey, took a roll of hard sausage from his satchel and laid it, with his clasp knife, on the table. He cut himself a slice and ate it standing; and then, noticing the thin, lean rebbe, he invited him, by a gesture, to help himself to the sausage. The rebbe put his hands behind his coat tails, declining the traveller's hospitality. The traveller forgot the other, and walked up and down, ready in his fur coat and cap, till his carriage should arrive. The sausage remained on the table, thick and spicy and brown. No such sausage was known in Polotzk. Reb' Lebe looked at it. Reb' Lebe continued to look. The stranger stopped to cut another slice, and repeated his gesture of invitation. Reb' Lebe moved a step towards the table, but his hands stuck behind his coat tails. The traveller resumed his walk. Reb' Lebe moved another step. The stranger was not looking. The rebbe's courage rose, he advanced towards the table; he stretched out his hand for the knife. At that instant the door opened, the carriage was announced. The eager traveller, without noticing Reb' Lebe, swept up sausage and knife, just at the moment when the timid rebbe was about to cut himself a delicious slice. I saw his discomfiture from my corner, and I am obliged to confess that I enjoyed

---

[1] A piece of parchment inscribed with a passage of Scripture, rolled in a case and tacked to the doorpost. The pious touch or kiss this when leaving or entering a house.

it. His face always looked foolish to me after that; but, fortunately for us both, we did not study together much longer.

Two little girls dressed in their best, shining from their curls to their shoes. One little girl has rosy cheeks, the other has staring eyes. Rosy-Cheeks carries a carpet bag; Big-Eyes carries a new slate. Hand in hand they go into the summer morning, so happy and pretty a pair that it is no wonder people look after them, from window and door; and that other little girls, not dressed in their best and carrying no carpet bags, stand in the street gaping after them.

Let the folks stare; no harm can come to the little sisters. Did not grandmother tie pepper and salt into the corners of their pockets, to ward off the evil eye? The little maids see nothing but the road ahead, so eager are they upon their errand. Carpet bag and slate proclaim that errand: Rosy-Cheeks and Big-Eyes are going to school.

I have no words to describe the pride with which my sister and I crossed the threshold of Isaiah the Scribe. Hitherto we had been to heder, to a rebbe; now we were to study with a *lehrer*, a secular teacher. There was all the difference in the world between the two. The one taught you Hebrew only, which every girl learned; the other could teach Yiddish and Russian and, some said, even German; and how to write a letter, and how to do sums without a counting-frame, just on a piece of paper; accomplishments which were extremely rare among girls in Polotzk. But nothing was too high for the grandchildren of Raphael the Russian; they had "good heads," everybody knew. So we were sent to Reb' Isaiah.

My first school, where I was so proud to be received, was a hovel on the edge of a swamp. The schoolroom was gray within and without. The door was so low that Reb' Isaiah had to stoop in passing. The little windows were murky. The walls were bare, but the low ceiling was decorated with bundles of goose quills stuck in under the rafters. A rough table stood in the middle of the room, with a long bench on either side. That was the schoolroom complete. In my eyes, on that first morning, it shone with a wonderful light, a strange glory that penetrated every corner, and made the stained logs fair as tinted marble; and the windows were not too small to afford me a view of a large new world.

Room was made for the new pupils on the bench, beside the teacher. We found our inkwells, which were simply hollows scooped out in the thick table top. Reb' Isaiah made us very serviceable pens by tying the pen points securely to little twigs; though some of the pupils used quills. The teacher also ruled our paper for us, into little squares, like a surveyor's notebook. Then he set us a copy, and we copied, one letter in each square, all the way down the page. All the little girls and the middle-sized girls and the pretty big girls copied letters in little squares, just so. There were so few of us that Reb' Isaiah could see everybody's page by just leaning over. And if some of our cramped fingers were clumsy, and did not form the loops and curves accurately, all he had to do was to stretch out his hand and rap with his ruler on our respective knuckles. It was all very cosey, with the inkwells that could not be upset, and the pens that grew in the woods or strutted in the dooryard, and the teacher in the closest touch with his pupils, as I have just told. And as he labored with us, and the hours drew themselves out, he was comforted by the smell of his dinner cooking in some little hole adjoining the schoolroom, and by the sound of his good Leah or Rachel or Deborah (I don't remember her name) keeping order among his little ones. She kept very good order, too, so that most of the time you could hear the scratching of the laborious pens accompanied by the croaking of the frogs in the swamp.

Although my sister and I began our studies at the same time, and progressed together, my parents did not want me to take up new subjects as fast as Fetchke did. They thought my health too delicate for much study. So when Fetchke had her Russian lesson I was told to go and play. I am sorry to say that I was disobedient on these occasions, as on many others. I did not go and play; I looked on, I listened, when Fetchke rehearsed her lesson at home. And one evening I stole the Russian primer and repaired to a secret place I knew of. It was a storeroom for broken chairs and rusty utensils and dried apples. Nobody would look for me in that dusty hole. Nobody did look there, but they looked everywhere else, in the house, and in the yard, and in the barn, and down the street, and at our neighbors'; and while everybody was searching and calling for me, and telling each other when I was last seen, and what I was then doing, I, Mashke, was bending over the stolen book, rehearsing A, B, C, by the names my sister had given them; and before anybody hit upon my retreat, I could spell B-O-G, *Bog* (God) and K-A-Z-A, *Kaza* (goat). I did not mind in the least being caught, for I had my new accomplishment to show off.

I remember the littered place, and the high chest that served as my table, and the blue glass lamp that lighted my secret efforts. I remember being brought from there into the firelit room where the family was assembled, and confusing them all by my recital of the simple words, B-O-G, *Bog*, and K-A-Z-A, *Kaza*. I was not re-proached for going into hiding at bedtime, and the next day I was allowed to take part in the Russian lesson.

Alas! there were not many lessons more. Long before we had exhausted Reb' Isaiah's learning, my sister and I had to give up our teacher, because the family fortunes began to decline, and luxuries, such as schooling, had to be cut off. Isaiah the Scribe taught us, in all, perhaps two terms, in which time we learned Yiddish and Rus-sian, and a little arithmetic. But little good we had from our ability to read, for there were no books in our house except prayer-books and other religious writings, mostly in Hebrew. For our skill in writing we had as little use, as letter-writing was not an everyday exercise, and idle writing was not thought of. Our good teacher, however, who had taken pride in our progress, would not let us lose all that we had learned from him. Books he could not lend us, because he had none himself; but he could, and he did, write us out a beautiful "copy" apiece, which we could repeat over and over, from time to time, and so keep our hands in.

I wonder that I have forgotten the graceful sentences of my "copy"; for I wrote them out just about countless times. It was in the form of a letter, written on lovely pink paper (my sister's was blue), the lines taking the shape of semicircles across the page; and that without any guide lines showing. The script, of course, was perfect—in the best manner of Isaiah the Scribe—and the senti-ments therein expressed were entirely noble. I was supposed to be a high-school pupil away on my vacation; and I was writing to my "Respected Parents," to assure them of my welfare, and to tell them how, in the midst of my pleasures, I still longed for my friends, and looked forward with eagerness to the renewal of my studies. All this, in phrases half Yiddish, half German, and altogether for-eign to the ears of Polotzk. At least, I never heard such talk in the market, when I went to buy a kopeck's worth of sunflower seeds.

This was all the schooling I had in Russia. My father's plans fell to the ground, on account of the protracted illness of both my parents. All his hopes of leading his children beyond the intellectual limits of Polotzk were trampled down by the monster poverty who showed his evil visage just as my sister and I were fairly started on a broader path.

One chance we had, and that was quickly snatched away, of continuing our education in spite of family difficulties. Lozhe the Rav, hearing from various sources that Pinchus, son-in-law of Raphael the Russian, had two bright little girls, whose talents were going to waste for want of training, became much interested, and sent for the children, to see for himself what the gossip was worth. By a strange trick of memory I recall nothing of this important interview, nor indeed of the whole matter, although a thousand trifles of that period recur to me on the instant; so I report this anecdote on the authority of my parents.

They tell me how the rav lifted me up on a table in front of him, and asked me many questions, and encouraged me to ask questions in my turn. Reb' Lozhe came to the conclusion, as a result of this interview, that I ought by all means to be put to school. There was no public school for girls, as we know, but a few pupils were maintained in a certain private school by irregular contributions from city funds. Reb' Lozhe enlisted in my cause the influence of his son, who, by virtue of some municipal office which he held, had a vote in fixing this appropriation. But although he pleaded eloquently for my admission as a city pupil, the rav's son failed to win the consent of his colleagues, and my one little crack of opportunity was tightly stopped.

My father does not remember on what technicality my application was dismissed. My mother is under the impression that it was plainly refused on account of my religion, the authorities being unwilling to appropriate money for the tuition of a Jewish child. But little it matters now what the reason was; the result is what affected me. I was left without teacher or book just when my mind was most active. I was left without food just when the hunger of growth was creeping up. I was left to think and think, without direction; without the means of grappling with the contents of my own thought.

In a community which was isolated from the mass of the people on account of its religion; which was governed by special civil laws in recognition of that fact; in whose calendar there were twoscore days of religious observance; whose going and coming, giving and taking, living and dying, to the minutest details of social conduct, to the most intimate particulars of private life, were regulated by sacred laws, there could be no question of personal convictions in religion. One was a Jew, leading a righteous life; or one was a Gentile, existing to harass the Jews, while making a living off Jewish enterprise. In the vocabulary of the more intelligent part of Polotzk, it is true, there were such words as freethinker and apostate; but these were the names of men who had forsaken the Law in distant times or in distant parts, and whose evil fame had reached Polotzk by the circuitous route of tradition. Nobody looked for such monsters in his neighborhood. Polotzk was safely divided into Jews and Gentiles.

If any one in Polotzk had been idle and curious enough to inquire into the state of mind of a little child, I wonder if his findings would not have disturbed this simple classification.

There used to be a little girl in Polotzk who recited the long Hebrew prayers, morning and evening, before and after meals, and never skipped a word; who kissed the *mezuzah* when going or coming; who abstained from food and drink on fast days when she was no bigger than a sacrificial hen; who spent Sabbath mornings over the lengthy ritual for the day, and read the Psalms till daylight failed.

This pious child could give as good an account of the Creation as any boy of her age. She knew how God made the world. Undeterred by the fate of Eve, she wanted to know more. She asked her wise rebbe how God came to be in His place, and where He found the stuff to make the world of, and what was doing in the universe before God undertook His task. Finding from his unsatisfying replies that the rebbe was but a barren branch on the tree of knowledge, the good little girl never betrayed to the world, by look or word, her discovery of his limitations, but continued to accord him, outwardly, all the courtesy due to his calling.

Her teacher having failed her, the young student, with admirable persistence, carried her questions from one to another of her acquaintances, putting their answers to the test whenever it was possible. She established by this means two facts: first, that she knew as much as any of those who undertook to instruct her; second, that her oracles sometimes gave false answers. Did the little inquisitor charge her betrayers with the lie? Magnanimous creature, she kept their falseness a secret, and ceased to probe their shallow depths.

What you would know, find out for yourself: this became our student's motto; and she passed from the question to the experiment. Her grandmother told her that if she handled "blind flowers" she would be stricken blind. She found by test that the pretty flowers were harmless. She tested everything that could be tested, till she hit at last on an impious plan to put God Himself to the proof.

The pious little girl arose one Sabbath afternoon from her religious meditations, when all the house was taking its after-dinner nap, and went out in the yard, and stopped at the gate. She took out her pocket handkerchief. She looked at it. Yes, that would do for the experiment. She put it back into her pocket. She did not have to rehearse mentally the sacred admonition not to carry anything beyond the house-limits on the Sabbath day. She knew it as she knew that she was alive. And with her handkerchief in her pocket the audacious child stepped into the street!

She stood a moment, her heart beating so that it pained. Nothing happened! She walked quite across the street. The Sabbath peace still lay on everything. She felt again of the burden in her pocket. Yes, she certainly was committing a sin. With an access of impious boldness, the sinner walked—she ran as far as the corner, and stood still, fearfully expectant. What form would the punishment take? She stood breathing painfully for an eternity. How still everything was—how close and still the air! Would it be a storm? Would a sudden bolt strike her? She stood and waited. She could not bring her hand to her pocket again, but she felt that it bulged monstrously. She stood with no thought of moving again. Where were the thunders of Jehovah? No sacred word of all her long prayers came to her tongue—not even "Hear, O Israel." She felt that she was in direct communication with God—awful thought!—and He would read her mind and would send His answer.

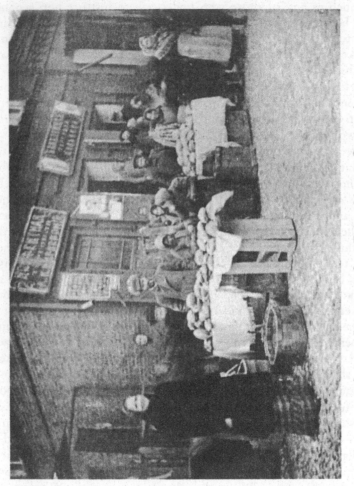

SABBATH LOAVES FOR SALE (BREAD MARKET, POLOTZK)

An age passed in blank expectancy. Nothing happened! Where was the wrath of God? *Where was God?*

When she turned to go home, the little philosopher had her handkerchief tied around her wrist in the proper way. The experiment was over, though the result was not clear. God had not punished her, but nothing was proved by His indifference. Either the act was no sin, and her preceptors were all deceivers; or it was indeed a sin in the eyes of God, but He refrained from stern justice for high reasons of His own. It was not a searching experiment she had made. She was bitterly disappointed, and perhaps that was meant as her punishment: God refused to give her a reply. She intended no sin for the sake of sin; so, being still in doubt, she tied her handkerchief around her wrist. Her eyes stared more than ever,—this was the child with the staring eyes,—but that was the only sign she gave of a consciousness suddenly expanded, of a self-consciousness intensified.

When she went back into the house, she gazed with a new curiosity at her mother, at her grandmother, dozing in their chairs. They looked *different.* When they awoke and stretched themselves and adjusted wig and cap, they looked *very* strange. As she went to get her grandmother her Bible, and dropped it accidentally, she kissed it by way of atonement just as a proper child should.

How, I wonder, would this Psalm-singing child have been labelled by the investigator of her mind? Would he have called her a Jew? She was too young to be called an apostate. Perhaps she would have been dismissed as a little fraud; and I should be content with that classification, if slightly modified. I should say the child was a piteously puzzled little fraud.

To return to the honest first person, I *was* something of a fraud. The days when I believed everything I was told did not run much beyond my teething time. I soon began to question if fire was really hot, if the cat would really scratch. Presently, as we have seen, I questioned God. And in those days my religion depended on my mood. I could believe anything I wanted to believe. I did believe, in all my moods, that there was a God who had made the world, in some fashion unexplained, and who knew about me and my doings; for there was the world all about me, and somebody must have made it. And it was conceivable that a being powerful enough to do such work could be aware of my actions at all times, and yet continue to me invisible. The question remained, what did He think of my conduct? Was He really angry when I broke the Sabbath, or pleased when I fasted on the Day of Atonement? My belief as to these matters wavered. When I swung the sacrifice around my head on Atonement Eve, repeating, "Be thou my sacrifice," etc., I certainly believed that I was bargaining with the Almighty for pardon, and that He was interested in the matter. But next day, when the fast was over, and I enjoyed all of my chicken that I could eat, I believed as certainly that God could not be party to such a foolish transaction, in which He got nothing but words, while I got both the feast and the pardon. The sacrifice of money, to be spent for the poor, seemed to me a more reliable insurance against damnation. The well-to-do pious offered up both living sacrifice and money for the poor-box, but it was a sign of poverty to offer only money. Even a lean rooster, to be killed, roasted, and garnished for the devotee's own table at the breaking of the fast, seemed to be considered a more respectable sacrifice than a groschen to increase the charity fund. All this was so illogical that it unsettled my faith in minor points of doctrine, and on these points I was quite happy to believe to-day one thing, to-morrow another.

As unwaveringly as I believed that we Jews had a God who was powerful and wise, I believed that the God of my Christian neighbors was impotent, cruel, and foolish. I understood that the god of the Gentiles was no better than a toy, to be dressed up in gaudy stuffs and carried in processions. I saw it often enough, and turned away in contempt. While the God of Abraham, Isaac, and Jacob— my God—enjoined on me honesty and kindness, the god of Vanka bade him beat me and spit on me whenever he caught me alone. And what a foolish god was that who taught the stupid Gentiles that we drank the blood of a murdered child at our Passover feast! Why, I, who was only a child, knew better. And so I hated and feared and avoided the great white church in the Platz, and hated every sign and symbol of that monstrous god who was kept there, and hated my own person, when, in our play of a Christian funeral, I imagined my body to be the corpse, over which was carried the hideous cross.

Perhaps I have established that I was more Jew than Gentile, though I can still prove that I was none the less a fraud. For instance, I remember how once, on the eve of the Ninth of Ab—the anniversary of the fall of the Temple—I was looking on at the lamentations of the women. A large circle had gathered around my mother, who was the only good reader among them, to listen to the story of the cruel destruction. Sitting on humble stools, in stocking feet, shabby clothes, and dishevelled hair, weeping in chorus, and wringing their hands, as if it was but yesterday that the sacred edifice fell and they were in the very dust and ashes of the ruin, the women looked to me enviously wretched and pious. I joined the circle in the candlelight. I wrung my hands, I moaned; but I was always slow of tears—I could not weep. But I wanted to look like the others. So I streaked my cheeks with the only moisture at hand.

Alas for my pious ambition! alas for the noble lament of the women! Somebody looked up and caught me in the act of manufacturing tears. I grinned, and she giggled. Another woman looked up. I grinned, and they giggled. Demoralization swept around the circle. Honest laughter snuffed out artificial grief. My mother at last looked up, with red and astonished eyes, and I was banished from the feast of tears.

I returned promptly to my playmates in the street, who were amusing themselves, according to the custom on that sad anniversary, by pelting each other with burrs. Here I was distinguished, more than I had been among my elders. My hair being curly, it caught a generous number of burrs, so that I fairly bristled with these emblems of mortification and woe.

Not long after that sinful experiment with the handkerchief I discovered by accident that I was not the only doubter in Polotzk. One Friday night I lay wakeful in my little bed, staring from the dark into the lighted room adjoining mine. I saw the Sabbath candles sputter and go out, one by one,—it was late,—but the lamp hanging from the ceiling still burned high. Everybody had gone to bed. The lamp would go out before morning if there was little oil; or else it would burn till Natasha, the Gentile chorewoman, came in the morning to put it out, and remove the candlesticks from the table, and unseal the oven, and do the dozen little tasks which no Jew could perform on the Sabbath. The simple prohibition to labor on the Sabbath day had been construed by zealous commentators to mean much more. One must not even touch any instrument of labor or commerce, as an axe or a coin. It was forbidden to light a fire, or to touch anything that contained a fire, or had contained fire, were it only a cold candlestick or a burned match. Therefore the lamp at which I was staring must burn till the Gentile woman came to put it out.

The light did not annoy me in the least; I was not thinking about it. But apparently it troubled somebody else. I saw my father come from his room, which also adjoined the living-room. What was he going to do? What was this he was doing? Could I believe my eyes? My father touched the lighted lamp!—yes, he shook it, as if to see how much oil there was left.

I was petrified in my place. I could neither move nor make a sound. It seemed to me he must feel my eyes bulging at him out of the dark. But he did not know that I was looking; he thought everybody was asleep. He turned down the light a very little, and waited. I did not take my eyes from him. He lowered the flame a little more, and waited again. I watched. By the slightest degrees he turned the light down. I understood. In case any one were awake, it would appear as if the lamp was going out of itself. I was the only one who lay so as to be able to see him, and I had gone to bed so early that he could not suppose I was awake. The light annoyed him, he wanted to put it out, but he would not risk having it known.

I heard my father find his bed in the dark before I dared to draw a full breath. The thing he had done was a monstrous sin. If his mother had seen him do it, it would have broken her heart—his mother who fasted half the days of the year, when he was a boy, to save his teacher's fee; his mother who walked almost barefoot in the cruel snow to carry him on her shoulders to school when she had no shoes for him; his mother who made it her pious pride to raise up a learned son, that most precious offering in the eyes of the great God, from the hand of a poor struggling woman. If my mother had seen it, it would have grieved her no less—my mother who was given to him, with her youth and good name and her dowry, in exchange for his learning and piety; my mother who was taken from her play to bear him children and feed them and keep them, while he sat on the benches of the scholars and repaid her labors with the fame of his learning. I did not put it to myself just so, but I understood that learning and piety were the things most valued in our family, that my father was a scholar, and that piety, of course, was the fruit of sacred learning. And yet my father had deliberately violated the Sabbath.

His act was not to be compared with my carrying the handkerchief. The two sins were of the same kind, but the sinners and their motives were different. I was a child, a girl at that, not yet of the age of moral responsibility. He was a man full grown, passing for one of God's elect, and accepting the reverence of the world as due tribute to his scholarly merits. I had by no means satisfied myself, by my secret experiment, that it was not sinful to carry a burden on the Sabbath day. If God did not punish me on the spot, perhaps it was because of my youth or perhaps it was because of my motive.

According to my elders, my father, by turning out the lamp, committed the sin of Sabbath-breaking. What did my father intend? I could not suppose that his purpose was similar to mine. Surely he, who had lived so long and studied so deeply, had by this time resolved all his doubts. Surely God had instructed *him*. I could not believe that he did wrong knowingly, so I came to the conclusion that he did not hold it a sin to touch a lighted lamp on Sabbath. Then why was he so secret in his action? That, too, became clear to me. I myself had instinctively adopted secret methods in all my little investigations, and had kept the results to myself. The way in which my questions were received had taught me much. I had a dim, inarticulate understanding of the horror and indignation which my father would excite if he, supposedly a man of piety, should publish the heretical opinion that it was not wrong to handle fire on the Sabbath. To see what remorse my mother suffered, or my father's mother, if by some accident she failed in any point of religious observance, was to know that she could never be brought to doubt the sacred importance of the thousand minutiæ of ancient Jewish practice. That which had been taught them as the truth by their fathers and mothers was the whole truth to my good friends and neighbors—that and nothing else. If there were any people in Polotzk who had strange private opinions, such as I concluded my father must hold, it was possible that he had a secret acquaintance with them. But it would never do, it was plain to me, to make public confession of his convictions. Such an act would not only break the hearts of his family, but it would also take the bread from the mouths of his children, and ruin them forever. My sister and my brother and I would come to be called the children of Israel

the Apostate, just as Gutke, my playmate, was called the granddaughter of Yankel the Informer. The most innocent of us would
be cursed and shunned for the sin of our father.

All this I came to understand, not all at once, but by degrees, as
I put this and that together, and brought my childish thoughts to
order. I was by no means absorbed in this problem. I played and
danced with the other children as heartily as ever, but I brooded
in my window corner when there was nothing else to do. I had
not the slightest impulse to go to my father, charge him with his
unorthodox conduct, and demand an explanation of him. I was
quite satisfied that I understood him, and I had not the habit of
confidences. I was still in the days when I was content to *find out*
things, and did not long to communicate my discoveries. Moreover,
I was used to living in two worlds, a real world and a make-believe
one, without ever knowing which was which. In one world I had
much company—father and mother and sister and friends—and did
as others did, and took everything for granted. In the other world
I was all alone, and I had to discover ways for myself; and I was
so uncertain that I did not attempt to bring a companion along.
And did I find my own father treading in the unknown ways? Then
perhaps some day he would come across me, and take me farther
than I had yet been; but I would not be the first to whisper that I
was there. It seems strange enough to me now that I should have
been so uncommunicative; but I remind myself that I have been
thoroughly made over, at least once, since those early days.

I recall with sorrow that I was sometimes as weak in morals as
I was in religion. I remember stealing a piece of sugar. It was long
ago—almost as long ago as anything that I remember. We were still
living in my grandfather's house when this dreadful thing happened, and I was only four or five years old when we moved from
there. Before my mother figured this out for me I scarcely had the
courage to confess my sin.

And it was thus: In a corner of a front room, by a window,
stood a high chest of drawers. On top of the chest stood a tin box,
decorated with figures of queer people with queer flat parasols; a
Chinese tea-box, in a word. The box had a lid. The lid was shut
tight. But I knew what was in that gorgeous box, and I coveted it.
I was very little—I never could reach anything. There stood a chair
suggestively near the chest. I pushed the chair a little and mounted

it. By standing on tiptoe I could now reach the box. I opened it and took out an irregular lump of sparkling sugar. I stood on the chair admiring it. I stood too long. My grandmother came in—or was it Itke, the housemaid?—and found me with the stolen morsel.

I saw that I was fairly caught. How could I hope to escape my captor, when I was obliged to turn on my stomach in order to descend safely, thus presenting my jailer with the most tempting opportunity for immediate chastisement? I took in the situation before my grandmother had found her voice for horror. Did I rub my eyes with my knuckles and whimper? I wish I could report that I was thus instantly struck with a sense of my guilt. I was impressed only with the absolute certainty of my impending doom, and I promptly seized on a measure of compensation. While my captor—I really think it was a grandmother—rehearsed her entire vocabulary of reproach, from a distance sufficient to enable her to hurl her voice at me with the best effect, I stuffed the lump of sugar into my mouth and munched it as fast as I could. And I had eaten it all, and had licked my sticky lips, before the avenging rod came down.

I remember no similar lapses from righteousness, but I sinned in lesser ways more times than there are years in my life. I sinned, and more than once I escaped punishment by some trick or sly speech. I do not mean that I lied outright, though that also I did, sometimes; but I would twist my naughty speech, if forced to repeat it, in such an artful manner, or give such ludicrous explanation of my naughty act, that justice was overcome by laughter and threw me, as often as not, a handful of raisins instead of a knotted strap. If by such successes I was encouraged to cultivate my natural slyness and duplicity, I throw the blame on my unwise preceptors, and am glad to be rid of the burden for once.

I have said that I used to lie. I recall no particular occasion when a lie was the cause of my disgrace; but I know that it was always my habit, when I had some trifling adventure to report, to garnish it up with so much detail and circumstance that nobody who had witnessed my small affair could have recognized it as the same, had I not insisted on my version with such fervid conviction. The truth is that everything that happened to me really loomed great and shone splendid in my eyes, and I could not, except by conscious effort, reduce my visions to their actual shapes and colors. If I saw a pair of geese leading about a lazy goose girl, they went through all sorts of antics before my eyes that fat geese are not known to indulge in. If I met poor Blind Munye with a frown on his face, I thought that a cloud of wrath overspread his countenance; and I ran home to relate, panting, how narrowly I had escaped his fury. I will not pretend that I was absolutely unconscious of my exaggerations; but if you insist, I will say that things as I reported them might have been so, and would have been much more interesting had they been so.

The noble reader who never told a lie, or never confessed one, will be shocked at these revelations of my childish depravity. What proof has he, he will cry, that I am not lying on every page of this chronicle, if, by my own confession, my childhood was spent in a maze of lies and dreams? I shall say to the saint, when I am challenged, that the proof of my conversion to veracity is engraven in his own soul. Do you not remember, you spotless one, how you used to steal and lie and cheat and rob? Oh, not with your own hand, of course! It was your remote ancestor who lived by plunder, and was honored for the blood upon his hairy hands. By and by he discovered that cunning was more effective than violence, and less troublesome. Still later he became convinced that the greatest cunning was virtue, and made him a moral code, and subdued the world. Then, when you came along, stumbling through the wilderness of cast-off errors, your wise ancestor gave you a thrust that landed you in the clearing of modernity, at the same time bellowing in your ear, "Now be good! It pays!"

This is the whole history of your saintliness. But all people do not take up life at the same point of human development. Some are backward at birth, and have to make up, in the brief space of their individual history, the stages they missed on their way out of the black past. With me, for example, it actually comes to this: that I have to recapitulate in my own experience all the slow steps of the progress of the race. I seem to learn nothing except by the prick of life on my own skin. I am saved from living in ignorance and dying in darkness only by the sensitiveness of my skin. Some men learn through borrowed experience. Shut them up in a glass tower, with an unobstructed view of the world, and they will go through every adventure of life by proxy, and be able to furnish you with a complete philosophy of life; and you may safely bring up your children by it. But I am not of that godlike organization. I am a thinking animal. Things are as important to me as ideas. I imbibe wisdom through every pore of my body. There are times, indeed, when the doctor in his study is less intelligible to me than a cricket far off in the field. The earth was my mother, the earth is my teacher. I am a dutiful pupil: I listen ever with my ear close to her lips. It seems to me I do not know a single thing that I did not learn, more or less directly, through the corporal senses. As long as I have my body, I need not despair of salvation.

CHAPTER VII

THE BOUNDARIES STRETCH

THE LONG CHAPTER OF TROUBLES which led to my father's emigration to America began with his own illness. The doctors sent him to Courland to consult expensive specialists, who prescribed tedious courses of treatment. He was far from cured when my mother also fell ill, and my father had to return to Polotzk to look after the business.

Trouble begets trouble. After my mother took to her bed everything continued to go wrong. The business gradually declined, as too much money was withdrawn to pay the doctors' and apothecaries' bills; and my father, himself in poor health, and worried about my mother, was not successful in coping with the growing difficulties. At home, the servants were dismissed, for the sake of economy, and all the housework and the nursing fell on my grandmother and my sister. Fetchke, as a result, was overworked, and fell ill of a fever. The baby, suffering from unavoidable neglect, developed the fractious temper of semi-illness. And by way of a climax, the old cow took it into her head to kick my grandmother, who was laid up for a week with a bruised leg.

Neighbors and cousins pulled us through till grandma got up, and after her, Fetchke. But my mother remained on her bed. Weeks, months, a year she lay there, and half of another year. All the doctors in Polotzk attended her in turn, and one doctor came all the way from Vitebsk. Every country practitioner for miles around was consulted, every quack, every old wife who knew a charm. The apothecaries ransacked their shops for drugs the names of which they had forgotten, and kind neighbors brought in their favorite remedies. There were midnight prayers in the synagogue for my mother, and petitions at the graves of her parents; and one awful night when she was near death, three pious mothers who had never lost a child came to my mother's bedside and bought her, for a few kopecks, for their own, so that she might gain the protection of their luck, and so be saved.

Still my poor mother lay on her bed, suffering and wasting. The house assumed a look of desolation. Everybody went on tiptoe; we talked in whispers; for weeks at a time there was no laughter in our home. The ominous night lamp was never extinguished. We slept in our clothes night after night, so as to wake the more easily in case of sudden need. We watched, we waited, but we scarcely hoped.

Once in a while I was allowed to take a short turn in the sickroom. It was awful to sit beside my mother's bed in the still night and see her helplessness. She had been so strong, so active. She used to lift sacks and barrels that were heavy for a man, and now she could not raise a spoon to her mouth. Sometimes she did not know me when I gave her the medicine, and when she knew me, she did not care. Would she ever care any more? She looked strange and small in the shadows of the bed. Her hair had been cut off after the first few months; her short curls were almost covered by the ice bag. Her cheeks were red, red, but her hands were so white as they had never been before. In the still night I wondered if she cared to live.

The night lamp burned on. My father grew old. He was always figuring on a piece of paper. We children knew the till was empty when the silver candlesticks were taken away to be pawned. Next, superfluous featherbeds were sold for what they would bring, and then there came a day when grandma, with eyes blinded by tears, groped in the big wardrobe for my mother's satin dress and velvet mantle; and after that it did not matter any more what was taken out of the house.

Then everything took a sudden turn. My mother began to improve, and at the same time my father was offered a good position as superintendent of a gristmill.

As soon as my mother could be moved, he took us all out to the mill, about three versts out of town, on the Polota. We had a pleasant cottage there, with the miller's red-headed, freckled family for our only neighbors. If our rooms were barer than they used to be, the sun shone in at all the windows; and as the leaves on the trees grew denser and darker, my mother grew stronger on her feet, and laughter returned to our house as the song bird to the grove.

We children had a very happy summer. We had never lived in the country before, and we liked the change. It was endless fun to explore the mill; to squeeze into forbidden places, and be pulled out by the angry miller; to tyrannize over the mill hands, and be worshipped by them in return; to go boating on the river, and discover unvisited nooks, and search the woods and fields for kitchen herbs, and get lost, and be found, a hundred times a week. And what an adventure it was to walk the three versts into town, leaving a trail of perfume from the wild-flower posies we carried to our city friends!

But these things did not last. The mill changed hands, and the new owner put a protégé of his own in my father's place. So, after a short breathing spell, we were driven back into the swamp of growing poverty and trouble.

The next year or so my father spent in a restless and fruitless search for a permanent position. My mother had another serious illness, and his own health remained precarious. What he earned did not more than half pay the bills in the end, though we were living very humbly now. Polotzk seemed to reject him, and no other place invited him.

Just at this time occurred one of the periodic anti-Semitic movements whereby government officials were wont to clear the forbidden cities of Jews, whom, in the intervals of slack administration of the law, they allowed to maintain an illegal residence in places outside the Pale, on payment of enormous bribes and at the cost of nameless risks and indignities.

It was a little before Passover that the cry of the hunted thrilled the Jewish world with the familiar fear. The wholesale expulsion of Jews from Moscow and its surrounding district at cruelly short notice was the name of this latest disaster. Where would the doom strike next? The Jews who lived illegally without the Pale turned their possessions into cash and slept in their clothes, ready for immediate flight. Those who lived in the comparative security of the Pale trembled for their brothers and sisters without, and opened wide their doors to afford the fugitives refuge. And hundreds of fugitives, preceded by a wail of distress, flocked into the open district, bringing their trouble where trouble was never absent, mingling their tears with the tears that never dried.

The open cities becoming thus suddenly crowded, every man's chance of making a living was diminished in proportion to the number of additional competitors. Hardship, acute distress, ruin for many: thus spread the disaster, ring beyond ring, from the stone thrown by a despotic official into the ever-full river of Jewish persecution.

Passover was celebrated in tears that year. In the story of the Exodus we would have read a chapter of current history, only for us there was no deliverer and no promised land.

But what said some of us at the end of the long service? Not "May we be next year in Jerusalem," but "Next year—in America!" So there was our promised land, and many faces were turned towards the West. And if the waters of the Atlantic did not part for them, the wanderers rode its bitter flood by a miracle as great as any the rod of Moses ever wrought.

My father was carried away by the westward movement, glad of his own deliverance, but sore at heart for us whom he left behind. It was the last chance for all of us. We were so far reduced in circumstances that he had to travel with borrowed money to a German port, whence he was forwarded to Boston, with a host of others, at the expense of an emigrant aid society.

I was about ten years old when my father emigrated. I was used to his going away from home, and "America" did not mean much more to me than "Kherson," or "Odessa," or any other names of distant places. I understood vaguely, from the gravity with which his plans were discussed, and from references to ships, societies, and other unfamiliar things, that this enterprise was different from previous ones; but my excitement and emotion on the morning of my father's departure were mainly vicarious.

I know the day when "America" as a world entirely unlike Polotzk lodged in my brain, to become the centre of all my dreams and speculations. Well I know the day. I was in bed, sharing the measles with some of the other children. Mother brought us a thick letter from father, written just before boarding the ship. The letter was full of excitement. There was something in it besides the description of travel, something besides the pictures of crowds of people, of foreign cities, of a ship ready to put out to sea. My father was travelling at the expense of a charitable organization, without means of his own, without plans, to a strange world where he had no friends; and yet he wrote with the confidence of a well-equipped soldier going into battle. The rhetoric is mine. Father simply wrote that the emigration committee was taking good care of everybody, that the weather was fine, and the ship comfortable. But I heard something, as we read the letter together in the darkened room, that was more than the words seemed to say. There was an elation, a hint of triumph, such as had never been in my father's letters before. I cannot tell how I knew it. I felt a stirring, a straining in my father's letter. It was there, even though my mother stumbled over strange words, even though she cried, as women will when somebody is going away. My father was inspired by a vision. He saw something—he promised us something. It was this "America." And "America" became my dream.

While it was nothing new for my father to go far from home in search of his fortune, the circumstances in which he left us were unlike anything we had experienced before. We had absolutely no reliable source of income, no settled home, no immediate prospects. We hardly knew where we belonged in the simple scheme of our society. My mother, as a bread-winner, had nothing like her former success. Her health was permanently impaired, her place in the business world had long been filled by others, and there was no capital to start her anew. Her brothers did what they could for her. They were well-to-do, but they all had large families, with marriageable daughters and sons to be bought out of military service. The allowance they made her was generous compared to their means,—affection and duty could do no more,—but there were four of us growing children, and my mother was obliged to make every effort within her power to piece out her income.

How quickly we came down from a large establishment, with servants and retainers, and a place among the best in Polotzk, to a single room hired by the week, and the humblest associations, and the averted heads of former friends! But oftenest it was my mother who turned away her head. She took to using the side streets, to avoid the pitiful eyes of the kind, and the scornful eyes of the haughty. Both were turned on her as she trudged from store to store, and from house to house, peddling tea or other ware; and both were hard to bear. Many a winter morning she arose in the dark, to tramp three or four miles in the gripping cold, through the dragging snow, with a pound of tea for a distant customer; and her profit was perhaps twenty kopecks. Many a time she fell on the ice, as she climbed the steep bank on the far side of the Dvina, a heavy basket on each arm. More than once she fainted at the doors of her customers, ashamed to knock as suppliant where she had used to be received as an honored guest. I hope the angels did not have to count the tears that fell on her frost-bitten, aching hands as she counted her bitter earnings at night.

And who took care of us children while my mother tramped the streets with her basket? Why, who but Fetchke? Who but the little housewife of twelve? Sure of our safety was my mother with Fetchke to watch; sure of our comfort with Fetchke to cook the soup and divide the scrap of meat and remember the next meal. Joseph was in heder all day; the baby was a quiet little thing; Mashke was no worse than usual. But still there was plenty to do, with order to keep in a crowded room, and the washing, and the mending. And Fetchke did it all. She went to the river with the women to wash the clothes, and tucked up her dress and stood bare-legged in the water, like the rest of them, and beat and rubbed with all her might, till our miserable rags gleamed white again.

And I? I usually had a cold, or a cough, or something to disable me; and I never had any talent for housework. If I swept and sanded the floor, polished the samovar, and ran errands, I was doing much. I minded the baby, who did not need much minding. I was willing enough, I suppose, but the hard things were done without my help.

Not that I mean to belittle the part that I played in our reduced domestic economy. Indeed, I am very particular to get all the credit due me. I always remind my sister Deborah, who was the baby of those humble days, that it was I who pierced her ears. Earrings were a requisite part of a girl's toilet. Even a beggar girl must have earrings, were they only loops of thread with glass beads. I heard my mother bemoan the baby because she had not time to pierce her ears. Promptly I armed myself with a coarse needle and a spool of thread, and towed Deborah out into the woodshed. The operation was entirely successful, though the baby was entirely ungrateful. And I am proud to this day of the unflinching manner in which I did what I conceived to be my duty. If Deborah chooses to go with ungarnished ears, it is her affair; my conscience is free of all reproach.

I had a direct way in everything. I rushed right in—I spoke right out. My mother sent me sometimes to deliver a package of tea, and I was proud to help in business. One day I went across the Dvina and far up "the other side." It was a good-sized expedition for me

WINTER SCENE ON THE DVINA

to make alone, and I was not a little pleased with myself when I delivered my package, safe and intact, into the hands of my customer. But the storekeeper was not pleased at all. She sniffed and sniffed, she pinched the tea, she shook it all out on the counter.

"*Na*, take it back," she said in disgust; "this is not the tea I always buy. It's a poorer quality."

I knew the woman was mistaken. I was acquainted with my mother's several grades of tea. So I spoke up manfully.

"Oh, no," I said; "this is the tea my mother always sends you. There is no worse tea."

Nothing in my life ever hurt me more than that woman's answer to my argument. She laughed—she simply laughed. But I understood, even before she controlled herself sufficiently to make verbal remarks, that I had spoken like a fool, had lost my mother a customer. I had only spoken the truth, but I had not expressed it diplomatically. That was no way to make business.

I felt very sore to be returning home with the tea still in my hand, but I forgot my trouble in watching a summer storm gather up the river. The few passengers who took the boat with me looked scared as the sky darkened, and the boatman grasped his oars very soberly. It took my breath away to see the signs, but I liked it; and I was much disappointed to get home dry.

When my mother heard of my misadventure she laughed, too; but that was different, and I was able to laugh with her.

This is the way I helped in the housekeeping and in business. I hope it does not appear as if I did not take our situation to heart, for I did—in my own fashion. It was plain, even to an idle dreamer like me, that we were living on the charity of our friends, and barely living at that. It was plain, from my father's letters, that he was scarcely able to support himself in America, and that there was no immediate prospect of our joining him. I realized it all, but I considered it temporary, and I found plenty of comfort in writing long letters to my father—real, original letters this time, not copies of Reb' Isaiah's model—letters which my father treasured for years.

As an instance of what I mean by my own fashion of taking trouble to heart, I recall the day when our household effects were attached for a debt. We had plenty of debts, but the stern creditor who set the law on us this time was none of ours. The claim was against a family to whom my mother sublet two of our three rooms, furnished with her own things. The police officers, who swooped down upon us without warning, as was their habit, asked no questions and paid no heed to explanations. They affixed a seal to every lame chair and cracked pitcher in the place; aye, to every faded petticoat found hanging in the wardrobe. These goods, comprising all our possessions and all our tenant's, would presently be removed, to be sold at auction, for the benefit of the creditor.

Lame chairs and faded petticoats, when they are the last one has, have a vital value in the owner's eyes. My mother moved about, weeping distractedly, all the while the officers were in the house. The frightened children cried. Our neighbors gathered to bemoan our misfortune. And over everything was the peculiar dread which only Jews in Russia feel when agents of the Government invade their homes.

The fear of the moment was in my heart, as in every other heart there. It was a horrid, oppressive fear. I retired to a quiet corner to grapple with it. I was not given to weeping, but I must think things out in words. I repeated to myself that the trouble was all about money. Somebody wanted money from our tenant, who had none to give. Our furniture was going to be sold to make this money. It was a mistake, but then the officers would not believe my mother. Still, it was only about money. Nobody was dead, nobody was ill. It was all about *money.* Why, there was plenty of money in Polotzk! My own uncle had many times as much as the creditor claimed. He could buy all our things back, or somebody else could. What did it matter? It was only *money,* and money was got by working, and we were all willing to work. There was nothing gone, nothing lost, as when somebody died. This furniture could be moved from place to place, and so could money be moved, and nothing was lost out of the world by the transfer. *That* was all. If anybody—

Why, what do I see at the window? Breine Malke, our next-door neighbor, is—yes, she is smuggling something out of the window! If she is caught—! Oh, I must help! Breine Malke beckons. She wants me to do something. I see—I understand. I must stand in the doorway, to obstruct the view of the officers, who are all engaged in the next room just now. I move readily to my post, but I cannot resist my curiosity. I must look over my shoulder a last time, to see what it is Breine Malke wants to smuggle out.

I can scarcely stifle my laughter. Of all our earthly goods, our neighbor has chosen for salvation a dented bandbox containing a moth-eaten bonnet from my mother's happier days! And I laugh not only from amusement but also from lightness of heart. For I have succeeded in reducing our catastrophe to its simplest terms, and I find that it is only a trifle, and no matter of life and death.

I could not help it. That was the way it looked to me.

I am sure I made as serious efforts as anybody to prepare myself for life in America on the lines indicated in my father's letters. In America, he wrote, it was no disgrace to work at a trade. Workmen and capitalists were equal. The employer addressed the employee as *you*, not, familiarly, as *thou*. The cobbler and the teacher had the same title, "Mister." And all the children, boys and girls, Jews and Gentiles, went to school! Education would be ours for the asking, and economic independence also, as soon as we were prepared. He wanted Fetchke and me to be taught some trade; so my sister was apprenticed to a dressmaker and I to a milliner.

Fetchke, of course, was successful, and I, of course, was not. My sister managed to learn her trade, although most of the time at the dressmaker's she had to spend in sweeping, running errands, and minding the babies; the usual occupations of the apprentice in any trade.

But I—I had to be taken away from the milliner's after a couple of months. I did try, honestly. With all my eyes I watched my mistress build up a chimney pot of straw and things. I ripped up old bonnets with enthusiasm. I picked up everybody's spools and thimbles, and other far-rolling objects. I did just as I was told, for I was determined to become a famous milliner, since America honored the workman so. But most of the time I was sent away on errands—to the market to buy soup greens, to the corner store to get change, and all over town with bandboxes half as round again as I. It was winter, and I was not very well dressed. I froze; I coughed; my mistress said I was not of much use to her. So my mother kept me at home, and my career as a milliner was blighted.

This was during our last year in Russia, when I was between twelve and thirteen years of age. I was old enough to be ashamed of my failures, but I did not have much time to think about them, because my Uncle Solomon took me with him to Vitebsk.

It was not my first visit to that city. A few years before I had spent some days there, in the care of my father's cousin Rachel, who journeyed periodically to the capital of the province to replenish her stock of spools and combs and like small wares, by the sale of which she was slowly earning her dowry.

On that first occasion, Cousin Rachel, who had developed in business that dual conscience, one for her Jewish neighbors and one for the Gentiles, decided to carry me without a ticket. I was so small, though of an age to pay half-fare, that it was not difficult. I remember her simple stratagem from beginning to end. When we approached the ticket office she whispered to me to stoop a little, and I stooped. The ticket agent passed me. In the car she bade me curl up in the seat, and I curled up. She threw a shawl over me and bade me pretend to sleep, and I pretended to sleep. I heard the conductor collect the tickets. I knew when he was looking at me. I heard him ask my age and I heard Cousin Rachel lie about it. I was allowed to sit up when the conductor was gone, and I sat up and looked out of the window and saw everything, and was perfectly, perfectly happy. I was fond of my cousin, and I smiled at her in perfect understanding and admiration of her cleverness in beating the railroad company.

I knew then, as I know now, beyond a doubt, that my Uncle David's daughter was an honorable woman. With the righteous she dealt squarely; with the unjust, as best she could. She was in duty bound to make all the money she could, for money was her only protection in the midst of the enemy. Every kopeck she earned or saved was a scale in her coat of armor. We learned this code early in life, in Polotzk; so I was pleased with the success of our ruse on this occasion, though I should have been horrified if I had seen Cousin Rachel cheat a Jew.

We made our headquarters in that part of Vitebsk where my father's numerous cousins and aunts lived, in more or less poverty, or at most in the humblest comfort; but I was taken to my Uncle Solomon's to spend the Sabbath. I remember a long walk, through magnificent avenues and past splendid shops and houses and gardens. Vitebsk was a metropolis beside provincial Polotzk; and I was very small, even without stooping.

Uncle Solomon lived in the better part of the city, and I found his place very attractive. Still, after a night's sleep, I was ready for further travel and adventures, and I set out, without a word to anybody, to retrace my steps clear across the city.

The way was twice as long as on the preceding day, perhaps because such small feet set the pace, perhaps because I lingered as long as I pleased at the shop windows. At some corners, too, I had to stop and study my route. I do not think I was frightened at all, though I imagine my back was very straight and my head very high all the way; for I was well aware that I was out on an adventure.

I did not speak to any one till I reached my Aunt Leah's; and then I hardly had a chance to speak, I was so much hugged and laughed over and cried over, and questioned and cross-questioned, without anybody waiting to hear my answers. I had meant to surprise Cousin Rachel, and I had frightened her. When she had come to Uncle Solomon's to take me back, she found the house in an uproar, everybody frightened at my disappearance. The neighborhood was searched, and at last messengers were sent to Aunt Leah's. The messengers in their haste quite overlooked me. It was their fault if they took a short cut unknown to me. I was all the time faithfully steering by the sign of the tobacco shop, and the shop with the jumping-jack in the window, and the garden with the iron fence, and the sentry box opposite a drug store, and all the rest of my landmarks, as carefully entered on my mental chart the day before.

All this I told my scared relatives as soon as they let me, till they were convinced that I was not lost, nor stolen by the gypsies, nor otherwise done away with. Cousin Rachel was so glad that she would not have to return to Polotzk empty-handed that she would not let anybody scold me. She made me tell over and over what I had seen on the way, till they all laughed and praised my acuteness for seeing so much more than they had supposed there was to see. Indeed, I was made a heroine, which was just what I intended to be when I set out on my adventure. And thus ended most of my unlawful escapades; I was more petted than scolded for my insubordination.

My second journey to Vitebsk, in the company of Uncle Solomon, I remember as well as the first. I had been up all night, dancing at a wedding, and had gone home only to pick up my small bundle and be picked up, in turn, by my uncle. I was a little taller now, and had my own ticket, like a real traveller.

It was still early in the morning when the train pulled out of the station, or else it was a misty day. I know the fields looked soft and gray when we got out into the country, and the trees were blurred. I did not want to sleep. A new day had begun—a new adventure. I would not miss any of it.

But the last day, so unnaturally prolonged, was entangled in the skirts of the new. When did yesterday end? Why was not this new day the same day continued? I looked up at my uncle, but he was smiling at me in that amused way of his—he always seemed to be amused at me, and he would make me talk and then laugh at me —so I did not ask my question. Indeed, I could not formulate it, so I kept staring out on the dim country, and thinking, and thinking; and all the while the engine throbbed and lurched, and the wheels ground along, and I was astonished to hear that they were keeping perfectly the time of the last waltz I had danced at the wedding. I sang it through in my head. Yes, that was the rhythm. The engine knew it, the whole machine repeated it, and sent vibrations through my body that were just like the movements of the waltz. I was so much interested in this discovery that I forgot the problem of the Continuity of Time; and from that day to this, whenever I have heard that waltz,—one of the sweet Danube waltzes,—I have lived through that entire experience: the festive night, the misty morning, the abnormal consciousness of time, as if I had existed forever, without a break; the journey, the dim landscape, and the tune singing itself in my head. Never can I hear that waltz without the accompaniment of engine wheels grinding rhythmically along speeding tracks.

I remained in Vitebsk about six months. I do not believe I was ever homesick during all that time. I was too happy to be homesick. The life suited me extremely well. My life in Polotzk had grown meaner and duller, as the family fortunes declined. For years there had been no lessons, no pleasant excursions, no jolly gatherings with uncles and aunts. Poverty, shadowed by pride, trampled down our simple ambitions and simpler joys. I cannot honestly say that I was very sensitive to our losses. I do not remember suffering because there was no jam on my bread, and no new dress for the holidays. I do not know whether I was hurt when some of our playmates abandoned us. I remember myself oftener in the attitude of an onlooker, as on the occasion of the attachment of our furniture, when I went off into a corner to think about it. Perhaps I was not able to cling to negations. The possession of the bread was a more absorbing fact than the loss of the jam. If I were to read my character backwards, I ought to believe that I did miss what I lacked in our days of privation; for I know, to my shame, that in more recent years I have cried for jam. But I am trying not to reason, only to remember; and from many scattered and shadowy memories, that glimmer and fade away so fast that I cannot fix them on this page, I form an idea, almost a conviction, that it was with me as I say.

However indifferent I may have been to what I had not, I was fully alive to what I had. So when I came to Vitebsk I eagerly seized on the many new things that I found around me; and these new impressions and experiences affected me so much that I count that visit as an epoch in my Russian life.

I was very much at home in my uncle's household. I was a little afraid of my aunt, who had a quick temper, but on the whole I liked her. She was fair and thin and had a pretty smile in the wake of her tempers. Uncle Solomon was an old friend. I was fond of him and he made much of me. His fine brown eyes were full of smiles, and there always was a pleasant smile for me, or a teasing one.

Uncle Solomon was comparatively prosperous, so I soon forgot whatever I had known at home of sordid cares. I do not remember that I was ever haunted by the thought of my mother, who slaved to keep us in bread; or of my sister, so little older than myself, who bent her little back to a woman's work. I took up the life around me as if there were no other life. I did not play all the time, but I enjoyed whatever work I found because I was so happy. I helped my Cousin Dinke help her mother with the housework. I put it this way because I think my aunt never set me any tasks; but Dinke was glad to have me help wash dishes and sweep and make beds. My cousin was a gentle, sweet girl, blue-eyed and fair, and altogether attractive. She talked to me about grown-up things, and I liked it. When her friends came to visit her she did not mind having me about, although my skirts were so short.

My helping hand was extended also to my smaller cousins, Mendele and Perele. I played lotto with Mendele and let him beat me; I found him when he was lost, and I helped him play tricks on our elders. Perele, the baby, was at times my special charge, and I think she did not suffer in my hands. I was a good nurse, though my methods were somewhat original.

Uncle Solomon was often away on business, and in his absence Cousin Hirshel was my hero. Hirshel was only a little older than I, but he was a pupil in the high school, and wore the student's uniform, and knew nearly as much as my uncle, I thought. When he buckled on his satchel of books in the morning, and strode away straight as a soldier,—no heder boy ever walked like that,—I stood in the doorway and worshipped his retreating steps. I met him on his return in the late afternoon, and hung over him when he laid out his books for his lessons. Sometimes he had long Russian pieces to commit to memory. He would walk up and down repeating the lines out loud, and I learned as fast as he. He would let me hold the book while he recited, and a proud girl was I if I could correct him.

My interest in his lessons amused him; he did not take me seriously. He looked much like his father, and twinkled his eyes at me in the same way and made fun of me, too. But sometimes he condescended to set me a lesson in spelling or arithmetic,—in reading I was as good as he,—and if I did well, he praised me and went and told the family about it; but lest I grow too proud of my achievements, he would sit down and do mysterious sums—I now believe it was algebra—to which I had no clue whatever, and which duly impressed me with a sense of my ignorance.

There were other books in the house than schoolbooks. The Hebrew books, of course, were there, as in other Jewish homes; but I was no longer devoted to the Psalms. There were a few books about in Russian and in Yiddish, that were neither works of devotion nor of instruction. These were story-books and poems. They were a great surprise to me and a greater delight. I read them hungrily, all there were—a mere handful, but to me an overwhelming treasure. Of all those books I remember by name only "Robinson Crusoe." I think I preferred the stories to the poems, though poetry was good to recite, walking up and down, like Cousin Hirshel. That was my introduction to secular literature, but I did not understand it at the time.

When I had exhausted the books, I began on the old volumes

of a Russian periodical which I found on a shelf in my room. There was a high stack of these paper volumes, and I was so hungry for books that I went at them greedily, fearing that I might not get through before I had to return to Polotzk.

I read every spare minute of the day, and most of the night. I scarcely ever stopped at night until my lamp burned out. Then I would creep into bed beside Dinke, but often my head burned so from excitement that I did not sleep at once. And no wonder. The violent romances which rushed through the pages of that periodical were fit to inflame an older, more sophisticated brain than mine. I must believe that it was a thoroughly respectable magazine, because I found it in my Uncle Solomon's house; but the novels it printed were certainly sensational, if I dare judge from my lurid recollections. These romances, indeed, may have had their literary qualities, which I was too untrained to appreciate. I remember nothing but startling adventures of strange heroes and heroines, violent catastrophes in every chapter, beautiful maidens abducted by cruel Cossacks, inhuman mothers who poisoned their daughters for jealousy of their lovers; and all these unheard-of things happening in a strange world, the very language of which was unnatural to me. I was quick enough to fix meanings to new words, however, so keen was my interest in what I read. Indeed, when I recall the zest with which I devoured those fearful pages, the thrill with which I followed the heartless mother or the abused maiden in her adventures, my heart beating in my throat when my little lamp began to flicker; and then, myself, big-eyed and shivery in the dark, stealing to bed like a guilty ghost,—when I remember all this, I have an unpleasant feeling, as of one hearing of another's debauch; and I would be glad to shake the little bony culprit that I was then.

My uncle was away so much of the time that I doubt if he knew how I spent my nights. My aunt, poor hard-worked housewife, knew too little of books to direct my reading. My cousins were not enough older than myself to play mentors to me. Besides all this, I think it was tacitly agreed, at my uncle's as at home, that Mashke was best let alone in such matters. So I burnt my midnight lamp, and filled my mind with a conglomeration of images entirely unsuited to my mental digestion; and no one can say what they would have bred in me, besides headache and nervousness, had they not been so soon dispelled and superseded by a host of strong new impressions. For these readings ended with my visit, which was closely followed by the preparations for our emigration.

On the whole, then, I do not feel that I was seriously harmed by my wild reading. I have not been told that my taste was corrupted, and my morals, I believe, have also escaped serious stricture. I would even say that I have never been hurt by any revelation, however distorted or untimely, that I found in books, good or poor; that I have never read an idle book that was entirely useless; and that I have never quite lost whatever was significant to my spirit in any book, good or bad, even though my conscious memory can give no account of it.

One lived, at Uncle Solomon's, not only one's own life, but the life of all around. My uncle, when he returned after a short absence, had stories to tell and adventures to describe; and I learned that one might travel considerably and see things unknown even in Vitebsk, without going as far as America. My cousins sometimes went to the theatre, and I listened with rapture to their account of what they had seen, and I learned the songs they had heard. Once Cousin Hirshel went to see a giant, who exhibited himself for three kopecks, and came home with such marvellous accounts of his astonishing proportions, and his amazing feats of strength, that little Mendele cried for envy, and I had to play lotto with him and let him beat me oh, so easily! till he felt himself a man again.

And sometimes I had adventures of my own. I explored the city to some extent by myself, or else my cousins took me with them on their errands. There were so many fine people to see, such wonderful shops, such great distances to go. Once they took me to a bookstore. I saw shelves and shelves of books, and people buying them, and taking them away to keep. I was told that some people had in their own houses more books than were in the store. Was not that wonderful? It was a great city, Vitebsk; I never could exhaust its delights.

Although I did not often think of my people at home, struggling desperately to live while I revelled in abundance and pleasure and excitement, I did do my little to help the family by giving lessons in lacemaking. As this was the only time in my life that I earned money by the work of my hands, I take care not to forget it and I like to give an account of it.

I was always, as I have elsewhere admitted, very clumsy with my hands, counting five thumbs to the hand. Knitting and embroidery, at which my sister was so clever, I could never do with any degree of skill. The blue peacock with the red tail that I achieved in cross-stitch was not a performance of any grace. Neither was I very much downcast at my failures in this field; I was not an ambitious needlewoman. but when the fad for "Russian lace" was introduced into Polotzk by a family of sisters who had been expelled from St. Petersburg, and all feminine Polotzk, on both sides of the Dvina, dropped knitting and crochet needles and embroidery frames to take up pillow and bobbins, I, too, was carried away by the novelty, and applied myself heartily to learn the intricate art, with the result that I did master it. The Russian sisters charged enormous fees for lessons, and made a fortune out of the sale of patterns while they held the monopoly. Their pupils passed on the art at reduced fees, and their pupils' pupils charged still less; until even the humblest cottage rang with the pretty click of the bobbins, and my Cousin Rachel sold steel pins by the ounce, instead of by the dozen, and the women exchanged cardboard patterns from one end of town to the other.

My teacher, who taught me without fee, being a friend of our prosperous days, lived "on the other side." It was winter, and many a time I crossed the frozen river, carrying a lace pillow as big as myself, till my hands were numb with cold. But I persisted, afraid as I was of cold; and when I came to Vitebsk I was glad of my one accomplishment. For Vitebsk had not yet seen "Russian lace," and I was an acceptable teacher of the new art, though I was such a mite, because there was no other. I taught my Cousin Dinke, of course, and I had a number of paying pupils. I gave lessons at my pupils' homes, and was very proud, going thus about town and being received as a person of importance. If my feet did not reach the floor when I sat in a chair, my hands knew their business for once; and I was such a conscientious and enthusiastic teacher that I had the satisfaction of seeing all my pupils execute difficult pieces before I left Vitebsk.

I never have seen money that was half so bright to look at, half so pretty to clink, as the money I earned by these lessons. And it was easy to decide what to do with my wealth. I bought presents for everybody I knew. I remember to this day the pattern of the shawl I bought for my mother. When I came home and unpacked my treasures, I was the proudest girl in Polotzk.

The proudest, but not the happiest. I found my family in such a pitiful state that all my joy was stifled by care, if only for a while.

Unwilling to spoil my holiday, my mother had not written me how things had gone from bad to worse during my absence, and I was not prepared. Fetchke met me at the station, and conducted me to a more wretched hole than I had ever called home before.

I went into the room alone, having been greeted outside by my mother and brother. It was evening, and the shabbiness of the apartment was all the gloomier for the light of a small kerosene lamp standing on the bare deal table. At one end of the table—is this Deborah? My little sister, dressed in an ugly gray jacket, sat motionless in the lamplight, her fair head drooping, her little hands folded on the edge of the table. At sight of her I grew suddenly old. It was merely that she was a shy little girl, unbecomingly dressed, and perhaps a little pale from underfeeding. But to me, at that moment, she was the personification of dejection, the living symbol of the fallen family state.

Of course my sober mood did not last long. Even "fallen family state" could be interpreted in terms of money—absent money—and that, as once established, was a trifling matter. Had n't I earned money myself? Heaps of it! Only look at this, and this, and this that I brought from Vitebsk, bought with my own money! No, I did not remain old. For many years more I was a very childish child.

Perhaps I had spent my time in Vitebsk to better advantage than at the milliner's, from any point of view. When I returned to my native town I *saw* things. I saw the narrowness, the stifling narrowness, of life in Polotzk. My books, my walks, my visits, as teacher, to many homes, had been so many doors opening on a wider world; so many horizons, one beyond the other. The boundaries of life had stretched, and I had filled my lungs with the thrilling air from a great Beyond. Child though I was, Polotzk, when I came back, was too small for me.

And even Vitebsk, for all its peepholes into a Beyond, presently began to shrink in my imagination, as America loomed near. My father's letters warned us to prepare for the summons, and we lived in a quiver of expectation.

Not that my father had grown suddenly rich. He was so far from rich that he was going to borrow every cent of the money for our third-class passage; but he had a business in view which he could carry on all the better for having the family with him; and, besides, we were borrowing right and left anyway, and to no definite purpose. With the children, he argued, every year in Russia was a year lost. They should be spending the precious years in school, in learning English, in becoming Americans. United in America, there were ten chances of our getting to our feet again to one chance in our scattered, aimless state.

So at last I was going to America! Really, really going, at last! The boundaries burst. The arch of heaven soared. A million suns shone out for every star. The winds rushed in from outer space, roaring in my ears, "America! America!"

CHAPTER VIII

THE EXODUS

ON THE DAY when our steamer ticket arrived, my mother did not go out with her basket, my brother stayed out of heder, and my sister salted the soup three times. I do not know what I did to celebrate the occasion. Very likely I played tricks on Deborah, and wrote a long letter to my father.

Before sunset the news was all over Polotzk that Hannah Hayye had received a steamer ticket for America. Then they began to come. Friends and foes, distant relatives and new acquaintances, young and old, wise and foolish, debtors and creditors, and mere neighbors,—from every quarter of the city, from both sides of the Dvina, from over the Polota, from nowhere,—a steady stream of them poured into our street, both day and night, till the hour of our departure. And my mother gave audience. Her faded kerchief halfway off her head, her black ringlets straying, her apron often at her eyes, she received her guests in a rainbow of smiles and tears. She was the heroine of Polotzk, and she conducted herself appropriately. She gave her heart's thanks for the congratulations and blessings that poured in on her; ready tears for condolences; patient answers to monotonous questions; and handshakes and kisses and hugs she gave gratis.

What did they not ask, the eager, foolish, friendly people? They wanted to handle the ticket, and mother must read them what is written on it. How much did it cost? Was it all paid for? Were we going to have a foreign passport or did we intend to steal across the border? Were we not all going to have new dresses to travel in? Was it sure that we could get kosher food on the ship? And with the questions poured in suggestions, and solid chunks of advice were rammed in by nimble prophecies. Mother ought to make a pilgrimage to a "Good Jew"—say, the Rebbe of Lubavitch—to get his blessing on our journey. She must be sure and pack her prayer books and Bible, and twenty pounds of zwieback at the least. If they did serve trefah on the ship, she and the four children would have to starve, unless she carried provisions from home.—

Oh, she must take all the featherbeds! Featherbeds are scarce in America. In America they sleep on hard mattresses, even in winter. Haveh Mirel, Yachne the dressmaker's daughter, who emigrated to New York two years ago, wrote her mother that she got up from childbed with sore sides, because she had no featherbed.—Mother must n't carry her money in a pocketbook. She must sew it into the lining of her jacket. The policemen in Castle Garden take all their money from the passengers as they land, unless the travellers deny having any.

And so on, and so on, till my poor mother was completely bewildered. And as the day set for our departure approached, the people came oftener and stayed longer, and rehearsed my mother in long messages for their friends in America, praying that she deliver them promptly on her arrival, and without fail, and might God bless her for her kindness, and she must be sure and write them how she found their friends.

Hayye Dvoshe, the wig-maker, for the eleventh time repeating herself, to my mother, still patiently attentive, thus:—

"Promise me, I beg you. I don't sleep nights for thinking of him. Emigrated to America eighteen months ago, fresh and well and strong, with twenty-five ruble in his pocket, besides his steamer ticket, with new phylacteries, and a silk skull-cap, and a suit as good as new,—made it only three years before,—everything respectable, there could be nothing better;—sent one letter, how he arrived in Castle Garden, how well he was received by his uncle's son-in-law, how he was conducted to the baths, how they bought him an American suit, everything good, fine, pleasant;—wrote how his relative promised him a position in his business—a clothing merchant is he—makes gold,—and since then not a postal card, not a word, just as if he had vanished, as if the earth had swallowed him. *Oi, weh!* what have n't I imagined, what have n't I dreamed, what have n't I lamented! Already three letters have I sent—the last one, you know, you yourself wrote for me, Hannah Hayye, dear—and no answer. Lost, as if in the sea!"

And after the application of a corner of her shawl to eyes and nose, Hayye Dvoshe, continuing:—

"So you will go into the newspaper, and ask them what has become of my Möshele, and if he is n't in Castle Garden, maybe he went up to Balti-moreh,—it's in the neighborhood, you know,

—and you can tell them, for a mark, that he has a silk handkerchief with his monogram in Russian, that his betrothed embroidered for him before the engagement was broken. And may God grant you an easy journey, and may you arrive in a propitious hour, and may you find your husband well, and strong, and rich, and may you both live to lead your children to the wedding canopy, and may America shower gold on you. Amen."

The weeks skipped, the days took wing, an hour was a flash of thought; so brimful of events was the interval before our departure. And no one was more alive than I to the multiple significance of the daily drama. My mother, full of grief at the parting from home and family and all things dear, anxious about the journey, uncertain about the future, but ready, as ever, to take up what new burdens awaited her; my sister, one with our mother in every hope and apprehension; my brother, rejoicing in his sudden release from heder; and the little sister, vaguely excited by mysteries afoot; the uncles and aunts and devoted neighbors, sad and solemn over their coming loss; and my father away over in Boston, eager and anxious about us in Polotzk,—an American citizen impatient to start his children on American careers,—I knew the minds of every one of these, and I lived their days and nights with them after an apish fashion of my own.

But at bottom I was aloof from them all. What made me silent and big-eyed was the sense of being in the midst of a tremendous adventure. From morning till night I was all attention. I must credit myself with some pang of parting; I certainly felt the thrill of expectation; but keener than these was my delight in the progress of the great adventure. It was delightful just to be myself. I rejoiced, with the younger children, during the weeks of packing and preparation, in the relaxation of discipline and the general demoralization of our daily life. It was pleasant to be petted and spoiled by favorite cousins and stuffed with belated sweets by unfavorite ones. It was distinctly interesting to catch my mother weeping in corner cupboards over precious rubbish that could by no means be carried to America. It was agreeable to have my Uncle Moses stroke my hair and regard me with affectionate eyes, while he told me that I would soon forget him, and asked me, so coaxingly, to write him an account of our journey. It was delicious to be notorious through the length and breadth of Polotzk; to be stopped and questioned at every shop-door, when I ran out to buy two kopecks' worth of butter; to be treated with respect by my former playmates, if ever I found time to mingle with them; to be pointed at by my enemies, as I passed them importantly on the street. And all my delight and pride and interest were steeped in a super-feeling, the sense that it was I, Mashke, *I myself,* that was moving and acting in the midst of unusual events. Now that I was sure of America, I was in no hurry to depart, and not impatient to arrive. I was willing to linger over every detail of our progress, and so cherish the flavor of the adventure.

The last night in Polotzk we slept at my uncle's house, having disposed of all our belongings, to the last three-legged stool, except such as we were taking with us. I could go straight to the room where I slept with my aunt that night, if I were suddenly set down in Polotzk. But I did not really sleep. Excitement kept me awake, and my aunt snored hideously. In the morning I was going away from Polotzk, forever and ever. I was going on a wonderful journey. I was going to America. How could I sleep?

My uncle gave out a false bulletin, with the last batch that the gossips carried away in the evening. He told them that we were not going to start till the second day. This he did in the hope of smuggling us quietly out, and so saving us the wear and tear of a public farewell. But his ruse failed of success. Half of Polotzk was at my uncle's gate in the morning, to conduct us to the railway station, and the other half was already there before we arrived.

The procession resembled both a funeral and a triumph. The women wept over us, reminding us eloquently of the perils of the sea, of the bewilderment of a foreign land, of the torments of home-sickness that awaited us. They bewailed my mother's lot, who had to tear herself away from blood relations to go among strangers; who had to face gendarmes, ticket agents, and sailors, unprotected by a masculine escort; who had to care for four young children in the confusion of travel, and very likely feed them trefah or see them starve on the way. Or they praised her for a brave pilgrim, and expressed confidence in her ability to cope with gendarmes and ticket agents, and blessed her with every other word, and all but carried her in their arms.

At the station the procession disbanded and became a mob. My uncle and my tall cousins did their best to protect us, but we wanderers were almost torn to pieces. They did get us into a car at last, but the riot on the station platform continued unquelled. When the warning bell rang out, it was drowned in a confounding babel of voices,—fragments of the oft-repeated messages, admonitions, lamentations, blessings, farewells. "Don't forget!"—"Take care of—" "Keep your tickets—" "Möshele—newspapers!" "Garlick is best!" "Happy journey!" "God help you!" "Good-bye! Good-bye!" "Remember—"

The last I saw of Polotzk was an agitated mass of people, waving colored handkerchiefs and other frantic bits of calico, madly gesticulating, falling on each other's necks, gone wild altogether. Then the station became invisible, and the shining tracks spun out from sky to sky. I was in the middle of the great, great world, and the longest road was mine.

Memory may take a rest while I copy from a contemporaneous document the story of the great voyage. In accordance with my promise to my uncle, I wrote, during my first months in America, a detailed account of our adventures between Polotzk and Boston. Ink was cheap, and the epistle, in Yiddish, occupied me for many hot summer hours. It was a great disaster, therefore, to have a lamp upset on my writing-table, when I was near the end, soaking the thick pile of letter sheets in kerosene. I was obliged to make a fair copy for my uncle, and my father kept the oily, smelly original. After a couple of years' teasing, he induced me to translate the letter into English, for the benefit of a friend who did not know Yiddish; for the benefit of the present narrative, which was not thought of thirteen years ago. I can hardly refrain from moralizing as I turn to the leaves of my childish manuscript, grateful at last for the calamity of the overturned lamp.

Our route lay over the German border, with Hamburg for our port. On the way to the frontier we stopped for a farewell visit in Vilna, where my mother had a brother. Vilna is slighted in my description. I find special mention of only two things, the horse-cars and the bookstores.

On a gray wet morning in early April we set out for the frontier. This was the real beginning of our journey, and all my faculties of observation were alert. I took note of everything,—the weather, the trains, the bustle of railroad stations, our fellow passengers, and the family mood at every stage of our progress.

The bags and bundles which composed our travelling outfit were much more bulky than valuable. A trifling sum of money, the steamer ticket, and the foreign passport were the magic agents by means of which we hoped to span the five thousand miles of earth and water between us and my father. The passport was supposed to pass us over the frontier without any trouble, but on account of the prevalence of cholera in some parts of the country, the poorer sort of travellers, such as emigrants, were subjected, at this time, to more than ordinary supervision and regulation.

At Versbolovo, the last station on the Russian side, we met the first of our troubles. A German physician and several gendarmes boarded the train and put us through a searching examination as to our health, destination, and financial resources. As a result of the inquisition we were informed that we would not be allowed to cross the frontier unless we exchanged our third-class steamer ticket for second-class, which would require two hundred rubles more than we possessed. Our passport was taken from us, and we were to be turned back on our journey.

My letter describes the situation:—

We were homeless, houseless, and friendless in a strange place. We had hardly money enough to last us through the voyage for which we had hoped and waited for three long years. We had suffered much that the reunion we longed for might come about; we had prepared ourselves to suffer more in order to bring it about, and had parted with those we loved, with places that were dear to us in spite of what we passed through in them, never again to see them, as we were convinced—all for the same dear end. With strong hopes and high spirits that hid the sad parting, we had started on our long journey. And now we were checked so unexpectedly but surely, the blow coming from where we little expected it, being, as we believed, safe in that quarter. When my mother had recovered enough to speak, she began to argue with the gendarme, telling him our story and begging him to be kind. The children were frightened and all but I cried. I was only wondering what would happen.

Moved by our distress, the German officers gave us the best advice they could. We were to get out at the station of Kibart, on

the Russian side, and apply to one Herr Schidorsky, who might
help us on our way.

The letter goes on:—

> We are in Kibart, at the depot. The least important particular,
> even, of that place, I noticed and remembered. How the porter—he
> was an ugly, grinning man—carried in our things and put them away
> in the southern corner of the big room, on the floor; how we sat
> down on a settee near them, a yellow settee; how the glass roof let
> in so much light that we had to shade our eyes because the car had
> been dark and we had been crying; how there were only a few people
> besides ourselves there, and how I began to count them and stopped
> when I noticed a sign over the head of the fifth person—a little
> woman with a red nose and a pimple on it—and tried to read the
> German, with the aid of the Russian translation below. I noticed all
> this and remembered it, as if there were nothing else in the world
> for me to think of.

The letter dwells gratefully on the kindness of Herr Schidorsky,
who became the agent of our salvation. He procured my mother a
pass to Eidtkuhnen, the German frontier station, where his older
brother, as chairman of a well-known emigrant aid association, arranged for our admission into Germany. During the negotiations,
which took several days, the good man of Kibart entertained us in
his own house, shabby emigrants though we were. The Schidorsky
brothers were Jews, but it is not on that account that their name
has been lovingly remembered for fifteen years in my family.

On the German side our course joined that of many other emigrant groups, on their way to Hamburg and other ports. We were
a clumsy enough crowd, with wide, unsophisticated eyes, with
awkward bundles hugged in our arms, and our hearts set on
America.

The letter to my uncle faithfully describes every stage of our
bustling progress. Here is a sample scene of many that I recorded:—

> There was a terrible confusion in the baggage-room where we
> were directed to go. Boxes, baskets, bags, valises, and great, shapeless
> things belonging to no particular class, were thrown about by por-
> ters and other men, who sorted them and put tickets on all but those
> containing provisions, while others were opened and examined in
> haste. At last our turn came, and our things, along with those of all

other American-bound travellers, were taken away to be steamed and smoked and other such processes gone through. We were told to wait till notice should be given us of something else to be done.

The phrases "we were told to do this" and "told to do that" occur again and again in my narrative, and the most effective handling of the facts could give no more vivid picture of the proceedings. We emigrants were herded at the stations, packed in the cars, and driven from place to place like cattle.

At the expected hour we all tried to find room in a car indicated by the conductor. We tried, but could only find enough space on the floor for our baggage, on which we made-believe sitting comfortably. For now we were obliged to exchange the comparative comforts of a third-class passenger train for the certain discomforts of a fourth-class one. There were only four narrow benches in the whole car, and about twice as many people were already seated on these as they were probably supposed to accommodate. All other space, to the last inch, was crowded by passengers or their luggage. It was very hot and close and altogether uncomfortable, and still at every new station fresh passengers came crowding in, and actually made room, spare as it was, for themselves. It became so terrible that all glared madly at the conductor as he allowed more people to come into that prison, and trembled at the announcement of every station. I cannot see even now how the officers could allow such a thing; it was really dangerous.

The following is my attempt to describe a flying glimpse of a metropolis:—

Towards evening we came into Berlin. I grow dizzy even now when I think of our whirling through that city. It seemed we were going faster and faster all the time, but it was only the whirl of trains passing in opposite directions and close to us that made it seem so. The sight of crowds of people such as we had never seen before, hurrying to and fro, in and out of great depots that danced past us, helped to make it more so. Strange sights, splendid buildings, shops, people, and animals, all mingled in one great, confused mass of a disposition to continually move in a great hurry, wildly, with no other aim but to make one's head go round and round, in following its dreadful motions. Round and round went my head. It was nothing but trains, depots, crowds,—crowds, depots, trains,—again and again, with no beginning, no end, only a mad dance! Faster and faster we go, faster still, and the noise increases with the speed. Bells, whistles, hammers, locomotives shrieking madly, men's voices, peddlers' cries, horses' hoofs, dogs' barkings—all united in doing their best to drown every other sound but their own, and made such a deafening uproar in the attempt that nothing could keep it out.

The plight of the bewildered emigrant on the way to foreign parts is always pitiful enough, but for us who came from plague-ridden Russia the terrors of the way were doubled.

In a great lonely field, opposite a solitary house within a large yard, our train pulled up at last, and a conductor commanded the passengers to make haste and get out. He need not have told us to hurry; we were glad enough to be free again after such a long imprisonment in the uncomfortable car. All rushed to the door. We breathed more freely in the open field, but the conductor did not wait for us to enjoy our freedom. He hurried us into the one large room which made up the house, and then into the yard. Here a great many men and women, dressed in white, received us, the women attending to the women and girls of the passengers, and the men to the others.

This was another scene of bewildering confusion, parents losing their children, and little ones crying; baggage being thrown together in one corner of the yard, heedless of contents, which suffered in consequence; those white-clad Germans shouting commands, always accompanied with "Quick! Quick!"—the confused passengers obeying all orders like meek children, only questioning now and then what was going to be done with them.

And no wonder if in some minds stories arose of people being captured by robbers, murderers, and the like. Here we had been taken to a lonely place where only that house was to be seen; our things were taken away, our friends separated from us; a man came to inspect us, as if to ascertain our full value; strange-looking people driving us about like dumb animals, helpless and unresisting; children we could not see crying in a way that suggested terrible things; ourselves driven into a little room where a great kettle was boiling on a little stove; our clothes taken off, our bodies rubbed with a slippery substance that might be any bad thing; a shower of warm water let down on us without warning; again driven to another little room where we sit, wrapped in woollen blankets till large, coarse bags are brought in, their contents turned out, and we see only a cloud of steam, and hear the women's orders to dress ourselves,— "Quick! Quick!"—or else we'll miss—something we cannot hear.

We are forced to pick out our clothes from among all the others, with the steam blinding us; we choke, cough, entreat the women to give us time; they persist, "Quick! Quick!—or you'll miss the train!"—Oh, so we really won't be murdered! They are only making us ready for the continuing of our journey, cleaning us of all suspicions of dangerous sickness. Thank God!

In Polotzk, if the cholera broke out, as it did once or twice in every generation, we made no such fuss as did these Germans. Those who died of the sickness were buried, and those who lived ran to the synagogues to pray. We travellers felt hurt at the way the Germans treated us. My mother nearly died of cholera once, but she was given a new name, a lucky one, which saved her; and that was when she was a small girl. None of us were sick now, yet hear how we were treated! Those gendarmes and nurses always shouted their commands at us from a distance, as fearful of our touch as if we had been lepers.

We arrived in Hamburg early one morning, after a long night in the crowded cars. We were marched up to a strange vehicle, long and narrow and high, drawn by two horses and commanded by a mute driver. We were piled up on this wagon, our baggage was thrown after us, and we started on a sight-seeing tour across the city of Hamburg. The sights I faithfully enumerate for the benefit of my uncle include little carts drawn by dogs, and big cars that run of themselves, later identified as electric cars.

The humorous side of our adventures did not escape me. Again and again I come across a laugh in the long pages of the historic epistle. The description of the ride through Hamburg ends with this:—

> The sight-seeing was not all on our side. I noticed many people stopping to look at us as if amused, though most passed by us as though used to such sights. We did make a queer appearance all in a long row, up above people's heads. In fact, we looked like a flock of giant fowls roosting, only wide awake.

The smiles and shivers fairly crowded each other in some parts of our career.

> Suddenly, when everything interesting seemed at an end, we all recollected how long it was since we had started on our funny ride. Hours, we thought, and still the horses ran. Now we rode through

quieter streets where there were fewer shops and more wooden houses. Still the horses seemed to have but just started. I looked over our perch again. Something made me think of a description I had read of criminals being carried on long journeys in uncomfortable things—like this? Well, it was strange—this long, long drive, the conveyance, no word of explanation; and all, though going different ways, being packed off together. We were strangers; the driver knew it. He might take us anywhere—how could we tell? I was frightened again as in Berlin. The faces around me confessed the same.

Yes, we are frightened. We are very still. Some Polish women over there have fallen asleep, and the rest of us look such a picture of woe, and yet so funny, it is a sight to see and remember.

Our mysterious ride came to an end on the outskirts of the city, where we were once more lined up, cross-questioned, disinfected, labelled, and pigeonholed. This was one of the occasions when we suspected that we were the victims of a conspiracy to extort money from us; for here, as at every repetition of the purifying operations we had undergone, a fee was levied on us, so much per head. My mother, indeed, seeing her tiny hoard melting away, had long since sold some articles from our baggage to a fellow passenger richer than she, but even so she did not have enough money to pay the fee demanded of her in Hamburg. Her statement was not accepted, and we all suffered the last indignity of having our persons searched.

This last place of detention turned out to be a prison. "Quarantine" they called it, and there was a great deal of it—two weeks of it. Two weeks within high brick walls, several hundred of us herded in half a dozen compartments,—numbered compartments, —sleeping in rows, like sick people in a hospital; with roll-call morning and night, and short rations three times a day; with never a sign of the free world beyond our barred windows; with anxiety and longing and homesickness in our hearts, and in our ears the unfamiliar voice of the invisible ocean, which drew and repelled us at the same time. The fortnight in quarantine was not an episode; it was an epoch, divisible into eras, periods, events.

The greatest event was the arrival of some ship to take some of the waiting passengers. When the gates were opened and the lucky ones said good-bye, those left behind felt hopeless of ever seeing the gates open for them. It was both pleasant and painful, for the strangers grew to be fast friends in a day, and really rejoiced in each other's fortune; but the regretful envy could not be helped either.

Our turn came at last. We were conducted through the gate of departure, and after some hours of bewildering manœuvres, described in great detail in the report to my uncle, we found ourselves—we five frightened pilgrims from Polotzk—on the deck of a great big steamship afloat on the strange big waters of the ocean.

For sixteen days the ship was our world. My letter dwells solemnly on the details of the life at sea, as if afraid to cheat my uncle of the smallest circumstance. It does not shrink from describing the torments of seasickness; it notes every change in the weather. A rough night is described, when the ship pitched and rolled so that people were thrown from their berths; days and nights when we crawled through dense fogs, our foghorn drawing answering warnings from invisible ships. The perils of the sea were not minimized in the imaginations of us inexperienced voyagers. The captain and his officers ate their dinners, smoked their pipes and slept soundly in their turns, while we frightened emigrants turned our faces to the wall and awaited our watery graves.

All this while the seasickness lasted. Then came happy hours on deck, with fugitive sunshine, birds atop the crested waves, band music and dancing and fun. I explored the ship, made friends with officers and crew, or pursued my thoughts in quiet nooks. It was my first experience of the ocean, and I was profoundly moved.

Oh, what solemn thoughts I had! How deeply I felt the greatness, the power of the scene! The immeasurable distance from horizon to horizon; the huge billows forever changing their shapes—now only a wavy and rolling plain, now a chain of great mountains, coming and going farther away; then a town in the distance, perhaps, with spires and towers and buildings of gigantic dimensions; and mostly a vast mass of uncertain shapes, knocking against each other in fury, and seething and foaming in their anger; the gray sky, with its mountains of gloomy clouds, flying, moving with the waves, as it seemed, very near them; the absence of any object besides the one ship; and the deep, solemn groans of the sea, sounding as if all the voices of the world had been turned into sighs and then gathered into that one mournful sound—so deeply did I feel the presence of these things, that the feeling became one of awe, both painful and sweet, and stirring and warming, and deep and calm and grand.

I would imagine myself all alone on the ocean, and Robinson Crusoe was very real to me. I was alone sometimes. I was aware of no human presence; I was conscious only of sea and sky and something I did not understand. And as I listened to its solemn voice, I felt as if I had found a friend, and knew that I loved the ocean. It seemed as if it were within as well as without, part of myself; and I wondered how I had lived without it, and if I could ever part with it.

And so suffering, fearing, brooding, rejoicing, we crept nearer and nearer to the coveted shore, until, on a glorious May morning, six weeks after our departure from Polotzk, our eyes beheld the Promised Land, and my father received us in his arms.

CHAPTER IX

THE PROMISED LAND

HAVING MADE SUCH GOOD TIME across the ocean, I ought to be able to proceed no less rapidly on *terra firma*, where, after all, I am more at home. And yet here is where I falter. Not that I hesitated, even for the space of a breath, in my first steps in America. There was no time to hesitate. The most ignorant immigrant, on landing, proceeds to give and receive greetings, to eat, sleep, and rise, after the manner of his own country; wherein he is corrected, admonished, and laughed at, whether by interested friends or the most indifferent strangers; and his American experience is thus begun. The process is spontaneous on all sides, like the education of the child by the family circle. But while the most stupid nursery maid is able to contribute her part toward the result, we do not expect an analysis of the process to be furnished by any member of the family, least of all by the engaging infant. The philosophical maiden aunt alone, or some other witness equally psychological and aloof, is able to trace the myriad efforts by which the little Johnnie or Nellie acquires a secure hold on the disjointed parts of the huge plaything, life.

Now I was not exactly an infant when I was set down, on a May day some fifteen years ago, in this pleasant nursery of America. I had long since acquired the use of my faculties, and had collected some bits of experience, practical and emotional, and had even learned to give an account of them. Still, I had very little perspective, and my observations and comparisons were superficial. I was too much carried away to analyze the forces that were moving me. My Polotzk I knew well before I began to judge it and experiment with it. America was bewilderingly strange, unimaginably complex, delightfully unexplored. I rushed impetuously out of the cage of my provincialism and looked eagerly about the brilliant universe. My question was, What have we here?—not, What does this mean? That query came much later. When I now become retrospectively introspective, I fall into the predicament of the centi-

pede in the rhyme, who got along very smoothly until he was asked
which leg came after which, whereupon he became so rattled that
he could n't take a step. I know I have come on a thousand feet,
on wings, winds, and American machines,—I have leaped and run
and climbed and crawled,—but to tell which step came after which
I find a puzzling matter. Plenty of maiden aunts were present during my second infancy, in the guise of immigrant officials, school-
teachers, settlement workers, and sundry other unprejudiced and
critical observers. Their statistics I might properly borrow to fill
the gaps in my recollections, but I am prevented by my sense of
harmony. The individual, we know, is a creature unknown to the
statistician, whereas I undertook to give the personal view of everything. So I am bound to unravel, as well as I can, the tangle of
events, outer and inner, which made up the first breathless years of
my American life.

During his three years of probation, my father had made a number of false starts in business. His history for that period is the
history of thousands who come to America, like him, with pockets
empty, hands untrained to the use of tools, minds cramped by centuries of repression in their native land. Dozens of these men pass
under your eyes every day, my American friend, too absorbed in
their honest affairs to notice the looks of suspicion which you cast
at them, the repugnance with which you shrink from their touch.
You see them shuffle from door to door with a basket of spools
and buttons, or bending over the sizzling irons in a basement tailor
shop, or rummaging in your ash can, or moving a pushcart from
curb to curb, at the command of the burly policeman. "The Jew
peddler!" you say, and dismiss him from your premises and from
your thoughts, never dreaming that the sordid drama of his days
may have a moral that concerns you. What if the creature with the
untidy beard carries in his bosom his citizenship papers? What if
the cross-legged tailor is supporting a boy in college who is one
day going to mend your state constitution for you? What if the
ragpicker's daughters are hastening over the ocean to teach your
children in the public schools? Think, every time you pass the
greasy alien on the street, that he was born thousands of years
before the oldest native American; and he may have something to
communicate to you, when you two shall have learned a common

language. Remember that his very physiognomy is a cipher the key to which it behooves you to search for most diligently.

By the time we joined my father, he had surveyed many avenues of approach toward the coveted citadel of fortune. One of these, heretofore untried, he now proposed to essay, armed with new courage, and cheered on by the presence of his family. In partnership with an energetic little man who had an English chapter in his history, he prepared to set up a refreshment booth on Crescent Beach. But while he was completing arrangements at the beach we remained in town, where we enjoyed the educational advantages of a thickly populated neighborhood; namely, Wall Street, in the West End of Boston.

Anybody who knows Boston knows that the West and North Ends are the wrong ends of that city. They form the tenement district, or, in the newer phrase, the slums of Boston. Anybody who is acquainted with the slums of any American metropolis knows that that is the quarter where poor immigrants foregather, to live, for the most part, as unkempt, half-washed, toiling, unaspiring foreigners; pitiful in the eyes of social missionaries, the despair of boards of health, the hope of ward politicians, the touchstone of American democracy. The well-versed metropolitan knows the slums as a sort of house of detention for poor aliens, where they live on probation till they can show a certificate of good citizenship.

He may know all this and yet not guess how Wall Street, in the West End, appears in the eyes of a little immigrant from Polotzk. What would the sophisticated sight-seer say about Union Place, off Wall Street, where my new home waited for me? He would say that it is no place at all, but a short box of an alley. Two rows of three-story tenements are its sides, a stingy strip of sky is its lid, a littered pavement is the floor, and a narrow mouth its exit.

But I saw a very different picture on my introduction to Union Place. I saw two imposing rows of brick buildings, loftier than any dwelling I had ever lived in. Brick was even on the ground for me to tread on, instead of common earth or boards. Many friendly windows stood open, filled with uncovered heads of women and children. I thought the people were interested in us, which was very neighborly. I looked up to the topmost row of windows, and my eyes were filled with the May blue of an American sky!

In our days of affluence in Russia we had been accustomed to upholstered parlors, embroidered linen, silver spoons and candlesticks, goblets of gold, kitchen shelves shining with copper and brass. We had featherbeds heaped halfway to the ceiling; we had clothes presses dusky with velvet and silk and fine woollen. The three small rooms into which my father now ushered us, up one flight of stairs, contained only the necessary beds, with lean mattresses; a few wooden chairs; a table or two; a mysterious iron structure, which later turned out to be a stove; a couple of unornamental kerosene lamps; and a scanty array of cooking-utensils and crockery. And yet we were all impressed with our new home and its furniture. It was not only because we had just passed through our seven lean years, cooking in earthen vessels, eating black bread on holidays and wearing cotton; it was chiefly because these wooden chairs and tin pans were American chairs and pans that they shone glorious in our eyes. And if there was anything lacking for comfort or decoration we expected it to be presently supplied—at least, we children did. Perhaps my mother alone, of us newcomers, appreciated the shabbiness of the little apartment, and realized that for her there was as yet no laying down of the burden of poverty.

Our initiation into American ways began with the first step on the new soil. My father found occasion to instruct or correct us even on the way from the pier to Wall Street, which journey we made crowded together in a rickety cab. He told us not to lean out of the windows, not to point, and explained the word "greenhorn." We did not want to be "greenhorns," and gave the strictest attention to my father's instructions. I do not know when my parents found opportunity to review together the history of Polotzk in the three years past, for we children had no patience with the subject; my mother's narrative was constantly interrupted by irrelevant questions, interjections, and explanations.

The first meal was an object lesson of much variety. My father produced several kinds of food, ready to eat, without any cooking, from little tin cans that had printing all over them. He attempted to introduce us to a queer, slippery kind of fruit, which he called "banana," but had to give it up for the time being. After the meal,

UNION PLACE (BOSTON), WHERE MY NEW HOME WAITED FOR ME

he had better luck with a curious piece of furniture on runners, which he called "rocking-chair." There were five of us newcomers, and we found five different ways of getting into the American machine of perpetual motion, and as many ways of getting out of it. One born and bred to the use of a rocking-chair cannot imagine how ludicrous people can make themselves when attempting to use it for the first time. We laughed immoderately over our various experiments with the novelty, which was a wholesome way of letting off steam after the unusual excitement of the day.

In our flat we did not think of such a thing as storing the coal in the bathtub. There was no bathtub. So in the evening of the first day my father conducted us to the public baths. As we moved along in a little procession, I was delighted with the illumination of the streets. So many lamps, and they burned until morning, my father said, and so people did not need to carry lanterns. In America, then, everything was free, as we had heard in Russia. Light was free; the streets were as bright as a synagogue on a holy day. Music was free; we had been serenaded, to our gaping delight, by a brass band of many pieces, soon after our installation on Union Place.

Education was free. That subject my father had written about repeatedly, as comprising his chief hope for us children, the essence of American opportunity, the treasure that no thief could touch, not even misfortune or poverty. It was the one thing that he was able to promise us when he sent for us; surer, safer than bread or shelter. On our second day I was thrilled with the realization of what this freedom of education meant. A little girl from across the alley came and offered to conduct us to school. My father was out, but we five between us had a few words of English by this time. We knew the word school. We understood. This child, who had never seen us till yesterday, who could not pronounce our names, who was not much better dressed than we, was able to offer us the freedom of the schools of Boston! No application made, no questions asked, no examinations, rulings, exclusions; no machinations, no fees. The doors stood open for every one of us. The smallest child could show us the way.

This incident impressed me more than anything I had heard in advance of the freedom of education in America. It was a concrete proof—almost the thing itself. One had to experience it to understand it.

It was a great disappointment to be told by my father that we were not to enter upon our school career at once. It was too near the end of the term, he said, and we were going to move to Crescent Beach in a week or so. We had to wait until the opening of the schools in September. What a loss of precious time—from May till September!

Not that the time was really lost. Even the interval on Union Place was crowded with lessons and experiences. We had to visit the stores and be dressed from head to foot in American clothing; we had to learn the mysteries of the iron stove, the washboard, and the speaking-tube; we had to learn to trade with the fruit peddler through the window, and not to be afraid of the policeman; and, above all, we had to learn English.

The kind people who assisted us in these important matters form a group by themselves in the gallery of my friends. If I had never seen them from those early days till now, I should still have remembered them with gratitude. When I enumerate the long list of my American teachers, I must begin with those who came to us on Wall Street and taught us our first steps. To my mother, in her perplexity over the cookstove, the woman who showed her how to make the fire was an angel of deliverance. A fairy godmother to us children was she who led us to a wonderful country called "uptown," where, in a dazzlingly beautiful palace called a "department store," we exchanged our hateful homemade European costumes, which pointed us out as "greenhorns" to the children on the street, for real American machine-made garments, and issued forth glorified in each other's eyes.

With our despised immigrant clothing we shed also our impossible Hebrew names. A committee of our friends, several years ahead of us in American experience, put their heads together and concocted American names for us all. Those of our real names that had no pleasing American equivalents they ruthlessly discarded, content if they retained the initials. My mother, possessing a name that was not easily translatable, was punished with the undignified nickname of Annie. Fetchke, Joseph, and Deborah issued as Frieda, Joseph, and Dora, respectively. As for poor me, I was simply cheated. The name they gave me was hardly new. My Hebrew name being Maryashe in full, Mashke for short, Russianized into Marya (*Mar-ya*), my friends said that it would hold good in English as

Mary; which was very disappointing, as I longed to possess a strange-sounding American name like the others.

I am forgetting the consolation I had, in this matter of names, from the use of my surname, which I have had no occasion to mention until now. I found on my arrival that my father was "Mr. Antin" on the slightest provocation, and not, as in Polotzk, on state occasions alone. And so I was "Mary Antin," and I felt very important to answer to such a dignified title. It was just like America that even plain people should wear their surnames on week days.

As a family we were so diligent under instruction, so adaptable, and so clever in hiding our deficiencies, that when we made the journey to Crescent Beach, in the wake of our small wagon-load of household goods, my father had very little occasion to admonish us on the way, and I am sure he was not ashamed of us. So much we had achieved toward our Americanization during the two weeks since our landing.

Crescent Beach is a name that is printed in very small type on the maps of the environs of Boston, but a lifesize strip of sand curves from Winthrop to Lynn; and that is historic ground in the annals of my family. The place is now a popular resort for holiday crowds, and is famous under the name of Revere Beach. When the reunited Antins made their stand there, however, there were no boulevards, no stately bath-houses, no hotels, no gaudy amusement places, no illuminations, no showmen, no tawdry rabble. There was only the bright clean sweep of sand, the summer sea, and the summer sky. At high tide the whole Atlantic rushed in, tossing the seaweeds in his mane; at low tide he rushed out, growling and gnashing his granite teeth. Between tides a baby might play on the beach, digging with pebbles and shells, till it lay asleep on the sand. The whole sun shone by day, troops of stars by night, and the great moon in its season.

Into this grand cycle of the seaside day I came to live and learn and play. A few people came with me, as I have already intimated; but the main thing was that *I* came to live on the edge of the sea —I, who had spent my life inland, believing that the great waters of the world were spread out before me in the Dvina. My idea of the human world had grown enormously during the long journey; my idea of the earth had expanded with every day at sea; my idea of the world outside the earth now budded and swelled during my prolonged experience of the wide and unobstructed heavens.

Not that I got any inkling of the conception of a multiple world. I had had no lessons in cosmogony, and I had no spontaneous revelation of the true position of the earth in the universe. For me, as for my fathers, the sun set and rose, and I did not feel the earth rushing through space. But I lay stretched out in the sun, my eyes level with the sea, till I seemed to be absorbed bodily by the very materials of the world around me; till I could not feel my hand as separate from the warm sand in which it was buried. Or I crouched on the beach at full moon, wondering, wondering, between the two splendors of the sky and the sea. Or I ran out to meet the incoming storm, my face full in the wind, my being a-tingle with an awesome delight to the tips of my fog-matted locks flying behind; and stood clinging to some stake or upturned boat, shaken by the roar and rumble of the waves. So clinging, I pretended that I was in danger, and was deliciously frightened; I held on with both hands, and shook my head, exulting in the tumult around me, equally ready to laugh or sob. Or else I sat, on the stillest days, with my back to the sea, not looking at all, but just listening to the rustle of the waves on the sand; not thinking at all, but just breathing with the sea.

Thus courting the influence of sea and sky and variable weather, I was bound to have dreams, hints, imaginings. It was no more than this, perhaps: that the world as I knew it was not large enough to contain all that I saw and felt; that the thoughts that flashed through my mind, not half understood, unrelated to my utterable thoughts, concerned something for which I had as yet no name. Every imaginative growing child has these flashes of intuition, especially one that becomes intimate with some one aspect of nature. With me it was the growing time, that idle summer by the sea, and I grew all the faster because I had been so cramped before. My mind, too, had so recently been worked upon by the impressive experience of a change of country that I was more than commonly alive to impressions, which are the seeds of ideas.

Let no one suppose that I spent my time entirely, or even chiefly, in inspired solitude. By far the best part of my day was spent in play—frank, hearty, boisterous play, such as comes natural to

American children. In Polotzk I had already begun to be considered too old for play, excepting set games or organized frolics. Here I found myself included with children who still played, and I willingly returned to childhood. There were plenty of playfellows. My father's energetic little partner had a little wife and a large family. He kept them in the little cottage next to ours; and that the shanty survived the tumultuous presence of that brood is a wonder to me to-day. The young Wilners included an assortment of boys, girls, and twins, of every possible variety of age, size, disposition, and sex. They swarmed in and out of the cottage all day long, wearing the door-sill hollow, and trampling the ground to powder. They swung out of windows like monkeys, slid up the roof like flies, and shot out of trees like fowls. Even a small person like me could n't go anywhere without being run over by a Wilner; and I could never tell which Wilner it was because none of them ever stood still long enough to be identified; and also because I suspected that they were in the habit of interchanging conspicuous articles of clothing, which was very confusing.

You would suppose that the little mother must have been utterly lost, bewildered, trodden down in this horde of urchins; but you are mistaken. Mrs. Wilner was a positively majestic little person. She ruled her brood with the utmost coolness and strictness. She had even the biggest boy under her thumb, frequently under her palm. If they enjoyed the wildest freedom outdoors, indoors the young Wilners lived by the clock. And so at five o'clock in the evening, on seven days in the week, my father's partner's children could be seen in two long rows around the supper table. You could tell them apart on this occasion, because they all had their faces washed. And this is the time to count them: there are twelve little Wilners at table.

I managed to retain my identity in this multitude somehow, and while I was very much impressed with their numbers, I even dared to pick and choose my friends among the Wilners. One or two of the smaller boys I liked best of all, for a game of hide-and-seek or a frolic on the beach. We played in the water like ducks, never taking the trouble to get dry. One day I waded out with one of the boys, to see which of us dared go farthest. The tide was extremely low, and we had not wet our knees when we began to look back to see if familiar objects were still in sight. I thought we had been wading for hours, and still the water was so shallow and quiet. My companion was marching straight ahead, so I did the same. Suddenly a swell lifted us almost off our feet, and we clutched at each other simultaneously. There was a lesser swell, and little waves began to run, and a sigh went up from the sea. The tide was turning—perhaps a storm was on the way—and we were miles, dreadful miles from dry land.

Boy and girl turned without a word, four determined bare legs ploughing through the water, four scared eyes straining toward the land. Through an eternity of toil and fear they kept dumbly on, death at their heels, pride still in their hearts. At last they reach high-water mark—six hours before full tide.

Each has seen the other afraid, and each rejoices in the knowledge. But only the boy is sure of his tongue.

"You was scared, war n't you?" he taunts.

The girl understands so much, and is able to reply:—

"You can schwimmen, I not."

"Betcher life I can schwimmen," the other mocks.

And the girl walks off, angry and hurt.

"An' I can walk on my hands," the tormentor calls after her. "Say, you greenhorn, why don'tcher look?"

The girl keeps straight on, vowing that she would never walk with that rude boy again, neither by land nor sea, not even though the waters should part at his bidding.

I am forgetting the more serious business which had brought us to Crescent Beach. While we children disported ourselves like mermaids and mermen in the surf, our respective fathers dispensed cold lemonade, hot peanuts, and pink popcorn, and piled up our respective fortunes, nickel by nickel, penny by penny. I was very proud of my connection with the public life of the beach. I admired greatly our shining soda fountain, the rows of sparkling glasses, the pyramids of oranges, the sausage chains, the neat white counter, and the bright array of tin spoons. It seemed to me that none of the other refreshment stands on the beach—there were a few— were half so attractive as ours. I thought my father looked very well in a long white apron and shirt sleeves. He dished out ice cream with enthusiasm, so I supposed he was getting rich. It never occurred to me to compare his present occupation with the position for which he had been originally destined; or if I thought about it,

I was just as well content, for by this time I had by heart my father's saying, "America is not Polotzk." All occupations were respectable, all men were equal, in America.

If I admired the soda fountain and the sausage chains, I almost worshipped the partner, Mr. Wilner. I was content to stand for an hour at a time watching him make potato chips. In his cook's cap and apron, with a ladle in his hand and a smile on his face, he moved about with the greatest agility, whisking his raw materials out of nowhere, dipping into his bubbling kettle with a flourish, and bringing forth the finished product with a caper. Such potato chips were not to be had anywhere else on Crescent Beach. Thin as tissue paper, crisp as dry snow, and salt as the sea—such thirst-producing, lemonade-selling, nickel-bringing potato chips only Mr. Wilner could make. On holidays, when dozens of family parties came out by every train from town, he could hardly keep up with the demand for his potato chips. And with a waiting crowd around him our partner was at his best. He was as voluble as he was skilful, and as witty as he was voluble; at least so I guessed from the laughter that frequently drowned his voice. I could not understand his jokes, but if I could get near enough to watch his lips and his smile and his merry eyes, I was happy. That any one could talk so fast, and in English, was marvel enough, but that this prodigy should belong to *our* establishment was a fact to thrill me. I had never seen anything like Mr. Wilner, except a wedding jester; but then he spoke common Yiddish. So proud was I of the talent and good taste displayed at our stand that if my father beckoned to me in the crowd and sent me on an errand, I hoped the people noticed that I, too, was connected with the establishment.

And all this splendor and glory and distinction came to a sudden end. There was some trouble about a license—some fee or fine— there was a storm in the night that damaged the soda fountain and other fixtures—there was talk and consultation between the houses of Antin and Wilner—and the promising partnership was dissolved. No more would the merry partner gather the crowd on the beach; no more would the twelve young Wilners gambol like mermen and mermaids in the surf. And the less numerous tribe of Antin must also say farewell to the jolly seaside life; for men in such humble business as my father's carry their families, along with their other earthly goods, wherever they go, after the manner of the gypsies. We had driven a feeble stake into the sand. The jealous Atlantic, in conspiracy with the Sunday law, had torn it out. We must seek our luck elsewhere.

In Polotzk we had supposed that "America" was practically synonymous with "Boston." When we landed in Boston, the horizon was pushed back, and we annexed Crescent Beach. And now, espying other lands of promise, we took possession of the province of Chelsea, in the name of our necessity.

In Chelsea, as in Boston, we made our stand in the wrong end of the town. Arlington Street was inhabited by poor Jews, poor Negroes, and a sprinkling of poor Irish. The side streets leading from it were occupied by more poor Jews and Negroes. It was a proper locality for a man without capital to do business. My father rented a tenement with a store in the basement. He put in a few barrels of flour and of sugar, a few boxes of crackers, a few gallons of kerosene, an assortment of soap of the "save the coupon" brands; in the cellar, a few barrels of potatoes, and a pyramid of kindling-wood; in the showcase, an alluring display of penny candy. He put out his sign, with a gilt-lettered warning of "Strictly Cash," and proceeded to give credit indiscriminately. That was the regular way to do business on Arlington Street. My father, in his three years' apprenticeship, had learned the tricks of many trades. He knew when and how to "bluff." The legend of "Strictly Cash" was a protection against notoriously irresponsible customers; while none of the "good" customers, who had a record for paying regularly on Saturday, hesitated to enter the store with empty purses.

If my father knew the tricks of the trade, my mother could be counted on to throw all her talent and tact into the business. Of course she had no English yet, but as she could perform the acts of weighing, measuring, and mental computation of fractions mechanically, she was able to give her whole attention to the dark mysteries of the language, as intercourse with her customers gave her opportunity. In this she made such rapid progress that she soon lost all sense of disadvantage, and conducted herself behind the counter very much as if she were back in her old store in Polotzk. It was far more cosey than Polotzk—at least, so it seemed to me; for behind the store was the kitchen, where, in the intervals of slack trade, she did her cooking and washing. Arlington Street customers were used to waiting while the storekeeper salted the soup or rescued a loaf from the oven.

Once more Fortune favored my family with a thin little smile, and my father, in reply to a friendly inquiry, would say, "One makes a living," with a shrug of the shoulders that added "but nothing to boast of." It was characteristic of my attitude toward bread-and-butter matters that this contented me, and I felt free to devote myself to the conquest of my new world. Looking back to those critical first years, I see myself always behaving like a child let loose in a garden to play and dig and chase the butterflies. Occasionally, indeed, I was stung by the wasp of family trouble; but I knew a healing ointment—my faith in America. My father had come to America to make a living. America, which was free and fair and kind, must presently yield him what he sought. I had come to America to see a new world, and I followed my own ends with the utmost assiduity; only, as I ran out to explore, I would look back to see if my house were in order behind me—if my family still kept its head above water.

In after years, when I passed as an American among Americans, if I was suddenly made aware of the past that lay forgotten,—if a letter from Russia, or a paragraph in the newspaper, or a conversation overheard in the street-car, suddenly reminded me of what I might have been,—I thought it miracle enough that I, Mashke, the granddaughter of Raphael the Russian, born to a humble destiny, should be at home in an American metropolis, be free to fashion my own life, and should dream my dreams in English phrases. But in the beginning my admiration was spent on more concrete embodiments of the splendors of America; such as fine houses, gay shops, electric engines and apparatus, public buildings, illuminations, and parades. My early letters to my Russian friends were filled with boastful descriptions of these glories of my new country. No native citizen of Chelsea took such pride and delight in its institutions as I did. It required no fife and drum corps, no Fourth of July procession, to set me tingling with patriotism. Even the common agents and instruments of municipal life, such as the letter carrier and the fire engine, I regarded with a measure of respect. I know what I thought of people who said that Chelsea was a very small, dull, unaspiring town, with no discernible excuse for a separate name or existence.

The apex of my civic pride and personal contentment was reached on the bright September morning when I entered the public school. That day I must always remember, even if I live to be so old that I cannot tell my name. To most people their first day at school is a memorable occasion. In my case the importance of the day was a hundred times magnified, on account of the years I had waited, the road I had come, and the conscious ambitions I entertained.

I am wearily aware that I am speaking in extreme figures, in superlatives. I wish I knew some other way to render the mental life of the immigrant child of reasoning age. I may have been ever so much an exception in acuteness of observation, powers of comparison, and abnormal self-consciousness; none the less were my thoughts and conduct typical of the attitude of the intelligent immigrant child toward American institutions. And what the child thinks and feels is a reflection of the hopes, desires, and purposes of the parents who brought him overseas, no matter how precocious and independent the child may be. Your immigrant inspectors will tell you what poverty the foreigner brings in his baggage, what want in his pockets. Let the overgrown boy of twelve, reverently drawing his letters in the baby class, testify to the noble dreams and high ideals that may be hidden beneath the greasy caftan of the immigrant. Speaking for the Jews, at least, I know I am safe in inviting such an investigation.

Who were my companions on my first day at school? Whose hand was in mine, as I stood, overcome with awe, by the teacher's desk, and whispered my name as my father prompted? Was it Frieda's steady, capable hand? Was it her loyal heart that throbbed, beat for beat with mine, as it had done through all our childish adventures? Frieda's heart did throb that day, but not with my emotions. My heart pulsed with joy and pride and ambition; in her heart longing fought with abnegation. For I was led to the schoolroom, with its sunshine and its singing and the teacher's cheery smile; while she was led to the workshop, with its foul air, care-lined faces, and the foreman's stern command. Our going to school was the fulfilment of my father's best promises to us, and

Frieda's share in it was to fashion and fit the calico frocks in which the baby sister and I made our first appearance in a public school-room.

I remember to this day the gray pattern of the calico, so affectionately did I regard it as it hung upon the wall—my consecration robe awaiting the beatific day. And Frieda, I am sure, remembers it, too, so longingly did she regard it as the crisp, starchy breadths of it slid between her fingers. But whatever were her longings, she said nothing of them; she bent over the sewing-machine humming an Old-World melody. In every straight, smooth seam, perhaps, she tucked away some lingering impulse of childhood; but she matched the scrolls and flowers with the utmost care. If a sudden shock of rebellion made her straighten up for an instant, the next instant she was bending to adjust a ruffle to the best advantage. And when the momentous day arrived, and the little sister and I stood up to be arrayed, it was Frieda herself who patted and smoothed my stiff new calico; who made me turn round and round, to see that I was perfect; who stooped to pull out a disfiguring basting-thread. If there was anything in her heart besides sisterly love and pride and good-will, as we parted that morning, it was a sense of loss and a woman's acquiescence in her fate; for we had been close friends, and now our ways would lie apart. Longing she felt, but no envy. She did not grudge me what she was denied. Until that morning we had been children together, but now, at the fiat of her destiny, she became a woman, with all a woman's cares; whilst I, so little younger than she, was bidden to dance at the May festival of untroubled childhood.

I wish, for my comfort, that I could say that I had some notion of the difference in our lots, some sense of the injustice to her, of the indulgence to me. I wish I could even say that I gave serious thought to the matter. There had always been a distinction between us rather out of proportion to the difference in our years. Her good health and domestic instincts had made it natural for her to become my mother's right hand, in the years preceding the emigration, when there were no more servants or dependents. Then there was the family tradition that Mary was the quicker, the brighter of the two, and that hers could be no common lot. Frieda was relied upon for help, and her sister for glory. And when I failed as a milliner's apprentice, while Frieda made excellent progress at the dressmak-

er's, our fates, indeed, were sealed. It was understood, even before
we reached Boston, that she would go to work and I to school. In
view of the family prejudices, it was the inevitable course. No injustice was intended. My father sent us hand in hand to school,
before he had ever thought of America. If, in America, he had been
able to support his family unaided, it would have been the culmi-
nation of his best hopes to see all his children at school, with equal
advantages at home. But when he had done his best, and was still
unable to provide even bread and shelter for us all, he was compelled to make us children self-supporting as fast as it was practi-
cable. There was no choosing possible; Frieda was the oldest, the
strongest, the best prepared, and the only one who was of legal age
to be put to work.

My father has nothing to answer for. He divided the world between his children in accordance with the laws of the country and
the compulsion of his circumstances. I have no need of defending
him. It is myself that I would like to defend, and I cannot. I remember that I accepted the arrangements made for my sister and
me without much reflection, and everything that was planned for
my advantage I took as a matter of course. I was no heartless monster, but a decidedly self-centred child. If my sister had seemed
unhappy it would have troubled me; but I am ashamed to recall
that I did not consider how little it was that contented her. I was
so preoccupied with my own happiness that I did not half perceive
the splendid devotion of her attitude towards me, the sweetness of
her joy in my good luck. She not only stood by approvingly when
I was helped to everything; she cheerfully waited on me herself.
And I took everything from her hand as if it were my due.

The two of us stood a moment in the doorway of the tenement
house on Arlington Street, that wonderful September morning
when I first went to school. It was I that ran away, on winged feet
of joy and expectation; it was she whose feet were bound in the
treadmill of daily toil. And I was so blind that I did not see that
the glory lay on her, and not on me.

Father himself conducted us to school. He would not have dele-
gated that mission to the President of the United States. He had
awaited the day with impatience equal to mine, and the visions he
saw as he hurried us over the sun-flecked pavements transcended

all my dreams. Almost his first act on landing on American soil, three years before, had been his application for naturalization. He had taken the remaining steps in the process with eager promptness, and at the earliest moment allowed by the law, he became a citizen of the United States. It is true that he had left home in search of bread for his hungry family, but he went blessing the necessity that drove him to America. The boasted freedom of the New World meant to him far more than the right to reside, travel, and work wherever he pleased; it meant the freedom to speak his thoughts, to throw off the shackles of superstition, to test his own fate, unhindered by political or religious tyranny. He was only a young man when he landed—thirty-two; and most of his life he had been held in leading-strings. He was hungry for his untasted manhood.

Three years passed in sordid struggle and disappointment. He was not prepared to make a living even in America, where the day laborer eats wheat instead of rye. Apparently the American flag could not protect him against the pursuing Nemesis of his limitations; he must expiate the sins of his fathers who slept across the seas. He had been endowed at birth with a poor constitution, a nervous, restless temperament, and an abundance of hindering prejudices. In his boyhood his body was starved, that his mind might be stuffed with useless learning. In his youth this dearly gotten learning was sold, and the price was the bread and salt which he had not been trained to earn for himself. Under the wedding canopy he was bound for life to a girl whose features were still strange to him; and he was bidden to multiply himself, that sacred learning might be perpetuated in his sons, to the glory of the God of his fathers. All this while he had been led about as a creature without a will, a chattel, an instrument. In his maturity he awoke, and found himself poor in health, poor in purse, poor in useful knowledge, and hampered on all sides. At the first nod of opportunity he broke away from his prison, and strove to atone for his wasted youth by a life of useful labor; while at the same time he sought to lighten the gloom of his narrow scholarship by freely partaking of modern ideas. But his utmost endeavor still left him far from his goal. In business, nothing prospered with him. Some fault of hand or mind or temperament led him to failure where other men found success. Wherever the blame for his disabilities be placed, he reaped their bitter fruit. "Give me bread!" he cried to America. "What will you do to earn it?" the challenge came back. And he found that he was master of no art, of no trade; that even his precious learning was of no avail, because he had only the most antiquated methods of communicating it.

So in his primary quest he had failed. There was left him the compensation of intellectual freedom. That he sought to realize in every possible way. He had very little opportunity to prosecute his education, which, in truth, had never been begun. His struggle for a bare living left him no time to take advantage of the public evening school; but he lost nothing of what was to be learned through reading, through attendance at public meetings, through exercising the rights of citizenship. Even here he was hindered by a natural inability to acquire the English language. In time, indeed, he learned to read, to follow a conversation or lecture; but he never learned to write correctly, and his pronunciation remains extremely foreign to this day.

If education, culture, the higher life were shining things to be worshipped from afar, he had still a means left whereby he could draw one step nearer to them. He could send his children to school, to learn all those things that he knew by fame to be desirable. The common school, at least, perhaps high school; for one or two, perhaps even college! His children should be students, should fill his house with books and intellectual company; and thus he would walk by proxy in the Elysian Fields of liberal learning. As for the children themselves, he knew no surer way to their advancement and happiness.

So it was with a heart full of longing and hope that my father led us to school on that first day. He took long strides in his eagerness, the rest of us running and hopping to keep up.

At last the four of us stood around the teacher's desk; and my father, in his impossible English, gave us over in her charge, with some broken word of his hopes for us that his swelling heart could no longer contain. I venture to say that Miss Nixon was struck by something uncommon in the group we made, something outside of Semitic features and the abashed manner of the alien. My little sister was as pretty as a doll, with her clear pink-and-white face, short golden curls, and eyes like blue violets when you caught them looking up. My brother might have been a girl, too, with his cherubic contours of face, rich red color, glossy black hair, and fine eyebrows. Whatever secret fears were in his heart, remembering his former teachers, who had taught with the rod, he stood up straight and uncringing before the American teacher, his cap respectfully doffed. Next to him stood a starved-looking girl with eyes ready to pop out, and short dark curls that would not have made much of a wig for a Jewish bride.

All three children carried themselves rather better than the common run of "green" pupils that were brought to Miss Nixon. But the figure that challenged attention to the group was the tall, straight father, with his earnest face and fine forehead, nervous hands eloquent in gesture, and a voice full of feeling. This foreigner, who brought his children to school as if it were an act of consecration, who regarded the teacher of the primer class with reverence, who spoke of visions, like a man inspired, in a common schoolroom, was not like other aliens, who brought their children in dull obedience to the law; was not like the native fathers, who brought their unmanageable boys, glad to be relieved of their care. I think Miss Nixon guessed what my father's best English could not convey. I think she divined that by the simple act of delivering our school certificates to her he took possession of America.

CHAPTER X

INITIATION

IT IS NOT WORTH WHILE to refer to voluminous school statistics to see just how many "green" pupils entered school last September, not knowing the days of the week in English, who next February will be declaiming patriotic verses in honor of George Washington and Abraham Lincoln, with a foreign accent, indeed, but with plenty of enthusiasm. It is enough to know that this hundred-fold miracle is common to the schools in every part of the United States where immigrants are received. And if I was one of Chelsea's hundred in 1894, it was only to be expected, since I was one of the older of the "green" children, and had had a start in my irregular schooling in Russia, and was carried along by a tremendous desire to learn, and had my family to cheer me on.

I was not a bit too large for my little chair and desk in the baby class, but my mind, of course, was too mature by six or seven years for the work. So as soon as I could understand what the teacher said in class, I was advanced to the second grade. This was within a week after Miss Nixon took me in hand. But I do not mean to give my dear teacher all the credit for my rapid progress, nor even half the credit. I shall divide it with her on behalf of my race and my family. I was Jew enough to have an aptitude for language in general, and to bend my mind earnestly to my task; I was Antin enough to read each lesson with my heart, which gave me an inkling of what was coming next, and so carried me along by leaps and bounds. As for the teacher, she could best explain what theory she followed in teaching us foreigners to read. I can only describe the method, which was so simple that I wish holiness could be taught in the same way.

There were about half a dozen of us beginners in English, in age from six to fifteen. Miss Nixon made a special class of us, and aided us so skillfully and earnestly in our endeavors to "see-a-cat," and "hear-a-dog-bark," and "look-at-the-hen," that we turned over page after page of the ravishing history, eager to find out how the common world looked, smelled, and tasted in the strange speech.

The teacher knew just when to let us help each other out with a word in our own tongue,—it happened that we were all Jews,—and so, working all together, we actually covered more ground in a lesson than the native classes, composed entirely of the little tots.

But we stuck—stuck fast—at the definite article; and sometimes the lesson resolved itself into a species of lingual gymnastics, in which we all looked as if we meant to bite our tongues off. Miss Nixon was pretty, and she must have looked well with her white teeth showing in the act; but at the time I was too solemnly occupied to admire her looks. I did take great pleasure in her smile of approval, whenever I pronounced well; and her patience and perseverance in struggling with us over that thick little word are becoming to her even now, after fifteen years. It is not her fault if any of us to-day give a buzzing sound to the dreadful English *th*.

I shall never have a better opportunity to make public declaration of my love for the English language. I am glad that American history runs, chapter for chapter, the way it does; for thus America came to be the country I love so dearly. I am glad, most of all, that the Americans began by being Englishmen, for thus did I come to inherit this beautiful language in which I think. It seems to me that in any other language happiness is not so sweet, logic is not so clear. I am not sure that I could believe in my neighbors as I do if I thought about them in un-English words. I could almost say that my conviction of immortality is bound up with the English of its promise. And as I am attached to my prejudices, I must love the English language!

Whenever the teachers did anything special to help me over my private difficulties, my gratitude went out to them, silently. It meant so much to me that they halted the lesson to give me a lift, that I needs must love them for it. Dear Miss Carrol, of the second grade, would be amazed to hear what small things I remember, all because I was so impressed at the time with her readiness and sweetness in taking notice of my difficulties.

Says Miss Carrol, looking straight at me:—

"If Johnnie has three marbles, and Charlie has twice as many, how many marbles has Charlie?"

I raise my hand for permission to speak.

"Teacher, I don't know vhat is tvice."

Teacher beckons me to her, and whispers to me the meaning of the strange word, and I am able to write the sum correctly. It's all in the day's work with her; with me, it is a special act of kindness and efficiency.

She whom I found in the next grade became so dear a friend that I can hardly name her with the rest, though I mention none of them lightly. Her approval was always dear to me, first because she was "Teacher," and afterwards, as long as she lived, because she was my Miss Dillingham. Great was my grief, therefore, when, shortly after my admission to her class, I incurred discipline, the first, and next to the last, time in my school career.

The class was repeating in chorus the Lord's Prayer, heads bowed on desks. I was doing my best to keep up by the sound; my mind could not go beyond the word "hallowed," for which I had not found the meaning. In the middle of the prayer a Jewish boy across the aisle trod on my foot to get my attention. "You must not say that," he admonished in a solemn whisper; "it's Christian." I whispered back that it wasn't, and went on to the "Amen." I did not know but what he was right, but the name of Christ was not in the prayer, and I was bound to do everything that the class did. If I had any Jewish scruples, they were lagging away behind my interest in school affairs. How American this was: two pupils side by side in the schoolroom, each holding to his own opinion, but both submitting to the common law; for the boy at least bowed his head as the teacher ordered.

But all Miss Dillingham knew of it was that two of her pupils whispered during morning prayer, and she must discipline them. So I was degraded from the honor row to the lowest row, and it was many a day before I forgave that young missionary; it was not enough for my vengeance that he suffered punishment with me. Teacher, of course, heard us both defend ourselves, but there was a time and a place for religious arguments, and she meant to help us remember that point.

I remember to this day what a struggle we had over the word "water," Miss Dillingham and I. It seemed as if I could not give the sound of w; I said "vater" every time. Patiently my teacher worked with me, inventing mouth exercises for me, to get my stubborn lips to produce that w; and when at last I could say "village" and "water" in rapid alternation, without misplacing the two initials, that memorable word was sweet on my lips. For we had conquered, and Teacher was pleased.

Getting a language in this way, word by word, has a charm that may be set against the disadvantages. It is like gathering a posy blossom by blossom. Bring the bouquet into your chamber, and these nasturtiums stand for the whole flaming carnival of them tumbling over the fence out there; these yellow pansies recall the velvet crescent of color glowing under the bay window; this spray of honeysuckle smells like the wind-tossed masses of it on the porch, ripe and bee-laden; the whole garden in a glass tumbler. So it is with one who gathers words, loving them. Particular words remain associated with important occasions in the learner's mind. I could thus write a history of my English vocabulary that should be at the same time an account of my comings and goings, my mistakes and my triumphs, during the years of my initiation.

If I was eager and diligent, my teachers did not sleep. As fast as my knowledge of English allowed, they advanced me from grade to grade, without reference to the usual schedule of promotions. My father was right, when he often said, in discussing my prospects, that ability would be promptly recognized in the public schools. Rapid as was my progress, on account of the advantages with which I started, some of the other "green" pupils were not far behind me; within a grade or two, by the end of the year. My brother, whose childhood had been one hideous nightmare, what with the stupid rebbe, the cruel whip, and the general repression of life in the Pale, surprised my father by the progress he made under intelligent, sympathetic guidance. Indeed, he soon had a reputation in the school that the American boys envied; and all through the school course he more than held his own with pupils of his age. So much for the right and wrong way of doing things.

There is a record of my early progress in English much better than my recollections, however accurate and definite these may be. I have several reasons for introducing it here. First, it shows what the Russian Jew can do with an adopted language; next, it proves that vigilance of our public-school teachers of which I spoke; and last, I am proud of it! That is an unnecessary confession, but I could not be satisfied to insert the record here, with my vanity unavowed.

This is the document, copied from an educational journal, a tattered copy of which lies in my lap as I write—treasured for fifteen years, you see, by my vanity.

EDITOR "PRIMARY EDUCATION":—

This is the uncorrected paper of a Russian child twelve years old, who had studied English only four months. She had never, until September, been to school even in her own country and has heard English spoken *only* at school. I shall be glad if the paper of my pupil and the above explanation may appear in your paper.

                    M. S. DILLINGHAM.

CHELSEA, MASS.

SNOW

Snow is frozen moisture which comes from the clouds.

Now the snow is coming down in feather-flakes, which makes nice snow-balls. But there is still one kind of snow more. This kind of snow is called snow-crystals, for it comes down in little curly balls. These snow-crystals aren't quiet as good for snow-balls as feather-flakes, for they (the snow-crystals) are dry: so they can't keep together as feather-flakes do.

The snow is dear to some children for they like sleighing.

As I said at the top—the snow comes from the clouds.

Now the trees are bare, and no flowers are to see in the fields and gardens, (we all know why) and the whole world seems like asleep without the happy birds songs which left us till spring. But the snow which drove away all these pretty and happy things, try, (as I think) not to make us at all unhappy; they covered up the branches of the trees, the fields, the gardens and houses, and the whole world looks like dressed in a beautiful white—instead of green—dress, with the sky looking down on it with a pale face.

And so the people can find some joy in it, too, without the happy summer.

                    MARY ANTIN.

And now that it stands there, with *her* name over it, I am ashamed of my flippant talk about vanity. More to me than all the praise I could hope to win by the conquest of fifty languages is the association of this dear friend with my earliest efforts at writing; and it pleases me to remember that to her I owe my very first appearance in print. Vanity is the least part of it, when I remember how she called me to her desk, one day after school was out, and showed me my composition—my own words, that I had written out of my own head—printed out, clear black and white, with my name at the end! Nothing so wonderful had ever happened to me before. My whole consciousness was suddenly transformed. I suppose that was the moment when I became a writer. I always loved to write,—I wrote letters whenever I had an excuse,—yet it had never occurred to me to sit down and write my thoughts for no person in particular, merely to put the word on paper. But now, as I read my own words, in a delicious confusion, the idea was born. I stared at my name: MARY ANTIN. Was that really I? The printed characters composing it seemed strange to me all of a sudden. If that was my name, and those were the words out of my own head, what relation did it all have to *me*, who was alone there with Miss Dillingham, and the printed page between us? Why, it meant that I could write again, and see my writing printed for people to read! I could write many, many, many things: I could write a book! The idea was so huge, so bewildering, that my mind scarcely could accommodate it.

I do not know what my teacher said to me; probably very little. It was her way to say only a little, and look at me, and trust me to understand. Once she had occasion to lecture me about living a shut-up life; she wanted me to go outdoors. I had been repeatedly scolded and reproved on that score by other people, but I had only laughed, saying that I was too happy to change my ways. But when Miss Dillingham spoke to me, I saw that it was a serious matter; and yet she only said a few words, and looked at me with that smile of hers that was only half a smile, and the rest a meaning. Another time she had a great question to ask me, touching my life to the quick. She merely put her question, and was silent; but I knew what answer she expected, and not being able to give it then, I went away sad and reproved. Years later I had my triumphant answer, but she was no longer there to receive it; and so her eyes look at me, from the picture on the mantel there, with a reproach I no longer merit.

I ought to go back and strike out all that talk about vanity. What reason have I to be vain, when I reflect how at every step I was petted, nursed, and encouraged? I did not even discover my own talent. It was discovered first by my father in Russia, and next by my friend in America. What did I ever do but write when they told me to write? I suppose my grandfather who drove a spavined horse through lonely country lanes sat in the shade of crisp-leaved oaks to refresh himself with a bit of black bread; and an acorn falling beside him, in the immense stillness, shook his heart with the echo, and left him wondering. I suppose my father stole away from the synagogue one long festival day, and stretched himself out in the sun-warmed grass, and lost himself in dreams that made the world of men unreal when he returned to them. And so what is there left for me to do, who do not have to drive a horse nor interpret ancient lore, but put my grandfather's question into words and set to music my father's dream? The tongue am I of those who lived before me, as those that are to come will be the voice of my unspoken thoughts. And so who shall be applauded if the song be sweet, if the prophecy be true?

I never heard of any one who was so watched and coaxed, so passed along from hand to helping hand, as was I. I always had friends. They sprang up everywhere, as if they had stood waiting for me to come. So here was my teacher, the moment she saw that I could give a good paraphrase of her talk on "Snow," bent on finding out what more I could do. One day she asked me if I had ever written poetry. I had not, but I went home and tried. I believe it was more snow, and I know it was wretched. I wish I could produce a copy of that early effusion; it would prove that my judgment is not severe. Wretched it was,—worse, a great deal, than reams of poetry that is written by children about whom there is no fuss made. But Miss Dillingham was not discouraged. She saw that I had no idea of metre, so she proceeded to teach me. We repeated miles of poetry together, smooth lines that sang themselves, mostly out of Longfellow. Then I would go home and write—oh, about the snow in our back yard!—but when Miss Dillingham came to read my verses, they limped and they lagged and they dragged, and there was no tune that would fit them.

At last came the moment of illumination: I saw where my trouble lay. I had supposed that my lines matched when they had an equal number of syllables, taking no account of accent. Now I knew better; now I could write poetry! The everlasting snow melted at last, and the mud puddles dried in the spring sun, and the grass on the common was green, and still I wrote poetry! Again I wish I had some example of my springtime rhapsodies, the veriest rubbish of the sort that ever a child perpetrated. Lizzie McDee, who had red hair and freckles, and a Sunday-school manner on weekdays, and was below me in the class, did a great deal better. We used to compare verses; and while I do not remember that I ever had the grace to own that she was the better poet, I do know that I secretly wondered why the teachers did not invite her to stay after school and study poetry, while they took so much pains with me. But so it was always with me: somebody did something for me all the time.

Making fair allowance for my youth, retarded education, and strangeness to the language, it must still be admitted that I never wrote good verse. But I loved to read it. My half-hours with Miss Dillingham were full of delight for me, quite apart from my new-born ambition to become a writer. What, then, was my joy, when Miss Dillingham, just before locking up her desk one evening, presented me with a volume of Longfellow's poems! It was a thin volume of selections, but to me it was a bottomless treasure. I had never owned a book before. The sense of possession alone was a source of bliss, and this book I already knew and loved. And so Miss Dillingham, who was my first American friend, and who first put my name in print, was also the one to start my library. Deep is my regret when I consider that she was gone before I had given much of an account of all her gifts of love and service to me.

About the middle of the year I was promoted to the grammar school. Then it was that I walked on air. For I said to myself that I was a *student* now, in earnest, not merely a school-girl learning to spell and cipher. I was going to learn out-of-the-way things, things that had nothing to do with ordinary life—things to *know*. When I walked home afternoons, with the great big geography book under my arm, it seemed to me that the earth was conscious of my step. Sometimes I carried home half the books in my desk, not because I should need them, but because I loved to hold them; and also because I loved to be seen carrying books. It was a badge of scholarship, and I was proud of it. I remembered the days in Vitebsk when I used to watch my cousin Hirshel start for school in the morning, every thread of his student's uniform, every worn copybook in his satchel, glorified in my envious eyes. And now I was myself as he: aye, greater than he; for I knew English, and I could write poetry.

If my head was not turned at this time it was because I was so busy from morning till night. My father did his best to make me vain and silly. He made much of me to every chance caller, boasting of my progress at school, and of my exalted friends, the teachers. For a school-teacher was no ordinary mortal in his eyes; she was a superior being, set above the common run of men by her erudition and devotion to higher things. That a school-teacher could be shallow or petty, or greedy for pay, was a thing that he could not have been brought to believe, at this time. And he was right, if he could only have stuck to it in later years, when a new-born pessimism, fathered by his perception that in America, too, some things needed mending, threw him to the opposite extreme of opinion, crying that nothing in the American scheme of society or government was worth tinkering.

He surely was right in his first appraisal of the teacher. The mean sort of teachers are not teachers at all; they are self-seekers who take up teaching as a business, to support themselves and keep their hands white. These same persons, did they keep store or drive a milk wagon or wash babies for a living, would be respectable. As trespassers on a noble profession, they are worth no more than the books and slates and desks over which they preside; so much furniture, to be had by the gross. They do not love their work. They contribute nothing to the higher development of their pupils. They busy themselves, not with research into the science of teaching, but with organizing political demonstrations to advance the cause of selfish candidates for public office, who promise them rewards. The true teachers are of another strain. Apostles all of an ideal, they go to their work in a spirit of love and inquiry, seeking not comfort, not position, not old-age pensions, but truth that is the soul of wisdom, the joy of big-eyed children, the food of hungry youth.

They were true teachers who used to come to me on Arlington Street, so my father had reason to boast of the distinction brought upon his house. For the school-teacher in her trim, unostentatious dress was an uncommon visitor in our neighborhood; and the talk that passed in the bare little "parlor" over the grocery store would not have been entirely comprehensible to our next-door neighbor.

In the grammar school I had as good teaching as I had had in the primary. It seems to me in retrospect that it was as good, on the whole, as the public school ideals of the time made possible. When I recall how I was taught geography, I see, indeed, that there was room for improvement occasionally both in the substance and in the method of instruction. But I know of at least one teacher of Chelsea who realized this; for I met her, eight years later, at a great metropolitan university that holds a summer session for the benefit of school-teachers who want to keep up with the advance in their science. Very likely they no longer teach geography entirely within doors, and by rote, as I was taught. Fifteen years is plenty of time for progress.

When I joined the first grammar grade, the class had had a half-year's start of me, but it was not long before I found my place near the head. In all branches except geography it was genuine progress. I overtook the youngsters in their study of numbers, spelling, reading, and composition. In geography I merely made a bluff, but I did not know it. Neither did my teacher. I came up to such tests as she put me.

The lesson was on Chelsea, which was right: geography, like charity, should begin at home. Our text ran on for a paragraph or so on the location, boundaries, natural features, and industries of the town, with a bit of local history thrown in. We were to learn all these interesting facts, and be prepared to write them out from memory the next day. I went home and learned—learned every word of the text, every comma, every footnote. When the teacher had read my paper she marked it "EE." "E" was for "excellent," but my paper was absolutely perfect, and must be put in a class by itself. The teacher exhibited my paper before the class, with some remarks about the diligence that could overtake in a week pupils who had had half a year's start. I took it all as modestly as I could, never doubting that I was indeed a very bright little girl, and getting to be very learned to boot. I was "perfect" in geography, a most erudite subject.

But what was the truth? The words that I repeated so accurately on my paper had about as much meaning to me as the words of the Psalms I used to chant in Hebrew. I got an idea that the city of Chelsea, and the world in general, was laid out flat, like the common, and shaved off at the ends, to allow the north, south, east, and west to snuggle up close, like the frame around a picture. If I looked at the map, I was utterly bewildered; I could find no correspondence between the picture and the verbal explanations. With words I was safe; I could learn any number of words by heart, and sometime or other they would pop out of the medley, clothed with meaning. Chelsea, I read, was bounded on all sides— "bounded" appealed to my imagination—by various things that I had never identified, much as I had roamed about the town. I immediately pictured these remote boundaries as a six-foot fence in a good state of preservation, with the Mystic River, the towns of Everett and Revere, and East Boston Creek, rejoicing, on the south, west, north, and east of it, respectively, that they had got inside; while the rest of the world peeped in enviously through a knot hole. In the middle of this cherished area piano factories—or was it shoe factories?—proudly reared their chimneys, while the population promenaded on a *rope walk*, saluted at every turn by the benevolent inmates of the Soldiers' Home on the top of Powderhorn Hill.

Perhaps the fault was partly mine, because I always would reduce everything to a picture. Partly it may have been because I had not had time to digest the general definitions and explanations at the beginning of the book. Still, I can take but little of the blame, when I consider how I fared through my geography, right to the end of the grammar-school course. I did in time disentangle the symbolism of the orange revolving on a knitting-needle from the astronomical facts in the case, but it took years of training under a master of the subject to rid me of my distrust of the map as a representation of the earth. To this day I sometimes blunder back to my early impression that any given portion of the earth's surface is constructed upon a skeleton consisting of two crossed bars, terminating in arrowheads which pin the cardinal points into place; and if I want to find any desired point of the compass, I am inclined to throw myself flat on my nose, my head due north, and my outstretched arms seeking the east and west respectively.

For in the schoolroom, as far as the study of the map went, we began with the symbol and stuck to the symbol. No teacher of geography I ever had, except the master I referred to, took the pains to ascertain whether I had any sense of the facts for which the symbols stood. Outside the study of maps, geography consisted of statistics: tables of population, imports and exports, manufactures, and degrees of temperature; dimensions of rivers, mountains, and political states; with lists of minerals, plants, and plagues native to any given part of the globe. The only part of the whole subject that meant anything to me was the description of the aspect of foreign lands, and the manners and customs of their peoples. The relation of physiography to human history—what might be called the moral of geography—was not taught at all, or was touched upon in an unimpressive manner. The prevalence of this defect in the teaching of school geography is borne out by the surprise of the college freshman, who remarked to the professor of geology that it was curious to note how all the big rivers and harbors on the Atlantic coastal plain occurred in the neighborhood of large cities! A little instruction in the elements of chartography—a little practice in the use of the compass and the spirit level, a topographical map of the town common, an excursion with a road map—would have given me a fat round earth in place of my paper ghost; would have illumined the one dark alley in my school life.

CHAPTER XI

"MY COUNTRY"

THE PUBLIC SCHOOL has done its best for us foreigners, and for the country, when it has made us into good Americans. I am glad it is mine to tell how the miracle was wrought in one case. You should be glad to hear of it, you born Americans; for it is the story of the growth of your country; of the flocking of your brothers and sisters from the far ends of the earth to the flag you love; of the recruiting of your armies of workers, thinkers, and leaders. And you will be glad to hear of it, my comrades in adoption; for it is a rehearsal of your own experience, the thrill and wonder of which your own hearts have felt.

How long would you say, wise reader, it takes to make an American? By the middle of my second year in school I had reached the sixth grade. When, after the Christmas holidays, we began to study the life of Washington, running through a summary of the Revolution, and the early days of the Republic, it seemed to me that all my reading and study had been idle until then. The reader, the arithmetic, the song book, that had so fascinated me until now, became suddenly sober exercise books, tools wherewith to hew a way to the source of inspiration. When the teacher read to us out of a big book with many bookmarks in it, I sat rigid with attention in my little chair, my hands tightly clasped on the edge of my desk; and I painfully held my breath, to prevent sighs of disappointment escaping, as I saw the teacher skip the parts between bookmarks. When the class read, and it came my turn, my voice shook and the book trembled in my hands. I could not pronounce the name of George Washington without a pause. Never had I prayed, never had I chanted the songs of David, never had I called upon the Most Holy, in such utter reverence and worship as I repeated the simple sentences of my child's story of the patriot. I gazed with adoration at the portraits of George and Martha Washington, till I could see them with my eyes shut. And whereas formerly my self-consciousness had bordered on conceit, and I thought myself an uncommon person, parading my schoolbooks through the streets, and swelling with pride when a teacher detained me in conversation, now I grew humble all at once, seeing how insignificant I was beside the Great.

As I read about the noble boy who would not tell a lie to save himself from punishment, I was for the first time truly repentant of my sins. Formerly I had fasted and prayed and made sacrifice on the Day of Atonement, but it was more than half play, in mimicry of my elders. I had no real horror of sin, and I knew so many ways of escaping punishment. I am sure my family, my neighbors, my teachers in Polotzk—all my world, in fact—strove together, by example and precept, to teach me goodness. Saintliness had a new incarnation in about every third person I knew. I did respect the saints, but I could not help seeing that most of them were a little bit stupid, and that mischief was much more fun than piety. Goodness, as I had known it, was respectable, but not necessarily admirable. The people I really admired, like my Uncle Solomon, and Cousin Rachel, were those who preached the least and laughed the most. My sister Frieda was perfectly good, but she did not think the less of me because I played tricks. What I loved in my friends was not inimitable. One could be downright good if one really wanted to. One could be learned if one had books and teachers. One could sing funny songs and tell anecdotes if one travelled about and picked up such things, like one's uncles and cousins. But a human being strictly good, perfectly wise, and unfailingly valiant, all at the same time, I had never heard or dreamed of. This wonderful George Washington was as inimitable as he was irreproachable. Even if I had never, never told a lie, I could not compare myself to George Washington; for I was not brave—I was afraid to go out when snowballs whizzed—and I could never be the First President of the United States.

So I was forced to revise my own estimate of myself. But the twin of my new-born humility, paradoxical as it may seem, was a sense of dignity I had never known before. For if I found that I was a person of small consequence, I discovered at the same time that I was more nobly related than I had ever supposed. I had relatives and friends who were notable people by the old standards,—I had never been ashamed of my family,—but this George Washington, who died long before I was born, was like a king in greatness, and he and I were Fellow Citizens. There was a great deal about Fellow Citizens in the patriotic literature we read at this time; and I knew from my father how he was a Citizen, through the process of naturalization, and how I also was a citizen, by virtue of my relation to him. Undoubtedly I was a Fellow Citizen, and George Washington was another. It thrilled me to realize what sudden greatness had fallen on me; and at the same time it sobered me, as with a sense of responsibility. I strove to conduct myself as befitted a Fellow Citizen.

Before books came into my life, I was given to stargazing and daydreaming. When books were given me, I fell upon them as a glutton pounces on his meat after a period of enforced starvation. I lived with my nose in a book, and took no notice of the alternations of the sun and stars. But now, after the advent of George Washington and the American Revolution, I began to dream again. I strayed on the common after school instead of hurrying home to read. I hung on fence rails, my pet book forgotten under my arm, and gazed off to the yellow-streaked February sunset, and beyond, and beyond. I was no longer the central figure of my dreams; the dry weeds in the lane crackled beneath the tread of Heroes.

What more could America give a child? Ah, much more! As I read how the patriots planned the Revolution, and the women gave their sons to die in battle, and the heroes led to victory, and the rejoicing people set up the Republic, it dawned on me gradually what was meant by *my country*. The people all desiring noble things, and striving for them together, defying their oppressors, giving their lives for each other—all this it was that made *my country*. It was not a thing that I *understood*; I could not go home and tell Frieda about it, as I told her other things I learned at school. But I knew one could say "my country" and *feel* it, as one felt "God" or "myself." My teacher, my schoolmates, Miss Dillingham, George Washington himself could not mean more than I when they said "my country," after I had once felt it. For the Country was for all the Citizens, and *I was a Citizen*. And when we stood up to sing "America," I shouted the words with all my might. I was in very earnest proclaiming to the world my love for my new-found country.

> "I love thy rocks and rills,
> Thy woods and templed hills."

Boston Harbor, Crescent Beach, Chelsea Square—all was hallowed ground to me. As the day approached when the school was to hold exercises in honor of Washington's Birthday, the halls resounded at all hours with the strains of patriotic songs; and I, who was a model of the attentive pupil, more than once lost my place in the lesson as I strained to hear, through closed doors, some neighboring class rehearsing "The Star-Spangled Banner." If the doors happened to open, and the chorus broke out unveiled—

> "O! say, does that Star-Spangled Banner yet wave
> O'er the land of the free, and the home of the brave?"—

delicious tremors ran up and down my spine, and I was faint with suppressed enthusiasm.

Where had been my country until now? What flag had I loved? What heroes had I worshipped? The very names of these things had been unknown to me. Well I knew that Polotzk was not my country. It was *goluth*—exile. On many occasions in the year we prayed to God to lead us out of exile. The beautiful Passover service closed with the words, "Next year, may we be in Jerusalem." On childish lips, indeed, those words were no conscious aspiration; we repeated the Hebrew syllables after our elders, but without their hope and longing. Still not a child among us was too young to feel in his own flesh the lash of the oppressor. We knew what it was to be Jews in exile, from the spiteful treatment we suffered at the hands of the smallest urchin who crossed himself; and thence we knew that Israel had good reason to pray for deliverance. But the story of the Exodus was not history to me in the sense that the story of the American Revolution was. It was more like a glorious myth, a belief in which had the effect of cutting me off from the actual world, by linking me with a world of phantoms. Those moments of exaltation which the contemplation of the Biblical past afforded us, allowing us to call ourselves the children of princes, served but to tinge with a more poignant sense of disinheritance the long humdrum stretches of our life. In very truth we were a people without a country. Surrounded by mocking foes and detractors, it was difficult for me to realize the persons of my people's heroes or the events in which they moved. Except in moments of abstraction from the world around me, I scarcely understood that Jerusalem was an actual spot on the earth, where once the Kings of the Bible, real people, like my neighbors in Polotzk, ruled in puissant majesty. For the conditions of our civil life did not permit us to cultivate a spirit of nationalism. The freedom of worship that was grudgingly granted within the narrow limits of the Pale by no means included the right to set up openly any ideal of a Hebrew State, any hero other than the Czar. What we children picked up of our ancient political history was confused with the miraculous story of the Creation, with the supernatural legends and hazy associations of Bible lore. As to our future, we Jews in Polotzk had no national expectations; only a life-worn dreamer here and there hoped to die in Palestine. If Fetchke and I sang, with my father, first making sure of our audience, "Zion, Zion, Holy Zion, not forever is it lost," we did not really picture to ourselves Judæa restored.

So it came to pass that we did not know what *my country* could mean to a man. And as we had no country, so we had no flag to love. It was by no far-fetched symbolism that the banner of the House of Romanoff became the emblem of our latter-day bondage in our eyes. Even a child would know how to hate the flag that we were forced, on pain of severe penalties, to hoist above our house-tops, in celebration of the advent of one of our oppressors. And as it was with country and flag, so it was with heroes of war. We hated the uniform of the soldier, to the last brass button. On the person of a Gentile, it was the symbol of tyranny; on the person of a Jew, it was the emblem of shame.

So a little Jewish girl in Polotzk was apt to grow up hungry-minded and empty-hearted; and if, still in her outreaching youth, she was set down in a land of outspoken patriotism, she was likely to love her new country with a great love, and to embrace its heroes in a great worship. Naturalization, with us Russian Jews, may mean more than the adoption of the immigrant by America. It may mean the adoption of America by the immigrant.

On the day of the Washington celebration I recited a poem that I had composed in my enthusiasm. But "composed" is not the word. The process of putting on paper the sentiments that seethed in my soul was really very discomposing. I dug the words out of my heart, squeezed the rhymes out of my brain, forced the missing syllables out of their hiding-places in the dictionary. May I never again know such travail of the spirit as I endured during the fevered

days when I was engaged on the poem. It was not as if I wanted
to say that snow was white or grass was green. I could do that
without a dictionary. It was a question now of the loftiest sentiments, of the most abstract truths, the names of which were very
new in my vocabulary. It was necessary to use polysyllables, and
plenty of them; and where to find rhymes for such words as "tyranny," "freedom," and "justice," when you had less than two
years' acquaintance with English! The name I wished to celebrate
was the most difficult of all. Nothing but "Washington" rhymed
with "Washington." It was a most ambitious undertaking, but my
heart could find no rest till it had proclaimed itself to the world;
so I wrestled with my difficulties, and spared not ink, till inspiration perched on my penpoint, and my soul gave up its best.

When I had done, I was myself impressed with the length, gravity, and nobility of my poem. My father was overcome with emotion as he read it. His hands trembled as he held the paper to the
light, and the mist gathered in his eyes. My teacher, Miss Dwight,
was plainly astonished at my performance, and said many kind
things, and asked many questions; all of which I took very solemnly, like one who had been in the clouds and returned to earth
with a sign upon him. When Miss Dwight asked me to read my
poem to the class on the day of celebration, I readily consented. It
was not in me to refuse a chance to tell my schoolmates what I
thought of George Washington.

I was not a heroic figure when I stood up in front of the class
to pronounce the praises of the Father of his Country. Thin, pale,
and hollow, with a shadow of short black curls on my brow, and
the staring look of prominent eyes, I must have looked more frightened than imposing. My dress added no grace to my appearance.
"Plaids" were in fashion, and my frock was of a red-and-green
"plaid" that had a ghastly effect on my complexion. I hated it when
I thought of it; but on the great day I did not know I had any
dress on. Heels clapped together, and hands glued to my sides, I
lifted up my voice in praise of George Washington. It was not much
of a voice; like my hollow cheeks, it suggested consumption. My
pronunciation was faulty, my declamation flat. But I had the courage of my convictions. I was face to face with twoscore Fellow
Citizens, in clean blouses and extra frills. I must tell them what

George Washington had done for their country—for *our* country
—for me.

I can laugh now at the impossible metres, the grandiose phrases,
the verbose repetitions of my poem. Years ago I must have laughed
at it, when I threw my only copy into the wastebasket. The copy
I am now turning over was loaned me by Miss Dwight, who faithfully preserved it all these years, for the sake, no doubt, of what I
strove to express when I laboriously hitched together those dozen
and more ungraceful stanzas. But to the forty Fellow Citizens sitting in rows in front of me it was no laughing matter. Even the
bad boys sat in attitudes of attention, hypnotized by the solemnity
of my demeanor. If they got any inkling of what the hail of big
words was about, it must have been through occult suggestion. I
fixed their eighty eyes with my single stare, and gave it to them,
stanza after stanza, with such emphasis as the lameness of the lines
permitted.

> He whose courage, will, amazing bravery,
>   Did free his land from a despot's rule,
> From man's greatest evil, almost slavery,
>   And all that's taught in tyranny's school,
> Who gave his land its liberty,
>   Who was he?

> 'T was he who e'er will be our pride,
>   Immortal Washington,
> Who always did in truth confide.
>   We hail our Washington!

The best of the verses were no better than these, but the children
listened. They had to. Presently I gave them news, declaring that
Washington

> Wrote the famous Constitution; sacred's the hand
> That this blessed guide to man had given, which says, "One
> And all of mankind are alike, excepting none."

This was received in respectful silence, possibly because the
other Fellow Citizens were as hazy about historical facts as I at
this point. "Hurrah for Washington!" they understood, and "Three
cheers for the Red, White, and Blue!" was only to be expected on

Twoscore of My Fellow Citizens—Public School, Chelsea

that occasion. But there ran a special note through my poem—a thought that only Israel Rubinstein or Beckie Aronovitch could have fully understood, besides myself. For I made myself the spokesman of the "luckless sons of Abraham," saying—

> Then we weary Hebrew children at last found rest
> In the land where reigned Freedom, and like a nest
> To homeless birds your land proved to us, and therefore
> Will we gratefully sing your praise evermore.

The boys and girls who had never been turned away from any door because of their father's religion sat as if fascinated in their places. But they woke up and applauded heartily when I was done, following the example of Miss Dwight, who wore the happy face which meant that one of her pupils had done well.

The recitation was repeated, by request, before several other classes, and the applause was equally prolonged at each repetition. After the exercises I was surrounded, praised, questioned, and made much of, by teachers as well as pupils. Plainly I had not poured my praise of George Washington into deaf ears. The teachers asked me if anybody had helped me with the poem. The girls invariably asked, "Mary Antin, how could you think of all those words?" None of them thought of the dictionary!

If I had been satisfied with my poem in the first place, the applause with which it was received by my teachers and schoolmates convinced me that I had produced a very fine thing indeed. So the person, whoever it was,—perhaps my father—who suggested that my tribute to Washington ought to be printed, did not find me difficult to persuade. When I had achieved an absolutely perfect copy of my verses, at the expense of a dozen sheets of blue-ruled note paper, I crossed the Mystic River to Boston and boldly invaded Newspaper Row.

It never occurred to me to send my manuscript by mail. In fact, it has never been my way to send a delegate where I could go myself. Consciously or unconsciously, I have always acted on the motto of a wise man who was one of the dearest friends that Boston kept for me until I came. "Personal presence moves the world," said the great Dr. Hale; and I went in person to beard the editor in his armchair.

From the ferry slip to the offices of the "Boston Transcript" the

way was long, strange, and full of perils; but I kept resolutely on
up Hanover Street, being familiar with that part of my route, till I
came to a puzzling corner. There I stopped, utterly bewildered by
the tangle of streets, the roar of traffic, the giddy swarm of pedestrians. With the precious manuscript tightly clasped, I balanced myself on the curbstone, afraid to plunge into the boiling vortex of
the crossing. Every time I made a start, a clanging street car
snatched up the way. I could not even pick out my street; the
unobtrusive street signs were lost to my unpractised sight, in the
glaring confusion of store signs and advertisements. If I accosted a
pedestrian to ask the way, I had to speak several times before I was
heard. Jews, hurrying by with bearded chins on their bosoms and
eyes intent, shrugged their shoulders at the name "Transcript," and
shrugged till they were out of sight. Italians sauntering behind their
fruit carts answered my inquiry with a lift of the head that made
their earrings gleam, and a wave of the hand that referred me to all
four points of the compass at once. I was trying to catch the eye
of the tall policeman who stood grandly in the middle of the
crossing, a stout pillar around which the waves of traffic broke,
when deliverance bellowed in my ear.

"Herald, Globe, Record, *Tra-avel-er!* Eh? Whatcher want, sis?"
The tall newsboy had to stoop to me. "Transcript? Sure!" And in
half a twinkling he had picked me out a paper from his bundle.
When I explained to him, he good-naturedly tucked the paper in
again, piloted me across, unravelled the end of Washington Street
for me, and with much pointing out of landmarks, headed me for
my destination, my nose seeking the spire of the Old South
Church.

I found the "Transcript" building a waste of corridors tunnelled
by a maze of staircases. On the glazed-glass doors were many signs
with the names or nicknames of many persons: "City Editor";
"Beggars and Peddlers not Allowed." The nameless world not included in these categories was warned off, forbidden to be or do:
"Private—No Admittance"; "Don't Knock." And the various in-
hospitable legends on the doors and walls were punctuated by frequent cuspidors on the floor. There was no sign anywhere of the
welcome which I, as an author, expected to find in the home of a
newspaper.

I was descending from the top story to the street for the seventh time, trying to decide what kind of editor a patriotic poem belonged to, when an untidy boy carrying broad paper streamers and whistling shrilly, in defiance of an express prohibition on the wall, bustled through the corridor and left a door ajar. I slipped in behind him, and found myself in a room full of editors.

I was a little surprised at the appearance of the editors. I had imagined my editor would look like Mr. Jones, the principal of my school, whose coat was always buttoned, and whose finger nails were beautiful. These people were in shirt sleeves, and they smoked, and they did n't politely turn in their revolving chairs when I came in, and ask, "What can I do for you?"

The room was noisy with typewriters, and nobody heard my "Please, can you tell me." At last one of the machines stopped, and the operator thought he heard something in the pause. He looked up through his own smoke. I guess he thought he saw something, for he stared. It troubled me a little to have him stare so. I realized suddenly that the hand in which I carried my manuscript was moist, and I was afraid it would make marks on the paper. I held out the manuscript to the editor, explaining that it was a poem about George Washington, and would he please print it in the "Transcript."

There was something queer about that particular editor. The way he stared and smiled made me feel about eleven inches high, and my voice kept growing smaller and smaller as I neared the end of my speech.

At last he spoke, laying down his pipe, and sitting back at his ease.

"So you have brought us a poem, my child?"

"It's about George Washington," I repeated impressively. "Don't you want to read it?"

"I should be delighted, my dear, but the fact is—"

He did not take my paper. He stood up and called across the room.

"Say, Jack! here is a young lady who has brought us a poem— about George Washington.—Wrote it yourself, my dear?—Wrote it all herself. What shall we do with her?"

Mr. Jack came over, and another man. My editor made me repeat my business, and they all looked interested, but nobody took my paper from me. They put their hands into their pockets, and my hand kept growing clammier all the time. The three seemed to be consulting, but I could not understand what they said, or why Mr. Jack laughed.

A fourth man, who had been writing busily at a desk near by, broke in on the consultation.

"That 's enough, boys," he said, "that 's enough. Take the young lady to Mr. Hurd."

Mr. Hurd, it was found, was away on a vacation, and of several other editors in several offices, to whom I was referred, none proved to be the proper editor to take charge of a poem about George Washington. At last an elderly editor suggested that as Mr. Hurd would be away for some time, I would do well to give up the "Transcript" and try the "Herald," across the way.

A little tired by my wanderings, and bewildered by the complexity of the editorial system, but still confident about my mission, I picked my way across Washington Street and found the "Herald" offices. Here I had instant good luck. The first editor I addressed took my paper and invited me to a seat. He read my poem much more quickly than I could myself, and said it was very nice, and asked me some questions, and made notes on a slip of paper which he pinned to my manuscript. He said he would have my piece printed very soon, and would send me a copy of the issue in which it appeared. As I was going, I could not help giving the editor my hand, although I had not experienced any handshaking in Newspaper Row. I felt that as author and editor we were on a very pleasant footing, and I gave him my hand in token of comradeship.

I had regained my full stature and something over, during this cordial interview, and when I stepped out into the street and saw the crowd intently studying the bulletin board I swelled out of all proportion. For I told myself that I, Mary Antin, was one of the inspired brotherhood who made newspapers so interesting. I did not know whether my poem would be put upon the bulletin board; but at any rate, it would be in the paper, with my name at the bottom, like my story about "Snow" in Miss Dillingham's school journal. And all these people in the streets, and more, thousands of people—all Boston!—would read my poem, and learn my name, and wonder who I was. I smiled to myself in delicious amusement when a man deliberately put me out of his path, as I dreamed my way through the jostling crowd; if he only *knew* whom he was treating so unceremoniously!

When the paper with my poem in it arrived, the whole house pounced upon it at once. I was surprised to find that my verses were not all over the front page. The poem was a little hard to find, if anything, being tucked away in the middle of the voluminous sheet. But when we found it, it looked wonderful, just like real poetry, not at all as if somebody we knew had written it. It occupied a gratifying amount of space, and was introduced by a flattering biographical sketch of the author—the *author!*—the material for which the friendly editor had artfully drawn from me during that happy interview. And my name, as I had prophesied, was at the bottom!

When the excitement in the house had subsided, my father took all the change out of the cash drawer and went to buy up the "Herald." He did not count the pennies. He just bought "Heralds," all he could lay his hands on, and distributed them gratis to all our friends, relatives, and acquaintances; to all who could read, and to some who could not. For weeks he carried a clipping from the "Herald" in his breast pocket, and few were the occasions when he did not manage to introduce it into the conversation. He treasured that clipping as for years he had treasured the letters I wrote him from Polotzk.

Although my father bought up most of the issue containing my poem, a few hundred copies were left to circulate among the general public, enough to spread the flame of my patriotic ardor and to enkindle a thousand sluggish hearts. Really, there was something more solemn than vanity in my satisfaction. Pleased as I was with my notoriety—and nobody but I knew how exceedingly pleased —I had a sober feeling about it all. I enjoyed being praised and admired and envied; but what gave a divine flavor to my happiness was the idea that I had publicly borne testimony to the goodness of my exalted hero, to the greatness of my adopted country. I did not discount the homage of Arlington Street, because I did not properly rate the intelligence of its population. I took the admiration of my schoolmates without a grain of salt; it was just so much honey to me. I could not know that what made me great in the eyes of my neighbors was that "there was a piece about me in the paper"; it mattered very little to them what the "piece" was about. I thought they really admired my sentiments. On the street, in the schoolyard, I was pointed out. The people said, "That's Mary Antin. She had her name in the paper." *I* thought they said, "This is she who loves her country and worships George Washington."

To repeat, I was well aware that I was something of a celebrity, and took all possible satisfaction in the fact; yet I gave my schoolmates no occasion to call me "stuck-up." My vanity did not express itself in strutting or wagging the head. I played tag and puss-in-the-corner in the schoolyard, and did everything that was comradelike. But in the schoolroom I conducted myself gravely, as befitted one who was preparing for the noble career of a poet.

I am forgetting Lizzie McDee. I am trying to give the impression that I behaved with at least outward modesty during my schoolgirl triumphs, whereas Lizzie could testify that she knew Mary Antin as a vain boastful, curly-headed little Jew. For I had a special style of deportment for Lizzie. If there was any girl in the school besides me who could keep near the top of the class all the year through, and give bright answers when the principal or the school committee popped sudden questions, and write rhymes that almost always rhymed, *I* was determined that that ambitious person should not soar unduly in her own estimation. So I took care to show Lizzie all my poetry, and when she showed me hers I did not admire it too warmly. Lizzie, as I have already said, was in a Sunday-school mood even on week days; her verses all had morals. My poems were about the crystal snow, and the ocean blue, and sweet spring, and fleecy clouds; when I tried to drag in a moral it kicked so that the music of my lines went out in a groan. So I had a sweet revenge when Lizzie, one day, volunteered to bolster up the eloquence of Mr. Jones, the principal, who was lecturing the class for bad behavior, by comparing the bad boy in the schoolroom to the rotten apple that spoils the barrelful. The groans, coughs, a-hem's, feet shufflings, and paper pellets that filled the room as Saint Elizabeth sat down, even in the principal's presence, were sweet balm to my smart of envy; I did n't care if I did n't know how to moralize.

When my teacher had visitors I was aware that I was the show pupil of the class. I was always made to recite, my compositions were passed around, and often I was called up on the platform—oh, climax of exaltation!—to be interviewed by the distinguished strangers; while the class took advantage of the teacher's distraction, to hold forbidden intercourse on matters not prescribed in the curriculum. When I returned to my seat, after such public audience with the great, I looked to see if Lizzie McDee was taking notice; and Lizzie, who was a generous soul, her Sunday-school airs notwithstanding, generally smiled, and I forgave her her rhymes.

Not but what I paid a price for my honors. With all my self-possession I had a certain capacity for shyness. Even when I arose to recite before the customary audience of my class I suffered from incipient stage fright, and my voice trembled over the first few words. When visitors were in the room I was even more troubled; and when I was made the special object of their attention my triumph was marred by acute distress. If I was called up to speak to the visitors, forty pairs of eyes pricked me in the back as I went. I stumbled in the aisle, and knocked down things that were not at all in my way; and my awkwardness increasing my embarrassment I would gladly have changed places with Lizzie or the bad boy in the back row; anything, only to be less conspicuous. When I found myself shaking hands with an august School-Committeeman, or a teacher from New York, the remnants of my self-possession vanished in awe; and it was in a very husky voice that I repeated, as I was asked, my name, lineage, and personal history. On the whole, I do not think that the School-Committeeman found a very forward creature in the solemn-faced little girl with the tight curls and the terrible red-and-green "plaid."

These awful audiences did not always end with the handshaking. Sometimes the great personages asked me to write to them, and exchanged addresses with me. Some of these correspondences continued through years, and were the source of much pleasure, on one side at least. And Arlington Street took notice when I received letters with important-looking or aristocratic-looking letterheads. Lizzie McDee also took notice. *I* saw to that.

CHAPTER XII

MIRACLES

IT WAS NOT ALWAYS in admiration that the finger was pointed at me. One day I found myself the centre of an excited group in the middle of the schoolyard, with a dozen girls interrupting each other to express their disapproval of me. For I had coolly told them, in answer to a question, that I did not believe in God.

How had I arrived at such a conviction? How had I come, from praying and fasting and Psalm-singing, to extreme impiety? Alas! my backsliding had cost me no travail of spirit. Always weak in my faith, playing at sanctity as I played at soldiers, just as I was in the mood or not, I had neglected my books of devotion and given myself up to profane literature at the first opportunity, in Vitebsk; and I never took up my prayer book again. On my return to Polotzk, America loomed so near that my imagination was fully occupied, and I did not revive the secret experiments with which I used to test the nature and intention of Deity. It was more to me that I was going to America than that I might not be going to Heaven. And when we joined my father, and I saw that he did not wear the sacred fringes, and did not put on the phylacteries and pray, I was neither surprised nor shocked, remembering the Sabbath night when he had with his own hand turned out the lamp. When I saw him go out to work on Sabbath exactly as on a week day, I understood why God had not annihilated me with his lightnings that time when I purposely carried something in my pocket on Sabbath: there was no God, and there was no sin. And I ran out to play, pleased to find that I was free, like other little girls in the street, instead of being hemmed about with prohibitions and obligations at every step. And yet if the golden truth of Judaism had not been handed me in the motley rags of formalism, I might not have been so ready to put away my religion.

It was Rachel Goldstein who provoked my avowal of atheism. She asked if I was n't going to stay out of school during Passover, and I said no. Was n't I a Jew? she wanted to know. No, I was n't; I was a Freethinker. What was that? I did n't believe in God. Rachel was horrified. Why, Kitty Maloney believed in God, and Kitty was only a Catholic! She appealed to Kitty.

"Kitty Maloney! Come over here. Don't you believe in God?—There, now, Mary Antin!—Mary Antin says she does n't believe in God!"

Rachel Goldstein's horror is duplicated. Kitty Maloney, who used to mock Rachel's Jewish accent, instantly becomes her voluble ally, and proceeds to annihilate me by plying me with crucial questions.

"You don't believe in God? Then who made you, Mary Antin?"

"Nature made me."

"*Nature* made you! What's that?"

"It's—everything. It's the trees—no, it's what makes the trees grow. *That 's* what it is."

"But *God* made the trees, Mary Antin," from Rachel and Kitty in chorus. "Maggie O'Reilly! Listen to Mary Antin. She says there is n't any God. She says the trees made her!"

Rachel and Kitty and Maggie, Sadie and Annie and Beckie, made a circle around me, and pressed me with questions, and mocked me, and threatened me with hell flames and utter extinction. I held my ground against them all obstinately enough, though my argument was exceedingly lame. I glibly repeated phrases I had heard my father use, but I had no real understanding of his atheistic doctrines. I had been surprised into this dispute. I had no spontaneous interest in the subject; my mind was occupied with other things. But as the number of my opponents grew, and I saw how unanimously they condemned me, my indifference turned into a heat of indignation. The actual point at issue was as little as ever to me, but I perceived that a crowd of Free Americans were disputing the right of a Fellow Citizen to have any kind of God she chose. I knew, from my father's teaching, that this persecution was contrary to the Constitution of the United States, and I held my ground as befitted the defender of a cause. George Washington would not have treated me as Rachel Goldstein and Kitty Maloney were doing! "This is a free country," I reminded them in the middle of the argument.

The excitement in the yard amounted to a toy riot. When the school bell rang and the children began to file in, I stood out there as long as any of my enemies remained, although it was my habit to go to my room very promptly. And as the foes of American Liberty crowded and pushed in the line, whispering to those who had not heard that a heretic had been discovered in their midst, the teacher who kept the line in the corridor was obliged to scold and pull the noisy ones into order; and Sadie Cohen told her, in tones of awe, what the commotion was about.

Miss Bland waited till the children had filed in before she asked me, in a tone encouraging confidence, to give my version of the story. This I did, huskily but fearlessly; and the teacher, who was a woman of tact, did not smile or commit herself in any way. She was sorry that the children had been rude to me, but she thought they would not trouble me any more if I let the subject drop. She made me understand, somewhat as Miss Dillingham had done on the occasion of my whispering during prayer, that it was proper American conduct to avoid religious arguments on school territory. I felt honored by this private initiation into the doctrine of the separation of Church and State, and I went to my seat with a good deal of dignity, my alarm about the safety of the Constitution allayed by the teacher's calmness.

This is not so strictly the story of the second generation that I may not properly give a brief account of how it fared with my mother when my father undertook to purge his house of superstition. The process of her emancipation, it is true, was not obvious to me at the time, but what I observed of her outward conduct has been interpreted by my subsequent experience; so that to-day I understand how it happens that all the year round my mother keeps the same day of rest as her Gentile neighbors; but when the ram's horn blows on the Day of Atonement, calling upon Israel to cleanse its heart from sin and draw nearer to the God of its fathers, her soul is stirred as of old, and she needs must join in the ancient service. It means, I have come to know, that she has dropped the husk and retained the kernel of Judaism; but years were required for this process of instinctive selection.

My father, in his ambition to make Americans of us, was rather headlong and strenuous in his methods. To my mother, on the eve of departure for the New World, he wrote boldly that progressive Jews in America did not spend their days in praying; and he urged her to leave her wig in Polotzk, as a first step of progress. My mother, like the majority of women in the Pale, had all her life taken her religion on authority; so she was only fulfilling her duty to her husband when she took his hint, and set out upon her journey in her own hair. Not that it was done without reluctance; the Jewish faith in her was deeply rooted, as in the best of Jews it always is. The law of the Fathers was binding to her, and the outward symbols of obedience inseparable from the spirit. But the breath of revolt against orthodox externals was at this time beginning to reach us in Polotzk from the greater world, notably from America. Sons whose parents had impoverished themselves by paying the fine for non-appearance for military duty, in order to save their darlings from the inevitable sins of violated Judaism while in the service, sent home portraits of themselves with their faces shaved; and the grieved old fathers and mothers, after offering up special prayers for the renegades, and giving charity in their name, exhibited the significant portraits on their parlor tables. My mother's own nephew went no farther than Vilna, ten hours' journey from Polotzk, to learn to cut his beard; and even within our town limits young women of education were beginning to reject the wig after marriage. A notorious example was the beautiful daughter of Lozhe the Rav, who was not restrained by her father's conspicuous relation to Judaism from exhibiting her lovely black curls like a maiden; and it was a further sign of the times that the rav did not disown his daughter. What wonder, then, that my poor mother, shaken by these foreshadowings of revolution in our midst, and by the express authority of her husband, gave up the emblem of matrimonial chastity with but a passing struggle? Considering how the heavy burdens which she had borne from childhood had never allowed her time to think for herself at all, but had obliged her always to tread blindly in the beaten paths, I think it greatly to her credit that in her puzzling situation she did not lose her poise entirely. Bred to submission, submit she must; and when she perceived a conflict of authorities, she prepared to accept the new order of things under which her children's future was to be formed; wherein she showed her native adaptability, the readiness to fall into line, which is one of the most charming traits of her gentle, self-effacing nature.

My father gave my mother very little time to adjust herself. He was only three years from the Old World with its settled prejudices. Considering his education, he had thought out a good deal for himself, but his line of thinking had not as yet brought him to include woman in the intellectual emancipation for which he himself had been so eager even in Russia. This was still in the day when he was astonished to learn that women had written books—had used their minds, their imaginations, unaided. He still rated the mental capacity of the average woman as only a little above that of the cattle she tended. He held it to be a wife's duty to follow her husband in all things. He could do all the thinking for the family, he believed; and being convinced that to hold to the outward forms of orthodox Judaism was to be hampered in the race for Americanization, he did not hesitate to order our family life on unorthodox lines. There was no conscious despotism in this; it was only making manly haste to realize an ideal the nobility of which there was no one to dispute.

My mother, as we know, had not the initial impulse to depart from ancient usage that my father had in his habitual scepticism. He had always been a nonconformist in his heart; she bore lovingly the yoke of prescribed conduct. Individual freedom, to him, was the only tolerable condition of life; to her it was confusion. My mother, therefore, gradually divested herself, at my father's bidding, of the mantle of orthodox observance; but the process cost her many a pang, because the fabric of that venerable garment was interwoven with the fabric of her soul.

My father did not attempt to touch the fundamentals of her faith. He certainly did not forbid her to honor God by loving her neighbor, which is perhaps not far from being the whole of Judaism. If his loud denials of the existence of God influenced her to reconsider her creed, it was merely an incidental result of the freedom of expression he was so eager to practise, after his life of enforced hypocrisy. As the opinions of a mere woman on matters so abstract as religion did not interest him in the least, he counted it no particular triumph if he observed that my mother weakened in her faith as the years went by. He allowed her to keep a Jewish kitchen as long as she pleased, but he did not want us children to refuse invitations to the table of our Gentile neighbors. He would have no bar to our social intercourse with the world around us, for only by freely sharing the life of our neighbors could we come into our full inheritance of American freedom and opportunity. On the holy days he bought my mother a ticket for the synagogue, but the children he sent to school. On Sabbath eve my mother might light the consecrated candles, but he kept the store open until Sunday morning. My mother might believe and worship as she pleased, up to the point where her orthodoxy began to interfere with the American progress of the family.

The price that all of us paid for this disorganization of our family life has been levied on every immigrant Jewish household where the first generation clings to the traditions of the Old World, while the second generation leads the life of the New. Nothing more pitiful could be written in the annals of the Jews; nothing more inevitable; nothing more hopeful. Hopeful, yes; alike for the Jew and for the country that has given him shelter. For Israel is not the only party that has put up a forfeit in this contest. The nations may well sit by and watch the struggle, for humanity has a stake in it. I say this, whose life has borne witness, whose heart is heavy with revelations it has not made. And I speak for thousands; oh, for thousands!

My gray hairs are too few for me to let these pages trespass the limit I have set myself. That part of my life which contains the climax of my personal drama I must leave to my grandchildren to record. My father might speak and tell how, in time, he discovered that in his first violent rejection of everything old and established he cast from him much that he afterwards missed. He might tell to what extent he later retraced his steps, seeking to recover what he had learned to value anew; how it fared with his avowed irreligion when put to the extreme test; to what, in short, his emancipation amounted. And he, like myself, would speak for thousands. My grandchildren, for all I know, may have a graver task than I have set them. Perhaps they may have to testify that the faith of Israel is a heritage that no heir in the direct line has the power to alienate from his successors. Even I, with my limited perspective, think it doubtful if the conversion of the Jew to any alien belief or disbelief is ever thoroughly accomplished. What positive affirmation of the persistence of Judaism in the blood my descendants may have to make, I may not be present to hear.

It would be superfluous to state that none of these hints and prophecies troubled me at the time when I horrified the schoolyard by denying the existence of God, on the authority of my father; and defended my right to my atheism, on the authority of the Constitution. I considered myself absolutely, eternally, delightfully emancipated from the yoke of indefensible superstitions. I was wild with indignation and pity when I remembered how my poor brother had been cruelly tormented because he did not want to sit in heder and learn what was after all false or useless. I knew now why poor Reb' Lebe had been unable to answer my questions; it was because the truth was not whispered outside America. I was very much in love with my enlightenment, and eager for opportunities to give proof of it.

It was Miss Dillingham, she who helped me in so many ways, who unconsciously put me to an early test, the result of which gave me a shock that I did not get over for many a day. She invited me to tea one day, and I came in much trepidation. It was my first entrance into a genuine American household; my first meal at a Gentile—yes, a Christian—board. Would I know how to behave properly? I do not know whether I betrayed my anxiety; I am certain only that I was all eyes and ears, that nothing should escape me which might serve to guide me. This, after all, was a normal state for me to be in, so I suppose I looked natural, no matter how much I stared. I had been accustomed to consider my table manners irreproachable, but America was not Polotzk, as my father was ever saying; so I proceeded very cautiously with my spoons and forks. I was cunning enough to try to conceal my uncertainty; by being just a little bit slow, I did not get to any given spoon until the others at table had shown me which it was.

All went well, until a platter was passed with a kind of meat that was strange to me. Some mischievous instinct told me that it was ham—forbidden food; and I, the liberal, the free, was afraid to touch it! I had a terrible moment of surprise, mortification, self-contempt; but I helped myself to a slice of ham, nevertheless, and hung my head over my plate to hide my confusion. I was furious with myself for my weakness. I to be afraid of a pink piece of pig's flesh, who had defied at least two religions in defence of free thought! And I began to reduce my ham to indivisible atoms, determined to eat more of it than anybody at the table.

Alas! I learned that to eat in defence of principles was not so easy as to talk. I ate, but only a newly abnegated Jew can understand with what squirming, what protesting of the inner man, what exquisite abhorrence of myself. That Spartan boy who allowed the stolen fox hidden in his bosom to consume his vitals rather than be detected in the theft, showed no such miracle of self-control as did I, sitting there at my friend's tea-table, eating unjewish meat.

And to think that so ridiculous a thing as a scrap of meat should be the symbol and test of things so august! To think that in the mental life of a half-grown child should be reflected the struggles and triumphs of ages! Over and over and over again I discover that I am a wonderful thing, being human; that I am the image of the universe, being myself; that I am the repository of all the wisdom in the world, being alive and sane at the beginning of this twentieth century. The heir of the ages am I, and all that has been is in me, and shall continue to be in my immortal self.

CHAPTER XIII

A CHILD'S PARADISE

ALL THIS WHILE that I was studying and exploring in the border-land between the old life and the new; leaping at conclusions, and sometimes slipping; finding inspiration in common things, and interpretations in dumb things; eagerly scaling the ladder of learning, my eyes on star-diademmed peaks of ambition; building up friendships that should support my youth and enrich my womanhood; learning to think much of myself, and much more of my world,— while I was steadily gathering in my heritage, sowed in the dim past, and ripened in the sun of my own day, what was my sister doing?

Why, what she had always done: keeping close to my mother's side on the dreary marches of a humdrum life; sensing sweet gardens of forbidden joy, but never turning from the path of duty. I cannot believe but that her sacrifices tasted as dust and ashes to her at times; for Frieda was a mere girl, whose childhood, on the whole, had been gray, while her appetite for happy things was as great as any normal girl's. She had a fine sense for what was best in the life about her, though she could not articulate her appreciation. She longed to possess the good things, but her position in the family forbidding possession, she developed a talent for vicarious enjoyment which I never in this life hope to imitate. And her simple mind did not busy itself with self-analysis. She did not even know why she was happy; she thought life was good to her. Still, there must have been moments when she perceived that the finer things were not in themselves unattainable, but were kept from her by a social tyranny. This I can only surmise, as in our daily intercourse she never gave a sign of discontent.

We continued to have part of our life in common for some time after she went to work. We formed ourselves into an evening school, she and I and the two youngsters, for the study of English and arithmetic. As soon as the supper dishes were put away, we gathered around the kitchen table, with books borrowed from school, and pencils supplied by my father with eager willingness. I

was the teacher, the others the diligent pupils; and the earnestness
with which we labored was worthy of the great things we meant
to achieve. Whether the results were commensurate with our efforts
I cannot say. I only know that Frieda's cheeks flamed with the
excitement of reading English monosyllables; and her eyes shone
like stars on a moonless night when I explained to her how she and
I and George Washington were Fellow Citizens together.

Inspired by our studious evenings, what Frieda Antin would not
be glad to sit all day bent over the needle, that the family should
keep on its feet, and Mary continue at school? The morning ride
on the ferryboat, when spring winds dimpled the river, may have
stirred her heart with nameless longings, but when she took her
place at the machine her lot was glorified to her, and she wanted
to sing; for the girls, the foreman, the boss, all talked about Mary
Antin, whose poems were printed in an American newspaper.
Wherever she went on her humble business, she was sure to hear
her sister's name. For, with characteristic loyalty, the whole Jewish
community claimed kinship with me, simply because I was a Jew;
and they made much of my small triumphs, and pointed to me
with pride, just as they always do when a Jew distinguishes himself
in any worthy way. Frieda, going home from work at sunset, when
rosy buds beaded the shining stems, may have felt the weariness of
those who toil for bread; but when we opened our books after
supper, her spirit revived afresh, and it was only when the lamp
began to smoke that she thought of taking rest.

At bedtime she and I chatted as we used to do when we were
little girls in Polotzk; only now, instead of closing our eyes to see
imaginary wonders, according to a bedtime game of ours, we exchanged anecdotes about the marvellous adventures of our American life. My contributions on these occasions were boastful
accounts, I have no doubt, of what I did at school, and in the
company of school-committee men, editors, and other notables;
and Frieda's delight in my achievements was the very flower of her
fine sympathy. As formerly, when I had been naughty and I invited
her to share in my repentance, she used to join me in spiritual
humility and solemnly dedicate herself to a better life; so now,
when I was full of pride and ambition, she, too, felt the crown on
her brows, and heard the applause of future generations murmuring
in her ear. And so partaking of her sister's glory, what Frieda Antin

would not say that her portion was sufficient reward for a youth of toil?

I did not, like my sister, earn my bread in those days; but let us say that I earned my salt, by sweeping, scrubbing, and scouring, on Saturdays, when there was no school. My mother's housekeeping was necessarily irregular, as she was pretty constantly occupied in the store; so there was enough for us children to do to keep the bare rooms shining. Even here Frieda did the lion's share; it used to take me all Saturday to accomplish what Frieda would do with half a dozen turns of her capable hands. I did not like housework, but I loved order; so I polished windows with a will, and even got some fun out of scrubbing, by laying out the floor in patterns and tracing them all around the room in a lively flurry of soapsuds.

There is a joy that comes from doing common things well, especially if they seem hard to us. When I faced a day's housework I was half paralyzed with a sense of inability, and I wasted precious minutes walking around it, to see what a very hard task I had. But having pitched in and conquered, it gave me an exquisite pleasure to survey my work. My hair tousled and my dress tucked up, streaked arms bare to the elbow, I would step on my heels over the damp, clean boards, and pass my hand over chair rounds and table legs, to prove that no dust was left. I could not wait to put my dress in order before running out into the street to see how my windows shone. Every workman who carries a dinner pail has these moments of keen delight in the product of his drudgery. Men of genius, likewise, in their hours of relaxation from their loftier tasks, prove this universal rule. I know a man who fills a chair at a great university. I have seen him hold a roomful of otherwise restless youths spellbound for an hour, while he discoursed about the respective inhabitants of the earth and sea at a time when nothing walked on fewer than four legs. And I have seen this scholar, his ponderous tomes shelved for a space, turning over and over with cherishing hands a letter-box that he had made out of card-board and paste, and exhibiting it proudly to his friends. For the hand was the first instrument of labor, that distinctive accomplishment by which man finally raised himself above his cousins, the lower animals; and a respect for the work of the hand survives as an instinct in all of us.

The stretch of weeks from June to September, when the schools were closed, would have been hard to fill in had it not been for the public library. At first I made myself a calendar of the vacation months, and every morning I tore off a day, and comforted myself with the decreasing number of vacation days. But after I discovered the public library I was not impatient for the reopening of school. The library did not open till one o'clock in the afternoon, and each reader was allowed to take out only one book at a time. Long before one o'clock I was to be seen on the library steps, waiting for the door of paradise to open. I spent hours in the reading-room, pleased with the atmosphere of books, with the order and quiet of the place, so unlike anything on Arlington Street. The sense of these things permeated my consciousness even when I was absorbed in a book, just as the rustle of pages turned and the tiptoe tread of the librarian reached my ear, without distracting my attention. Anything so wonderful as a library had never been in my life. It was even better than school in some ways. One could read and read, and learn and learn, as fast as one knew how, without being obliged to stop for stupid little girls and inattentive little boys to catch up with the lesson. When I went home from the library I had a book under my arm; and I would finish it before the library opened next day, no matter till what hours of the night I burned my little lamp.

What books did I read so diligently? Pretty nearly everything that came to my hand. I dare say the librarian helped me select my books, but, curiously enough, I do not remember. Something must have directed me, for I read a great many of the books that are written for children. Of these I remember with the greatest delight Louisa Alcott's stories. A less attractive series of books was of the Sunday School type. In volume after volume a very naughty little girl by the name of Lulu was always going into tempers, that her father might have opportunity to lecture her and point to her an-gelic little sister, Gracie, as an example of what she should be; after which they all felt better and prayed. Next to Louisa Alcott's books in my esteem were boys' books of adventure, many of them by Horatio Alger; and I read all, I suppose, of the Rollo books, by Jacob Abbott.

But that was not all. I read every kind of printed rubbish that came into the house, by design or accident. A weekly story paper of a worse than worthless character, that circulated widely in our neighborhood because subscribers were rewarded with a premium of a diamond ring, warranted I don't know how many karats, occupied me for hours. The stories in this paper resembled, in breathlessness of plot, abundance of horrors, and improbability of characters, the things I used to read in Vitebsk. The text was illustrated by frequent pictures, in which the villain generally had his hands on the heroine's throat, while the hero was bursting in through a graceful drapery to the rescue of his beloved. If a bundle came into the house wrapped in a stained old newspaper, I laboriously smoothed out the paper and read it through. I enjoyed it all, and found fault with nothing that I read. And, as in the case of the Vitebsk readings, I cannot find that I suffered any harm. Of course, reading so many better books, there came a time when the diamond-ring story paper disgusted me; but in the beginning my appetite for print was so enormous that I could let nothing pass through my hands unread, while my taste was so crude that nothing printed could offend me.

Good reading matter came into the house from one other source besides the library. The Yiddish newspapers of the day were excellent, and my father subscribed to the best of them. Since that time Yiddish journalism has sadly degenerated, through imitation of the vicious "yellow journals" of the American press.

There was one book in the library over which I pored very often, and that was the encyclopædia. I turned usually to the names of famous people, beginning, of course, with George Washington. Oftenest of all I read the biographical sketches of my favorite authors, and felt that the worthies must have been glad to die just to have their names and histories printed out in the book of fame. It seemed to me the apotheosis of glory to be even briefly mentioned in an encyclopædia. And there grew in me an enormous ambition that devoured all my other ambitions, which was no less than this: that I should live to know that after my death my name would surely be printed in the encyclopædia. It was such a prodigious thing to expect that I kept the idea a secret even from myself, just letting it lie where it sprouted, in an unexplored corner of my busy brain. But it grew on me in spite of myself, till finally I could not resist the temptation to study out the exact place in the encyclopædia where my name would belong. I saw that it would come not far from "Alcott, Louisa M."; and I covered my face with my hands, to hide the silly, baseless joy in it. I practised saying my name in the encyclopædic form, "Antin, Mary"; and I realized that it sounded chopped off, and wondered if I might not annex a middle initial. I wanted to ask my teacher about it, but I was afraid I might betray my reasons. For, infatuated though I was with the idea of the greatness I might live to attain, I knew very well that thus far my claims to posthumous fame were ridiculously unfounded, and I did not want to be laughed at for my vanity.

Spirit of all childhood! Forgive me, forgive me, for so lightly betraying a child's dream-secrets. I that smile so scoffingly to-day at the unsophisticated child that was myself, have I found any nobler thing in life than my own longing to be noble? Would I not rather be consumed by ambitions that can never be realized than live in stupid acceptance of my neighbor's opinion of me? The statue in the public square is less a portrait of a mortal individual than a symbol of the immortal aspiration of humanity. So do not laugh at the little boy playing at soldiers, if he tells you he is going to hew the world into good behavior when he gets to be a man. And do, by all means, write my name in the book of fame, saying, She was one who aspired. For that, in condensed form, is the story of the lives of the great.

Summer days are long, and the evenings, we know, are as long as the lamp-wick. So, with all my reading, I had time to play; and, with all my studiousness, I had the will to play. My favorite playmates were boys. It was but mild fun to play theatre in Bessie Finklestein's back yard, even if I had leading parts, which I made impressive by recitations in Russian, no word of which was intelligible to my audience. It was far better sport to play hide-and-seek with the boys, for I enjoyed the use of my limbs—what there was of them. I was so often reproached and teased for being little, that it gave me great satisfaction to beat a five-foot boy to the goal.

Once a great, hulky colored boy, who was the torment of the neighborhood, treated me roughly while I was playing on the street. My father, determined to teach the rascal a lesson for once, had him arrested and brought to court. The boy was locked up overnight, and he emerged from his brief imprisonment with a respect for the rights and persons of his neighbors. But the moral of this incident lies not herein. What interested me more than my revenge on a bully was what I saw of the way in which justice was actually administered in the United States. Here we were gathered in the little courtroom, bearded Arlington Street against wool-headed Arlington Street; accused and accuser, witnesses, sympathizers, sight-seers, and all. Nobody cringed, nobody was bullied, nobody lied who did n't want to. We were all free, and all treated equally, just as it said in the Constitution! The evil-doer was actually punished, and not the victim, as might very easily happen in a similar case in Russia. "Liberty and justice for all." Three cheers for the Red, White, and Blue!

There was one occasion in the week when I was ever willing to put away my book, no matter how entrancing were its pages. That was on Saturday night, when Bessie Finklestein called for me; and Bessie and I, with arms entwined, called for Sadie Rabinowitch; and Bessie and Sadie and I, still further entwined, called for Annie Reilly; and Bessie, etc., etc., inextricably wound up, marched up Broadway, and took possession of all we saw, heard, guessed, or desired, from end to end of that main thoroughfare of Chelsea.

Parading all abreast, as many as we were, only breaking ranks to let people pass; leaving the imprints of our noses and fingers on plate-glass windows ablaze with electric lights and alluring with display; inspecting tons of cheap candy, to find a few pennies' worth of the most enduring kind, the same to be sucked and chewed by the company, turn and turn about, as we continued our promenade; loitering wherever a crowd gathered, or running for a block or so to cheer on the fire-engine or police ambulance; getting into everybody's way, and just keeping clear of serious mischief,— we were only girls,— we enjoyed ourselves as only children can whose fathers keep a basement grocery store, whose mothers do their own washing, and whose sisters operate a machine for five dollars a week. Had we been boys, I suppose Bessie and Sadie and the rest of us would have been a "gang," and would have popped into the Chinese laundry to tease "Chinky Chinaman," and been chased by the "cops" from comfortable doorsteps, and had a "bully" time of it. Being what we were, we called ourselves a "set," and we had a "lovely" time, as people who passed us on Broadway could not fail to see. And hear. For we were at the giggling age, and Broadway on Saturday night was full of giggles for us. We stayed out till all hours, too; for Arlington Street had no strict domestic programme, not even in the nursery, the inmates of which were as likely to be found in the gutter as in their cots, at any time this side of one o'clock in the morning.

There was an element in my enjoyment that was yielded neither by the sights, the adventures, nor the chewing-candy. I had a keen feeling for the sociability of the crowd. All plebeian Chelsea was abroad, and a bourgeois population is nowhere unneighborly. Women shapeless with bundles, their hats awry over thin, eager faces, gathered in knots on the edge of the curb, boasting of their bargains. Little girls in curlpapers and little boys in brimless hats clung to their skirts, whining for pennies, only to be silenced by absent-minded cuffs. A few disconsolate fathers strayed behind these family groups, the rest being distributed between the barber shops and the corner lamp-posts. I understood these people, being one of them, and I liked them, and I found it all delightfully sociable.

Saturday night is the workman's wife's night, but that does not entirely prevent my lady from going abroad, if only to leave an order at the florist's. So it happened that Bellingham Hill and Washington Avenue, the aristocratic sections of Chelsea, mingled with Arlington Street on Broadway, to the further enhancement of my enjoyment of the occasion. For I always loved a mixed crowd. I loved the contrasts, the high lights and deep shadows, and the gradations that connect the two, and make all life one. I saw many, many things that I was not aware of seeing at the time. I only found out afterwards what treasures my brain had stored up, when, coming to the puzzling places in life, light and meaning would suddenly burst on me, the hidden fruit of some experience that had not impressed me at the time.

How many times, I wonder, did I brush past my destiny on Broadway, foolishly staring after it, instead of going home to pray? I wonder did a stranger collide with me, and put me patiently out of his way, wondering why such a mite was not at home and abed at ten o'clock in the evening, and never dreaming that one day he might have to reckon with me? Did some one smile down on my childish glee, I wonder, unwarned of a day when we should weep together? I wonder—I wonder. A million threads of life and love and sorrow was the common street; and whether we would or not, we entangled ourselves in a common maze, without paying the homage of a second glance to those who would some day master us; too dull to pick that face from out the crowd which one day would bend over us in love or pity or remorse. What company of skipping, laughing little girls is to be reproached for careless hours, when men and women on every side stepped heedlessly into the traps of fate? Small sin it was to annoy my neighbor by getting in his way, as I stared over my shoulder, if a grown man knew no better than to drop a word in passing that might turn the course of another's life, as a boulder rolled down from the mountain-side deflects the current of a brook.

CHAPTER XIV

MANNA

So went the life in Chelsea for the space of a year or so. Then my father, finding a discrepancy between his assets and liabilities on the wrong side of the ledger, once more struck tent, collected his flock, and set out in search of richer pastures.

There was a charming simplicity about these proceedings. Here to-day, apparently rooted; there to-morrow, and just as much at home. Another basement grocery, with a freshly painted sign over the door; the broom in the corner, the loaf on the table—these things made home for us. There were rather more Negroes on Wheeler Street, in the lower South End of Boston, than there had been on Arlington Street, which promised more numerous outstanding accounts; but they were a neighborly folk, and they took us strangers in—sometimes very badly. Then there was the school three blocks away, where "America" was sung to the same tune as in Chelsea, and geography was made as dark a mystery. It was impossible not to feel at home.

And presently, lest anything be lacking to our domestic bliss, there was a new baby in a borrowed crib; and little Dora had only a few more turns to take with her battered doll carriage before a life-size vehicle with a more animated dolly was turned over to her constant care.

The Wheeler Street neighborhood is not a place where a refined young lady would care to find herself alone, even in the cheery daylight. If she came at all, she would be attended by a trusty escort. She would not get too close to people on the doorsteps, and she would shrink away in disgust and fear from a blear-eyed creature careering down the sidewalk on many-jointed legs. The delicate damsel would hasten home to wash and purify and perfume herself till the foul contact of Wheeler Street was utterly eradicated, and her wonted purity restored. And I do not blame her. I only wish that she would bring a little soap and water and perfumery into Wheeler Street next time she comes; for some people there

Wheeler Street, in the Lower South End of Boston

may be smothering in the filth which they abhor as much as she, but from which they cannot, like her, run away.

Many years after my escape from Wheeler Street I returned to see if the place was as bad as I remembered it. I found the narrow street grown even narrower, the sidewalk not broad enough for two to walk abreast, the gutter choked with dust and refuse, the dingy row of tenements on either side unspeakably gloomy. I discovered, what I had not realized before, that Wheeler Street was a crooked lane connecting a corner saloon on Shawmut Avenue with a block of houses of ill repute on Corning Street. It had been the same in my day, but I had not understood much, and I lived unharmed.

On this later visit I walked slowly up one side of the street, and down the other, remembering many things. It was eleven o'clock in the evening, and sounds of squabbling coming through doors and windows informed my experienced ear that a part of Wheeler Street was going to bed. The grocery store in the basement of Number 11—my father's old store—was still open for business; and in the gutter in front of the store, to be sure, was a happy baby, just as there used to be.

I was not alone on this tour of inspection. I was attended by a trusty escort. But I brought soap and water with me. I am applying them now.

I found no fault with Wheeler Street when I was fourteen years old. On the contrary, I pronounced it good. We had never lived so near the car tracks before, and I delighted in the moonlike splendor of the arc lamp just in front of the saloon. The space illumined by this lamp and enlivened by the passage of many thirsty souls was the favorite playground for Wheeler Street youth. On our street there was not room to turn around; here the sidewalk spread out wider as it swung around to Shawmut Avenue.

I played with the boys by preference, as in Chelsea. I learned to cut across the tracks in front of an oncoming car, and it was great fun to see the motorman's angry face turn scared, when he thought I was going to be shaved this time sure. It was amusing, too, to watch the side door of the saloon, which opened right opposite the grocery store, and see a drunken man put out by the bartender. The fellow would whine so comically, and cling to the doorpost so like a damp leaf to a twig, and blubber so like a red-faced baby, that it was really funny to see him.

And there was Morgan Chapel. It was worth coming to Wheeler Street just for that. All the children of the neighborhood, except the most rowdyish, flocked to Morgan Chapel at least once a week. This was on Saturday evening, when a free entertainment was given, consisting of music, recitations, and other parlor accomplishments. The performances were exceedingly artistic, according to the impartial judgment of juvenile Wheeler Street. I can speak with authority for the crowd of us from Number 11. We hung upon the lips of the beautiful ladies who read or sang to us; and they in turn did their best, recognizing the quality of our approval. We admired the miraculously clean gentlemen who sang or played, as heartily as we applauded their performance. Sometimes the beautiful ladies were accompanied by ravishing little girls who stood up in a glory of golden curls, frilled petticoats, and silk stockings, to recite pathetic or comic pieces, with trained expression and practised gestures that seemed to us the perfection of the elocutionary art. We were all a little bit stage-struck after these entertainments; but what was more, we were genuinely moved by the glimpses of a fairer world than ours which we caught through the music and poetry; the world in which the beautiful ladies dwelt with the fairy children and the clean gentlemen.

Brother Hotchkins, who managed these entertainments, knew what he was there for. His programmes were masterly. Classics of the lighter sort were judiciously interspersed with the favorite street songs of the day. Nothing that savored of the chapel was there: the hour was honestly devoted to entertainment. The total effect was an exquisitely balanced compound of pleasure, wonder, and longing. Knock-kneed men with purple noses, bristling chins, and no collars, who slouched in sceptically and sat tentatively on the edge of the rear settees at the beginning of the concert, moved nearer the front as the programme went on, and openly joined in the applause at the end. Scowling fellows who came in with defiant faces occasionally slunk out shamefaced; and both the knock-kneed and the defiant sometimes remained to hear Brother Tompkins pray and preach. And it was all due to Brother Hotchkins's masterly programme. The children behaved very well, for the most part; the few "toughs" who came in on purpose to make trouble were promptly expelled by Brother Hotchkins and his lieutenants.

I could not help admiring Brother Hotchkins, he was so eminently efficient in every part of the hall, at every stage of the proceedings. I always believed that he was the author of the alluring notices that occupied the bulletin board every Saturday, though I never knew it for a fact. The way he handled the bad boys was masterly. The way he introduced the performers was inimitable. The way he did everything was the best way. And yet I did not like Brother Hotchkins. I could not. He was too slim, too pale, too fair. His voice was too encouraging, his smile was too restrained. The man was a missionary, and it stuck out all over him. I could not abide a missionary. That was the Jew in me, the European Jew, trained by the cruel centuries of his outcast existence to distrust any one who spoke of God by any other name than *Adonai.* But I should have resented the suggestion that inherited distrust was the cause of my dislike for good Brother Hotchkins; for I considered myself freed from racial prejudices, by the same triumph of my infallible judgment which had lifted from me the yoke of credulity. An uncompromising atheist, such as I was at the age of fourteen, was bound to scorn all those who sought to implant religion in their fellow men, and thereby prolong the reign of superstition. Of course that was the explanation.

Brother Hotchkins, happily unconscious of my disapproval of his complexion, arose at intervals behind the railing, to announce, from a slip of paper, that "the next number on our programme will be a musical selection by," etc., etc.; until he arrived at "I am sure you will all join me in thanking the ladies and gentlemen who have entertained us this evening." And as I moved towards the door with my companions, I would hear his voice raised for the inevitable "You are all invited to remain to a short prayer service, after which—"a little louder—"refreshments will be served in the vestry. I will ask Brother Tompkins to—" The rest was lost in the shuffle of feet about the door and the roar of electric cars glancing past each other on opposite tracks. I always got out of the chapel before Brother Tompkins could do me any harm. As if there was anything he could steal from me, now that there was no God in my heart!

If I were to go back to Morgan Chapel now, I should stay to

hear Brother Tompkins, and as many other brethren as might have anything to say. I would sit very still in my corner seat and listen to the prayer, and silently join in the Amen. For I know now what Wheeler Street is, and I know what Morgan Chapel is there for, in the midst of those crooked alleys, those saloons, those pawnshops, those gloomy tenements. It is there to apply soap and water, and it is doing that all the time. I have learned, since my deliverance from Wheeler Street, that there is more than one road to any given goal. I should look with respect at Brother Hotchkins applying soap and water in his own way, convinced at last that my way is not the only way. Men must work with those tools to the use of which they are best fitted by nature. Brother Hotchkins must pray, and I must bear witness, and another must nurse a feeble infant. We are all honest workmen, and deserve standing-room in the workshop of sweating humanity. It is only the idle scoffers who stand by and jeer at our efforts to cleanse our house that should be kicked out of the door, as Brother Hotchkins turned out the rowdies.

It was characteristic of the looseness of our family discipline at this time that nobody was seriously interested in our visits to Morgan Chapel. Our time was our own, after school duties and household tasks were done. Joseph sold newspapers after school; I swept and washed dishes; Dora minded the baby. For the rest, we amused ourselves as best we could. Father and mother were preoccupied with the store day and night; and not so much with weighing and measuring and making change as with figuring out how long it would take the outstanding accounts to ruin the business entirely. If my mother had scruples against her children resorting to a building with a cross on it, she did not have time to formulate them. If my father heard us talking about Morgan Chapel, he dismissed the subject with a sarcastic characterization, and wanted to know if we were going to join the Salvation Army next; but he did not seriously care, and he was willing that the children should have a good time. And if my parents had objected to Morgan Chapel, was the sidewalk in front of the saloon a better place for us children to spend the evening? They could not have argued with us very long, so they hardly argued at all.

In Polotzk we had been trained and watched, our days had been regulated, our conduct prescribed. In America, suddenly, we were let loose on the street. Why? Because my father having renounced his faith, and my mother being uncertain of hers, they had no particular creed to hold us to. The conception of a system of ethics independent of religion could not at once enter as an active principle in their life; so that they could give a child no reason why to be truthful or kind. And as with religion, so it fared with other branches of our domestic education. Chaos took the place of system; uncertainty, inconsistency undermined discipline. My parents knew only that they desired us to be like American children; and seeing how their neighbors gave their children boundless liberty, they turned us also loose, never doubting but that the American way was the best way. In public deportment, in etiquette, in all matters of social intercourse, they had no standards to go by, seeing that America was not Polotzk. In their bewilderment and uncertainty they needs must trust us children to learn from such models as the tenements afforded. More than this, they must step down from their throne of parental authority, and take the law from their children's mouths; for they had no other means of finding out what was good American form. The result was that laxity of domestic organization, that inversion of normal relations which makes for friction, and which sometimes ends in breaking up a family that was formerly united and happy.

This sad process of disintegration of home life may be observed in almost any immigrant family of our class and with our traditions and aspirations. It is part of the process of Americanization; an upheaval preceding the state of repose. It is the cross that the first and second generations must bear, an involuntary sacrifice for the sake of the future generations. These are the pains of adjustment, as racking as the pains of birth. And as the mother forgets her agonies in the bliss of clasping her babe to her breast, so the bent and heart-sore immigrant forgets exile and homesickness and ridicule and loss and estrangement, when he beholds his sons and daughters moving as Americans among Americans.

On Wheeler Street there were no real homes. There were miserable flats of three or four rooms, or fewer, in which families that did not practise race suicide cooked, washed, and ate; slept from two to four in a bed, in windowless bedrooms; quarrelled in the gray morning, and made up in the smoky evening; tormented each other, supported each other, saved each other, drove each other out of the house. But there was no common life in any form that means life. There was no room for it, for one thing. Beds and cribs took up most of the floor space, disorder packed the interspaces. The centre table in the "parlor" was not loaded with books. It held, invariably, a photograph album and an ornamental lamp with a paper shade; and the lamp was usually out of order. So there was as little motive for a common life as there was room. The yard was only big enough for the perennial rubbish heap. The narrow side-walk was crowded. What were the people to do with themselves? There were the saloons, the missions, the libraries, the cheap amuse-ment places, and the neighborhood houses. People selected their resorts according to their tastes. The children, let it be thankfully recorded, flocked mostly to the clubs; the little girls to sew, cook, dance, and play games; the little boys to hammer and paste, mend chairs, debate, and govern a toy republic. All these, of course, are forms of baptism by soap and water.

Our neighborhood went in search of salvation to Morgan Me-morial Hall, Barnard Memorial, Morgan Chapel aforementioned, and some other clean places that lighted a candle in their window. My brother, my sister Dora, and I were introduced to some of the clubs by our young neighbors, and we were glad to go. For our home also gave us little besides meals in the kitchen and beds in the dark. What with the six of us, and the store, and the baby, and sometimes a "greener" or two from Polotzk, whom we lodged as a matter of course till they found a permanent home—what with such a company and the size of our tenement, we needed to get out almost as much as our neighbors' children. I say almost; for our parlor we managed to keep pretty clear, and the lamp on our centre table was always in order, and its light fell often on an open book. Still, it was part of the life of Wheeler Street to belong to clubs, so we belonged.

I did n't care for sewing or cooking, so I joined a dancing-club; and even here I was a failure. I had been a very good dancer in Russia, but here I found all the steps different, and I did not have the courage to go out in the middle of the slippery floor and mince it and toe it in front of the teacher. When I retired to a corner and tried to play dominoes, I became suddenly shy of my partner; and I never could win a game of checkers, although formerly I used to beat my father at it. I tried to be friends with a little girl I had known in Chelsea, but she met my advances coldly. She lived on Appleton Street, which was too aristocratic to mix with Wheeler Street. Geraldine was studying elocution, and she wore a scarlet cape and hood, and she was going on the stage by and by. I acknowledged that her sense of superiority was well-founded, and retired farther into my corner, for the first time conscious of my shabbiness and lowliness.

I looked on at the dancing until I could endure it no longer. Overcome by a sense of isolation and unfitness, I slipped out of the room, avoiding the teacher's eye and went home to write melancholy poetry.

What had come over me? Why was I, the confident, the ambitious, suddenly grown so shy and meek? Why was the candidate for encyclopædic immortality overawed by a scarlet hood? Why did I, a very tomboy yesterday, suddenly find my playmates stupid, and hide-and-seek a bore? I did not know why. I only knew that I was lonely and troubled and sore; and I went home to write sad poetry.

I shall never forget the pattern of the red carpet in our parlor, —we had achieved a carpet since Chelsea days,—because I lay for hours face down on the floor, writing poetry on a screechy slate. When I had perfected my verses, and copied them fair on the famous blue-lined note paper, and saw that I had made a very pathetic poem indeed, I felt better. And this happened over and over again. I gave up the dancing-club, I ceased to know the rowdy little boys, and I wrote melancholy poetry oftener, and felt better. The centre table became my study. I read much, and mooned between chapters, and wrote long letters to Miss Dillingham.

For some time I wrote to her almost daily. That was when I found in my heart such depths of woe as I could not pack into rhyme. And finally there came a day when I could utter my trouble in neither verse nor prose, and I implored Miss Dillingham to come to me and hear my sorrowful revelations. But I did not want her to come to the house. In the house there was no privacy; I could not talk. Would she meet me on Boston Common at such and such a time?

Would she? She was a devoted friend, and a wise woman. She met me on Boston Common. It was a gray autumn day—was it not actually drizzling?—and I was cold sitting on the bench; but I was thrilled through and through with the sense of the magnitude of my troubles, and of the romantic nature of the rendezvous.

Who that was even half awake when he was growing up does not know what all these symptoms betokened? Miss Dillingham understood, and she wisely gave me no inkling of her diagnosis. She let me talk and kept a grave face. She did not belittle my troubles—I made specific charges against my home, members of my family, and life in general; she did not say that I would get over them, that every growing girl suffers from the blues; that I was, in brief, a little goose stretching my wings for flight. She told me rather that it would be noble to bear my sorrows bravely, to soothe those who irritated me, to live each day with all my might. She reminded me of great men and women who have suffered, and who overcame their troubles by living and working. And she sent me home amazingly comforted, my pettiness and self-consciousness routed by the quiet influence of her gray eyes searching mine. This, or something like this, had to be repeated many times, as anybody will know who was present at the slow birth of his manhood. From now on, for some years, of course, I must weep and laugh out of season, stand on tiptoe to pluck the stars in heaven, love and hate immoderately, propound theories of the destiny of man, and not know what is going on in my own heart.

CHAPTER XV

TARNISHED LAURELS

In the intervals of harkening to my growing-pains I was, of course, still a little girl. As a little girl, in many ways immature for my age, I finished my course in the grammar school, and was graduated with honors, four years after my landing in Boston.

Wheeler Street recognizes five great events in a girl's life: namely, christening, confirmation, graduation, marriage, and burial. These occasions all require full dress for the heroine, and full dress is forthcoming, no matter if the family goes into debt for it. There was not a girl who came to school in rags all the year round that did not burst forth in sudden glory on Graduation Day. Fine muslin frocks, lace-trimmed petticoats, patent-leather shoes, perishable hats, gloves, parasols, fans—every girl had them. A mother who had scrubbed floors for years to keep her girl in school was not going to have her shamed in the end for want of a pretty dress. So she cut off the children's supply of butter and worked nights and borrowed and fell into arrears with the rent; and on Graduation Day she felt magnificently rewarded, seeing her Mamie as fine as any girl in the school. And in order to preserve for posterity this triumphant spectacle, she took Mamie, after the exercises, to be photographed, with her diploma in one hand, a bouquet in the other, and the gloves, fan, parasol, and patent-leather shoes in full sight around a fancy table. Truly, the follies of the poor are worth studying.

It did not strike me as folly, but as the fulfilment of the portent of my natal star, when I saw myself, on Graduation Day, arrayed like unto a princess. Frills, lace, patent-leather shoes—I had everything. I even had a sash with silk fringes.

Did I speak of folly? Listen, and I will tell you quite another tale. Perhaps when you have heard it you will not be too hasty to run and teach The Poor. Perhaps you will admit that The Poor may have something to teach you.

Before we had been two years in America, my sister Frieda was engaged to be married. This was under the old dispensation: Frieda came to America too late to avail herself of the gifts of an American girlhood. Had she been two years younger she might have dodged her circumstances, evaded her Old-World fate. She would have gone to school and imbibed American ideas. She might have clung to her girlhood longer instead of marrying at seventeen. I am so fond of the American way that it has always seemed to me a pitiful accident that my sister should have come so near and missed by so little the fulfilment of my country's promise to women. A long girlhood, a free choice in marriage, and a brimful womanhood are the precious rights of an American woman.

My father was too recently from the Old World to be entirely free from the influence of its social traditions. He had put Frieda to work out of necessity. The necessity was hardly lifted when she had an offer of marriage, but my father would not stand in the way of what he considered her welfare. Let her escape from the workshop, if she had a chance, while the roses were still in her cheeks. If she remained for ten years more bent over the needle, what would she gain? Not even her personal comfort; for Frieda never called her earnings her own, but spent everything on the family, denying herself all but necessities. The young man who sued for her was a good workman, earning fair wages, of irreproachable character, and refined manners. My father had known him for years.

So Frieda was to be released from the workshop. The act was really in the nature of a sacrifice on my father's part, for he was still in the woods financially, and would sorely miss Frieda's wages. The greater the pity, therefore, that there was no one to counsel him to give America more time with my sister. She attended the night school; she was fond of reading. In books, in a slowly ripening experience, she might have found a better answer to the riddle of a girl's life than a premature marriage.

My sister's engagement pleased me very well. Our confidences were not interrupted, and I understood that she was happy. I was very fond of Moses Rifkin myself. He was the nicest young man of my acquaintance, not at all like other workmen. He was very kind to us children, bringing us presents and taking us out for excursions. He had a sense of humor, and he was going to marry our Frieda. How could I help being pleased?

The marriage was not to take place for some time, and in the interval Frieda remained in the shop. She continued to bring home all her wages. If she was going to desert the family, she would not let them feel it sooner than she must.

Then all of a sudden she turned spendthrift. She appropriated I do not know what fabulous sums, to spend just as she pleased, for once. She attended bargain sales, and brought away such finery as had never graced our flat before. Home from work in the evening, after a hurried supper, she shut herself up in the parlor, and cut and snipped and measured and basted and stitched as if there were nothing else in the world to do. It was early summer, and the air had a wooing touch, even on Wheeler Street. Moses Rifkin came, and I suppose he also had a wooing touch. But Frieda only smiled and shook her head; and as her mouth was full of pins, it was physically impossible for Moses to argue. She remained all evening in a white disorder of tucked breadths, curled ruffles, dismembered sleeves, and swirls of fresh lace; her needle glancing in the lamplight, and poor Moses picking up her spools.

Her trousseau, was it not? No, not her trousseau. It was my graduation dress on which she was so intent. And when it was finished, and was pronounced a most beautiful dress, and she ought to have been satisfied, Frieda went to the shops once more and bought the sash with the silk fringes.

The improvidence of the poor is a most distressing spectacle to all right-minded students of sociology. But please spare me your homily this time. It does not apply. The poor are the poor in spirit. Those who are rich in spiritual endowment will never be found bankrupt.

Graduation Day was nothing less than a triumph for me. It was not only that I had two pieces to speak, one of them an original composition; it was more because I was known in my school district as the "smartest" girl in the class, and all eyes were turned on the prodigy, and I was aware of it. I was aware of everything. That is why I am able to tell you everything now.

The assembly hall was crowded to bursting, but my friends had no trouble in finding seats. They were ushered up to the platform, which was reserved for guests of honor. I was very proud to see my friends treated with such distinction. My parents were there, and Frieda, of course; Miss Dillingham, and some others of my Chelsea teachers. A dozen or so of my humbler friends and acquaintances were scattered among the crowd on the floor.

When I stepped up on the stage to read my composition I was seized with stage fright. The floor under my feet and the air around me were oppressively present to my senses, while my own hand I could not have located. I did not know where my body began or ended, I was so conscious of my gloves, my shoes, my flowing sash. My wonderful dress, in which I had taken so much satisfaction, gave me the most trouble. I was suddenly paralyzed by a conviction that it was too short, and it seemed to me I stood on absurdly long legs. And ten thousand people were looking up at me. It was horrible!

I suppose I no more than cleared my throat before I began to read, but to me it seemed that I stood petrified for an age, an awful silence booming in my ears. My voice, when at last I began, sounded far away. I thought that nobody could hear me. But I kept on, mechanically; for I had rehearsed many times. And as I read I gradually forgot myself, forgot the place and the occasion. The people looking up at me heard the story of a beautiful little boy, my cousin, whom I had loved very dearly, and who died in far-distant Russia some years after I came to America. My composition was not a masterpiece; it was merely good for a girl of fifteen. But I had written that I still loved the little cousin, and I made a thousand strangers feel it. And before the applause there was a moment of stillness in the great hall.

After the singing and reading by the class, there were the customary addresses by distinguished guests. We girls were reminded that we were going to be women, and happiness was promised to those of us who would aim to be noble women. A great many trite and obvious things, a great deal of the rhetoric appropriate to the occasion, compliments, applause, general satisfaction; so went the programme. Much of the rhetoric, many of the fine sentiments did not penetrate to the thoughts of us for whom they were intended, because we were in such a flutter about our ruffles and ribbons, and could hardly refrain from openly prinking. But we applauded very heartily every speaker and every would-be speaker, understanding that by a consensus of opinion on the platform we were very fine young ladies, and much was to be expected of us.

One of the last speakers was introduced as a member of the School Board. He began like all the rest of them, but he ended differently. Abandoning generalities, he went on to tell the story of a particular schoolgirl, a pupil in a Boston school, whose phenomenal career might serve as an illustration of what the American system of free education and the European immigrant could make of each other. He had not got very far when I realized, to my great surprise and no small delight, that he was telling my story. I saw my friends on the platform beaming behind the speaker, and I heard my name whispered in the audience. I had been so much of a celebrity, in a small local way, that identification of the speaker's heroine was inevitable. My classmates, of course, guessed the name, and they turned to look at me, and nudged me, and all but pointed at me; their new muslins rustling and silk ribbons hissing.

One or two nearest me forgot etiquette so far as to whisper to me. "Mary Antin," they said, as the speaker sat down, amid a burst of the most enthusiastic applause,—"Mary Antin, why don't you get up and thank him?"

I was dazed with all that had happened. Bursting with pride I was, but I was moved, too, by nobler feelings. I realized, in a vague, far-off way, what it meant to my father and mother to be sitting there and seeing me held up as a paragon, my history made the theme of an eloquent discourse; what it meant to my father to see his ambitious hopes thus gloriously fulfilled, his judgment of me verified; what it meant to Frieda to hear me all but named with such honor. With all these things choking my heart to overflowing, my wits forsook me, if I had had any at all that day. The audience was stirring and whispering so that I could hear: "Who is it?" "Is that so?" And again they prompted me:—

"Mary Antin, get up. Get up and thank him, Mary."

And I rose where I sat, and in a voice that sounded thin as a fly's after the oratorical bass of the last speaker, I began:—

"I want to thank you—"

That is as far as I got. Mr. Swan, the principal, waved his hand to silence me; and then, and only then, did I realize the enormity of what I had done.

My eulogist had had the good taste not to mention names, and I had been brazenly forward, deliberately calling attention to myself when there was no need. Oh, it was sickening! I hated myself, I hated with all my heart the girls who had prompted me to such immodest conduct. I wished the ground would yawn and snap me up. I was ashamed to look up at my friends on the platform. What was Miss Dillingham thinking of me? Oh, what a fool I had been! I had ruined my own triumph. I had disgraced myself, and my friends, and poor Mr. Swan, and the Winthrop School. The monster vanity had sucked out my wits, and left me a staring idiot.

It is easy to say that I was making a mountain out of a mole hill, a catastrophe out of a mere breach of good manners. It is easy to say that. But I know that I suffered agonies of shame. After the exercises, when the crowd pressed in all directions in search of friends, I tried in vain to get out of the hall. I was mobbed, I was lionized. Everybody wanted to shake hands with the prodigy of the day, and they knew who it was. I had made sure of that; I had exhibited myself. The people smiled on me, flattered me, passed me on from one to another. I smirked back, but I did not know what I said. I was wild to be clear of the building. I thought everybody mocked me. All my roses had turned to ashes, and all through my own brazen conduct.

I would have given my diploma to have Miss Dillingham know how the thing had happened, but I could not bring myself to speak first. If she would ask me—But nobody asked. Nobody looked away from me. Everybody congratulated me, and my father and mother and my remotest relations. But the sting of shame smarted just the same; I could not be consoled. I had made a fool of myself: Mr. Swan had publicly put me down.

Ah, so that was it! Vanity was the vital spot again. It was wounded vanity that writhed and squirmed. It was not because I had been bold, but because I had been pronounced bold, that I suffered so monstrously. If Mr. Swan, with an eloquent gesture, had not silenced me, I might have made my little speech—good heavens! what *did* I mean to say?—and probably called it another feather in my bonnet. But he had stopped me promptly, disgusted with my forwardness, and he had shown before all those hundreds what he thought of me. Therein lay the sting.

With all my talent for self-analysis, it took me a long time to realize the essential pettiness of my trouble. For years—actually for years—after that eventful day of mingled triumph and disgrace, I could not think of the unhappy incident without inward squirming.

I remember distinctly how the little scene would suddenly flash upon me at night, as I lay awake in bed, and I would turn over impatiently, as if to shake off a nightmare; and this so long after the occurrence that I was myself amazed at the persistence of the nightmare. I had never been reproached by any one for my conduct on Graduation Day. Why could I not forgive myself? I studied the matter deeply—it wearies me to remember how deeply—till at last I understood that it was wounded vanity that hurt so, and no nobler remorse. Then, and only then, was the ghost laid. If it ever tried to get up again, after that, I only had to call it names to see it scurry back to its grave and pull the sod down after it.

Before I had laid my ghost, a friend told me of a similar experience of his boyhood. He was present at a small private entertainment, and a violinist who should have played being absent, the host asked for a volunteer to take his place. My friend, then a boy in his teens, offered himself, and actually stood up with the violin in his hands, as if to play. But he could not even hold the instrument properly—he had never been taught the violin. He told me he never knew what possessed him to get up and make a fool of himself before a roomful of people; but he was certain that ten thousand imps possessed him and tormented him for years and years after, if only he remembered the incident.

My friend's confession was such a consolation to me that I could not help thinking I might do some other poor wretch a world of good by offering him my company and that of my friend in his misery. For if it took me a long time to find out that I was a vain fool, the corollary did not escape me: there must be other vain fools.

CHAPTER XVI

DOVER STREET

WHAT HAPPENED NEXT was Dover Street.

And what was Dover Street?

Ask rather, What was it not? Dover Street was my fairest garden of girlhood, a gate of paradise, a window facing on a broad avenue of life. Dover Street was a prison, a school of discipline, a battle-field of sordid strife. The air in Dover Street was heavy with evil odors of degradation, but a breath from the uppermost heavens rippled through, whispering of infinite things. In Dover Street the dragon poverty gripped me for a last fight, but I overthrew the hideous creature, and sat on his neck as on a throne. In Dover Street I was shackled with a hundred chains of disadvantage, but with one free hand I planted little seeds, right there in the mud of shame, that blossomed into the honeyed rose of widest freedom. In Dover Street there was often no loaf on the table, but the hand of some noble friend was ever in mine. The night in Dover Street was rent with the cries of wrong, but the thunders of truth crashed through the pitiful clamor and died out in prophetic silences.

Outwardly, Dover Street is a noisy thoroughfare cut through a South End slum, in every essential the same as Wheeler Street. Turn down any street in the slums, at random, and call it by whatever name you please, you will observe there the same fashions of life, death, and endurance. Every one of those streets is a rubbish heap of damaged humanity, and it will take a powerful broom and an ocean of soapsuds to clean it out.

Dover Street is intersected, near its eastern end, where we lived, by Harrison Avenue. That street is to the South End what Salem Street is to the North End. It is the heart of the South End ghetto, for the greater part of its length; although its northern end belongs to the realm of Chinatown. Its multifarious business bursts through the narrow shop doors, and overruns the basements, the sidewalk, the street itself, in pushcarts and open-air stands. Its multitudinous population bursts through the greasy tenement doors, and floods the corridors, the doorsteps, the gutters, the side streets, pushing in and out among the pushcarts, all day long and half the night besides.

Rarely as Harrison Avenue is caught asleep, even more rarely is it found clean. Nothing less than a fire or flood would cleanse this street. Even Passover cannot quite accomplish this feat. For although the tenements may be scrubbed to their remotest corners, on this one occasion, the cleansing stops at the curbstone. A great deal of the filthy rubbish accumulated in a year is pitched into the street, often through the windows; and what the ashman on his daily round does not remove is left to be trampled to powder, in which form it steals back into the houses from which it was so lately removed.

The City Fathers provide soap and water for the slums, in the form of excellent schools, kindergartens, and branch libraries. And there they stop: at the curb-stone of the people's life. They cleanse and discipline the children's minds, but their bodies they pitch into the gutter. For there are no parks and almost no playgrounds in the Harrison Avenue district,—in my day there were none,—and such as there are have been wrenched from the city by public-spirited citizens who have no offices in City Hall. No wonder the ashman is not more thorough: he learns from his masters.

It is a pity to have it so, in a queen of enlightened cities like Boston. If we of the twentieth century do not believe in baseball as much as in philosophy, we have not learned the lesson of modern science, which teaches, among other things, that the body is the nursery of the soul; the instrument of our moral development; the secret chart of our devious progress from worm to man. The great achievement of recent science, of which we are so proud, has been the deciphering of the hieroglyphic of organic nature. To worship the facts and neglect the implications of the message of science is to applaud the drama without taking the moral to heart. And we certainly are not taking the moral to heart when we try to make a hero out of the boy by such foreign appliances as grammar and algebra, while utterly despising the fittest instrument for his uplifting—the boy's own body.

We had no particular reason for coming to Dover Street. It might just as well have been Applepie Alley. For my father had sold, with the goods, fixtures, and good-will of the Wheeler Street store, all his hopes of ever making a living in the grocery trade; and I doubt

if he got a silver dollar the more for them. We had to live somewhere, even if we were not making a living, so we came to Dover
Street, where tenements were cheap; by which I mean that rent was
low. The ultimate cost of life in those tenements, in terms of human
happiness, is high enough.

Our new home consisted of five small rooms up two flights of
stairs, with the right of way through the dark corridors. In the
"parlor" the dingy paper hung in rags and the plaster fell in chunks.
One of the bedrooms was absolutely dark and air-tight. The
kitchen windows looked out on a dirty court, at the back of which
was the rear tenement of the estate. To us belonged, along with the
five rooms and the right of way aforesaid, a block of upper space
the length of a pulley line across this court, and the width of an
arc described by a windy Monday's wash in its remotest
wanderings.

The little front bedroom was assigned to me, with only one partner, my sister Dora. A mouse could not have led a cat much of a
chase across this room; still we found space for a narrow bed, a
crazy bureau, and a small table. From the window there was an
unobstructed view of a lumberyard, beyond which frowned the
blackened walls of a factory. The fence of the lumberyard was gay
with theatre posters and illustrated advertisements of tobacco,
whiskey, and patent baby foods. When the window was open, there
was a constant clang and whirr of electric cars, varied by the screech
of machinery, the clatter of empty wagons, or the rumble of heavy
trucks.

There was nothing worse in all this than we had had before since
our exile from Crescent Beach; but I did not take the same delight
in the propinquity of electric cars and arc lights that I had till now.
I suppose the tenement began to pall on me.

It must not be supposed that I enjoyed any degree of privacy,
because I had half a room to myself. We were six in the five rooms;
we were bound to be always in each other's way. And as it was
within our flat, so it was in the house as a whole. All doors, beginning with the street door, stood open most of the time; or if
they were closed, the tenants did not wear out their knuckles
knocking for admittance. I could stand at any time in the unswept
entrance hall and tell, from an analysis of the medley of sounds and
smells that issued from doors ajar, what was going on in the several

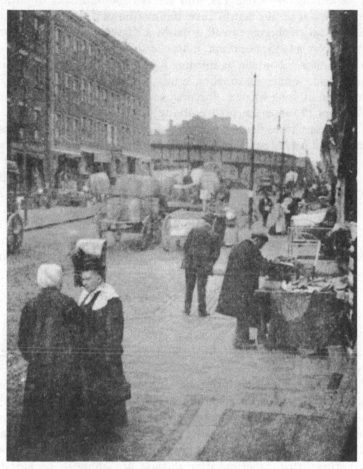

HARRISON AVENUE IS THE HEART OF THE SOUTH END GHETTO

flats from below up. That guttural, scolding voice, unremittent as the hissing of a steam pipe, is Mrs. Rasnosky. I make a guess that she is chastising the infant Isaac for taking a second lump of sugar in his tea. *Spam! Bam!* Yes, and she is rubbing in her objections with the flat of her hand. That blubbering and moaning, accompanying an elephantine tread, is fat Mrs. Casey, second floor, home drunk from an afternoon out, in fear of the vengeance of Mr. Casey; to propitiate whom she is burning a pan of bacon, as the choking fumes and outrageous sizzling testify. I hear a feeble whining, interrupted by long silences. It is that scabby baby on the third floor, fallen out of bed again, with nobody home to pick him up.

To escape from these various horrors I ascend to the roof, where bacon and babies and child-beating are not. But there I find two figures in calico wrappers, with bare red arms akimbo, a basket of wet clothes in front of each, and only one empty clothes-line between them. I do not want to be dragged in as a witness in a case of assault and battery, so I descend to the street again, grateful to note, as I pass, that the third-floor baby is still.

In front of the door I squeeze through a group of children. They are going to play tag, and are counting to see who should be "it":—

> "My-mother-and-your-mother-went-out-to-hang-clothes;
> My-mother-gave-your-mother-a-punch-in-the-nose."

If the children's couplet does not give a vivid picture of the life, manners, and customs of Dover Street, no description of mine can ever do so.

Frieda was married before we came to Dover Street, and went to live in East Boston. This left me the eldest of the children at home. Whether on this account, or because I was outgrowing my childish carelessness, or because I began to believe, on the cumulative evidence of the Crescent Beach, Chelsea, and Wheeler Street adventures, that America, after all, was not going to provide for my father's family,—whether for any or all of these reasons, I began at this time to take bread-and-butter matters more to heart, and to ponder ways and means of getting rich. My father sought employment wherever work was going on. His health was poor; he aged very fast. Nevertheless he offered himself for every kind of labor; he offered himself for a boy's wages. Here he was found too

weak, here too old; here his imperfect English was in the way, here
his Jewish appearance. He had a few short terms of work at this or
that; I do not know the name of the form of drudgery that my
father did not practise. But all told, he did not earn enough to pay
the rent in full and buy a bone for the soup. The only steady source
of income, for I do not know what years, was my brother's earnings from his newspapers.

Surely this was the time for me to take my sister's place in the
workshop. I had had every fair chance until now: school, my time
to myself, liberty to run and play and make friends. I had graduated
from grammar school; I was of legal age to go to work. What was
I doing, sitting at home and dreaming?

I was minding my business, of course; with all my might I was
minding my business. As I understood it, my business was to go
to school, to learn everything there was to know, to write poetry,
become famous, and make the family rich. Surely it was not shirk-
ing to lay out such a programme for myself. I had boundless faith
in my future. I was certainly going to be a great poet; I was certainly going to take care of the family.

Thus mused I, in my arrogance. And my family? They were as
bad as I. My father had not lost a whit of his ambition for me.
Since Graduation Day, and the school-committeeman's speech, and
half a column about me in the paper, his ambition had soared even
higher. He was going to keep me at school till I was prepared for
college. By that time, he was sure, I would more than take care of
myself. It never for a moment entered his head to doubt the wisdom or justice of this course. And my mother was just as loyal to
my cause, and my brother, and my sister.

It is no wonder if I got along rapidly: I was helped, encouraged,
and upheld by every one. Even the baby cheered me on. When I
asked her whether she believed in higher education, she answered,
without a moment's hesitation, "Ducka-ducka-da!" Against her I
remember only that one day, when I read her a verse out of a most
pathetic piece I was composing, she laughed right out, a most disrespectful laugh; for which I revenged myself by washing her face
at the faucet, and rubbing it red on the roller towel.

It was just like me, when it was debated whether I would be
best fitted for college at the High or the Latin School, to go in
person to Mr. Tetlow, who was principal of both schools, and so

get the most expert opinion on the subject. I never send a messenger, you may remember, where I can go myself. It was vacation time, and I had to find Mr. Tetlow at his home. Away out to the wilds of Roxbury I found my way—perhaps half an hour's ride on the electric car from Dover Street. I grew an inch taller and broader between the corner of Cedar Street and Mr. Tetlow's house, such was the charm of the clean, green suburb on a cramped waif from the slums. My faded calico dress, my rusty straw sailor hat, the color of my skin and all bespoke the waif. But never a bit daunted was I. I went up the steps to the porch, rang the bell, and asked for the great man with as much assurance as if I were a daily visitor on Cedar Street. I calmly awaited the appearance of Mr. Tetlow in the reception room, and stated my errand without trepidation.

And why not? I was a solemn little person for the moment, earnestly seeking advice on a matter of great importance. That is what Mr. Tetlow saw, to judge by the gravity with which he discussed my business with me, and the courtesy with which he showed me to the door. He saw, too, I fancy, that I was not the least bit conscious of my shabby dress; and I am sure he did not smile at my appearance, even when my back was turned.

A new life began for me when I entered the Latin School in September. Until then I had gone to school with my equals, and as a matter of course. Now it was distinctly a feat for me to keep in school, and my schoolmates were socially so far superior to me that my poverty became conspicuous. The pupils of the Latin School, from the nature of the institution, are an aristocratic set. They come from refined homes, dress well, and spend the recess hour talking about parties, beaux, and the matinée. As students they are either very quick or very hard-working; for the course of study, in the lingo of the school world, is considered "stiff." The girl with half her brain asleep, or with too many beaux, drops out by the end of the first year; or a one and only beau may be the fatal element. At the end of the course the weeding process has reduced the once numerous tribe of academic candidates to a cosey little family.

By all these tokens I should have had serious business on my hands as a pupil in the Latin School, but I did not find it hard. To make myself letter-perfect in my lessons required long hours of study, but that was my delight. To make myself at home in an alien world was also within my talents; I had been practising it day and night for the past four years. To remain unconscious of my shabby and ill-fitting clothes when the rustle of silk petticoats in the schoolroom protested against them was a matter still within my moral reach. Half a dress a year had been my allowance for many seasons; even less, for as I did not grow much I could wear my dresses as long as they lasted. And I had stood before editors, and exchanged polite calls with school-teachers, untroubled by the detestable colors and archaic design of my garments. To stand up and recite Latin declensions without trembling from hunger was something more of a feat, because I sometimes went to school with little or no breakfast; but even that required no special heroism,—at most it was a matter of self-control. I had the advantage of a poor appetite, too; I really did not need much breakfast. Or if I was hungry it would hardly show; I coughed so much that my unsteadiness was self-explained.

Everything helped, you see. My schoolmates helped. Aristocrats though they were, they did not hold themselves aloof from me. Some of the girls who came to school in carriages were especially cordial. They rated me by my scholarship, and not by my father's occupation. They teased and admired me by turns for learning the footnotes in the Latin grammar by heart; they never reproached me for my ignorance of the latest comic opera. And it was more than good breeding that made them seem unaware of the incongruity of my presence. It was a generous appreciation of what it meant for a girl from the slums to be in the Latin School, on the way to college. If our intimacy ended on the steps of the school-house, it was more my fault than theirs. Most of the girls were democratic enough to have invited me to their homes, although to some, of course, I was "impossible." But I had no time for visiting; school work and reading and family affairs occupied all the daytime, and much of the night time. I did not "go with" any of the girls, in the school-girl sense of the phrase. I admired some of them, either for good looks, or beautiful manners, or more subtle attributes; but always at a distance. I discovered something inimitable in the way the Back Bay girls carried themselves; and I should have been the first to perceive the incongruity of Commonwealth Avenue entwining arms with Dover Street. Some day, perhaps, when I should be famous and rich; but not just then. So my companions and I parted on the steps of the school-house, in mutual respect; they

guiltless of snobbishness, I innocent of envy. It was a graciously
American relation, and I am happy to this day to recall it.

The one exception to this rule of friendly distance was my chum,
Florence Connolly. But I should hardly have said "chum." Florence and I occupied adjacent seats for three years, but we did not
walk arm in arm, nor call each other nicknames, nor share our
lunch, nor correspond in vacation time. Florence was quiet as a
mouse, and I was reserved as an oyster; and perhaps we two had
no more in common fundamentally than those two creatures in
their natural state. Still, as we were both very studious, and never
strayed far from our desks at recess, we practised a sort of intimacy
of propinquity. Although Florence was of my social order, her father presiding over a cheap lunch room, I did not on that account
feel especially drawn to her. I spent more time studying Florence
than loving her, I suppose. And yet I ought to have loved her; she
was such a good girl. Always perfect in her lessons, she was so
modest that she recited in a noticeable tremor, and had to be told
frequently to raise her voice. Florence wore her light brown hair
brushed flatly back and braided in a single plait, at a time when
pompadours were six inches high and braids hung in pairs. Florence
had a pocket in her dress for her handkerchief, in a day when pockets were repugnant to fashion. All these things ought to have made
me feel the kinship of humble circumstances, the comradeship of
intellectual earnestness; but they did not.

The truth is that my relation to persons and things depended
neither on social distinctions nor on intellectual or moral affinities.
My attitude, at this time, was determined by my consciousness of
the unique elements in my character and history. It seemed to me
that I had been pursuing a single adventure since the beginning of
the world. Through highways and byways, underground, over-
ground, by land, by sea, ever the same star had guided me, I
thought, ever the same purpose had divided my affairs from other
men's. What that purpose was, where was the fixed horizon beyond
which my star would not recede, was an absorbing mystery to me.
But the current moment never puzzled me. What I chose instinctively to do I knew to be right and in accordance with my destiny.
I never hesitated over great things, but answered promptly to the
call of my genius. So what was it to me whether my neighbors
spurned or embraced me, if my way was no man's way? Nor

should any one ever reject me whom I chose to be my friend, because I would make sure of a kindred spirit by the coincidence of our guiding stars.

When, where in the harum-scarum life of Dover Street was there time or place for such self-communing? In the night, when everybody slept; on a solitary walk, as far from home as I dared to go.

I was not unhappy on Dover Street; quite the contrary. Everything of consequence was well with me. Poverty was a superficial, temporary matter; it vanished at the touch of money. Money in America was plentiful; it was only a matter of getting some of it, and I was on my way to the mint. If Dover Street was not a pleasant place to abide in, it was only a wayside house. And I was really happy, actively happy, in the exercise of my mind in Latin, mathematics, history, and the rest; the things that suffice a studious girl in the middle teens.

Still I had moments of depression, when my whole being protested against the life of the slum. I resented the familiarity of my vulgar neighbors. I felt myself defiled by the indecencies I was compelled to witness. Then it was I took to running away from home. I went out in the twilight and walked for hours, my blind feet leading me. I did not care where I went. If I lost my way, so much the better; I never wanted to see Dover Street again.

But behold, as I left the crowds behind, and the broader avenues were spanned by the open sky, my grievances melted away, and I fell to dreaming of things that neither hurt nor pleased. A fringe of trees against the sunset became suddenly the symbol of the whole world, and I stood and gazed and asked questions of it. The sunset faded; the trees withdrew. The wind went by, but dropped no hint in my ear. The evening star leaped out between the clouds, and sealed the secret with a seal of splendor.

A favorite resort of mine, after dark, was the South Boston Bridge, across South Bay and the Old Colony Railroad. This was so near home that I could go there at any time when the confusion in the house drove me out, or I felt the need of fresh air. I liked to stand leaning on the bridge railing, and look down on the dim tangle of railroad tracks below. I could barely see them branching out, elbowing, winding, and sliding out into the night in pairs. I was fascinated by the dotted lights, the significant red and green of signal lamps. These simple things stood for a complexity that it made me dizzy to think of. Then the blackness below me was split by the fiery eye of a monster engine, his breath enveloped me in blinding clouds, his long body shot by, rattling a hundred claws of steel; and he was gone, with an imperative shriek that shook me where I stood.

So would I be, swift on my rightful business, picking out my proper track from the million that cross it, pausing for no obstacles, sure of my goal.

After my watches on the bridge I often stayed up to write or study. It is late before Dover Street begins to go to bed. It is past midnight before I feel that I am alone. Seated in my stiff little chair before my narrow table, I gather in the night sounds through the open window, curious to assort and define them. As, little by little, the city settles down to sleep, the volume of sound diminishes, and the qualities of particular sounds stand out. The electric car lurches by with silent gong, taking the empty track by leaps, humming to itself in the invisible distance. A benighted team swings recklessly around the corner, sharp under my rattling window panes, the staccato pelting of hoofs on the cobblestones changed suddenly to an even pounding on the bridge. A few pedestrians hurry by, their heavy boots all out of step. The distant thoroughfares have long ago ceased their murmur, and I know that a million lamps shine idly in the idle streets.

My sister sleeps quietly in the little bed. The rhythmic dripping of a faucet is audible through the flat. It is so still that I can hear the paper crackling on the wall. Silence upon silence is added to the night; only the kitchen clock is the voice of my brooding thoughts,—ticking, ticking, ticking.

Suddenly the distant whistle of a locomotive breaks the stillness with a long-drawn wail. Like a threatened trouble, the sound comes nearer, piercingly near; then it dies out in a mangled silence, complaining to the last.

The sleepers stir in their beds. Somebody sighs, and the burden of all his trouble falls upon my heart. A homeless cat cries in the alley, in the voice of a human child. And the ticking of the kitchen clock is the voice of my troubled thoughts.

Many things are revealed to me as I sit and watch the world asleep. But the silence asks me many questions that I cannot answer; and I am glad when the tide of sound begins to return, by

I Liked to Stand and Look Down on the Dim Tangle of Railroad Tracks Below little and little, and I welcome the clatter of tin cans that announces the milkman. I cannot see him in the dusk, but I know his wholesome face has no problem in it.

It is one flight up to the roof; it is a leap of the soul to the sunrise. The morning mist rests lightly on chimneys and roofs and walls, wreathes the lamp-posts, and floats in gauzy streamers down the streets. Distant buildings are massed like palace walls, with turrets and spires lost in the rosy clouds. I love my beautiful city spreading all about me. I love the world. I love my place in the world.

CHAPTER XVII

THE LANDLADY

FROM SUNRISE TO SUNSET the day was long enough for many things besides school, which occupied five hours. There was time for me to try to earn my living; or at least the rent of our tenement. Rent was a standing trouble. We were always behind, and the landlady was very angry; so I was particularly ambitious to earn the rent. I had had one or two poems published since the celebrated eulogy of George Washington, but nobody had paid for my poems—yet. I was coming to that, of course, but in the mean time I could not pay the rent with my writing. To be sure, my acquaintance with men of letters gave me an opening. A friend of mine introduced me to a slightly literary lady, who introduced me to the editor of the "Boston Searchlight," who offered me a generous commission for subscriptions to his paper.

If our rent was three and one-half dollars per week, payable on strong demand, and the annual subscription to the "Searchlight" was one dollar, and my commission was fifty per cent, how many subscribers did I need? How easy! Seven subscribers a week—one a day! Anybody could do that. Mr. James, the editor, said so. He said I could get two or three any afternoon, between the end of school and supper. If I worked all Saturday—my head went dizzy computing the amount of my commissions. It would be rent and shoes and bonnets and everything for everybody.

Bright and early one Saturday morning in the fall I started out canvassing, in my hand a neatly folded copy of the "Searchlight," in my heart, faith in my lucky star and good-will towards all the world. I began with one of the great office buildings on Tremont Street, as Mr. James had advised. The first half-hour I lost, wandering through the corridors, reading the names on the doors. There were so many people in the same office, how should I know, when I entered, which was Wilson & Reed, Solicitors, and which C. Jenkins Smith, Mortgages and Bonds? I decided that it did not matter: I would call them all "Sir."

I selected a door and knocked. After waiting some time, I

knocked a little louder. The building buzzed with noise,—swift footsteps echoed on the stone floors, snappy talk broke out with the opening of every door, bells tinkled, elevators hummed,—no wonder they did not hear me knock. But I noticed that other people went in without knocking, so after a while I did the same.

There were several men and two women in the small, brightly lighted room. They were all busy. It was very confusing. Should I say "Sir" to the roomful?

"Excuse me, sir," I began. That was a very good beginning, I felt sure, but I must speak louder. Lately my voice had been poor in school—gave out, sometimes, in the middle of a recitation. I cleared my throat, but I did not repeat myself. The back of the bald head that I had addressed revolved and presented its complement, a bald front.

"Will you—would you like—I'd like—"

I stared in dismay at the bald gentleman, unable to recall a word of what I meant to say; and he stared in impatience at me.

"Well, well!" he snapped, "What is it? What is it?"

That reminded me.

"It's the 'Boston Searchlight,' sir. I take sub—"

"Take it away—take it away. We're busy here." He waved me away over his shoulder, the back of his head once more presented to me.

I stole out of the room in great confusion. Was that the way I was going to be received? Why, Mr. James had said nobody would hesitate to subscribe. It was the best paper in Boston, the "Searchlight," and no business man could afford to be without it. I must have made some blunder. Was "Mortgages and Bonds" a business? I'd never heard of it, and very likely I had spoken to C. Jenkins Smith. I must try again—of course I must try again.

I selected a real estate office next. A real estate broker, I knew for certain, was a business man. Mr. George A. Hooker must be just waiting for the "Boston Searchlight."

Mr. Hooker was indeed waiting, and he was telling "Central" about it.

"Yes, Central; waiting, waiting—What?—Yes, yes; ring *four*— What's that?—Since when?—Why did n't you say so at first, then, instead of keeping me on the line—What?—Oh, is that so? Well, never mind this time, Central.—I see, I see.—All right."

I had become so absorbed in this monologue that when Mr. Hooker swung around on me in his revolving chair I was startled, feeling that I had been caught eavesdropping. I thought he was going to rebuke me, but he only said, "What can I do for you, Miss?"

Encouraged by his forbearance, I said:—

"Would you like to subscribe to the 'Boston Searchlight,' sir?" —"Sir" was safer, after all.—"It's a dollar a year."

I was supposed to say that it was the best paper in Boston, etc., but Mr. Hooker did not look interested, though he was not cross.

"No, thank you, Miss; no new papers for me. Excuse me, I am very busy." And he began to dictate to a stenographer.

Well, that was not so bad. Mr. Hooker was at least polite. I must try to make a better speech next time. I stuck to real estate now. O'Lair & Kennedy were both in, in my next office, and both apparently enjoying a minute of relaxation, tilted back in their chairs behind a low railing. Said I, determined to be businesslike at last, and addressing myself to the whole firm:—

"Would you like to subscribe to the 'Boston Searchlight?' It's a very good paper. No business man can afford it—afford to be without it, I mean. It's only a dollar a year."

Both men smiled at my break, and I smiled, too. I wondered would they subscribe separately, or would they take one copy for the firm.

"The 'Boston Searchlight,' " repeated one of the partners. "Never heard of it. Is that the paper you have there?"

He unfolded the paper I gave him, looked over it, and handed it to his partner.

"Ever heard of the 'Searchlight,' O'Lair? What do you think— can we afford to be without it?"

"I guess we'll make out somehow," replied Mr. O'Lair, handing me back my paper. "But I'll buy this copy of you, Miss," he added, from second thoughts.

"And I'll go partner on the bargain," said Mr. Kennedy.

But I objected.

"This is a sample," I said; "I don't sell single papers. I take subscriptions for the year. It's one dollar."

"And no business man can afford it, you know." Mr. Kennedy

winked as he said it, and we all smiled again. It would have been stupid not to see the joke.

"I'm sorry I can't sell my sample," I said, with my hand on the doorknob.

"That's all right, my dear," said Mr. Kennedy, with a gracious wave of the hand. And his partner called after me, "Better luck next door!"

Well, I was getting on! The people grew friendlier all the time. But I skipped "next door"; it was "Mortgages and Bonds." I tried "Insurance."

"The best paper in Boston, is it?" remarked Mr. Thomas F. Dix, turning over my sample. "And who told you that, young lady?"

"Mr. James," was my prompt reply.

"Who is Mr. James?—The *editor!* Oh, I see. And do you also think the 'Searchlight' the best paper in Boston?"

"I don't know, sir. I like the 'Herald' much better, and the 'Transcript.'"

At that Mr. Dix laughed. "That's right," he said. "Business is business, but you tell the truth. One dollar, is it? Here you are. My name is on the door. Good-day."

I think I spent twenty minutes copying the name and room number from the door. I did not trust myself to read plain English. What if I made a mistake, and the "Searchlight" went astray, and good Mr. Dix remained unilluminated? He had paid for the year —it would be dreadful to make a mistake.

Emboldened by my one success, I went into the next office without considering the kind of business announced on the door. I tried brokers, lawyers, contractors, and all, just as they came around the corridor; but I copied no more addresses. Most of the people were polite. Some men waved me away, like C. Jenkins Smith. Some looked impatient at first, but excused themselves politely in the end. Almost everybody said, "We're busy here," as if they suspected I wanted them to read a whole year's issue of the "Searchlight" at once. At last one man told me he did not think it was a nice business for a girl, going through the offices like that.

This took me aback. I had not thought anything about the nature of the business. I only wanted the money to pay the rent. I wandered through miles of stone corridors, unable to see why it was not a nice business, and yet reluctant to go on with it, with the doubt in my mind. Intent on my new problem, I walked into a messenger boy; and looking back to apologize to him, I collided softly with a cushion-shaped gentleman getting out of an elevator. I was making up my mind to leave the building forever, when I saw an office door standing open. It was the first open door I had come across since morning—it was past noon now—and it was a sign to me to keep on. I must not give up so easily.

Mr. Frederick A. Strong was alone in the office, surreptitiously picking his teeth. He had been to lunch. He heard me out good-naturedly.

"How much is your commission, if I may ask?" It was the first thing he had said.

"Fifty cents, sir."

"Well, I'll tell you what I will do. I don't care to subscribe, but here's a quarter for you."

If I did not blush, it was because it is not my habit, but all of a sudden I choked. A lump jumped into my throat; almost the tears were in my eyes. That man was right who said it was not nice to go through the offices. I was taken for a beggar: a stranger offered me money for nothing.

I could not say a word. I started to go out. But Mr. Strong jumped up and prevented me.

"Oh, don't go like that!" he cried. "I did n't mean to offend you; upon my word, I did n't. I beg your pardon. I did n't know —you see—Won't you sit down a minute to rest? That's kind of you."

Mr. Strong was so genuinely repentant that I could not refuse him. Besides, I felt a little weak. I had been on my feet since morning, and had had no lunch. I sat down, and Mr. Strong talked. He showed me a picture of his wife and little girl, and said I must go and see them some time. Pretty soon I was chatting, too, and I told Mr. Strong about the Latin School; and of course he asked me if I was French, the way people always did when they wanted to say that I had a foreign accent. So we got started on Russia, and had such an interesting time that we both jumped up, surprised, when a fine young lady in a beautiful hat came in to take possession of the idle typewriter.

Mr. Strong introduced me very formally, thanked me for an interesting hour, and shook hands with me at the door. I did not add his name to my short subscription list, but I counted it a greater triumph that I had made a friend.

It would have been seeking an anticlimax to solicit any more in the building. I went out, into the roar of Tremont Street, and across the Common, still green and leafy. I rested a while on a bench, debating where to go next. It was past two by the clock on Park Street Church. I had had a long day already, but it was too early to quit work, with only one half dollar of my own in my pocket. It was Saturday—in the evening the landlady would come. I must try a little longer.

I went out along Columbus Avenue, a popular route for bicyclists at that time. The bicycle stores all along the way looked promising to me. The people did not look so busy as in the office building: they would at least be polite.

They were not particularly rude, but they did not subscribe. Nobody wanted the "Searchlight." They had never heard of it—they made jokes about it—they did not want it at any price.

I began to lose faith in the paper myself. I got tired of its name. I began to feel dizzy. I stopped going into the stores. I walked straight along, looking at nothing. I wanted to go back, go home, but I would n't. I felt like doing myself spite. I walked right along, straight as the avenue ran. I did not know where it would lead me. I did not care. Everything was horrid. I would go right on until night. I would get lost. I would fall in a faint on a strange doorstep, and be found dead in the morning, and be pitied.

Would n't that be interesting! The adventure might even end happily. I might faint at the door of a rich old man's house, who would take me in, and order his housekeeper to nurse me, just like in the story books. In my delirium—of course I would have a fever—I would talk about the landlady, and how I had tried to earn the rent; and the old gentleman would wipe his spectacles for pity. Then I would wake up, and ask plaintively, "Where am I?" And when I got strong, after a delightfully long convalescence, the old gentleman would take me to Dover Street—in a carriage!—and we would all be reunited, and laugh and cry together. The old gentleman, of course, would engage my father as his steward, on the spot, and we would all go to live in one of his houses, with a garden around it.

I walked on and on, gleefully aware that I had not eaten since morning. Was n't I beginning to feel shaky? Yes; I should certainly faint before long. But I did n't like the houses I passed. They did not look fit for my adventure. I must keep up till I reached a better neighborhood.

Anybody who knows Boston knows how cheaply my adventure ended. Columbus Avenue leads out to Roxbury Crossing. When I saw that the houses were getting shabbier, instead of finer, my heart sank. When I came out on the noisy, thrice-commonplace street-car centre, my spirit collapsed utterly.

I did not swoon. I woke up from my foolish, childish dream with a shock. I was disgusted with myself, and frightened besides. It was evening now, and I was faint and sick in good earnest, and I did not know where I was. I asked a starter at the transfer station the way to Dover Street, and he told me to get on a car that was just coming in.

"I'll walk," I said, "if you will please tell me the shortest way." How could I spend five cents out of the little I had made?

But the starter discouraged me.

"You can't walk it before midnight—the way you look, my girl. Better hop on that car before it goes."

I could not resist the temptation. I rode home in the car, and felt like a thief when I paid the fare. Five cents gone to pay for my folly!

I was grateful for a cold supper; thrice grateful to hear that Mrs. Hutch, the landlady, had been and gone, content with two dollars that my father had brought home.

Mrs. Hutch seldom succeeded in collecting the full amount of the rents from her tenants. I suppose that made the bookkeeping complicated, which must have been wearing on her nerves; and hence her temper. We lived, on Dover Street, in fear of her temper. Saturday had a distinct quality about it, derived from the imminence of Mrs. Hutch's visit. Of course I awoke on Saturday morning with the no-school feeling; but the grim thing that leaped to its feet and glowered down on me, while the rest of my consciousness was still yawning on its back, was the Mrs.-Hutch-is-coming-and-there's-no-rent feeling.

It is hard, if you are a young girl, full of life and inclined to be glad, to go to sleep in anxiety and awake in fear. It is apt to interfere with the circulation of the vital ether of happiness in the young, which is damaging to the complexion of the soul. It is bitter, when you are middle-aged and unsuccessful, to go to sleep in self-reproach and awake unexonerated. It is likely to cause fermentation in the sweetest nature; it is certain to breed gray hairs and a premature longing for death. It is pitiful, if you are the home-keeping mother of an impoverished family, to drop in your traces helpless at night, and awake unstrengthened in the early morning. The haunting consciousness of rooted poverty is an improper bedfellow for a woman who still bears. It has been known to induce physical and spiritual malformations in the babies she nurses.

It did require strength to lift the burden of life, in the gray morning, on Dover Street; especially on Saturday morning. Perhaps my mother's pack was the heaviest to lift. To the man of the house, poverty is a bulky dragon with gripping talons and a poisonous breath; but he bellows in the open, and it is possible to give him knightly battle, with the full swing of the angry arm that cuts to the enemy's vitals. To the housewife, want is an insidious myriapod creature that crawls in the dark, mates with its own offspring, breeds all the year round, persists like leprosy. The woman has an endless, inglorious struggle with the pest; her triumphs are too petty for applause, her failures too mean for notice. Care, to the man, is a hound to be kept in leash and mastered. To the woman, care is a secret parasite that infects the blood.

Mrs. Hutch, of course, was only one symptom of the disease of poverty, but there were times when she seemed to me the sharpest tooth of the gnawing canker. Surely as sorrow trails behind sin, Saturday evening brought Mrs. Hutch. The landlady did not trail. Her movements were anything but impassive. She climbed the stairs with determination and landed at the top with emphasis. Her knock on the door was clear, sharp, unfaltering; it was impossible to pretend not to hear it. Her "Good-evening" announced business; her manner of taking a chair suggested the throwing-down of the gauntlet. Invariably she asked for my father, calling him Mr. Anton, and refusing to be corrected; almost invariably he was not at home—was out looking for work. Had he left her the rent? My mother's gentle "No, ma'am" was the signal for the storm. I do not want to repeat what Mrs. Hutch said. It would be hard on her, and hard on me. She grew red in the face; her voice grew shriller with every word. My poor mother hung her head where she stood;

the children stared from their corners; the frightened baby cried. The angry landlady rehearsed our sins like a prophet foretelling doom. We owed so many weeks' rent; we were too lazy to work; we never intended to pay; we lived on others; we deserved to be put out without warning. She reproached my mother for having too many children; she blamed us all for coming to America. She enumerated her losses through nonpayment of her rents; told us that she did not collect the amount of her taxes; showed us how our irregularities were driving a poor widow to ruin.

My mother did not attempt to excuse herself, but when Mrs. Hutch began to rail against my absent father, she tried to put in a word in his defence. The landlady grew all the shriller at that, and silenced my mother impatiently. Sometimes she addressed herself to me. I always stood by, if I was at home, to give my mother the moral support of my dumb sympathy. I understood that Mrs. Hutch had a special grudge against me, because I did not go to work as a cash girl and earn three dollars a week. I wanted to explain to her how I was preparing myself for a great career, and I was ready to promise her the payment of the arrears as soon as I began to get rich. But the landlady would not let me put in a word. And I was sorry for her, because she seemed to be having such a bad time.

At last Mrs. Hutch got up to leave, marching out as determinedly as she had marched in. At the door she turned, in undiminished wrath, to shoot her parting dart:—

"And if Mr. Anton does not bring me the rent on Monday, I will serve notice of eviction on Tuesday, without fail."

We breathed when she was gone. My mother wiped away a few tears, and went to the baby, crying in the windowless, air-tight room.

I was the first to speak.

"Is n't she queer, mamma!" I said. "She never remembers how to say our name. She insists on saying *Anton—Anton.* Celia, say *Anton.*" And I made the baby laugh by imitating the landlady, who had made her cry.

But when I went to my little room I did not mock Mrs. Hutch. I thought about her, thought long and hard, and to a purpose. I decided that she must hear me out once. She must understand about my plans, my future, my good intentions. It was too irrational to go on like this, we living in fear of her, she in distrust of us. If Mrs. Hutch would only trust me, and the tax collectors would trust her, we could all live happily forever.

I was the more certain that my argument would prevail with the landlady, if only I could make her listen, because I understood her point of view. I even sympathized with her. What she said about the babies, for instance, was not all unreasonable to me. There was this last baby, my mother's sixth, born on Mrs. Hutch's premises —yes, in the windowless, air-tight bedroom. Was there any need of this baby? When May was born, two years earlier, on Wheeler Street, I had accepted her; after a while I even welcomed her. She was born an American, and it was something to me to have one genuine American relative. I had to sit up with her the whole of her first night on earth, and I questioned her about the place she came from, and so we got acquainted. As my mother was so ill that my sister Frieda, who was nurse, and the doctor from the dispensary had all they could do to take care of her, the baby remained in my charge a good deal, and so I got used to her. But when Celia came I was two years older, and my outlook was broader; I could see around a baby's charms, and discern the disadvantages of possessing the baby. I was supplied with all kinds of relatives now— I had a brother-in-law, and an American-born nephew, who might become a President. Moreover, I knew there was not enough to eat before the baby's advent, and she did not bring any supplies with her that I could see. The baby was one too many. There was no need of her. I resented her existence. I recorded my resentment in my journal.

I was pleased with my broad-mindedness, that enabled me to see all sides of the baby question. I could regard even the rent question disinterestedly, like a philosopher reviewing natural phenomena. It seemed not unreasonable that Mrs. Hutch should have a craving for the rent as such. A school-girl dotes on her books, a baby cries for its rattle, and a landlady yearns for her rents. I could easily believe that it was doing Mrs. Hutch spiritual violence to withhold the rent from her; and hence the vehemence with which she pursued the arrears.

Yes, I could analyze the landlady very nicely. I was certainly qualified to act as peacemaker between her and my family. But I must go to her own house, and *not* on a rent day. Saturday evening,

when she was embittered by many disappointments, was no time
to approach her with diplomatic negotiations. I must go to her
house on a day of good omen.

And I went, as soon as my father could give me a week's rent
to take along. I found Mrs. Hutch in the gloom of a long, faded
parlor. Divested of the ample black coat and widow's bonnet in
which I had always seen her, her presence would have been less
formidable had I not been conscious that I was a mere rumpled
sparrow fallen into the lion's den. When I had delivered the money,
I should have begun my speech; but I did not know what came
first of all there was to say. While I hesitated, Mrs. Hutch observed
me. She noticed my books, and asked about them. I thought this
was my opening, and I showed her eagerly my Latin grammar, my
geometry, my Virgil. I began to tell her how I was to go to college,
to fit myself to write poetry, and get rich, and pay the arrears. But
Mrs. Hutch cut me short at the mention of college. She broke out
with her old reproaches, and worked herself into a worse fury than
I had ever witnessed before. I was all alone in the tempest, and a
very old lady was sitting on a sofa, drinking tea; and the tidy on
the back of the sofa was sliding down.

I was so bewildered by the suddenness of the onslaught, I felt
so helpless to defend myself, that I could only stand and stare at
Mrs. Hutch. She kept on railing without stopping for breath, repeating herself over and over. At last I ceased to hear what she said;
I became hypnotized by the rapid motions of her mouth. Then the
moving tidy caught my eye and the spell was broken. I went over
to the sofa with a decided step and carefully replaced the tidy.

It was now the landlady's turn to stare, and I stared back, surprised at my own action. The old lady also stared, her teacup sus-
pended under her nose. The whole thing was so ridiculous! I had
come on such a grand mission, ready to dictate the terms of a noble
peace. I was met with anger and contumely; the dignity of the
ambassador of peace rubbed off at a touch, like the golden dust
from the butterfly's wing. I took my scolding like a meek child;
and then, when she was in the middle of a trenchant phrase, her
eye fixed daggerlike on mine, I calmly went to put the enemy's
house in order! It was ridiculous, and I laughed.

Immediately I was sorry. I wanted to apologize, but Mrs. Hutch
did n't give me a chance. If she had been harsh before, she was

terrific now. Did I come there to insult her?—she wanted to know.
Was n't it enough that I and my family lived on her, that I must
come to her on purpose to rile her with my talk about college—
college! these beggars!—and laugh in her face? "What did you come
for? Who sent you? Why do you stand there staring? Say something! *College!* these beggars! And do you think I'll keep you till
you go to college? *You,* learning geometry! Did you ever figure
out how much rent your father owes me? You are all too lazy—
Don't say a word! Don't speak to me! Coming here to laugh in
my face! I don't believe you can say one sensible word. *Latin*—
and *French!* Oh, these beggars! You ought to go to work, if you
know enough to do one sensible thing. *College!* Go home and tell
your father never to send you again. Laughing in my face—and
staring! Why don't you say something? How old are you?"

Mrs. Hutch actually stopped, and I jumped into the pause.

"I'm seventeen," I said quickly, "and I feel like seventy."

This was too much, even for me who had spoken. I had not
meant to say the last. It broke out, like my wicked laugh. I was
afraid, if I stayed any longer, Mrs. Hutch would have the apoplexy;
and I felt that I was going to cry. I moved towards the door, but
the landlady got in another speech before I had escaped.

"Seventeen—seventy! And looks like twelve! The child is silly.
Can't even tell her own age. No wonder, with her Latin, and
French, and—"

I did cry when I got outside, and I did n't care if I was noticed.
What was the use of anything? Everything I did was wrong. Everything I tried to do for Mrs. Hutch turned out bad. I tried to sell
papers, for the sake of the rent, and nobody wanted the "Searchlight," and I was told it was not a nice business. I wanted to take
her into my confidence, and she would n't hear a word, but scolded
and called me names. She was an unreasonable, ungrateful landlady.
I wished she *would* put us out, then we should be rid of her.—But
was n't it funny about that tidy? What made me do that? I never
meant to. Curious, the way we sometimes do things we don't want
to at all.—The old lady must be deaf; she did n't say anything all
that time.—Oh, I have a whole book of the "Æneid" to review,
and it's getting late. I must hurry home.

It was impossible to remain despondent long. The landlady came
only once a week, I reflected, as I walked, and the rest of the time

I was surrounded by friends. Everybody was good to me, at home, of course, and at school; and there was Miss Dillingham, and her friend who took me out in the country to see the autumn leaves, and her friend's friend who lent me books, and Mr. Hurd, who put my poems in the "Transcript," and gave me books almost every time I came, and a dozen others who did something good for me all the time, besides the several dozen who wrote me such nice letters. Friends? If I named one for every block I passed I should not get through before I reached home. There was Mr. Strong, too, and he wanted me to meet his wife and little girl. And Mr. Pastor! I had almost forgotten Mr. Pastor. I arrived at the corner of Washington and Dover Streets, on my way home, and looked into Mr. Pastor's showy drug store as I passed, and that reminded me of the history of my latest friendship.

My cough had been pretty bad—kept me awake nights. My voice gave out frequently. The teachers had spoken to me several times, suggesting that I ought to see a doctor. Of course the teachers did not know that I could not afford a doctor, but I could go to the free dispensary, and I did. They told me to come again, and again, and I lost precious hours sitting in the waiting-room, watching for my turn. I was examined, thumped, studied, and sent out with prescriptions and innumerable directions. All that was said about food, fresh air, sunny rooms, etc., was, of course, impossible; but I would try the medicine. A bottle of medicine was a definite thing with a fixed price. You either could or could not afford it, on a given day. Once you began with milk and eggs and such things, there was no end of it. You were always going around the corner for more, till the grocer said he could give no more credit. No; the medicine bottle was the only safe thing.

I had taken several bottles, and was told that I was looking better, when I went, one day, to have my prescription renewed. It was just after a hard rain, and the pools on the broken pavements were full of blue sky. I was delighted with the beautiful reflections; there were even the white clouds moving across the blue, there, at my feet, on the pavement! I walked with my head down all the way to the drug store, which was all right; but I should not have done it going back, with the new bottle of medicine in my hand.

In front of a cigar store, halfway between Washington Street and Harrison Avenue, stood a wooden Indian with a package of wooden cigars in his hand. My eyes on the shining rain pools, I walked plump into the Indian, and the bottle was knocked out of my hand and broke with a crash.

I was horrified at the catastrophe. The medicine cost fifty cents. My mother had given me the last money in the house. I must not be without my medicine; the dispensary doctor was very emphatic about that. It would be dreadful to get sick and have to stay out of school. What was to be done?

I made up my mind in less than five minutes. I went back to the drug store and asked for Mr. Pastor himself. He knew me; he often sold me postage stamps, and joked about my large correspondence, and heard a good deal about my friends. He came out, on this occasion, from his little office in the back of the store; and I told him of my accident, and that there was no more money at home, and asked him to give me another bottle, to be paid for as soon as possible. My father had a job as night watchman in a store. I should be able to pay very soon.

"Certainly, my dear, certainly," said Mr. Pastor; "very glad to oblige you. It's doing you good, is n't it?—That's right. You're such a studious young lady, with all those books, and so many letters to write—you need something to build you up. There you are.—Oh, don't mention it! Any time at all. And look out for wild Indians!"

Of course we were great friends after that, and this is the way my troubles often ended on Dover Street. To bump into a wooden Indian was to bump into good luck, a hundred times a week. No wonder I was happy most of the time.

CHAPTER XVIII

THE BURNING BUSH

Just when Mrs. Hutch was most worried about the error of my ways, I entered on a new chapter of adventures, even more remote from the cash girl's career than Latin and geometry. But I ought not to name such harsh things as landladies at the opening of the fairy story of my girlhood. I have reached what was the second transformation of my life, as truly as my coming to America was the first great transformation.

Robert Louis Stevenson, in one of his delightful essays, credits the lover with a feeling of remorse and shame at the contemplation of that part of his life which he lived without his beloved, content with his barren existence. It is with just such a feeling of remorse that I look back to my bookworm days, before I began the study of natural history outdoors; and with a feeling of shame akin to the lover's I confess how late in my life nature took the first place in my affections.

The subject of nature study is better developed in the public schools to-day than it was in my time. I remember my teacher in the Chelsea grammar school who encouraged us to look for different kinds of grasses in the empty lots near home, and to bring to school samples of the cereals we found in our mothers' pantries. I brought the grasses and cereals, as I did everything the teacher ordered, but I was content when nature study was over and the arithmetic lesson began. I was not interested, and the teacher did not make it interesting.

In the boys' books I was fond of reading I came across all sorts of heroes, and I sympathized with them all. The boy who ran away to sea; the boy who delighted in the society of ranchmen and cowboys; the stage-struck boy, whose ambition was to drive a pasteboard chariot in a circus; the boy who gave up his holidays in order to earn money for books; the bad boy who played tricks on people; the clever boy who invented amusing toys for his blind little sister—all these boys I admired. I could put myself in the place of any one of these heroes, and delight in their delights. But there was one sort of hero I never could understand, and that was the boy whose favorite reading was natural history, who kept an aquarium, collected beetles, and knew all about a man by the name of Agassiz. This style of boy always had a seafaring uncle, or a missionary aunt, who sent him all sorts of queer things from China and the South Sea Islands; and the conversation between this boy and the seafaring uncle home on a visit, I was perfectly willing to skip. The impossible hero usually kept snakes in a box in the barn, where his little sister was fond of playing with her little friends. The snakes escaped at least once before the end of the story; and the things the boy said to the frightened little girls, about the harmless and fascinating qualities of snakes, was something I had no patience to read.

No, I did not care for natural history. I would read about travels, about deserts, and nameless islands, and strange peoples; but snakes and birds and minerals and butterflies did not interest me in the least. I visited the Natural History Museum once or twice, because it was my way to enter every open door, so as to miss nothing that was free to the public; but the curious monsters that filled the glass cases and adorned the walls and ceilings failed to stir my imagination, and the slimy things that floated in glass vessels were too horrid for a second glance.

Of all the horrid things that ever passed under my eyes when I lifted my nose from my book, spiders were the worst. Mice were bad enough, and so were flies and worms and June bugs; but spiders were absolutely the most loathsome creatures I knew. And yet it was the spider that opened my eyes to the wonders of nature, and touched my girlish happiness with the hues of the infinite.

And it happened at Hale House.

It was not Dr. Hale, though it might have been, who showed me the way to the settlement house on Garland Street which bears his name. Hale House is situated in the midst of the labyrinth of narrow streets and alleys that constitutes the slum of which Harrison Avenue is the backbone, and of which Dover Street is a member.

Bearing in mind the fact that there are almost no playgrounds in all this congested district, you will understand that Hale House has plenty of work on its hands to carry a little sunshine into the grimy tenement homes. The beautiful story of how that is done cannot be told here, but what Hale House did for me I may not omit to mention.

It was my brother Joseph who discovered Hale House. He started a debating club, and invited his chums to help him settle the problems of the Republic on Sunday afternoons. The club held its first session in our empty parlor on Dover Street, and the United States Government was in a fair way to be put on a sound basis at last, when the numerous babies belonging to our establishment broke up the meeting, leaving the Administration in suspense as to its future course.

The next meeting was held in Isaac Maslinsky's parlor, and the orators were beginning to jump to their feet and shake their fists at each other, in excellent parliamentary form, when Mrs. Maslinsky sallied in, to smile at the boys' excitement. But at the sight of seven pairs of boys' boots scuffling on her cherished parlor carpet, the fringed cover of the centre table hanging by one corner, and the plush photograph album unceremoniously laid aside, indignation took the place of good humor in Mrs. Maslinsky's ample bosom, and she ordered the boys to clear out, threatening "Ike" with dire vengeance if ever again he ventured to enter the parlor with ungentle purpose.

On the following Sunday Harry Rubinstein offered the club the hospitality of *his* parlor, and the meeting began satisfactorily. The subject on the table was the Tariff, and the pros and antis were about evenly divided. Congress might safely have taken a nap, with the Hub Debating Club to handle its affairs, if Harry Rubinstein's big brother Jake had not interfered. He came out of the kitchen, where he had been stuffing the baby with peanuts, and stood in the doorway of the parlor and winked at the dignified chairman. The chairman turned his back on him, whereupon Jake pelted him with peanut shells. He mocked the speakers, and called them "kids," and wanted to know how they could tell the Tariff from a sunstroke, anyhow. "We've got to have free trade," he mocked. "Pa, listen to the kids! 'In the interests of the American laborer.' Hoo-ray! Listen to the kids, pa!"

Flesh and blood could not bear this. The political reformers adjourned indefinitely, and the club was in danger of extinction for want of a sheltering roof, when one of the members discovered that

Hale House, on Garland Street, was waiting to welcome the club.

How the debating-club prospered in the genial atmosphere of the settlement house; how from a little club it grew to be a big club, as the little boys became young men; how Joseph and Isaac and Harry and the rest won prizes in public debates; how they came to be a part of the multiple influence for good that issues from Garland Street—all this is a piece of the history of Hale House, whose business in the slums is to mould the restless children on the street corners into noble men and women. I brought the debating-club into my story just to show how naturally the children of the slums drift toward their salvation, if only some island of safety lies in the course of their innocent activities. Not a child in the slums is born to be lost. They are all born to be saved, and the raft that carries them unharmed through the perilous torrent of tenement life is the child's unconscious aspiration for the best. But there must be lighthouses to guide him midstream.

Dora followed Joseph to Hale House, joining a club for little girls which has since become famous in the Hale House district. The leader of this club, under pretence of teaching the little girls the proper way to sweep and make beds, artfully teaches them how to beautify a tenement home by means of noble living.

Joseph and Dora were so enthusiastic about Hale House that I had to go over and see what it was all about. And I found the Natural History Club.

I do not know how Mrs. Black, who was then the resident, persuaded me to try the Natural History Club, in spite of my aversion for bugs. I suppose she tried me in various girls' clubs, and found that I did not fit, any more than I fitted in the dancing-club that I attempted years before. I dare say she decided that I was an old maid, and urged me to come to the meetings of the Natural History Club, which was composed of adults. The members of this club were not people from the neighborhood, I understood, but workers at Hale House and their friends; and they often had eminent naturalists, travellers, and other notables lecture before them. My curiosity to see a real live naturalist probably induced me to accept Mrs. Black's invitation in the end; for up to that time I had never met any one who enjoyed the creepy society of snakes and worms, except in books.

The Natural History Club sat in a ring around the reception

room, facing the broad doorway of the adjoining room. Mrs. Black introduced me, and I said "Glad to meet you" all around the circle, and sat down in a kindergarten chair beside the piano. It was Friday evening, and I had the sense of leisure which pervades the school-girl's consciousness when there is to be no school on the morrow. I liked the pleasant room, pleasanter than any at home. I liked the faces of the company I was in. I was prepared to have an agreeable evening, even if I was a little bored.

The tall, lean gentleman with the frank blue eyes got up to read the minutes of the last meeting. I did not understand what he read, but I noticed that it gave him great satisfaction. This man had greeted me as if he had been waiting for my coming all his life. What did Mrs. Black call him? He looked and spoke as if he was happy to be alive. I liked him. Oh, yes! this was Mr. Winthrop.

I let my thoughts wander, with my eyes, all around the circle, trying to read the characters of my new friends in their faces. But suddenly my attention was arrested by a word. Mr. Winthrop had finished reading the minutes, and was introducing the speaker of the evening. "We are very fortunate in having with us Mr. Emerson, whom we all know as an authority on spiders."

Spiders! What hard luck! Mr. Winthrop pronounced the word "spiders" with unmistakable relish, as if he doted on the horrid creatures; but I— My nerves contracted into a tight knot. I gripped the arms of my little chair, determined *not* to run, with all those strangers looking on. I watched Mr. Emerson, to see when he would open a box of spiders. I recalled a hideous experience of long ago, when, putting on a dress that had hung on the wall for weeks, I felt a thing with a hundred legs crawling down my bare arm, and shook a spider out of my sleeve. I watched the lecturer, but I was *not* going to run. It was too bad that Mrs. Black had not warned me.

After a while I realized that the lecturer had no menagerie in his pockets. He talked, in a familiar way, about different kinds of spiders and their ways; and as he talked, he wove across the doorway, where he stood, a gigantic spider's web, unwinding a ball of twine in his hand, and looping various lengths on invisible tacks he had ready in the door frame.

I was fascinated by the progress of the web. I forgot my terrors; I began to follow Mr. Emerson's discourse. I was surprised to hear

how much there was to know about a dusty little spider, besides
that he could spin his webs as fast as my broom could sweep them
away. The drama of the spider's daily life became very real to me
as the lecturer went on. His struggle for existence; his wars with
his enemies; his wiles, his traps, his patient labors; the intricate safe-
guards of his simple existence; the fitness of his body for his surroundings, of his instincts for his vital needs—the whole picture of
the spider's pursuit of life under the direction of definite laws filled
me with a great wonder and left no room in my mind for repugnance or fear. It was the first time the natural history of a living
creature had been presented to me under such circumstances that I
could not avoid hearing and seeing, and I was surprised at my dul-
ness in the past when I had rejected books on natural history.

I did not become an enthusiastic amateur naturalist at once; I
did not at once begin to collect worms and bugs. But on the next
sweeping-day I stood on a chair, craning my neck, to study the
spider webs I discovered in the corners of the ceiling; and one or
two webs of more than ordinary perfection I suffered to remain
undisturbed for weeks, although it was my duty, as a housecleaner,
to sweep the ceiling clean. I began to watch for the mice that were
wont to scurry across the floor when the house slept and I alone
waked. I even placed a crust for them on the threshold of my room,
and cultivated a breathless intimacy with them, when the little gray
beasts acknowledged my hospitality by nibbling my crust in full
sight. And so by degrees I came to a better understanding of my
animal neighbors on all sides, and I began to look forward to the
meetings of the Natural History Club.

The club had frequent field excursions, in addition to the regular
meetings. At the seashore, in the woods, in the fields; at high tide
and low tide, in summer and winter, by sunlight and by moonlight,
the marvellous story of orderly nature was revealed to me, in fragments that allured the imagination and made me beg for more.
Some of the members of the club were school-teachers, accustomed
to answering questions. All of them were patient; some of them
took special pains with me. But nobody took me seriously as a
member of the club. They called me the club mascot, and appointed
me curator of the club museum, which was not in existence, at a
salary of ten cents a year, which was never paid. And I was well

The Natural History Club Had Frequent Field Excursions

pleased with my unique position in the club, delighted with my new friends, enraptured with my new study.

More and more, as the seasons rolled by, and page after page of the book of nature was turned before my eager eyes, did I feel the wonder and thrill of the revelations of science, till all my thoughts became colored with the tints of infinite truths. My days arranged themselves around the meetings of the club as a centre. The whole structure of my life was transfigured by my novel experiences outdoors. I realized, with a shock at first, but afterwards with complacency, that books were taking a secondary place in my life, my irregular studies in natural history holding the first place. I began to enjoy the Natural History rooms; and I was obliged to admit to myself that my heart hung with a more thrilling suspense over the fate of some beans I had planted in a window box than over the fortunes of the classic hero about whom we were reading at school.

But for all my enthusiasm about animals, plants, and rocks,— for all my devotion to the Natural History Club,—I did not become a thorough naturalist. My scientific friends were right not to take me seriously. Mr. Winthrop, in his delightfully frank way, called me a fraud; and I did not resent it. I dipped into zoölogy, botany, geology, ornithology, and an infinite number of other ologies, as the activities of the club or of particular members of it gave me opportunity, but I made no systematic study of any branch of science; at least not until I went to college. For what enthralled my imagination in the whole subject of natural history was not the orderly array of facts, but the glimpse I caught, through this or that fragment of science, of the grand principles underlying the facts. By asking questions, by listening when my wise friends talked, by reading, by pondering and dreaming, I slowly gathered together the kaleidoscopic bits of the stupendous panorama which is painted in the literature of Darwinism. Everything I had ever learned at school was illumined by this new knowledge; the world lay newly made under my eyes. Vastly as my mind had stretched to embrace the idea of a great country, when I exchanged Polotzk for America, it was no such enlargement as I now experienced, when in place of the measurable earth, with its paltry tale of historic centuries, I was given the illimitable universe to contemplate, with the numberless æons of infinite time.

As the meaning of nature was deepened for me, so was its aspect beautified. Hitherto I had loved in nature the spectacular,—the blazing sunset, the whirling tempest, the flush of summer, the snow-wonder of winter. Now, for the first time, my heart was satisfied with the microscopic perfection of a solitary blossom. The harmonious murmur of autumn woods broke up into a hundred separate melodies, as the pelting acorn, the scurrying squirrel, the infrequent chirp of the lingering cricket, and the soft speed of ripe pine cones through dense-grown branches, each struck its discriminate chord in the scented air. The outdoor world was magnified in every dimension; inanimate things were vivified; living things were dignified.

No two persons set the same value on any given thing, and so it may very well be that I am boasting of the enrichment of my life through the study of natural history to ears that hear not. I need only recall my own obtuseness to the subject, before the story of the spider sharpened my senses, to realize that these confessions of a nature lover may bore every other person who reads them. But I do not pretend to be concerned about the reader at this point. I never hope to explain to my neighbor the exact value of a winter sunrise in my spiritual economy, but I know that my life has grown better since I learned to distinguish between a butterfly and a moth; that my faith in man is the greater because I have watched for the coming of the song sparrow in the spring; and my thoughts of immortality are the less wavering because I have cherished the winter chickweed on my lawn.

Those who find their greatest intellectual and emotional satisfaction in the study of nature are apt to refer their spiritual problems also to science. That is how it went with me. Long before my introduction to natural history I had realized, with an uneasy sense of the breaking of peace, that the questions which I thought to have been settled years before were beginning to tease me anew. In Russia I had practised a prescribed religion, with little faith in what I professed, and a restless questioning of the universe. When I came to America I lightly dropped the religious forms that I had half mocked before, and contented myself with a few novel phrases employed by my father in his attempt to explain the riddle of existence. The busy years flew by, when from morning till night I was preoccupied with the process of becoming an American; and no question arose in my mind that my books or my teachers could not fully answer. Then came a time when the ordinary business of my girl's life discharged itself automatically, and I had leisure once more to look over and around things. This period coinciding with my moody adolescence, I rapidly entangled myself in a net of doubts and questions, after the well-known manner of a growing girl. I asked once more, How did I come to be?—and I found that I was no whit wiser than poor Reb' Lebe, whom I had despised for his ignorance. For all my years of America and schooling, I could give no better answer to my clamoring questions than the teacher of my childhood. Whence came the fair world? Was there a God, after all? And if so, what did He intend when He made me?

It was always my way, if I wanted anything, to turn my daily life into a pursuit of that thing. "Have you seen the treasure I seek?" I asked of every man I met. And if it was God that I desired, I made all my friends search their hearts for evidence of His being. I asked all the wise people I knew what they were going to do with themselves after death; and if the wise failed to satisfy me, I questioned the simple, and listened to the babies talking in their sleep.

Still the imperative clamor of my mind remained unallayed. Was all my life to be a hunger and a questioning? I complained of my teachers, who stuffed my head with facts and gave my soul no crumb to feed on. I blamed the stars for their silence. I sat up nights brooding over the emptiness of knowledge, and praying for revelations.

Sometimes I lived for days in a chimera of doubts, feeling that it was hardly worth while living at all if I was never to know why I was born and why I could not live forever. It was in one of these prolonged moods that I heard that a friend of mine, a distinguished man of letters whom I greatly admired, was coming to Boston for a short visit. A terrific New England blizzard arrived some hours in advance of my friend's train, but so intent was I on questioning him that I disregarded the weather, and struggled through towering snowdrifts, in the teeth of the wild wind, to the railroad station. There I nearly perished of weariness while waiting for the train, which was delayed by the storm. But when my friend emerged from one of the snow-crusted cars I was rewarded; for the blizzard had kept the reporters away, and the great man could give me his undivided attention.

No doubt he understood the pressing importance of the matter to me, from the trouble I had taken to secure an early interview with him. He heard me out very soberly, and answered my questions as honestly as a thinking man could. Not a word of what he said remains in my mind, but I remember going away with the impression that it was possible to live without knowing everything, after all, and that I might even try to be happy in a world full of riddles.

In such ways as this I sought peace of mind, but I never achieved more than a brief truce. I was coming to believe that only the stupid could be happy, and that life was pretty hard on the philosophical, when the great new interest of science came into my life, and scattered my blue devils as the sun scatters the night damps.

Some of my friends in the Natural History Club were deeply versed in the principles of evolutionary science, and were able to guide me in my impetuous rush to learn everything in a day. I was in a hurry to deduce, from the conglomeration of isolated facts that I picked up in the lectures, the final solution of all my problems. It took both patience and wisdom to check me and at the same time satisfy me, I have no doubt; but then I was always fortunate in my friends. Wisdom and patience in plenty were spent on me, and I was instructed and inspired and comforted. Of course my wisest teacher was not able to tell me how the original spark of life was kindled, nor to point out, on the starry map of heaven, my future abode. The bread of absolute knowledge I do not hope to taste in this life. But all creation was remodelled on a grander scale by the utterances of my teachers; and my problems, though they deepened with the expansion of all namable phenomena, were carried up to the heights of the impersonal, and ceased to torment me. Seeing how life and death, beginning and end, were all parts of the process of being, it mattered less in what particular ripple of the flux of existence I found myself. If past time was a trooping of similar yesterdays, back over the unbroken millenniums, to the first moment, it was simple to think of future time as a trooping of knowable to-days, on and on, to infinity. Possibly, also, the spark of life that had persisted through the geological ages, under a million million disguises, was vital enough to continue for another earth-age, in some shape as potent as the first or last. Thinking in æons and in races, instead of in years and individuals, somehow lightened the burden of intelligence, and filled me anew with a sense of youth and well-being, that I had almost lost in the pit of my narrow personal doubts.

No one who understands the nature of youth will be misled, by this summary of my intellectual history, into thinking that I actually arranged my newly acquired scientific knowledge into any such orderly philosophy as, for the sake of clearness, I have outlined above. I had long passed my teens, and had seen something of life that is not revealed to poetizing girls, before I could give any logical account of what I read in the book of cosmogony. But the high peaks of the promised land of evolution did flash on my vision in the earlier days, and with these to guide me I rebuilt the world, and found it much nobler than it had ever been before, and took great comfort in it.

I did not become a finished philosopher from hearing a couple of hundred lectures on scientific subjects. I did not even become a finished woman. If anything, I grew rather more girlish. I remember myself as very merry in the midst of my serious scientific friends, and I can think of no time when I was more inclined to play the tomboy than when off for a day in the woods, in quest of botanical and zoölogical specimens. The freedom of outdoors, the society of congenial friends, the delight of my occupation—all acted as a strong wine on my mood, and sent my spirits soaring to immoderate heights. I am very much afraid I made myself a nuisance, at times, to some of the more sedate of my grown-up companions. I wish they could know that I have truly repented. I wish they had known at the time that it was the exuberance of my happiness that played tricks, and no wicked desire to annoy kind friends. But I am sure that those who were offended have long since forgotten or forgiven, and I need remember nothing of those wonderful days other than that a new sun rose above a new earth for me, and that my happiness was like unto the iridescent dews.

CHAPTER XIX

A KINGDOM IN THE SLUMS

I DID NOT ALWAYS WAIT for the Natural History Club to guide me to delectable lands. Some of the happiest days of that happy time I spent with my sister in East Boston. We had a merry time at supper, Moses making clever jokes, without cracking a smile himself; and the baby romping in his high chair, eating what was n't good for him. But the best of the evening came later, when father and baby had gone to bed, and the dishes were put away, and there was not a crumb left on the red-and-white checked tablecloth. Frieda took out her sewing, and I took a book; and the lamp was between us, shining on the table, on the large brown roses on the wall, on the green and brown diamonds of the oil cloth on the floor, on the baby's rattle on a shelf, and on the shining stove in the corner. It was such a pleasant kitchen—such a cosey, friendly room—that when Frieda and I were left alone I was perfectly happy just to sit there. Frieda had a beautiful parlor, with plush chairs and a velvet carpet and gilt picture frames; but we preferred the homely, homelike kitchen.

I read aloud from Longfellow, or Whittier, or Tennyson; and it was as great a treat to me as it was to Frieda. Her attention alone was inspiring. Her delight, her eager questions doubled the meaning of the lines I read. Poor Frieda had little enough time for reading, unless she stole it from the sewing or the baking or the mending. But she was hungry for books, and so grateful when I came to read to her that it made me ashamed to remember all the beautiful things I had and did not share with her.

It is true I shared what could be shared. I brought my friends to her. At her wedding were some of the friends of whom I was most proud. Miss Dillingham came, and Mr. Hurd; and the humbler guests stared in admiration at our school-teachers and editors. But I had so many delightful things that I could not bring to Frieda—my walks, my dreams, my adventures of all sorts. And yet when I told her about them, I found that she partook of everything. For she had her talent for vicarious enjoyment, by means of which she entered as an actor into my adventures, was present as a witness at the frolic of my younger life. Or if I narrated things that were beyond her, on account of her narrower experience, she listened with an eager longing to understand that was better than some people's easy comprehension. My world ever rang with good tidings, and she was grateful if I brought her the echo of them, to ring again within the four walls of the kitchen that bounded her life. And I, who lived on the heights, and walked with the learned, and bathed in the crystal fountains of youth, sometimes climbed the sublimest peak in my sister's humble kitchen, there caught the unfaltering accents of inspiration, and rejoiced in silver pools of untried happiness.

The way she reached out for everything fine was shown by her interest in the incomprehensible Latin and French books that I brought. She liked to hear me read my Cicero, pleased by the movement of the sonorous periods. I translated Ovid and Virgil for her; and her pleasure illumined the difficult passages, so that I seldom needed to have recourse to the dictionary. I shall never forget the evening I read to her, from the "Æneid," the passage in the fourth book describing the death of Dido. I read the Latin first, and then my own version in English hexameters, that I had prepared for a recitation at school. Frieda forgot her sewing in her lap, and leaned forward in rapt attention. When I was through, there were tears of delight in her eyes; and I was surprised myself at the beauty of the words I had just pronounced.

I do not dare to confess how much of my Latin I have forgotten, lest any of the devoted teachers who taught me should learn the sad truth; but I shall always boast of some acquaintance with Virgil, through that scrap of the "Æneid" made memorable by my sister's enjoyment of it.

Truly my education was not entirely in the hands of persons who had licenses to teach. My sister's fat baby taught me things about the origin and ultimate destiny of dimples that were not in any of my school-books. Mr. Casey, of the second floor, who was drunk whenever his wife was sober, gave me an insight into the psychology of the beer mug that would have added to the mental furniture of my most scholarly teacher. The bold-faced girls who passed the evening on the corner, in promiscuous flirtation with the cock-eyed youths of the neighborhood, unconsciously revealed to me the eternal secrets of adolescence. My neighbor of the third floor, who sat on the curbstone with the scabby baby in her bedraggled lap, had things to say about the fine ladies who came in carriages to inspect the public bathhouse across the street that ought to be repeated in the lecture halls of every school of philanthropy. Instruction poured into my brain at such a rate that I could not digest it all at the time; but in later years, when my destiny had led me far from Dover Street, the emphatic moral of those lessons became clear. The memory of my experience on Dover Street became the strength of my convictions, the illumined index of my purpose, the aureola of my happiness. And if I paid for those lessons with days of privation and dread, with nights of tormenting anxiety, I count the price cheap. Who would not go to a little trouble to find out what life is made of? Life in the slums spins busily as a schoolboy's top, and one who has heard its humming never forgets. I look forward to telling, when I get to be a master of language, what I read in the crooked cobblestones when I revisited Dover Street the other day.

Dover Street was never really my residence—at least, not the whole of it. It happened to be the nook where my bed was made, but I inhabited the City of Boston. In the pearl-misty morning, in the ruby-red evening, I was empress of all I surveyed from the roof of the tenement house. I could point in any direction and name a friend who would welcome me there. Off towards the northwest, in the direction of Harvard Bridge, which some day I should cross on my way to Radcliffe College, was one of my favorite palaces, whither I resorted every day after school.

A low, wide-spreading building with a dignified granite front it was, flanked on all sides by noble old churches, museums, and school-houses, harmoniously disposed around a spacious triangle, called Copley Square. Two thoroughfares that came straight from the green suburbs swept by my palace, one on either side, converged at the apex of the triangle, and pointed off, past the Public Garden, across the historic Common, to the domed State House sitting on a height.

It was my habit to go very slowly up the low, broad steps to the palace entrance, pleasing my eyes with the majestic lines of the building, and lingering to read again the carved inscriptions: *Public Library—Built by the People—Free to All.*

Did I not say it was my palace? Mine, because I was a citizen; mine, though I was born an alien; mine, though I lived on Dover Street. My palace—*mine!*

I loved to lean against a pillar in the entrance hall, watching the people go in and out. Groups of children hushed their chatter at the entrance, and skipped, whispering and giggling in their fists, up the grand stairway, patting the great stone lions at the top, with an eye on the aged policemen down below. Spectacled scholars came slowly down the stairs, loaded with books, heedless of the lofty arches that echoed their steps. Visitors from out of town lingered long in the entrance hall, studying the inscriptions and symbols on the marble floor. And I loved to stand in the midst of all this, and remind myself that I was there, that I had a right to be there, that I was at home there. All these eager children, all these fine-browed women, all these scholars going home to write learned books—I and they had this glorious thing in common, this noble treasure house of learning. It was wonderful to say, *This is mine;* it was thrilling to say, *This is ours.*

I visited every part of the building that was open to the public. I spent rapt hours studying the Abbey pictures. I repeated to myself lines from Tennyson's poem before the glowing scenes of the Holy Grail. Before the "Prophets" in the gallery above I was mute, but echoes of the Hebrew Psalms I had long forgotten throbbed somewhere in the depths of my consciousness. The Chavannes series around the main staircase I did not enjoy for years. I thought the pictures looked faded, and their symbolism somehow failed to move me at first.

Bates Hall was the place where I spent my longest hours in the library. I chose a seat far at one end, so that looking up from my books I would get the full effect of the vast reading-room. I felt the grand spaces under the soaring arches as a personal attribute of my being.

The courtyard was my sky-roofed chamber of dreams. Slowly strolling past the endless pillars of the colonnade, the fountain murmured in my ear of all the beautiful things in all the beautiful world. I imagined that I was a Greek of the classic days, treading on sandalled feet through the glistening marble porticoes of Athens. I expected to see, if I looked over my shoulder, a bearded philosopher in a drooping mantle, surrounded by beautiful youths with wreathed locks. Everything I read in school, in Latin or Greek, everything in my history books, was real to me here, in this courtyard set about with stately columns.

Here is where I liked to remind myself of Polotzk, the better to bring out the wonder of my life. That I who was born in the prison of the Pale should roam at will in the land of freedom was a marvel that it did me good to realize. That I who was brought up to my teens almost without a book should be set down in the midst of all the books that ever were written was a miracle as great as any on record. That an outcast should become a privileged citizen, that a beggar should dwell in a palace—this was a romance more thrilling than poet ever sung. Surely I was rocked in an enchanted cradle.

From the Public Library to the State House is only a step, and I found my way there without a guide. The State House was one of the places I could point to and say that I had a friend there to welcome me. I do not mean the representative of my district, though I hope he was a worthy man. My friend was no less a man than the Honorable Senator Roe, from Worcester, whose letters to me, written under the embossed letter head of the Senate Chamber, I could not help exhibiting to Florence Connolly.

How did I come by a Senator? Through being a citizen of Boston, of course. To be a citizen of the smallest village in the United States which maintains a free school and a public library is to stand in the path of the splendid processions of opportunity. And as Boston has rather better schools and a rather finer library than some other villages, it comes natural there for children in the slums to summon gentlemen from the State House to be their personal friends.

It is so simple, in Boston! You are a school-girl, and your teacher gives you a ticket for the annual historical lecture in the Old South Church, on Washington's Birthday. You hear a stirring discourse on some subject in your country's history, and you go home with a heart bursting with patriotism. You sit down and write a letter to the speaker who so moved you, telling him how glad you are to be an American, explaining to him, if you happen to be a recently made American, why you love your adopted country so much better than your native land. Perhaps the patriotic lecturer happens to be a Senator, and he reads your letter under the vast dome of the State House; and it occurs to him that he and his eminent colleagues

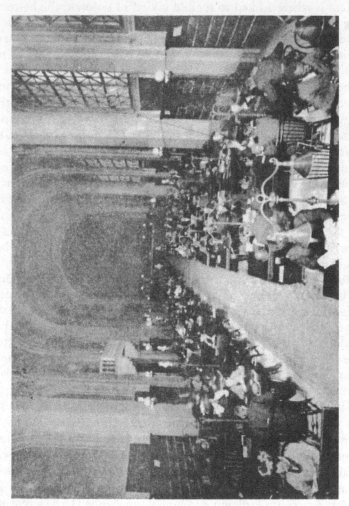

BATES HALL, WHERE I SPENT MY LONGEST HOURS IN THE LIBRARY

and the stately capitol and the glorious flag that floats above it, all gathered on the hill above the Common, do his country no greater honor than the outspoken admiration of an ardent young alien. The Senator replies to your letter, inviting you to visit him at the State House; and in the renowned chamber where the august business of the State is conducted, you, an obscure child from the slums, and he, a chosen leader of the people, seal a democratic friendship based on the love of a common flag.

Even simpler than to meet a Senator was it to become acquainted with a man like Edward Everett Hale. "The Grand Old Man of Boston," the people called him, from the manner of his life among them. He kept open house in every public building in the city. Whereever two citizens met to devise a measure for the public weal, he was a third. Wherever a worthy cause needed a champion, Dr. Hale lifted his mighty voice. At some time or another his colossal figure towered above an eager multitude from every pulpit in the city, from every lecture platform. And where is the map of Boston that gives the names of the lost alleys and back ways where the great man went in search of the lame in body, who could not join the public assembly, in quest of the maimed in spirit, who feared to show their faces in the open? If all the little children who have sat on Dr. Hale's knee were started in a procession on the State House steps, standing four abreast, there would be a lane of merry faces across the Common, out to the Public Library, over Harvard Bridge, and away beyond to remoter landmarks.

That I met Dr. Hale is no wonder. It was as inevitable as that I should be a year older every twelvemonth. He was a part of Boston, as the salt wave is a part of the sea. I can hardly say whether he came to me or I came to him. We met, and my adopted country took me closer to her breast.

A day or two after our first meeting I called on Dr. Hale, at his invitation. It was only eight o'clock in the morning, you may be sure, because he had risen early to attend to a hundred great affairs, and I had risen early so as to talk with a great man before I went to school. I think we liked each other a little the more for the fact that when so many people were still asleep, we were already busy in the interests of citizenship and friendship. We certainly liked each other.

I am sure I did not stay more than fifteen minutes, and all that

I recall of our conversation was that Dr. Hale asked me a great many questions about Russia, in a manner that made me feel that I was an authority on the subject; and with his great hand in good-bye he gave me a bit of homely advice, namely, that I should never study before breakfast!

That was all, but for the rest of the day I moved against a back-ground of grandeur. There was a noble ring to Virgil that day that even my teacher's firm translation had never brought out before. Obscure points in the history lesson were clear to me alone, of the thirty girls in the class. And it happened that the tulips in Copley Square opened that day, and shone in the sun like lighted lamps.

Any one could be happy a year on Dover Street, after spending half an hour on Highland Street. I enjoyed so many half-hours in the great man's house that I do not know how to convey the sense of my remembered happiness. My friend used to keep me in con-versation a few minutes, in the famous study that was fit to have been preserved as a shrine; after which he sent me to roam about the house, and explore his library, and take away what books I pleased. Who would feel cramped in a tenement, with such royal privileges as these?

Once I brought Dr. Hale a present, a copy of a story of mine that had been printed in a journal; and from his manner of accepting it you might have thought that I was a princess dispensing gifts from a throne. I wish I had asked him, that last time I talked with him, how it was that he who was so modest made those who walked with him so great.

Modest as the man was the house in which he lived. A gray old house of a style that New England no longer builds, with a pillared porch curtained by vines, set back in the yard behind the old trees. Whatever cherished flowers glowed in the garden behind the house, the common daisy was encouraged to bloom in front. And was there sun or snow on the ground, the most timid hand could open the gate, the most humble visitor was sure of a welcome. Out of that modest house the troubled came comforted, the fallen came uplifted, the noble came inspired.

My explorations of Dr. Hale's house might not have brought me to the gables, but for my friend's daughter, the artist, who had a studio at the top of the house. She asked me one day if I would sit for a portrait, and I consented with the greatest alacrity. It would be an interesting experience, and interesting experiences were the bread of life to me. I agreed to come every Saturday morning, and felt that something was going to happen to Dover Street.

When I came home from my talk with Miss Hale, I studied myself long in my blotched looking-glass. I saw just what I expected. My face was too thin, my nose too large, my complexion too dull. My hair, which was curly enough, was too short to be described as luxurious tresses; and the color was neither brown nor black. My hands were neither white nor velvety; the fingers ended decidedly, instead of tapering off like rosy dreams. I was disgusted with my wrists; they showed too far below the tight sleeves of my dress of the year before last, and they looked consumptive.

No, it was not for my beauty that Miss Hale wanted to paint me. It was because I was a girl, a person, a piece of creation. I understood perfectly. If I could write an interesting composition about a broom, why should not an artist be able to make an interesting picture of me? I had done it with the broom, and the milk wagon, and the rain spout. It was not what a thing was that made it interesting, but what I was able to draw out of it. It was exciting to speculate as to what Miss Hale was going to draw out of me.

The first sitting was indeed exciting. There was hardly any sitting to it. We did nothing but move around the studio, and move the easel around, and try on ever so many backgrounds, and ever so many poses. In the end, of course, we left everything just as it had been at the start, because Miss Hale had had the right idea from the beginning; but I understood that a preliminary tempest in the studio was the proper way to test that idea.

I was surprised to find that I should not be obliged to hold my breath, and should be allowed to wink all I wanted. Posing was just sitting with my hands in my lap, and enjoying the most interesting conversation with the artist. We hit upon such out-of-the-way topics—once, I remember, we talked about the marriage laws of different states! I had a glorious time, and I believe Miss Hale did too. I watched the progress of the portrait with utter lack of comprehension, and with perfect faith in the ultimate result. The morning flew so fast that I could have sat right on into the afternoon without tiring.

Once or twice I stayed to lunch, and sat opposite the artist's mother at table. It was like sitting face to face with Martha Wash-

The Famous Study, That Was Fit to Have Been Preserved as a Shrine ington, I thought. Everything was wonderful in that wonderful old house.

One thing disturbed my enjoyment of those Saturday mornings. It was a small thing, hardly as big as a pen-wiper. It was a silver coin which Miss Hale gave me regularly when I was going. I knew that models were paid for sitting, but I was not a professional model. When people sat for their portraits they usually paid the artist, instead of the artist paying them. Of course I had not ordered this portrait, but I had such a good time sitting that it did not seem to me I could be earning money. But what troubled me was not the suspicion that I did not earn the money, but that I did not know what was in my friend's mind when she gave it to me. Was it possible that Miss Hale had asked me to sit on purpose to be able to pay me, so that I could help pay the rent? Everybody knew about the rent sooner or later, because I was always asking my friends what a girl could do to make the landlady happy. Very possibly Miss Hale had my landlady in mind when she asked me to pose. I might have asked her—I dearly loved explanations, which cleared up hidden motives—but her answer would not have made any real difference. I should have accepted the money just the same. Miss Hale was not a stranger, like Mr. Strong when he offered me a quarter. She knew me, she believed in my cause, and she wanted to contribute to it. Thus I, in my hairsplitting analyses of persons and motives; while the portrait went steadily on.

It was Miss Hale who first found a use for our superfluous baby. She came to Dover Street several times to study our tiny Celia, in swaddling clothes improvised by my mother, after the fashion of the old country. Miss Hale wanted a baby for a picture of the Nativity which she was doing for her father's church; and of all the babies in Boston, our Celia, our little Jewish Celia, was posing for the Christ Child! It does not matter in this connection that the Infant that lies in the lantern light, brooded over by the Mother's divine sorrow of love, in the beautiful altar piece in Dr. Hale's church, was not actually painted from my mother's baby, in the end. The point is that my mother, in less than half a dozen years of America, had so far shaken off her ancient superstitions that she feared no evil consequence from letting her child pose for a Christian picture.

A busy life I led, on Dover Street; a happy, busy life. When I was not reciting lessons, nor writing midnight poetry, nor selling papers, nor posing, nor studying sociology, nor pickling bugs, nor interviewing statesmen, nor running away from home, I made long entries in my journal, or wrote forty-page letters to my friends. It was a happy thing that poor Mrs. Hutch did not know what sums I spent for stationery and postage stamps. She would have gone into consumption, I do believe, from inexpressible indignation; and she would have been in the right—to be indignant, not to go into consumption. I admit it; she would have been justified—from her point of view. From my point of view I was also in the right; of course I was. To make friends among the great was an important part of my education, and was not to be accomplished without a liberal expenditure of paper and postage stamps. If Mrs. Hutch had not repulsed my offer of confidences, I could have shown her long letters written to me by people whose mere signature was prized by autograph hunters. It is true that I could not turn those letters directly into rent-money,—or if I could, I would not,—but indirectly my interesting letters did pay a week's rent now and then. Through the influence of my friends my father sometimes found work that he could not have got in any other way. These practical results of my costly pursuit of friendships might have given Mrs. Hutch confidence in my ultimate solvency, had she not remained obstinately deaf to my plea for time, her heart being set on direct, immediate, convertible cash payment.

That was very narrow-minded, even though I say it who should not. The grocer on Harrison Avenue who supplied our table could have taught her to take a more liberal view. We were all anxious to teach her, if she only would have listened. Here was this poor grocer, conducting his business on the same perilous credit system which had driven my father out of Chelsea and Wheeler Street, supplying us with tea and sugar and strong butter, milk freely splashed from rusty cans, potent yeast, and bananas done to a turn,—with everything, in short, that keeps a poor man's family hearty in spite of what they eat,—and all this for the consideration of part payment, with the faintest prospect of a future settlement in full. Mr. Rosenblum had an intimate knowledge of the financial situation of every family that traded with him, from the gossip of his customers around his herring barrel. He knew without asking that my father had no regular employment, and that, consequently, it was risky to give us credit. Nevertheless he gave us credit by the week, by the month, accepted partial payment with thanks, and let the balance stand by the year.

We owed him as much as the landlady, I suppose, every time he balanced our account. But he never complained; nay, he even insisted on my mother's taking almonds and raisins for a cake for the holidays. He knew, as well as Mrs. Hutch, that my father kept a daughter at school who was of age to be put to work; but so far was he from reproaching him for it that he detained my father by the half-hour, inquiring about my progress and discussing my future. He knew very well, did the poor grocer, who it was that burned so much oil in my family; but when I came in to have my kerosene can filled, he did not fall upon me with harsh words of blame. Instead, he wanted to hear about my latest triumph at school, and about the great people who wrote me letters and even came to see me; and he called his wife from the kitchen behind the store to come and hear of these grand doings. Mrs. Rosenblum, who could not sign her name, came out in her faded calico wrapper, and stood with her hands folded under her apron, shy and respectful before the embryo scholar; and she nodded her head sideways in approval, drinking in with envious pleasure her husband's Yiddish version of my tale. If her black-eyed Goldie happened to be playing jackstones on the curb, Mrs. Rosenblum pulled her into the store, to hear what distinction Mr. Antin's daughter had won at school, bidding her take example from Mary, if she would also go far in education.

"Hear you, Goldie? She has the best marks, in everything, Goldie, all the time. She is only five years in the country, and she'll be in college soon. She beats them all in school, Goldie—her father says she beats them all. She studies all the time—all night—and she writes, it is a pleasure to hear. She writes in the paper, Goldie. You ought to hear Mr. Antin read what she writes in the paper. Long pieces—"

"You don't understand what he reads, ma," Goldie interrupts mischievously; and I want to laugh, but I refrain. Mr. Rosenblum does not fill my can; I am forced to stand and hear myself eulogized.

"Not understand? Of course I don't understand. How should I understand? I was not sent to school to learn. Of course I don't understand. But *you* don't understand, Goldie, and that's a shame. If you would put your mind on it, and study hard, like Mary Antin, you would also stand high, and you would go to high school, and be somebody."

"Would you send me to high school, pa?" Goldie asks, to test her mother's promises. "Would you really?"

"Sure as I am a Jew," Mr. Rosenblum promptly replies, a look of aspiration in his deep eyes. "Only show yourself worthy, Goldie, and I'll keep you in school till you get to something. In America everybody can get to something, if he only wants to. I would even send you farther than high school—to be a teacher, maybe. Why not? In America everything is possible. But you have to work hard, Goldie, like Mary Antin—study hard, put your mind on it."

"Oh, I know it, pa!" Goldie exclaims, her momentary enthusiasm extinguished at the thought of long lessons indefinitely prolonged. Goldie was a restless little thing who could not sit long over her geography book. She wriggled out of her mother's grasp now, and made for the door, throwing a "back-hand" as she went, without losing a single jackstone. "I hate long lessons," she said. "When I graduate grammar school next year I'm going to work in Jordan-Marsh's big store, and get three dollars a week, and have lots of fun with the girls. I can't write pieces in the paper, anyhow.—Beckie! Beckie Hurvich! Where you going? Wait a minute, I'll go along." And she was off, leaving her ambitious parents to shake their heads over her flightiness.

Mr. Rosenblum gave me my oil. If he had had postage stamps in stock, he would have given me all I needed, and felt proud to think that he was assisting in my important correspondences. And he was a poor man, and had a large family, and many customers who paid as irregularly as we. He ran the risk of ruin, of course, but he did not scold—not us, at any rate. For he *understood.* He was himself an immigrant Jew of the type that values education, and sets a great price on the higher development of the child. He would have done in my father's place just what my father was doing: borrow, beg, go without, run in debt—anything to secure for a promising child the fulfilment of the promise. That is what America was for. The land of opportunity it was, but opportunities must be used, must be grasped, held, squeezed dry. To keep a child of working age in school was to invest the meagre present for the sake of the opulent future. If there was but one child in a family of twelve who promised to achieve an intellectual career, the other eleven, and father, and mother, and neighbors must devote themselves to that one child's welfare, and feed and clothe and cheer it on, and be rewarded in the end by hearing its name mentioned with the names of the great.

So the poor grocer helped to keep me in school for I do not know how many years. And this is one of the things that is done on Harrison Avenue, by the people who pitch rubbish through their windows. Let the City Fathers strike the balance.

Of course this is wretched economics. If I had a son who wanted to go into the grocery business, I should take care that he was well grounded in the principles of sound bookkeeping and prudence. But I should not fail to tell him the story of the Harrison Avenue grocer, hoping that he would puzzle out the moral.

Mr. Rosenblum himself would be astonished to hear that any one was drawing morals from his manner of conducting his little store, and yet it is from men like him that I learn the true values of things. The grocer weighed me out a quarter of a pound of butter, and when the scales were even he threw in another scrap. "*Na!*" he said, smiling across the counter, "you can carry that much around the corner!" Plainly he was showing me that if I have not as many houses as my neighbor, that should not prevent me from cultivating as many graces. If I made some shame-faced reference to the unpaid balance, Mr. Rosenblum replied, "I guess you 're not thinking of running away from Boston yet. You have n't finished turning the libraries inside out, have you?" In this way he reminded me that there were things more important than conventional respectability. The world belongs to those who can use it to the best advantage, the grocer seemed to argue; and I found that I had the courage to test this philosophy.

From my little room on Dover Street I reached out for the world, and the world came to me. Through books, through the conversation of noble men and women, through communion with the stars in the depth of night, I entered into every noble chamber of the palace of life. I employed no charm to win admittance. The doors opened to me because I had a right to be within. My patent of nobility was the longing for the abundance of life with which I was endowed at birth; and from the time I could toddle unaided I had been gathering into my hand everything that was fine in the world around me. Given health and standing-room, I should have worked out my salvation even on a desert island. Being set down in the garden of America, where opportunity waits on ambition, I was bound to make my days a triumphal march toward my goal. The most unfriendly witness of my life will not venture to deny that I have been successful. For aside from subordinate desires for greatness or wealth or specific achievement, my chief ambition in life has been *to live*, and I have lived. A glowing life has been mine, and the fires that blazed highest in all my days were kindled on Dover Street.

I have never had a dull hour in my life; I have never had a livelier time than in the slums. In all my troubles I was thrilled through and through with a prophetic sense of how they were to end. A halo of romance floated before every to-morrow; the wings of future adventures rustled in the dead of night. Nothing could be quite common that touched my life, because I had a power for attracting uncommon things. And when my noblest dreams shall have been realized I shall meet with nothing finer, nothing more remote from the commonplace, than some of the things that came into my life on Dover Street.

Friends came to me bearing noble gifts of service, inspiration, and love. There came one, to talk with whom was to double the volume of life. She left roses on my pillow when I lay ill, and in my heart she planted a longing for greatness that I have yet to satisfy. Another came whose soul was steeped in sunshine, whose eyes saw through every pretence, whose lips mocked nothing holy. And one came who carried the golden key that unlocked the last secret chamber of life for me. Friends came trooping from everywhere, and some were poor, and some were rich, but all were devoted and true; and they left no niche in my heart unfilled, and no want unsatisfied.

To be alive in America, I found out long ago, is to ride on the central current of the river of modern life; and to have a conscious purpose is to hold the rudder that steers the ship of fate. I was alive to my finger tips, back there on Dover Street, and all my girlish purposes served one main purpose. It would have been amazing if I had stuck in the mire of the slum. By every law of my nature I was bound to soar above it, to attain the fairer places that wait for every emancipated immigrant.

A characteristic thing about the aspiring immigrant is the fact that he is not content to progress alone. Solitary success is imperfect success in his eyes. He must take his family with him as he rises. So when I refused to be adopted by a rich old man, and clung to my family in the slums, I was only following the rule; and I can tell it without boasting, because it is no more to my credit than that I wake refreshed after a night's sleep.

This suggests to me a summary of my virtues, through the exercise of which I may be said to have attracted my good fortune. I find that I have always given nature a chance, I have used my opportunities, and have practised self-expression. So much my enemies will grant me; more than this my friends cannot claim for me.

In the Dover Street days I did not philosophize about my private character, nor about the immigrant and his ways. I lived the life, and the moral took care of itself. And after Dover Street came Applepie Alley, Letterbox Lane, and other evil corners of the slums of Boston, till it must have looked to our neighbors as if we meant to go on forever exploring the underworld. But we found a short-cut—we found a short-cut! And the route we took from the tenements of the stifling alleys to a darling cottage of our own, where the sun shines in at every window, and the green grass runs up to our very doorstep, was surveyed by the Pilgrim Fathers, who transcribed their field notes on a very fine parchment and called it the Constitution of the United States.

It was good to get out of Dover Street—it was better for the growing children, better for my weary parents, better for all of us, as the clean grass is better than the dusty pavement. But I must never forget that I came away from Dover Street with my hands full of riches. I must not fail to testify that in America a child of the slums owns the land and all that is good in it. All the beautiful things I saw belonged to me, if I wanted to use them; all the beautiful things I desired approached me. I did not need to seek my kingdom. I had only to be worthy, and it came to me, even on Dover Street. Everything that was ever to happen to me in the future had its germ or impulse in the conditions of my life on Dover Street. My friendships, my advantages and disadvantages, my gifts, my habits, my ambitions—these were the materials out of

which I built my after life, in the open workshop of America. My
days in the slums were pregnant with possibilities; it only needed
the ripeness of events to make them fruit forth in realities. Steadily
as I worked to win America, America advanced to lie at my feet. I
was an heir, on Dover Street, awaiting maturity. I was a princess
waiting to be led to the throne.

CHAPTER XX

THE HERITAGE

ONE OF THE INHERENT DISADVANTAGES of premature biography is that it cannot go to the natural end of the story. This difficulty threatened me in the beginning, but now I find I do not need to tax my judgment to fix the proper stopping-place. Sudden qualms of reluctance warn me where the past and present meet. I have reached a point where my yesterdays lie in a quick heap, and I cannot bear to prod and turn them and set them up to be looked at. For that matter, I am not sure that I should add anything really new, even if I could force myself to cross the line of discretion. I have already shown what a real thing is this American freedom that we talk about, and in what manner a certain class of aliens make use of it. Anything that I might add of my later adventures would be a repetition, in substance, of what I have already described. Having traced the way an immigrant child may take from the ship through the public schools, passed on from hand to hand by the ready teachers; through free libraries and lecture halls, inspired by every occasion of civic consciousness; dragging through the slums the weight of private disadvantage, but heartened for the effort by public opportunity; welcomed at a hundred open doors of instruction, initiated with pomp and splendor and flags unfurled; seeking, in American minds, the American way, and finding it in the thoughts of the noble,—striving against the odds of foreign birth and poverty, and winning, through the use of abundant opportunity, a place as enviable as that of any native child,—having traced the footsteps of the young immigrant almost to the college gate, the rest of the course may be left to the imagination. Let us say that from the Latin School on I lived very much as my American schoolmates lived, having overcome my foreign idiosyncrasies, and the rest of my outward adventures you may read in any volume of American feminine statistics.

But lest I be reproached for a sudden affectation of reserve, after having trained my reader to expect the fullest particulars, I am willing to add a few details. I went to college, as I proposed, though not to Radcliffe. Receiving an invitation to live in New York that I did not like to refuse, I went to Barnard College instead. There I took all the honors that I deserved; and if I did not learn to write poetry, as I once supposed I should, I learned at least to think in English without an accent. Did I get rich? you may want to know, remembering my ambition to provide for the family. I can reply that I have earned enough to pay Mrs. Hutch the arrears, and satisfy all my wants. And where have I lived since I left the slums? My favorite abode is a tent in the wilderness, where I shall be happy to serve you a cup of tea out of a tin kettle, and answer further questions.

And is this really to be the last word? Yes, though a long chapter of the romance of Dover Street is left untold. I could fill another book with anecdotes, telling how I took possession of Beacon Street, and learned to distinguish the lord of the manor from the butler in full dress. I might trace my steps from my bare room overlooking the lumber-yard to the satin drawing-rooms of the Back Bay, where I drank afternoon tea with gentle ladies whose hands were as delicate as their porcelain cups. My journal of those days is full of comments on the contrasts of life, that I copied from my busy thoughts in the evening, after a visit to my aristocratic friends. Coming straight from the cushioned refinement of Beacon Street, where the maid who brought my hostess her slippers spoke in softer accents than the finest people on Dover Street, I sometimes stumbled over poor Mr. Casey lying asleep in the corridor; and the shock of the contrast was like a searchlight turned suddenly on my life, and I pondered over the revelation, and wrote touching poems, in which I figured as a heroine of two worlds.

I might quote from my journals and poems, and build up the picture of that double life. I might rehearse the names of the gracious friends who admitted me to their tables, although I came direct from the reeking slums. I might enumerate the priceless gifts they showered on me; gifts bought not with gold but with love. It would be a pleasant task to recall the high things that passed in the gilded drawing-rooms over the afternoon tea. It would add a splendor to my simple narrative to weave in the portraits of the distinguished men and women who busied themselves with the humble fortunes of a school-girl. And finally, it would relieve my heart of a burden of gratitude to publish, once for all, the amount of my indebtedness to the devoted friends who took me by the hand when I walked in the paths of obscurity, and led me, by a pleasanter lane than I could have found by myself, to the open fields where obstacles thinned and opportunities crowded to meet me. Outside America I should hardly be believed if I told how simply, in my experience, Dover Street merged into the Back Bay. These are matters to which I long to testify, but I must wait till they recede into the past.

I can conjure up no better symbol of the genuine, practical equality of all our citizens than the Hale House Natural History Club, which played an important part in my final emancipation from the slums. For all I was regarded as a plaything by the serious members of the club, the attention and kindness they lavished on me had a deep significance. Every one of those earnest men and women unconsciously taught me my place in the Commonwealth, as the potential equal of the best of them. Few of my friends in the club, it is true, could have rightly defined their benevolence toward me. Perhaps some of them thought they befriended me for charity's sake, because I was a starved waif from the slums. Some of them imagined they enjoyed my society, because I had much to say for myself, and a gay manner of meeting life. But all these were only secondary motives. I myself, in my unclouded perception of the true relation of things that concerned me, could have told them all why they spent their friendship on me. They made way for me because I was their foster sister. They opened their homes to me that I might learn how good Americans lived. In the least of their attentions to me, they cherished the citizen in the making.

The Natural History Club had spent the day at Nahant, studying marine life in the tide pools, scrambling up and down the cliffs with no thought for decorum, bent only on securing the starfish, limpets, sea-urchins, and other trophies of the chase. There had been a merry luncheon on the rocks, with talk and laughter between sandwiches, and strange jokes, intelligible only to the practising naturalist. The tide had rushed in at its proper time, stealing away our seaweed cushions, drowning our transparent pools, spouting in the crevices, booming and hissing, and tossing high the snowy foam.

From the deck of the jolly excursion steamer which was carrying

THE TIDE HAD RUSHED IN, STEALING AWAY OUR SEAWEED CUSHIONS

us home, we had watched the rosy sun dip down below the sea. The members of the club, grouped in twos and threes, discussed the day's successes, compared specimens, exchanged field notes, or watched the western horizon in sympathetic silence.

It had been a great day for me. I had seen a dozen new forms of life, had caught a hundred fragments of the song of nature by the sea; and my mind was seething with meanings that crowded in. I do not remember to which of my learned friends I addressed my questions on this occasion, but he surely was one of the most learned. For he took up all my fragments of dawning knowledge in his discourse, and welded them into a solid structure of wisdom, with windows looking far down the past and a tower overlooking the future. I was so absorbed in my private review of creation that I hardly realized when we landed, or how we got into the electric cars, till we were a good way into the city.

At the Public Library I parted from my friends, and stood on the broad stone steps, my jar of specimens in my hand, watching the car that carried them glide out of sight. My heart was full of a stirring wonder. I was hardly conscious of the place where I stood, or of the day, or the hour. I was in a dream, and the familiar world around me was transfigured. My hair was damp with sea spray; the roar of the tide was still in my ears. Mighty thoughts surged through my dreams, and I trembled with understanding.

I sank down on the granite ledge beside the entrance to the Library, and for a mere moment I covered my eyes with my hand. In that moment I had a vision of myself, the human creature, emerging from the dim places where the torch of history has never been, creeping slowly into the light of civilized existence, pushing more steadily forward to the broad plateau of modern life, and leaping, at last, strong and glad, to the intellectual summit of the latest century.

What an awful stretch of years to contemplate! What a weighty past to carry in memory! How shall I number the days of my life, except by the stars of the night, except by the salt drops of the sea?

But hark to the clamor of the city all about! This is my latest home, and it invites me to a glad new life. The endless ages have indeed throbbed through my blood, but a new rhythm dances in my veins. My spirit is not tied to the monumental past, any more than my feet were bound to my grandfather's house below the hill.

The past was only my cradle, and now it cannot hold me, because I am grown too big; just as the little house in Polotzk, once my home, has now become a toy of memory, as I move about at will in the wide spaces of this splendid palace, whose shadow covers acres. No! it is not I that belong to the past, but the past that belongs to me. America is the youngest of the nations, and inherits all that went before in history. And I am the youngest of America's children, and into my hands is given all her priceless heritage, to the last white star espied through the telescope, to the last great thought of the philosopher. Mine is the whole majestic past, and mine is the shining future.

ACKNOWLEDGEMENTS

To my mother who bore me; to my father who endowed me; to my brothers and sisters who believed in me; to my friends who loved me; to my teachers who inspired me; to my neighbors who befriended me; to my daughter who enlarged me; to my husband who opened the door of the greater life for me;—to all these who helped to make this book, I give my thanks.

GLOSSARY

KEY TO PRONUNCIATION

Explanations

The abbreviations *Germ.* (= German), *Hebr.* (= Hebrew), *Russ.* (= Russian), and *Yid.* (= Yiddish) indicate the origin of a word. Most of the names marked *Yiddish* are such in form only, the roots being for the most part Hebrew.

Prop. n. = proper name.

The endings *ke* and *le* of Yiddish proper names (Mashke, Perele) have a diminutive or endearing value, like the German *chen* (Helenchen)

Double names are given under the first name.

The religious customs described prevail among the Orthodox Jews of European countries. In the United States they have been considerably modified, especially among the Reformed Jews.

Ab (äb), *Hebr.* The fifth month of the Hebrew calendar. The ninth of Ab is a day of fasting and mourning, in commemoration of the destruction of Jerusalem and the Temple.

Adonai (ä-do-nai'), *Hebr.* An appellation of God.

Aleph (ä'-lef), *Hebr.* The first letter of the Hebrew alphabet.

Atonement, Day of (Hebrew, *Yom Kippur*). The most solemn of the Hebrew festivals, observed by fasting and an elaborate ceremonial.

Bachur (bä'-ḥur), *Hebr.* A young unmarried man, particularly a student of the Talmud. (See *Yeshibah bachur.*)

Berl (berl), *Yid.* Prop. n.

Cabala (käb-ä'-lä), *Hebr.* A system of Hebrew mystic philosophy which flourished in the Middle Ages.

Candle Prayer (Yiddish, *licht bentschen*). Prayer pronounced over lighted candles by the women and older girls of the household at the commencement of the Sabbath.

Canopy, wedding (Hebrew *huppah*). A portable canopy under which the marriage ceremony is performed, usually outdoors.

Cossaks (kos'-aks), *Russ.* A name given to certain Russian tribes, formerly distinguished for their freebooting habits, now best known for their position in the army.

Dayyan (dai'-an), *Hebr.* A judge to whom are submitted civil disputes, as distinguished from purely religious questions, which are decided by the Rav.

Dinke (din'-ke), *Yid.* Prop. n.

Dvina (dvē'-nä), *Russ.* Name of a river.

Dvornik (dvor'-nik), *Russ.* An outdoor man; a choreman.

Dvoshe (dvo'-she), *Yid.* Prop. n.

Earlocks (Hebrew *peath*). Two locks of hair allowed to grow long and hang in front of the ears. Among the fanatical Hasidim, a mark of piety.

Eidtkuhnen (eit-koo'-ñen), *Germ.* Name of a Russo-German frontier town.

Fetchke (fëtch'-ke), *Yid.* Prop. n.

Fringes, sacred (Hebrew *zizit*). Specially prepared fringes fastened to the four corners of the *arba kanfot* (literally, "four-corners"), a garment worn by all pious males underneath the jacket or frock coat, usually with the fringes showing. The latter play a part in the daily ritual.

Goluth (gol'-ùt), *Hebr.* Banishment; exile.

Good Jew (Yiddish *guter id*). Among the Hasidim, a title popularly accorded to more or less learned individuals distinguished for their piety, and credited with supernatural powers of healing, divination, etc. Pilgrimages to some renowned "Good Jew" were often undertaken by the very pious, on occasions of perplexity or trouble, for the purpose of obtaining his advice or help.

Groschen (gro'-shen), *Germ.* A popular name for various coins of small denomination, especially the half-kopeck.

Gutke (gùt'-ke), *Yid.* Prop. n.

Hannah Hayye (ḥän'-a ḥai'-e), *Hebr.* Prop. n.

Hasid, pl. Hasidim (ḥäs'-id, ḥas-id'-im), *Hebr.* A numerous sect of Jews distinguished for their enthusiasm in religious observance, a fanatical worship of their rabbis and many superstitious practices.

Haveh Mirel (ḥa'-ve mirl), *Hebr.* and *Yid.* Prop. n.

Hayye Dvoshe (ḥai'-e dvo'-she), *Hebr.* and *Yid.* Prop. n.

Hayyim (ḥai'-im), *Hebr.* Prop. n.

Hazzan (ḥäz-an), *Hebr.* Cantor in a synagogue.

Heder (ḥë'-der), *Hebr.* Elementary Hebrew school, usually held at the teacher's residence.

Henne Rösel (he'-ñe rözl), *Yid.* Prop. n.

Hirshel (hir'-shl), *Yid.* Prop. n.

Hode (ho'-de), *Yid.* Prop. n.

Horn, ram's (Hebrew *shofar*). Ritual horn, used in the synagogue during the great festivals.
Hossen (ḥo'-ssn), *Hebr.* Bridegroom; prospective bridegroom; betrothed.
Humesh (ḥu'-mesh), *Hebr.* The Pentateuch.

Icon (ī'-kon), *Russ.* A representation of Christ or some saint, usually in an elaborate frame, found in every orthodox Russian house.
Itke (it'-ke), *Yid.* Prop. n.

Jew, Good. See under Good.

Kibart (ki-bärt'), *Russ.* Name of a town.
Kiddush (kid'-ush), *Hebr.* Benediction pronounced over a cup of wine before the Sabbath evening meal.
Kimanye (ki-mä'-ñe), *Russ.* Name of a village.
Kimanyer (ki-mä'-ñer), *Yid.* Belonging to or hailing from the village of Kimanye.
Knupf (knùpf), *Yid.* A sort of turban.
Kopeck (ko'-pek), *Russ.* A copper coin, the 1/100 part of a ruble, worth about half a cent.
Kopistch (ko'-pistch), *Russ.* Name of a town.
Kosher (ko'-sher), *Hebr.* Clean, according to Jewish ritual law; opposed to **tref**, unclean. Applied chiefly to articles of diet and cooking and eating vessels.

Lamden (läm'-den), *Hebr.* Scholar; one versed in Hebrew learning.
Law, the (specifically used). The Mosaic Law; the Torah.
Lebe (lë'-be), *Yid.* Prop. n.
Loaf, Sabbath. See under **Sabbath**.
Lozhe (lo'-zhe), *Yid.* Prop. n.
Lubavitch (lù-bäv'-itch), *Russ.* Name of a town.

Maryashe (mär-yä'-she), *Yid.* Prop. n.
Mashinke (mä'-shin-ke), *Yid.* A diminutive of Mashke.
Mashke (mäsh'-ke), *Yid.* Prop. n.
Mendele (men'-del-e), *Yid.* Prop. n.
Mezuzah (me-zù'-zä), *Hebr.* A piece of parchment inscribed with a passage of Scripture, rolled in a case and tacked to the doorpost. The pious touch or kiss this when leaving or entering a house.
Mikweh (mik'-we), *Hebr.* Ritual bath, constructed and used according to minute directions.
Mirele (mir'-e-le), *Yid.* Prop. n.
Mishka (mish'-kä), *Russ.* Prop. n.
Moon, blessing of. Benediction pronounced at the appearance of the new moon.
Moshe (mo'-she), *Yid.* Prop. n., a form of Moses.
Möshele (mo'-she-le), *Yid.* Prop. n., diminutive of Moshe.
Mulke (mùl'-ke), *Yid.* Prop. n., diminutive of Mulye.
Mulye (mùl'-e), *Yid.* Prop. n.

Na! (nä), *Yid.* Here you are! Take it!
Nohem (no'-ḥem), *Hebr.* Prop. n.
Nu, nu! (nù, nù), *Yid.* Well, well.

Oi, weh! (oi, vë), *Yid.* Woe is me!
Oven, sealing of. As no fire is kindled on the Sabbath, the Sabbath dinner is cooked on Friday afternoon and left in the brick oven overnight. The oven is tightly closed with a board or sheet of metal, wet rags being stuffed into the interstices.

Passover (Hebrew, *pesech*). The feast of Unleavened Bread, commemorating the escape of the Israelites from Egypt.
Passport, foreign. A special passport required of any Russian subject wishing to go to a foreign country. To avoid the necessity of procuring such a passport, travellers often cross the border by stealth.
Perele (per'-e-le), *Yid.* Prop. n.
Phylacteries (fi-lak'-ter-is; Hebrew *tefillin*). Two small leathern boxes containing parchments inscribed with certain passages of Scripture, worn during morning prayer, one on the forehead and one on the left arm, where they are fastened by means of straps, in a manner carefully prescribed. The wearing of the *tefillin* is obligatory on all males over thirteen years of age (the age of confirmation).
Pinchus (pin'-chus), *Hebr.* Prop. n.
Pogrom (po-grom'), *Russ.* An organized massacre of Jews.
Poll (pol), *Yid.* A series of steps in the bathing-room, where cupping, etc., is done under a high temperature.
Polota (Po-lo-tä'), *Russ.* Name of a river.
Polotzk (po'-lotzk), *Russ.*, also spelled Polotsk. A town in the government of Vitebsk, Russia, since early times a stronghold of Jewish orthodoxy. *N. B.* Polotzk must not be confused with Plotzk (also spelled Plock), the capital of the government of Plotzk, in Russian Poland, about 400 miles southwest of Polotzk.
Praying Shawl (Hebrew, *tallit*). A fine white woollen shawl with sacred fringes (*zizit*), in the four corners, worn by males after marriage, during certain devotional exercises.
Purim (pù'-rim), *Hebr.* A feast in commemoration of the deliverance of the Persian Jews, through the intervention of Esther, from the massacre planned by Haman. Masquerading, feasting, exchange of presents, and general license make this celebration the jolliest of the Jewish year.

Questions, the Four. At the Passover feast, the youngest son (or, in the absence of a son of suitable age, a daughter) asks four questions as to the significance of various symbolic articles used in the ceremonial, in reply to which the family read the story of Exodus.

Rabbi (rab'-ī), *Hebr.* A title accorded to men distinguished for learning and authorized to teach the Law. As used in the present work, *rabbi* is identical with the official title of *rav*, which see.
Rabbonim (räb-on'-im), *Hebr.* Plural of *rabbi*.

Rav (räv), *Hebr.* The spiritual head of a Jewish community, whose duties include the settlement of ritualistic questions.

Reb' (reb), *Yid.* An abbreviation of *rebbe,* used as a title of respect, equivalent to the old-fashioned English "master."

Rebbe (reb'-e), *Yid.* Colloquial form of *rabbi.* A Hebrew teacher. Applied usually to teachers of lesser rank; also used as a title for a "Good Jew"; as, the Rebbe of Kopistch.

Rebbetzin (reb'-e-tzin), *Yid.* Female Hebrew teacher.

Riga (ri'-gä), *Russ.* Name of a city.

Ruble (rú'-bl), *Russ.* The monetary unit of Russia. A silver coin (or, more commonly, a paper bill) worth a little over fifty cents.

Sabbath Loaf (Hebrew, *hallah*). A wheaten loaf of peculiar shape used in the Sabbath ceremonial.

Sacred Fringes. See under **Fringes.**

Shadchan (shäd'-chan), *Hebr.* Professional match-maker; marriage broker.

Shawl, Praying. See under **Praying.**

Shema (shmä), *Hebr.* The verse recited as the Jewish confession of faith ("Hear, O Israel, the Lord our God, the Lord is One"); so called from the initial word. The "Shema" recurs constantly in the daily ritual, and is informally repeated on every occasion of distress, or as a charm to ward off evil influences.

Shohat (sho'-hat), *Hebr.* Slaughterer of cattle according to ritual law.

Succoth (sù'-kot), *Hebr.* The feast of Tabernacles, celebrated with many symbolic rites, among these being the eating of the festive meals outdoors, in a booth or bower of lattice work covered with evergreens.

Talakno (täl-äk-no'), *Russ.* Meal made of ground oats, often mixed with other grains or with weeds. An important article of diet among the peasants, generally moistened with cold water and eaten raw.

Talmudists (tal'-múd-ists; from Hebrew *talmud*). The compilers of the Talmud (the body of Jewish traditional lore); scholars versed in the teachings of the Talmud.

Tav (täv), *Hebr.* The last letter of the Hebrew alphabet.

Torah (tō'-rä), *Hebr.* The Mosaic Law; the book or scroll of the Law; sacred learning.

Trefah (trëf'-a), *Hebr.* Unclean, according to ritual law; opposed to **kosher,** clean. Chiefly applied to articles of food and eating and cooking vessels.

Versbolovo (vers-bo-lo'-vä), *Russ.* Name of a town.

Verst (vyerst), *Russ.* A measure of length, about two-thirds of an English mile.

Vilna (vil'-nä), *Russ.* Name of a city.

Vitebsk (vi'-tebsk), *Russ.* Name of a city.

Vodka (vod'-kä), *Russ.* A kind of whiskey distilled from barley or from potatoes, constantly indulged in by the lower classes in Russia, especially by the peasants.

Wedding Canopy. See under **Canopy.**

Yachne (Yäch'-ne), *Yid.* Prop. n.

Yakub (yä-kúb'), *Russ.* Prop. n.

Yankel (yän'-kl), *Yid.* Prop. n.

Yeshibah (ye-shib'-ä), *Hebr.* Rabbinical school or seminary.

—— **Bachur,** a student in a *yeshibah.*

Yiddish (yid'-ish), *Yid.* Judeo-German, the language of the Jews of Eastern Europe. The basis is an archaic form of German, on which are grafted many words of Hebrew origin, and words from the vernacular of the country.

Yochem (yo'-chem), *Yid.* Prop. n.

Yuchovitch (yù-chov-itch'), *Russ.* Name of a village.

Zaddik (tzä'-dik), *Hebr.* A man of piety; a holy man.

Zalmen (zäl'-men), *Yid.* Prop. n.

Zimbler (tzim'-bler), *Yid.* A performer on the *zimble,* an instrument constructed like a wooden tray, with several wires stretched across lengthwise, and played by means of two short rods.

APPENDIXES

HOW I WROTE *THE PROMISED LAND*

The author of an autobiography, of all writing folk, ought to be exempt from the importunities of the reporter. Any important questions the newsgatherer might ask the author has anticipated, and the unimportant ones—but nothing is unimportant to a newspaper man. If I were to answer all the questions that have been addressed to me since the publication of "The Promised Land" I should fill a volume twice as thick as the one which provoked them. "How did you come to write your book?" is a leading question. The answer is that in the fullness of time it wrote itself. I seldom meet anybody who is willing to believe this statement, but I can only go on repeating it, since it is the truth. From the time I was a schoolgirl in Boston till the day I began my autobiography somebody was always urging me to write the story of my life, but I was impervious to literary advice, and could not be hurried into any work for which I felt no inclination. The inner impulse came at last—born, to be sure, of certain outer circumstances—and that was when my early experiences marked themselves off from what came after, as the foundation may stand out from the superstructure. When the foundation was in place, I was ready to take account of the blocks that composed it, but not before. In the fullness of time, as I have said.

I had no plan when I began. "I thought so!" exclaims the critical reader, who has noticed certain repetitions and irregularities in my writing, and he thought right. One day I found myself thinking of the time I went to school in Polotzk, and I wrote about that. Another day I kept seeing the little girls I used to play with, and I put them in. Then it was the market-place that haunted me, or the Dvina gurgled in my ears all night, or there came into my mind a tale the women used to tell while picking feathers of a Winter evening. I put these things down just as they came, and so grew the book. When it came to putting these fragments together, I found that they fitted wonderfully well, considering their haphazard origin. A little re-arrangement of the loosed sheets, an introductory sentence here, a connecting phrase there, and the story fell into chapters that named themselves. I never knew what I was going to do till it was done. The only part of the book that was done consciously, with the sense that such and such matters ought to be included, were the first four chapters. These were written last of all, when I had exhausted my unprompted reminiscences. It is the only part of the book that I worked over. The rest, especially the American chapters, I dipped up from the bottom of my inkwell.

People express wonder at the minuteness of my early recollections, not realizing how much they could recall of their own childhood if they tried. You never know what you know till you try to tell it. Teachers understand this. I made more discoveries while writing my book than in all the years of which it is a record. I never knew my friends so well as when I had described them. The chapter called "My Country" has been much commented upon, and people have wondered how I could have known my own childish processes so well. But there is no miracle in this; as a piece of child psychology it has been duplicated many times. The creator of Emmy Lou knew every bit as much of her own mental development as I did, and so did the creator of Maggie Tulliver and of Tom Sawyer. These characters were not invented; they were remembered. I, too, might have written in the third person. Mark that most of my spiritual adventures were exactly those which all thoughtful children have known in some shape or other. Every child in time awakens to a sense of self, of friendship, of patriotism; but while normally these things come gradually, obscurely, in my case they came spectacularly. If a man who was born blind should suddenly behold the world, his descriptions of the common earth might excel the most fervid poetry, yet you would not say that he was speaking of unfamiliar things.

Granted that children's minds work alike the world over, just what is the nature of our childhood memories? It is probably different with different minds. I find that most of my early memories are physical. I see persons and objects, I hear sounds, songs, phrases, I mark movements and fleeting expressions on people's faces; literally see and hear and take note. In an early chapter of "The Promised Land" I describe a Spring walk by the river Polota. How was I able to reproduce the fleeting emotions engendered by that scene, which I last visited twenty years ago? By following the road to the river bank, and sitting in the same spot, in the very same attitude. Understand that in the very same attitude, so that the sun struck me at the same angle as before, and my palm rested on the identical lump of earth, and my head turned exactly as it did twenty years ago, to catch the song of the plowman on the opposite bank. I did all this while I was writing, and so the old feeling came, resuscitated by the impact of the original influences. This is what is called living one's old life over again, but most people make the mistake of taking the phrase as a metaphor, whereas some of us know that it is a statement of fact as true as anything in a standard natural history. Members of my family have told me that I looked wild after a session with my memories—that my hair bristled, my eyes bulged, and I did not answer when spoken to. What wonder if in the course of one morning I had been out of my grown-up skin back in my little-girl skin and home again for luncheon!

This is what it amounts to, then, this matter of recalling what you felt and thought twenty or forty or sixty years ago; your brain at the time registered certain attitudes of the world around you, which you, at the moment of recollecting, reconstruct, even to assuming the corresponding pose of your own body; then all the associated thought and feelings revive for the moment, and lo! what a wonderful memory you have.

One word of warning to prospective autobiographers: If you enjoy remembering things, don't put your memories on paper. If you do, you will never remember any more: you will know, but never more remember. Chasing elusive memories is like chasing butterflies. The captured butterfly, however delicately mounted, is no longer a butterfly; it is a beautiful carcass. Similarly, your living memories, flitting unexpectedly across your thoughts, now in this connection, now in that, now shining with tears, now quivering with ancient laughter, their capricious appearances splitting the flat surface of reality into the alluring caves and grottoes of illusion—what will be left of your magic memories when you have caught them and put them on paper? Facts—dead facts that you can share with your neighbor. Your neighbor may be the gainer by it, as one who cannot roam in the fields is the gainer by the exertions of the entomologist, but do not go into the business of writing your life's story unless you are willing to exchange quivering butterflies for dried specimens.

MALINKE'S ATONEMENT

I

It was not the fault of Breine Henne, the egg-woman, if her only daughter, Malinke, had to assume the burdens of housekeeping before she cast her milk teeth. Breine Henne made a fraction of a living for herself and her two children by a small trade in poultry; whence her nickname. As her business obliged her to stand all day in the market-place, it naturally fell to Malinke to cook and sweep and wash. The law of circumstance was potent in Polotzk, next to the law of the Czar.

Late one afternoon Malinke was kneeling on a chair by the window, watching for her mother's return. It had rained all day, a cold autumn drizzle, and she knew trade was dull in such weather; her mother ought to be coming home. Presently she saw the familiar figure, and ran out into the entry to open the door.

Breine Henne came up the yard with a flat, heavy tread. The water churned in her broken shoes. Her limp skirt was a fringe of rags at the bottom, dripping with the mud of the market-place. Her frayed jacket, whose original color the owner herself could scarcely recall, looked black on the shoulders from the rain it had soaked up, and the woolly shawl tied about her head was hoary with moisture. She walked with her red hands clasped on her stomach, a covered basket hanging on one arm.

Malinke hopped on the threshold, impatient for her mother's society. The child was much alone.

"Let me brush off the mud for you with the besom," she offered, as her mother stamped her feet in the entry. "I have scrubbed the floor and sanded it all afresh, and you must n't bring in any mud, mama."

"Good health to you, my little housewife!" the mother said, giving the child a wet caress. "And where did you get the sand? The box was empty yesterday."

"Oh, I ran errands for old Rachel, and she gave me a basin of sand. Is n't it bright, mama? But you are so wet! Did you sell the hen? What have you in the basket?"

Malinke paused in her chatter to lift the cover from the basket. She saw a ball of gray feathers, slightly speckled with white. A little sigh of disappointment escaped her, but she said nothing. Lifting the hen, she cut the rag that bound its feet and set it down on the floor. The bird shook out its feathers, stretched its wings, and pattered over to the corner behind the oven, to drink from the broken earthenware dish which Malinke hastened to fill with fresh water.

Breine Henne peeled off her wet garments and spread them around the hot oven, watching the child meanwhile with a smile half sad, half happy. How many times she had promised Malinke a treat—an apple or a pear—in case she disposed of the hen that did n't lay; and always she had disappointed her—until now. Her smile turned wholly happy as she thought of the treat in store for Malinke and Yösele.

"Feed her well, little daughter," she said. "Give her all the oats you have, and the others will get the scrapings Rachel gives you after supper."

"All the oats? Why all the oats for her alone?" Malinke looked for an explanation.

"Yes, stuff her all she'll hold. She's to be killed in the morning."

"You're joking, mama. You did n't sell her, so who's going to kill her?"

"The butcher, of course," laughed Breine Henne, as she tied a cotton head-kerchief under her chin, preparatory to sitting down to roast her bare feet. "Who else kills chickens? The butcher, of course."

Malinke's eyes grew large with conjecture, but she could not frame a guess.

"The butcher shall kill the hen, Malinke," Breine Henne repeated impressively, "*and you shall eat it!*"

The child changed color from surprise. Her mother was not jesting—she would not tease her so. There was to be a chicken cooked for her and Yösele and Mother. She was speechless for a quarter of a minute, then she broke into a laugh of pure happiness, and clapped her hands as if she were a real little girl of nine, instead of a responsible housekeeper and an understudy to her mother in bearing the troubles of their difficult existence.

"Oh, mama, it will be so good! For Sabbath, you mean, don't you? Won't Yösele be surprised! Let me tell him, mama, do. I'll run to meet him when I hear the boys coming home from *heder* [Hebrew school]. Oh, how good it will taste!"

Intoxicated with unlooked-for happiness, she caught one foot in her hand and danced around on the other till she lost her balance. Her eye fell on the devoted hen, who, unconscious of her impending doom, was polishing her yellow bill on a leg of the wooden bench against the wall. Malinke caught her up in her arms.

"Oh, you dear old hen! You poor old hen! You would n't lay, you would n't get fat, nobody wanted you, and now *I'm* going to eat you!"

She thrust her fingers knowingly through the soft feathers to the warm skin. The exuberance faded from her face. She turned to her mother with a wry little smile.

"She's *not* very fat, is she, mama? Do you think there will be *any* yellow rings on the soup? I saw the chicken soup the women from the sick-visiting society brought old Rachel when she was sick, and it was all yellow on top—*fat!*—and smelt so good!"

"If we live, we'll see," was Breine Henne's philosophic reply. "There will be the bones to lick, anyway. And now reach down under the bed and pull me out the sack of potatoes, and I'll peel some while you make the samovar. Yösele comes home all dried up—nothing hot to eat all day, poor boy."

One potato apiece was as much as Breine Henne could allow for supper, but her tongue being nimbler than her fingers, she had time, while preparing those few potatoes, to rehearse a good deal of domestic history.

"I don't know what people will say of such extravagance," she remarked to the pot in her lap. "Breine Henne the egg-woman, the destitute widow, to eat chicken, and not even a holiday for an excuse! It was Rebecca the apple-woman put it into my head, and I can't see but what she is right. 'How much longer will you lug around that hen?' she laughed at me. 'I have seen you six market days with the same lean hen,' she said. 'I know her by her single eye, and every housewife in Polotz knows her by this time. Naked bones, that's what she is. You'll never sell her. Take my advice, Breine Henne, go home and have her killed for Sabbath. You'll save all she'll ever bring you if you use her economically. You can stand another year in the rain and rot in your shoes, the hen will never be any plumper. Nobody wants to put a lean chip in the soup.'"

Malinke had been watching the much-criticized fowl peck at its food, rejoicing, with anticipatory relish, at every kernel that swelled its crop. Her pleasure was marred by her mother's quotation of the apple-woman's disparaging opinion.

"Is she as bad as that, mama?" she asked. "Won't there be any fat at all?"

"If there won't, there won't," replied the mother unemotionally. "I can't make the creature over now. Is it my fault that she always was lean, and would not lay? I stuffed her enough, I'm sure; more than the others. It was fated that we should eat her, else why wasn't she plump, so that I could sell her? Already last Atonement Day I had it in mind to kill the hen as a sacrifice, but I reconsidered, and decided it would be too great an extravagance. It is no trifle for a destitute widow to offer up a hen. So I offered a groschen, and you a groschen, and Yösele, being a scholar, and soon to be confirmed, offered a little dwarf rooster, the one the stray cat—a curse on her!—nearly chewed up when he was a chick. He wasn't fit for anything else, the crippled rooster, and God would accept him, I knew. Everything is acceptable to the Almighty that is offered Him by the poor man's self-denial."

Malinke showed interest in her mother's discourse.

"Then why didn't you sacrifice the hen?" she asked.

"I've told you why, you little fool. It would have been too much."

"Too much for God?"

"Silence, you imp! Don't let loose your tongue. I thought I could not afford the hen then. Extravagance is a sin. The Almighty knows how I have to struggle to keep body and soul together. I am behind with the rent, behind with the tuition. Reb' Zalmen Boruch sent me word last week that if I don't pay him at least half of what I owe he can't let Yösele come any more. I don't blame the *rebbe* [Hebrew teacher]; he is a poor man himself. If I have to take Yösele out of school, the Most High will know it was not because I did not value sacred learning."

Malinke saw that her mother was getting ready to cry, and tried to divert her thoughts.

"I can peel as close as that, mama," she said, fingering the little heap of potato parings in her mother's lap. "I make it so thin you can see the light through if you hold it up."

She cocked her head as she applied the test to a curl of the peel.

Breine Henne brightened at once.

"Sound be your little head!" she blessed as she emptied her lap before rising. "I know you are a good housewife. Now you watch me to-morrow when I cut up the hen, and you'll learn how to make the most of a fowl. There will be the soup for Sabbath, and the meat, and the bits will last a few days. And then the feathers—a handful; but I won't have as much as a little pillow to give you, Malinke, when you make a match, unless I fill it by handfuls."

Malinke laughed. "I don't want to make a match, and I don't want any feathers. I just want to eat chicken every Sabbath!"

When Yösele came home, the story of his good luck met him on the threshold, and nothing was talked of during the supper but the next day's feast.

"Oh, mama, will you give me the neck?" begged Malinke. "I once ate a chicken's neck, at Aunt Leah's, and it had so many little bones, you could suck and suck and never know when you were done. Will you give me the neck?"

Jumping up from her stool in her excitement, the little girl bumped her mother's elbow, causing her to spill the boiling water she was at that moment drawing from the samovar.

"See what you are doing, you little fool!" scolded Breine Henne. "Do you want to scald me? Don't jump in the air like that. I'll give you what I'll give you, and an end of it. In the meantime you have potatoes and herring; eat and be thankful. Ever see such a wild goat? Have the neck and the tail too, only quiet down."

Yösele put in a brotherly joke.

"Why don't you bid for the whole chicken at once, and be done with it? I don't expect anything but a couple of drumsticks, the feet, and maybe the breast and the liver."

But this rehearsal of the chicken's anatomy betrayed him into a slip from his dignity. "The liver, mama," he begged eagerly, "will you give me the liver? I think you ought to give me the liver, because there's only one, and I'm an only son, you know. Will you give me the liv—"

"But I'm an only daughter, you know!" cried Malinke, once more jumping up in her place. "Mama, you give me the liver!"

Breine Henne emptied her saucer at a gulp, and set it down on the bare table. "Children, children," she cried, spreading out her hands in appeal, "will you get quiet to-night? You, Yösele, ought to be ashamed to be so greedy—a great boy of twelve! And, anyway, a scholar ought to be sated with Torah [sacred learning], and ask for nothing more. You, Malinke, are out of your head to-night. An only daughter, indeed! What are daughters worth? They're only good to sit in the house, a burden on their parents' neck, until they're married off. A son, at least, prays for the souls of his parents when they're dead; it's a deed of piety to raise sons."

"That's just what I think, mama," Yösele caught at her words. "And so you'll give me the liver?"

Breine Henne shook her head angrily by way of answer. She had begun the long grace after meals, and she would not speak till after the amen.

Yösele, reproved, began to pray in a loud voice, swaying back and forth, and from time to time closing his eyes tight, as if the better to concentrate on the holy words. Malinke also began to mumble the prayer, sitting on the edge of her stool and surreptitiously brushing the few crumbs from the table with one bare hand, catching them in the other.

Before Yösele was half through, Malinke ended with an explosive "amen," causing her brother to open his eyes at her in an incredulous stare, while his lips mechanically progressed with the prayer.

"Mama, she skips!" the male of the house broke out, as soon as he could speak. "She slurs the words, and she skips. I don't think she knows the prayer at all."

"I don't—I do," his sister defended herself. "I know it all, but I can say it fast, can't I? When we have only half a herring and three potatoes, and say the whole prayer, what'll we say when we have a chicken? I'll pray slowly to-morrow, you'll see."

Yösele stared, amazed at his sister's audacity. Breine Henne gave her a couple of cuffs with the flat of her hand, and would have given more if Malinke had not skipped out of arm's reach.

"Hold your tongue, you bastard!" she cried, using a not uncommon epithet of reproach. "Ever hear such a mouth? Where does the imp get such words? What! will you measure the prayer according to your meal? You should thank God for every crumb that you put into your mouth. There are plenty in Polotzk who don't have any potatoes, nor any herring either. Already nine years old, and she has n't learned respect for the Almighty! One might think she was n't raised among Jews. Never let me hear you talk like that again, Malinke; do you hear?"

The culprit received this tirade at a safe distance, with an expression of forbearance rather than contrition. She traced patterns in the sand with one foot, where she stood, at the same time chewing on the end of a very thin pigtail, until her mother stopped for breath.

"But, mama," argued the bold child, unabashed, "I don't grudge the prayer,—I'll say it twice, if you want me to,—but it seems foolish to thank God just the same for a little as for much. I think He won't believe that we mean it. You don't do that way to anybody else—to people. When Aunt Leah brought fruit and wine for Yösele, when he had the fever, you thanked her and blessed her, and prayed for her in the synagogue; but when a neighbor lends you a spoonful of salt you don't say so much about it. Don't you think God knows the difference, too?"

Breine Henne had opened her mouth several times during Malinke's discourse, not to speak, but to catch her breath. Her pale eyes stared at the child as if they saw a strange monster. She made an ineffectual clutch at Malinke, and finally collapsed on her stool, crying from helplessness.

"Hear her—hear her!" she wailed, a corner of her kerchief at her eyes. "What kind of a renegade have I brought into the world? Let somebody talk to her who knows how. I can't argue with her any more. I'm a poor, struggling widow—a friendless female—I'm obliged to spend my days in the street, in the market-place. How do I know what the girl does here all day—where she gets such talk? No child in Polotzk ever had such audacity. Such a mouth! And to think how I wept when her twin sister died! A fine life I would have of it if I had two like her! The Supreme One will punish us all for her sinful mouth."

After one or two unsuccessful efforts to soothe her mother, Malinke went about her usual evening duties with a composure that bespoke a conscience at rest. Her critical young soul by no means yielded in the argument that so outraged her mother's piety; but she knew when it was useless to speak. Having washed the few dishes from the recent meal, she quickly made her toilet for the night, by slipping off her coarse flannel dress and removing the clumsy boots from her bare feet, and tumbled into the only bed in the room, burying herself up to the nose in the miscellaneous collection of rags that composed the bed covering.

Yösele, rather ostentatiously reading his bed-time prayers, watched her prompt proceedings out of a corner of his eye, wondering, in a parenthesis of his evening devotions, why Malinke was such a queer little girl. He knew no one who asked such strange questions as Malinke, and no one who could satisfy her. His own teacher, a pious scholar, caught in the toils of one of her impudent inquisitions, was obliged to silence her by the only argument that ever made Malinke hang her head in submission.

"You are only a girl," the rebbe had reminded her. "Girls don't need to know things out of books."

Malinke was asleep by the time Yösele had finished his devotions; she was snoring gently before he had composed himself to sleep on the narrow wooden bench by the oven. The latter process required some time and thought, as Yösele, in spite of years of experience, had not evolved a satisfactory way of arranging his bedding, which consisted of a tattered quilt, a couple of burlap sacks, and his own jacket.

"If I lie on the sacks and cover myself with the quilt, I am warm, but my sides get sore," he complained to his mother. "If I lie on the quilt and cover myself with the sacks, it's soft, but my feet freeze. If I put my jacket on my feet, I have nothing for a pillow."

The vexing problem was solved this evening in one of the few ways possible, and presently Malinke's solo became a duet, Yösele snoring an octave or two deeper than his sister.

II

Breine Henne sat up some time longer over a bit of hopeless mending. "Patch upon patch," she muttered to herself, "like a head of cabbage."

She was about to blow out the lamp, preparatory to going to bed, when Malinke, with a long-drawn sigh, turned over in her sleep. Breine Henne went over and looked at her. The child was a small hump under the bed-clothes. Her thin little face was turned to the wall, and her colorless pigtail, tied with a scarlet rag, straggled forlornly on the pillow.

"Seems like a baby, when she lies there like that," mused Breine Henne, stooping over the bed, her hands busy with the knotted fastenings of her undergarments. "No bigger than a baby, and speaks up like a man. And such queer ideas! God knows where she gets them."

She blew out the lamp and lay down beside Malinke. "May God refrain from punishing her for her talk!" she prayed as she fell asleep.

The next day was Friday—a short work-day, as the Sabbath began with the early sunset. It was the day appointed for the great feast, the children reminded each other on waking.

"Be sure you go to the butcher early, Malinke," Breine Henne called over her shoulder, as she was leaving for the day. "I'll be home at twelve to dress the chicken. That will give it plenty of time to cook."

Malinke, always a diligent little housewife, needed no prompting on this day. Returning from the butcher's, she passed a morning of volcanic activity. She had scrubbed and scoured only the day before, but in honor of the coming feast she scrubbed anew, first carefully brushing the sand from the floor into a basin, to be used over again. She repolished the almost spotless samovar with sand and cranberry juice,—she had to beg the cranberries from a neighbor,—and her small collection of cutlery came in for its share of rubbing. The little window-panes were so pieced that it was risky to touch them, but this was a supreme occasion, worthy of supreme daring. And looking through her clear window-panes, Malinke perceived that the street was very muddy. The street was no business of hers, because she was not a house-owner; but she cleaned the street for a generous distance to right and left of the house, exerting herself with besom and shovel till her little back ached. If she could have reached the sky to tear the clouds asunder, she would have set the sun to shine into her shining room. Nothing was too good for the occasion.

From time to time, as she busied herself in the room or outside, Malinke ran to peep at the slaughtered hen, which lay awaiting further operations. If something should happen to the chicken now—a cat or a dog! Malinke wished her fowl were safely in the pot, but she did not yet know how to dress a chicken. She had picked the feathers clean; that was as far as she could go. And what if her mother should be late, and the chicken not have time to cook! The anxious little housekeeper was making up her mind to ask a neighbor to prepare the fowl, when Breine Henne, breathless with haste, came into the room.

It was a tense little face, with two great eyes—two hungry eyes—that bent over the wretched carcass, as her mother slit and cut and tore, laying bare the creature's anatomy. The mother, herself not a little excited, kept up a running commentary on the subject of chickens, with special reference to the one in hand; but Malinke uttered no word. She was in an ecstasy of expectation beyond speech.

"Not so bad, after all," Breine Henne commented, cheerfully making the most of the lean carcass. "Upon my word, she's not as bad as I thought. I'm glad I did n't sell her. We'll have a nice soup, and chicken meat for two or three days. I've seen plumper chickens, but still this one—"

She broke off abruptly, a look of keen trouble in her face. Her bloodstained fingers trembled as she tore at the intestines. They had felt a lump where there should be none.

"Lord of All!" she breathed, "what is this?"

Malinke watched her with a face gone pale. Her hands clasped tightly over her thumping heart, she waited for her mother's explanation.

"Look, look!" Breine Henne cried, "a wire—a bit of crooked wire, right in the intestine! Oi, woe is me! the chicken is *tref!*"[1]

Malinke felt a sickening sinking of the heart. For a quarter of a minute she remained standing as if petrified, then she threw herself on the bench and cried aloud.

Breine Henne took no notice of her at first. She sat staring at the dismembered chicken, wringing her hands and bemoaning herself. Presently she became aware of Malinke, now sobbing with her face in her arms.

"Don't cry—don't cry, Malinke," she soothed. "Maybe it is n't *tref*, after all. Take your shawl and run to the *rav.*[2] Perhaps he will decide that the chicken is *kosher.*"

The little girl jumped up, a flame of hope in her tear-stained face.

"Oh, do you think so, mama? Do you really think it may be kosher? Oi, dear little mama! Where's my shawl? How shall I carry it? What shall I tell the rav? I'll run—I'll run."

[1] *Tref*, unclean, in conformity with Jewish dietary laws, as distinguished from *kosher*, clean.
[2] *Rav*, the religious head of a Jewish community.

Breine Henne wrapped the chicken in a cloth. "Don't lose any-thing," she cautioned, "and don't be gone long. This is where I found the wire; see? Show him. Now run, and God grant that the rav finds it kosher."

It was some distance to the rav's, but Malinke ran all the way. Arrived at her destination, she burst into the house and thrust her bundle under the nose of the astonished servant.

"A *shala*" [question], she panted. "My mother sent me to ask a shala. Is Reb' Nossen at home?"

"Mercy on us!" protested the servant, an elderly person who was not used to being hurried, "one would think the town were on fire, to see the child. And if it is a shala, what then? Must you rush in on people and take their breath away? It's nothing new, a shala. Reb' Nossen settles a dozen every day. Sit down there on the bench, and I'll go and see if he is not busy. There's a novelty for you—a shala!"

Malinke thought the woman was gone an age, but at last she saw her returning through the long living-room, where the table was already set for Sabbath.

"Come, he will see you at once. See that you do not touch the clean table cloth as you pass. You are—I guess you have n't got your Sabbath dress on yet."

Malinke did not notice the look of disapproval which her con-ductor cast over her ragged person. She saw only an open door at the end of the room, and went in, always holding out her bundle before her.

Reb' Nossen was busy arranging a pyramid of books on a table. He greeted the child over his shoulder.

"Well, little girl, what is your question?"

Malinke, in all her eagerness, remembered that she was in a great presence. She had never been in the rav's house before. A sudden shyness replaced her usual assurance.

"Well," repeated the rav, still without turning, "you came to ask a shala. What is it?"

Malinke advanced a step. "The chicken," she whispered. "My mother found a wire."

"So? Let's see it. Put it down here, by the window. This is the wire, is it? And how was it found? Show me exactly where it lay. H'm—h'm."

The rav poked the dismembered organs with a long forefinger, and carefully examined the spot where the bit of wire had been embedded. He peered long at the wire itself, with knitted brows and set mouth. Then, after wiping his fingers on a red bandana, he picked out a book from the pile he had been arranging, and began to turn its yellow leaves, humming a bit of Sabbath melody under his breath.

Malinke followed his movements with eyes of feverish expectancy. The rav's word was law in such a matter. Would he say tref or kosher?

Reb' Nossen turned the leaves and hummed to himself. His silvery ear-locks mingled with his beard, which swept the table. A silk skull-cap sat high on his broad brow. Face and hands were shining with health and cleanliness. The rav had just returned from the *mikweh*.[3] The peace of approaching Sabbath was in his soul.

Malinke did not take her hungry eyes from Reb' Nossen's face. Apparently the question was not a simple one, to be resolved at a glance. The rav ceased his humming. He pushed away his book and took another. He returned to the chicken, lying in the light of the window. Once he asked Malinke to show him again how the wire was found, and she answered that, and other questions, in a voice trembling with apprehension.

If Reb' Nossen had noticed the child's distress, and asked her questions about herself and her mother, he might have come to a conclusion promptly. Besides the nature of the foreign body, the position in which it was found, and the condition of the carcass, the rav had a right to take into consideration the circumstances of the owner of the animal. For the sacred office of the rav endows him with considerable latitude in the interpretation of the Law. If the question is one on which authorities differ, or even if the rav to whom it is submitted disagrees with recorded opinions, the owner of the property in question is entitled to the benefit of the doubt, especially if he be a poor man. The Jewish Law was not framed to oppress God's chosen people. It was meant to keep them clean, by guarding them against every disease of mind and body. In the mouths of wise and liberal scholars, it can be interpreted in two words: Be pure.

Reb' Nossen peered very closely at his book, following the lines across the page with his finger. He was a trifle short-sighted. Perhaps

---

[3] The ritual bath.

that was why he did not notice that Malinke's shawl was in rags, that her shoes gaped, and that she looked at him with frightened, hungry eyes.

"Little girl," he said, after an interval in which the child suffered agonies of doubt, "little girl, tell your mother the chicken is unclean."

Malinke felt again that horrid sinking of the heart. Mechanically she tied up her bundle, and went out. She did not hear the rav call "Good Sabbath" after her.

Her feet carried her homewards. She did not think of the way. The bitterness of her disappointment made her blind and deaf. But suddenly, as she turned a corner, she was brought back to life by a strong smell of cooking coming from an open kitchen door. Involuntarily she drew a deep breath. Fish, chicken, and fresh bread. Malinke gave a gulp and stuffed the corner of her shawl into her mouth. She would not be seen crying on the street.

Her knees trembled as she walked on. She had eaten black bread and tea for breakfast, and bread with salt for dinner. She was tired from exertion, and shaken by emotion. The miserable bundle in her hand became a grievous burden. And what were they going to have for supper?

Oh, if only Reb' Nossen had found the chicken clean! Why was it unclean? All sorts of things were found inside chickens, and yet they were pronounced clean. Yösele once told her about a chicken that his schoolmate's mother cooked for a holiday. An earring had been found in the gizzard, and the rav had pronounced the meat kosher. Why was not her chicken kosher? How did the rav know?

Malinke's thoughts climbed from the plaintive to the curious, from the curious to the rebellious, from the rebellious to the defiant. What was written in the books the rav consulted? She was only a girl—she would never know. Reb' Nossen said tref. How did he know? Suppose he had said kosher, then her mother would cook the chicken, they would all enjoy it, and no harm come to anybody.

Malinke stopped short in her walk, struck by an idea, a great and fearful idea. Nobody knew of the rav's decision but herself. *Suppose she should tell her mother it was kosher?* Her face flamed; the blood thumped in her ears. Stooping down, she undid the bundle in her lap. The chicken looked exactly as it had done when first opened by her mother. Why, why was it unclean? The rav's word made it so.

Oh, it was cruel! She was so hungry—half the time she was hungry. She never had good things to eat. Why should the rav rob her of the chicken? It was just like any other chicken. He should not rob her! He might have said kosher, and he did not. Suppose she told her mother it was kosher?

She began to run, frightened at her own thoughts. It was a heinous sin she contemplated. The rav was the voice of God. He had declared the chicken unfit for a Jewish table, and she proposed to eat of it, and impose it upon her mother and brother.

"But what if the rav were mistaken?" the rebel in her cried. Malinke, who went much from house to house doing errands, and heard much talk, and asked questions freely, knew that it was not impossible for a rav to make a mistake. Only the year before, Polotzk was torn into two factions, the one adhering to Reb' Nossen, the other to Reb' Isaac, when the two dignitaries disagreed in the settlement of a shala. Malinke did not know just what the point in dispute was,—something about a burial,—nor whose opinion prevailed in the end. But one thing was clear from the dispute: a rav may make a mistake. And if Reb' Nossen were wrong in her case, was it just that she and Yösele and her mother should suffer for his error?

"No, no, no!" she cried in her heart. "I won't tell—I won't. If it's unclean, God will punish me, and then I shall know."

She kept on running, but she was no longer frightened. Arrived at her own doorstep, she paused once more. Clasping her bundle tightly to her breast, she closed her eyes and prayed.

"Good God, if the chicken is tref, punish me, and nobody else. Amen."

Breine Henne opened the door the moment she heard Malinke in the entry.

"Well, well?" she questioned eagerly. "What does the rav say?"

Malinke answered firmly, "Kosher."

Her mother was too excited to notice how pale the child was.

III

It was a happy family that sat down to supper when Yösele returned from evening prayer in the synagogue.

Breine Henne had replaced the cotton kerchief by her wig, which she wore only on holy days and ceremonious occasions. Yösele's patched trousers were mercifully invisible under the table, and from his thighs to his neck he was conscious of his Sabbath jacket. It had belonged to his father, may he rest in peace! but Yösele was a big boy for his age, and the jacket fitted not so badly, if he puffed himself out a little in front, and sat firmly on the tails of the coat behind, and turned up the cuffs of the sleeves.

Malinke was even more splendid than Yösele. She wore a blue woolen dress, trimmed with rows of gold braid on the skirt and a double row of gilt buttons on the waist. The dress was frayed and stained and choky,—Malinke was obliged to leave the waist and the neck-buttons unfastened,—but the gold trimmings redeemed every fault. She had earned the dress by hulling quarts and quarts of strawberries for a neighbor, whose little girl's cast-off clothes fitted her well enough.

Dear to Malinke's heart was the dress, and dearer still the boots on her feet. Yes, a pair of Sabbath boots had Malinke, and such boots! They were whole, they were new, they were shiny. They had patent-leather tips, and patent-leather tops closing with three buttons on each side, and all the buttons were on. All the poor little girls in the neighborhood envied her those boots. They squeaked delightfully. They were the pride and joy of her heart.

How came Malinke by such superior footgear? "God is good," she somewhat tactlessly remarked, when Aunt Leah presented her with the boots, which had belonged to Cousin Fredke, who died of cholera. Aunt Leah never gave away anything till it was shabby enough for a beggar, but because poor Fredke had been fond of Malinke— "God is good," said the beneficiary of Aunt Leah's sorrow.

Arrayed in all her finery, Malinke sat down to the unwonted feast with a face of glowing happiness. There was no shadow in her heart. The anguish of the afternoon was washed away in a flood of peace. Having struggled so bitterly and come to a great resolution, she was abiding by it with all the courage of her fiery young soul. By her prayer on the doorstep she had bravely assumed all the responsibility for her conduct. If she had sinned, the punishment was to fall on her alone: no innocent person should suffer. She did not doubt for a moment that God had heard and would heed her petition. And until God gave her a sign of His displeasure, she would not call herself a sinner, but would enjoy herself to the utmost.

All joys come to an end, but the joy of sucking chicken-bones bade fair to outlast all others. The Sabbath candles, stuck in a basin of sand, for want of candlesticks, had burned down to half their length before Breine Henne could induce the children to give up the clean-picked bones to which they clung.

"M—m," protested Yösele, "there's more on it"; and "M—m," pleaded Malinke, "it still tastes of chicken."

The mother got up and brought the soup to the table, and set it steaming under their noses. Then, and not till then, did they consent to part with the bones.

"Oh!" triumphed Malinke, gloating over her plate, "there *is* a fat-spot in mine!"

"Take care," warned Breine Henne, "it's very hot. Blow on it, children."

The soup was pronounced delicious with every mouthful. Malinke dipped up very scant spoonfuls, to make it last. Yösele, finishing before her, made a dive at her plate to help himself.

"She had more than I," he grumbled, when his mother ordered him to let his sister's plate alone. And Malinke, not feeling safe enough even under her mother's protection, began to gulp her soup hastily, lest her brother rob her of any.

She had almost finished, when she gave a short cough, accompanied by a convulsive jerk of the head. She grew red in the face; her eyes started out; her tongue protruded. She was choking.

Breine Henne and Yösele jumped up in a fright, and began to thump and shake her.

"A bone!" wailed Breine Henne. "Oi, *weh!* She'll choke to death. Take a drink of water—there, try to drink. Woe is me, she's choking!"

Breine Henne set Malinke's plate on her head, while she and Yösele pounded her on the back and chest simultaneously. It was the best remedy they knew, and it failed to dislodge the bone. The mother next inserted her forefinger into the girl's throat as far as it would go, but without result. The child struggled convulsively. The sweat was on her blackening face, the tears in her eyes.

Yösele began to bawl with fright. His mother was out of her wits.

"Oi, weh! Woe is me! I always knew no good would come of that hen. Malinke! Malinke! little daughter! Take a drink of water. God Almighty, have pity on us! Run, Yösele, call the neighbors. Oh, Malinke, Malinke!"

Yösele ran out, calling, "Help! Help!"

Jacob the tailor, who occupied the rear of the house, answered the call, and his frightened family flocked after him to the scene of distress.

Jacob stopped in front of Malinke, helpless and aghast. Not so Peshe Frede, his wife. Without a word she grasped the strangling child by the ankles, and turning her upside down, swung her back and forth with all her might.

Presently Malinke gave a gasp, followed by a wailing "Oh—h!" Peshe Frede put her back in her chair, and everybody crowded around.

Slowly the red left Malinke's face. It faded and faded, till she was ashy white. She looked around the circle of faces, with a growing horror in her eyes. She tried to speak, but failed.

"There, there," her mother crooned, "sit still. You'll be better in a minute."

She began to fondle the child, wiping her moist face with a corner of her own apron. Malinke avoided her touch with a strange gesture, always staring with eyes of horror.

"God has punished me," she breathed in a strangled whisper. "I have sinned, and God has punished me."

"What is she saying?" they all asked one another. "Better put her to bed, Breine Henne. She will be all right when she has rested."

But Malinke pushed her mother away. Springing up, she threw out her hands in a gesture of despair, crying aloud, "God has punished me! God has punished me!"

The others drew away from her in amazement. "What do you mean? What does she mean?" they questioned.

Again Breine Henne tried to soothe the child, and again Malinke avoided her.

"Don't touch me!" she cried. "I am a great sinner. God has punished me."

Then she told them. Standing in the middle of the room, with wild eyes, panting and sobbing, she told them the whole story of the rav's decision and her false report. She did not excuse herself, although she tried to explain to them the thoughts and feelings that led up to her wicked resolution; but she saw that they did not understand.

"Do with me what you will," she cried. "I have sinned. God has punished me." With a sob that shook her whole frame, she threw herself prone on the floor in abject surrender.

No language but the Yiddish can reproduce the exclamations of horror, anger, reproach, that broke from the lips of the bystanders. Breine Henne sank upon a chair and threw out her arms across the table, moaning as one mortally hurt. Yösele shrank into a corner, his jaw hanging, his eyes roving around the room as if seeking support. The assembled neighbors turned horrified faces on one another, gasping and ejaculating. Jacob's two little girls clung to each other, backing away toward the door, as if they feared contamination. And the culprit shook the floor with her sobs.

"Oi!" moaned the unhappy mother, when she could speak. "Dark is my world; my eyes may not look upon the light of day. God in heaven, why didst Thou punish me with such a child? A monster—a renegade! Why dost Thou leave her in the world, such a wicked spirit? Woe is me, woe is me! dark is my world."

Peshe Frede, herself weeping from pious sorrow, tried to soothe her neighbor.

"What good will it do to cry? Calm yourself, Breine Henne. The Almighty knows it is not your fault. The girl is possessed by an evil spirit. I always warned you that she would grow up a renegade. A trifle is it, to impose *trefah* upon a clean house? Such treachery! An honest Gentile would not do such a thing. Mark my word, this will not be the end of her wickedness. She would poison all Polotzk if her evil heart told her to. But what is the use of crying? Calm yourself, Breine Henne. What is done, is done."

After a while, Breine Henne lifted her heavy head. Her eyes fell on the dishes standing on the table. She broke into fresh weeping.

"Tref—tref—everything tref! All the dishes defiled. Woe is me, she has ruined me!"

"Don't lose your head, Breine Henne," Jacob spoke up. "Defiled vessels can be purified. The crockery must be scalded, the knives must be stuck into the cracks of the floor for half an hour, the—the—the rest of the things must be taken to the rav to pass upon."

The tailor was not much of a scholar, but so far as he had ventured to advise, he was correct. Every housewife knew as much. A gleam of comfort came to Breine Henne's heart as Jacob spoke, but the mention of the rav brought her shame back to her. She wept and prayed and wrung her hands. Peshe Frede at last gave up the attempt to comfort her, and retired, followed by her family.

"The whole town will ring with this," the poor egg-woman wailed. "Peshe Frede will have it all over town to-morrow. They will call us *trefah fressers* [eaters of unclean food]. Everybody will point a finger at us. Where shall I bury myself? Good God, just God, I beg Thee open a grave for me, and let me sink in and hide my disgrace."

Far into the night Breine Henne wept, exhausting the vocabulary of lamentation. The candles burned out, the oil in the lamp was low, and still she rocked herself in her grief. Yösele had long since curled up on his bench, too stupefied by misery to bother with the bed-clothes. Finally she dragged herself over to the bed and fell asleep, exhausted. At Malinke she did not look.

Malinke had not moved since she had thrown herself on the floor. She heard the hubbub excited by her confession, as one hears the rustle of summer leaves on the brink of a cataract. The greater tumult was in her own heart. Her own conscience hurled the bitterest reproaches at her. She knew, better than all her censors, how often she had questioned the written Word of God, defied the authority of her elders, and set up her own unhallowed standards. Nobody knew but she of the foreign petitions she injected into her daily prayers. For weeks past she had prayed, morning and night, that her hair might grow long, so that her playmates could not twit her about her pigtail. Now, in her hour of repentance, she realized how irreverent were her prayers. She had mocked at Yösele's rebbe, a pious and learned man, because he could not answer her impertinent questions about the Creation. Finally, she had disregarded the express commands of the rav himself, and betrayed her own mother and brother, for the sake of a chicken-bone and a plate of watery soup. Her most pitiless judge could not have drawn up a more bitter indictment than Malinke's conscience presented to her.

Now that she had had a sign from God, her remorse was bottomless. With all her soul she repented. She knew she would never be wicked any more, but she longed for a means of immediate atonement for the past. She threw her soul at the feet of God in utter humility at last, and she prayed Him to trample upon her and leave the mark of His chastisement on her.

IV

Worn out by her agonized thoughts. Malinke finally fell asleep.
When she awoke, stiff with cold and sore from lying on the bare
boards, the windows were opaque with dawn. She sat up, amazed
to find herself on the floor. She made out her mother's figure lying
on the edge of the bed. There was a curious atmosphere of disorder
about the room.

Breine Henne moved on the bed with a groan. In a flash Malinke
remembered everything. Her tormenting thoughts of the evening
rushed back into her brain. The sense of guilt once more overwhelmed her. It seemed to her that she was not herself, but somebody else,—a monstrous, unclean creature, from whom the real
Malinke shrank in horror. She longed to cry out, to struggle, to
shake off the hideous thing that grappled her, but she was afraid
to wake the sleepers. She must get out of the house, or she would
stifle.

Slowly creeping across the floor, inch by inch, she reached the
door. Noiselessly she lifted the latch and stole out. The chill of the
autumn morning struck to her very bones. She wished she had
taken a shawl, but she dared not go back.

Like a ghost she wandered away through the empty streets. She
had never been abroad at such an hour in the autumn; she thought it
was her sins that had turned the world so gray and unfamiliar. The
watchmen had gone home with the first glimmer of day. In all the
sleeping city, she alone was awake. It was a symbol of her isolation
from the world of righteous men.

Her dress reminded her that it was Sabbath. The people would
sleep late, but presently they would awake. The men would go to
the synagogue, and so would some of the women. The children
would put on their best clothes, and call to one another from the
doorways, and go visiting until dinner-time. Where should she go
then, she that was neither man nor woman nor honest child?

Crying softly, she wandered blindly on. At the bottom of a steep
street, the river gleamed pale in the ghostly light. Malinke descended
to the edge, and being unable to go farther, looked about her for the
first time.

On the bank above her a low gray building was just visible
between the palings of a sagging fence. Beyond the fence she could

make out a gray ribbon trembling down a shallow gash in the bank. That was where the spring flowed out which was reputed among the Gentiles to cure blindness. The building behind the fence was the Old Synagogue. By these landmarks, Malinke identified the spot. It was where the Jewish women came on New Year's Day for the ceremony of shaking their sins into the river, that they might start the new year with clean hearts.

A sudden thought came to Malinke. A flash of hope lighted up the gloom of her troubled soul. Why could not she, like the pious women of Polotzk, shake her sins into the river and begin a holy life? Was repentance only for New Year? Did God grant pardons only on the Day of Atonement? She did not realize that she was once more committing the sin of religious innovation—once more reasoning outside the book. Swept away by a genuine longing to make her peace with God, she cast about for means to carry out the symbolic rites of the season of atonement, fervently praying that the Almighty should see and understand.

Contrition, prayer, fasting, and sacrifice. She could not think of any other processes that went to the solemn drama of annual repentance. Contrition? Her soul prostrated itself in deepest humility. And prayer? She prayed with all her being that God should have mercy on her and forgive her sins. Her every breath should be a prayer. Fasting also she could fulfill. She would fast as long as her body would hold out. A whole day—two days she would fast. Sacrifice was left. What could she sacrifice? What had she that would be acceptable to God?

Malinke's heart sank as she failed to find a solution to this problem. Was she to give up the hope of God's forgiveness because she had nothing to sacrifice? No, no! she must think of something.

Her pockets were empty, because it was Sabbath. She looked down on herself, and so got her inspiration. She would sacrifice her Sabbath clothes—the dress with the gold trimmings, *and the boots!*

Joy unspeakable lighted Malinke's pinched face. With feverish fingers she unfastened and tore off her dress, half laughing, half crying with excitement. Then, sitting down on the wet bank, she unlaced her boots and started to roll them up in her dress.

What pretty boots they were! The patent-leather trimmings were as shiny as water. They were almost new: the varnish was not all worn off from the instep. She had worn them very little, of

course: only on Sabbaths and holy days. It was the only pair of
boots she could remember that had come to her new. She always
had other people's cast-off boots. If they were too big, she stuffed
them with rags; if too small, she slit them in the tight spots. Her
Sabbath boots, now, fitted her as if made to her measure.

Malinke could not forbear trying them on once more, for the last
time. It was light enough now for her to make out the stitching on
the patent-leather tops. It was a pretty pattern, all scrolls. She wondered if Fredke had loved those boots as much as she did.

With a deep, deep sigh, Malinke pulled off the beautiful boots
again, and resolutely rolled them up in the blue dress. The sacrifice
was ready.

But now a new difficulty assailed her. In what manner was the
sacrifice to be performed? On Atonement Day, when money was
offered, it was put into the poor-box; if a fowl, it was cooked and
eaten at the close of the fast. What was she to do with her clothes?
And the formula—she could not remember the formula by which
the sacrifice was offered, because it was used only once a year. She
also suspected that it would not fit the novel sacrifice she proposed
to offer.

After some hard thinking she threw up her head with a gesture
of finality, and turned an appealing face to heaven.

"Good God," she prayed, her teeth chattering with cold, "I have
nothing to sacrifice except this. I don't know how to do it. I'll just
tie a stone to it and throw it into the river. I beg Thee to pardon me
if I do wrong, and accept my sacrifice like a real one. I would pray
from the prayer-book, but it's at home, and there is nothing in it
about atonement in the middle of the year. Forgive me for everything. Amen."

V

Malinke never knew how she got home that day, nor how the time
passed. Her faith in the validity of her atonement had lifted her into
a state of exaltation past all physical sensation. She heard herself, in
a voice not her own, communicate the great news to her mother:
that she had atoned, by prayer and sacrifice, and all was well. Her
mother seemed unaccountably affected by the news. Malinke dimly

perceived that her mother's fresh tears were not the tears of joy; but she was too far removed from the world to be troubled, or even puzzled. She was fasting, in accordance with her resolution. She felt as buoyant as a chip floating on the bosom of the river.

It was well along in the afternoon when Malinke awoke from her trance. She was lying on the bed, staring wide-eyed at the wall, when she became aware of some unusual commotion in the room. Presently her mother's voice penetrated her dazed consciousness.

"Do you hear, Malinke? Get up and go to the rav. He has sent for you. Do you hear?"

Breine Henne's voice, though on the verge of tears, expressed a sort of awestruck elation. Genuinely grieved by the sinful conduct of her untractable child, the poor mother yet felt a tinge of bitter pride in the enormity of Malinke's crime, that attracted the notice of the rav himself.

"Get up, Malinke," she urged in a deep voice. "Reb' Nossen wants to speak to you. His messenger is waiting."

The mention of the rav's name brought Malinke to her senses. She jumped up and looked about for the messenger. He was a sickly-faced youth, a poor student in the seminary, who lived on the charity of the community. As she looked into his dull, unspeculative eyes it came over Malinke that in the sight of the world she was still a sinner, a law-breaker at large, no matter how sure she was in her heart of God's forgiveness. She would have to answer to her neighbors for her backsliding. The rav's summons was only the beginning. With quick imagination she visualized the mocking children that would follow her in the street, the mothers who would scowl her out of all companionship with their good little daughters; and she heard the taunts and jibes of inventive enemies. The expiation of her sin would be the long punishment at the hands of her neighbors. It was well for Malinke that she had so promptly made her peace with God. She had courage now to face the disapproving world.

She suffered her mother to wrap a shawl about her head and shoulders, but of the messenger she took no notice. Did she not know the way? She kept several yards in front of her guide, and presented herself at Reb' Nossen's gate with brave promptness.

The elderly servant ushered her into the rav's presence without a word. Even the customary "Good Sabbath" stuck in her throat at sight of the juvenile sinner. The woman knew Malinke's story by this time, as did every person of sound hearing and fair understanding in Polotzk. For Peshe Frede, the tailor's wife, had been to the synagogue, and started the story on a town-wide career by a score of sure, unobstructed channels. Before the Gentile chorewomen had unsealed the Jewish ovens, to draw out the Sabbath pots, there was not a bit of stale gossip current in Polotzk. Malinke and her misconduct furnished the fresh topic for every domestic circle.

Reb' Nossen had heard the story from his good wife, who had it from her good neighbor, who overheard the women exclaim over it in the rear rows of the women's gallery in the synagogue after service. The rav was one of the most liberal that Polotzk had ever had. Hearing the story of Malinke, he was a little shocked, and more than a little interested. He had taken but scant notice of Malinke the day before, when she came with the chicken. Now he wanted to see what manner of child was this who could plot and deceive, and invite the wrath of God, and make public confession of her sins, all in one short Sabbath eve.

Malinke's heart beat quite evenly as the great man bent his shortsighted gaze on her. Her own look was clear and direct. She wished for nothing so much as that the rav should see to the very bottom of her soul. The peace that filled her heart—the gift of a forgiving God—would be the answer to his bitterest reproaches. And as Reb' Nossen continued to study her face, without speaking, Malinke's mind was flooded with a sudden intuition of the nature of the judge before whom she stood. She had tested his wisdom—God Himself had confirmed his judgment: how could he fail in understanding and mercy? She was eager to speak, to tell everything, but restrained her tongue out of respect.

At last the rav began to question her. Very earnestly he listened to her artless account of her family, and the history of the luckless fowl up to the time of Breine Henne's great resolution concerning it. He made her repeat certain details, and led her to quote freely from her mother's comments on their daily life. From time to time his fine head moved in a barely perceptible nod of comprehension, but he said nothing, except to direct the child's narrative, until she came to the account of her temptation and its tragic consequences.

Here, to Malinke's amazement, he took up the story himself.

"You were very hungry, little girl," he said, in as simple words as she herself would have used. "It seemed to you a cruel decision. You thought perhaps I had made a mistake, after all."

Malinke gasped. Such perfect comprehension she had never expected from anybody below God.

"Is that so, little girl?"

"Oh, yes, yes!" she affirmed eagerly. "I thought there might be a mistake. But I know now it was true—the chicken was unclean. That's why it choked me." A touch of confusion made her speech waver. She did not know just how to express her newer faith in the rav's wisdom. "But I know, Reb' Nossen, that it was true. You could n't make a mistake."

Reb' Nossen put up his white hand to silence her.

"Hush, my child; do not speak so. There was a great mistake—a great mistake. No man has a right to give judgment who does not know his people. A wise teacher is like a physician, who has one medicine for the strong, and another for the weak. The Law must be read with one eye on the scroll, and the other on the world, lest the Torah become a writ of bondage, and the pent people rebel. The rabbi alone cannot keep the Torah holy. The people must be with him, and he with them."

Reb' Nossen spoke as if to himself. Malinke gazed at him in wonder, not half comprehending his meaning. After some moments of silence, the rav came out of his reverie. The child had been respectfully standing all this time, but now he bade her be seated. He set a chair for her himself, in the light of the window, near his own. He had been blind long enough with respect to this poor, uninstructed child. He, too, wanted to atone.

He brought Malinke back to her story.

"And so you ate of the forbidden meat, and thought you had a sign from God when you choked." There was not a trace of reproof in his voice.

"Yes, and then I was so sorry, and in the morning I prayed, and I had nothing to sacrifice except my things."

She was not surprised at his knowing more of her story than she had told him. The rav seemed to read her thoughts of yesterday.

"And those were your Sabbath clothes?"

For answer Malinke looked down on her very shabby dress. Anybody might know *that* was not her Sabbath dress.

"You had a pair of good boots, eh?"

"Oh, they were beautiful!" Malinke grew loquacious again. "They were the best I ever had. They were almost new. Aunt Leah would n't have given them to me, but Fredke died, and the other girls could n't wear them, because Fredke was the smallest. They were trimmed with patent leather, and they fitted me—"

She broke off, unable to express the perfection of the relation between the now historic boots and her abused little feet. Unconsciously she looked down upon the ruinous boots that replaced them.

The rav's eyes followed hers.

"Do you regret the pretty boots, Malinke?"

The child jumped up in her excitable manner, her eyes full of protest.

"Oh, no, *no!*" she cried earnestly. "I'm glad they're at the bottom of the river. I shall never have such beautiful boots again as long as I live, but I'm *glad*, because it was my sacrifice, and God will forgive me. Reb' Nossen," she repeated, vehemently, "I'm *glad!*"

The rav put up his hand to hide his eyes from the little penitent. Short-sighted as he was, he had a sudden vision of spiritual vistas. After a moment, he raised his head and drew Malinke to him. Stroking her thin hair, he regarded her with grave, sad eyes. He reproached himself inwardly for his blindness on the occasion of their first interview. The signs of privation and suffering were plain in the little girl's pinched face, in the sharp angles of her figure, visible under her scanty apparel. And suddenly, across his vaguer speculations, shot a clear idea of the child's immediate want. If the chicken was rejected as unclean, what did those poor people have for dinner?

"Malinke," questioned Reb' Nossen, looking hard at the child, "what did you eat to-day?"

She returned his look with a smile of triumph.

"Nothing," she replied, with the least touch of pride in her voice. "I'm fasting, you know, for atonement."

"Fasting!" exclaimed the rav, in a tone of reproach, and rising as he spoke. "Why, you're too young to fast, my child, and too weak. Besides, it is wrong to fast on Sabbath. Your head is full of strange ideas. There are a great many things to explain to you—a great many.

But there will be time enough for that when you have had something to eat."

Pushing her gently back into her chair, he went to the door and called aloud, "Deborah! Tamareh!" Once aroused, the rav was practical enough.

"You shall eat," he said again to Malinke, going back to her chair and looking down upon her. "Why, you are as thin as a skeleton. What business has such a child with fasting? You shall eat, and then we can talk. There are a great many things we can learn together, my child, but the body comes before the mind."

Malinke's eyes, that had met his so bravely at the beginning of the interview, when she expected accusation and reproof, now wavered and fell, as the old man's sympathy focused in his gaze. And then, to her own amazement, a great sob broke from her, followed by a flood of tears.

The rav strode over to the door once more, the tails of his long frock coat flying back from his white-stockinged legs. He called impatiently, "Deborah! Tamareh!"

In answer to his summons came neither his wife nor the servant, but a strange, disheveled figure, with pale eyes in a tear-blotched face. It was Breine Henne, the egg-woman, impelled by a dozen contradictory impulses to be present at what she imagined to be her child's bitter trial. At sight of Reb' Nossen's stern face, and Malinke sobbing in her chair, all her motives resolved themselves into an overpowering instinct to defend her little girl, against the rav himself, against all the world, if need be.

"Reb' Nossen, Reb' Nossen," she began to plead, "listen to me, I beg you. Don't be too hard on the child. She is so young, and so ignorant. She has no father, and I am a poor, ignorant woman, and all day long she is among strangers, because there is nobody at home to take care of her. It was a great temptation—she was so hungry, poor child. She had hardly tasted meat for weeks. We cook nothing but grits when times are so bad. She was out of her head with disappointment. May you never know what it is to be hungry for a decent meal. And it was all my fault, anyway. I should have killed the chicken last Atonement Day, and then this dreadful thing would n't have happened. And oh, Reb' Nossen! as I am a Jewish woman, I believe the child is out of her head this day. She stole out of the house at daybreak, will you believe me? on purpose to throw her best clothes into the river, because she imagined that would be a sacrifice in atonement for her sins! You know, Reb' Nossen, that no sane child would do such a thing. It was her only decent dress, and the boots were the best she ever had in her life. If you had seen her when she came back, blue with cold, and saying such wild things—Oh, Reb' Nossen, don't, don't be hard on my poor child!"

The rav waited patiently for Breine Henne to stop.

"Calm yourself, my good woman," he said, as soon as he could speak. "Take a seat—here—and try to be calm. I did not mean to be harsh with the child. I do not blame her for anything. On the contrary—Ah, Tamareh! yes, I called. Bring this child something to eat. She has not eaten to-day, Tamareh. Bring it in here, and be quick."

While the famished child was eating, the rav drew from the mother many details bearing on Malinke's character and education, which Breine Henne adorned with numerous comments and apologies. She was very much puzzled at the rav's benign attitude toward the child,—the very opposite of what Malinke had earned,—but she would have thought it disrespectful to question him. No doubt he knew what he was about, and if she did not understand,—why, she was only a poor, ignorant female. So she babbled on in a happy excitement, her eyes resting now and then on Malinke, feasting there in the house of the rav, and at his own invitation.

There was little more than crumbs left on Malinke's tray when she leaned back, with a smile of utter contentment on her face, and remarked to the friendly air, "I really can't eat any more."

The rav turned and looked at the tray.

"That's good—that's good," he said. "Now come over here. I've been talking with your mother, and I find your education has been a little defective. I have caused you—I might have saved you much trouble. I should like to make amends." He embraced them both in his look. "I shall be very glad to provide for your tuition in the future, if you will let me choose the teacher—and if you care for lessons, Malinke."

The child drew in her breath.

Breine Henne broke out in a flood of thanks and blessings, which the good man did not hear. He was waiting for Malinke to speak. At last she opened her lips.

"Shall I begin to-morrow?" she asked.

The rav smiled, pleased with her directness.

"To-morrow," he said. "It is well to hasten to a good thing. And shall I name your teacher?"

Malinke ventured on a petition.

"I hope it will be a rebbe, not a *rebbetzin* [female teacher]," she said. "The rebbetzins don't know so much."

Breine Henne broke out in reproof.

"Hush, you bold child! There you go again, talking as a child should n't. That's her great fault, believe me, Reb' Nossen—that tongue of hers. You ought to be more respectful, and grateful, and, whatever you do, keep your tongue quiet."

The rav uttered no direct reproof.

"If the rebbe knows more than the rebbetzin, it is because he has spent more time in study, my dear. Perhaps a rebbe would be best for you. Well, now, I cannot afford to pay much; I am not known for my riches. I must choose some one who will not ask too much tuition. What would you say to taking a few lessons with me? I have never taught girls, but I can try."

It was Breine Henne who gasped now, and Malinke who babbled excitedly.

"Oh, will you teach me everything?" she cried, "the same as a boy—the same as Yösele? I'd like to read *everything*. Yösele says a girl can't understand, but I don't think that's true, do you? Do you mean you'll teach me the *Humesh*, and *Gemara*, and everything?"

The rav smiled again.

"Not all at once, my child, not all at once. We must make a beginning first. You come to-morrow before sunset prayer, and then we'll see. The Torah is inexhaustible. There are a great many things to learn—about conduct, and sacrifice, and many other things. I pray that I have the wisdom to teach you."

For the second time that day, Malinke walked home without touching the earth. But if she did not know the way she took, a third of Polotzk did. That much of the population followed her to her door, as a volunteer escort of honor.

For in the quiet of the Sabbath afternoon, the movements of the rav's messenger had been observed, and a knot of the most irrepressible gossips in Polotzk lay in wait for Malinke and her mother at Reb' Nossen's gate. Breine Henne, bursting with pride, was glad to fall upon the bosom of the first gossip with an apron who presented herself; and so the story of the great interview was out.

Before the first corner was turned, the original knot of gossips had become the indistinguishable nucleus of a rapidly growing procession, at the head of which a fairly straight version of Malinke's story was told, and at the tail of which it was rumored that Reb' Nossen was going to adopt Breine Henne's girl, and make a great scholar of her.

But Malinke heard nothing of what the people said. In the midst of the throng she was communing with herself about the mystery of divine justice. She who had sinned the most was the most blessed of all little girls in Polotzk. The Lord had accepted her atonement. In compensation for her blindness, that had led her into error, God had sent her a teacher.

THE LIE

I

The first thing about his American teachers that struck David Rudin-sky was the fact that they were women, and the second was that they did not get angry if somebody asked questions. This phenomenon subverted his previous experience. When he went to *heder* (Hebrew school), in Russia, his teachers were always men, and they did not like to be interrupted with questions that were not in the lesson. Everything was different in America, and David liked the difference.

The American teachers, on their part, also made comparisons. They said David was not like other children. It was not merely that his mind worked like lightning; those neglected Russian waifs were almost always quick to learn, perhaps because they had to make up for lost time. The quality of his interest, more than the rapidity of his progress, excited comment. Miss Ralston, David's teacher in the sixth grade, which he reached in his second year at school, said of him that he never let go of a lesson till he had got the soul of the matter. "I don't think grammar is grammar to him," she said, "or fractions mere arithmetic. I'm not satisfied with the way I teach these things since I've had David. I feel that if he were on the platform instead of me, geography and grammar would be spliced to the core of the universe."

One difficulty David's teachers encountered, and that was his extreme reserve. In private conversation it was hard to get anything out of him except "yes, ma'am" and "no, ma'am," or, "I don't understand, please." In the classroom he did not seem to be aware of the existence of anybody besides Teacher and himself. He asked questions as fast as he could formulate them, and Teacher had to exercise much tact in order to satisfy him without slighting the rest of her pupils. To advances of a personal sort he did not respond, as if friendship were not among the things he hungered for.

It was Miss Ralston who found the way to David's heart. Perhaps she was interested in such things; they sometimes are, in the public schools. After the Christmas holidays, the children were given as a subject for composition, "How I spent the Vacation." David wrote in a froth of enthusiasm about whole days spent in the public library. He covered twelve pages with an account of the books he had read. The list included many juvenile classics in American history and biography; and from his comments it was plain that the little alien worshiped the heroes of war.

When Miss Ralston had read David's composition, she knew what to do. She was one of those persons who always know what to do, and do it. She asked David to stay after school, and read to him, from a blue book with gilt lettering, "Paul Revere's Ride" and "Independence Bell." That hour neither of them ever forgot. To David it seemed as if all the heroes he had dreamed of crowded around him, so real did his teacher's reading make them. He heard the clash of swords and the flapping of banners in the wind. On the blackboard behind Miss Ralston troops of faces appeared and vanished, like the shadows that run across a hillside when clouds are moving in the sky. As for Miss Ralston, she said afterwards that she was the first person who had ever seen the real David Rudinsky. That was a curious statement to make, considering that his mother and father, and sundry other persons in the two hemispheres, had had some acquaintance with David previous to the reading of "Paul Revere's Ride." However, Miss Ralston had a way of saying curious things.

There were many readings out of school hours, after that memorable beginning. Miss Ralston did not seem to realize that the School Board did not pay her for those extra hours that she spent on David. David did not know that she was paid at all. He thought Teacher was born on purpose to read and tell him things and answer his questions, just as his mother existed to cook his favorite soup and patch his trousers. So he brought his pet book from the library, and when the last pupil was gone, he took it from his desk, and laid it on Miss Ralston's, without a word; and Miss Ralston read, and they were both happy. When a little Jewish boy from Russia goes to school in America, all sorts of things are likely to happen that the School Board does not provide for. It might be amusing to figure out the reasons.

David's reserve slowly melted in the glowing intimacy of these happy half-hours; still he seldom made any comment on the reading at the time; he basked mutely in the warmth of his teacher's sympathy. But what he did not say orally he was very likely to say on paper. That also was one of Miss Ralston's discoveries. When she gave out the theme, "What I Mean to Do When I Grow Up," David wrote that he was going to be an American citizen, and always vote for honest candidates, and belong to a society for arresting illegal voters. You see David was only a greenhorn, and an excitable one. He thought it a very great matter to be a citizen, perhaps because such a thing was not allowed in the country he came from. Miss Ralston probably knew how it was with him, or she guessed. She was great at guessing, as all her children knew. At any rate, she did not smile as she read of David's patriotic ambitions. She put his paper aside until their next quiet hour, and then she used it so as to get a great deal out of him that he would not have had the courage to tell if he had not believed that it was an exercise in composition.

This Miss Ralston was a crafty person. She learned from David about a Jewish restaurant where his father sometimes took him, a place where a group of ardent young Russians discussed politics over their inexpensive dinner. She heard about a mass meeting of Russian Jews to celebrate the death of Alexander III, "because he was a cruel tyrant, and was very bad to Jewish people." She even tracked some astonishing phrases in David's vocabulary to their origin in the Sunday orations he had heard on the Common, in his father's company.

Impressed by these and other signs of paternal interest in her pupil's education, Miss Ralston was not unprepared for the visit which David's father paid her soon after these revelations. It was a very cold day, and Mr. Rudinsky shivered in his thin, shabby overcoat; but his face glowed with inner warmth as he discovered David's undersized figure in one of the front seats.

"I don't know how to say it what I feel to see my boy sitting and learning like this," he said, with a vibration in his voice that told more than his words. "Do you know, ma'am, if I did n't have to make a living, I'd like to stay here all day and see my David get educated. I'm forty years old, and I've had much in my life, but it's worth nothing so much as this. The day I brought my children to school, it was the best day in my life. Perhaps you won't believe me, ma'am, but when I hear that David is a good boy and learns good in school, I would n't change places with Vanderbilt the millionaire."

He looked at Miss Ralston with the eyes of David listening to "Paul Revere's Ride."

"What do you think, ma'am," he asked, as he got up to leave, "my David will be a good American, no?"

"He ought to be," said Miss Ralston, warmly, "with such a father."

Mr. Rudinsky did not try to hide his gratification.

"I am a citizen," he said, unconsciously straightening. "I took out citizen papers as soon as I came to America, four years ago."

So they came to the middle of February, when preparations for Washington's Birthday were well along. One day the class was singing "America," when Miss Ralston noticed that David stopped and stared absently at the blackboard in front of him. He did not wake out of his reverie till the singing was over, and then he raised his hand.

"Teacher," he asked, when he had permission to speak, "what does it mean, 'Land where my fathers died'?"

Miss Ralston explained, wondering how many of her pupils cared to analyze the familiar words as David did.

A few days later, the national hymn was sung again. Miss Ralston watched David. His lips formed the words "Land where my fathers died," and then they stopped, set in the pout of childish trouble. His eyes fixed themselves on the teacher's, but her smile of encouragement failed to dispel his evident perplexity.

Anxious to help him over his unaccountable difficulty, Miss Ralston detained him after school.

"David," she asked him, when they were alone, "do you understand 'America' now?"

"Yes, ma'am."

"Do you understand 'Land where my fathers died'?"

"Yes, ma'am."

"You did n't sing with the others."

"No, ma'am."

Miss Ralston thought of a question that would rouse him.

"Don't you like 'America,' David?"

The boy almost jumped in his place.

"Oh, yes, ma'am, I do! I like 'America.' It's—fine."

He pressed his fist nervously to his mouth, a trick he had when excited.

"Then tell me, David, why you don't sing it."

David's eyes fixed themselves in a look of hopeless longing. He answered in a whisper, his pale face slowly reddening.

"*My* fathers did n't die here. How can I sing such a lie?"

Miss Ralston's impulse was to hug the child, but she was afraid to startle him. The attention she had lavished on the boy was rewarded at this moment, when her understanding of his nature inspired the answer to his troubled question. She saw how his mind worked. She realized, what a less sympathetic witness might have failed to realize, that behind the moral scruple expressed in his words, there was a sense of irreparable loss derived from the knowledge that he had no share in the national past. The other children could shout the American hymn in all the pride of proprietorship, but to him the words did not apply. It was a flaw in his citizenship, which he was so jealous to establish.

The teacher's words were the very essence of tact and sympathy. In her voice were mingled the yearning of a mother and the faith of a comrade.

"David Rudinsky, you have as much a right to those words as I or anybody else in America. Your ancestors did not die on our battlefields, but they would have if they'd had a chance. You used to spend all your time reading the Hebrew books, in Russia. Don't you know how your people—your ancestors, perhaps!—fought the Roman tyrants? Don't you remember the Maccabean brothers, and Bar Kochba, and—oh, you know about them more than I! I'm ashamed to tell you that I have n't read much Jewish history, but I'm sure if we begin to look it up, we'll find that people of your race—people like your father, David—took a part in the fight for freedom, wherever they were allowed. And even in this country— David, I'm going to find out for you how many Jews there were in the armies of the Revolution. We don't think about it here, you see, because we don't ask what a man's religion is, as long as he is brave and good."

David's eyes slowly lost their look of distress as his teacher talked. His tense little face, upturned to hers, reminded her of a withered blossom that revives in the rain. She went on with increasing earnestness, herself interested in the discoveries she was making, in her need.

"I tell you the truth, David, I never thought of these things before, but I do believe that the Pilgrim Fathers did n't all come here before the Revolution. Is n't your father just like them? Think of it, dear, how he left his home, and came to a strange land, where he could n't even speak the language. That was a great trouble, you know; something like the fear of the Indians in the old days. And did n't he come looking for the very same things? He wanted freedom for himself and his family, and a chance for his children to grow up wise and brave. You know your father cares more for such things than he does for money or anything. It's the same story over again. Every ship that brings your people from Russia and other countries where they are ill-treated is a *Mayflower*. If I were a Jewish child like you, I would sing 'America' louder than anybody else!"

David's adoring eyes gave her the thanks which his tongue would not venture to utter. Never since that moment, soon after his arrival from Russia, when his father showed him his citizenship papers, saying, "Look, my son, this makes you an American," had he felt so secure in his place in the world.

Miss Ralston studied his face in silence while she gathered up some papers on her desk, preparatory to leaving. In the back of her mind she asked herself to how many of the native children in her class the Fourth of July meant anything besides fire-crackers.

"Get your things, David," she said presently, as she locked her desk. "It's time we were going. Think if we should get locked up in the building!"

David smiled absently. In his ears rang the familiar line, "Land where my fathers died—my fathers died—fathers died."

"It's something like the Psalms!" he said suddenly, himself surprised at the discovery.

"What is like the Psalms, dear?"

He hesitated. Now that he had to explain, he was not sure any more. Miss Ralston helped him out.

"You mean 'America' sounds like the Psalms to you?"

David nodded. His teacher beamed her understanding. How did she guess wherein the similarity lay? David had in mind such moments as this when he said of Miss Ralston, "Teacher talks with her eyes."

Miss Ralston went to get her coat and hat from the closet.

"Get your things, David," she repeated. "The janitor will come to chase us out in a minute."

He was struggling with the torn lining of a coat-sleeve in the children's dressing-room, when he heard Miss Ralston exclaim,—

"Oh, David! I had almost forgotten. You must try this on. This is what you're going to wear when you speak the dialogue with Annie and Raymond. We used it in a play a few years ago. I thought it would do for you."

She held up a blue-and-buff jacket with tarnished epaulets. David hurried to put it on. He was to take the part of George Washington in the dialogue. At sight of the costume, his heart started off on a gallop.

Alas for his gallant aspirations! Nothing of David was visible outside the jacket except two big eyes above and two blunt boot-toes below. The collar reached to his ears; the cuffs dangled below his knees. He resembled a scarecrow in the cornfield more than the Father of his Country.

Miss Ralston suppressed her desire to laugh.

"It's a little big, is n't it?" she said cheerily, holding up the shoulders of the heroic garment. "I wonder how we can make it fit. Don't you think your mother would know how to take up the sleeves and do something to the back?"

She turned the boy around, more hopeless than she would let him see. Miss Ralston understood more about little boys' hearts than about their coats.

"How old are you, David?" she asked, absently, wondering for the hundredth time at his diminutive stature. "I thought the boy for whom this was made was about your age."

David's face showed that he felt reproved. "I'm twelve," he said, apologetically.

Miss Ralston reproached herself for her tactlessness, and proceeded to make amends.

"Twelve?" she repeated, patting the blue shoulders. "You speak the lines like a much older boy. I'm sure your mother can make the coat fit, and I'll bring the wig—a powdered wig—and the sword, David! You'll look just like George Washington!"

Her gay voice echoed in the empty room. Her friendly eyes challenged his. She expected to see him kindle, as he did so readily in these days of patriotic excitement. But David failed to respond. He remained motionless in his place, his eyes blank and staring.

Miss Ralston had the feeling that behind his dead front his soul was running away from her.

This is just what was happening. David was running away from her, and from himself, and from the image of George Washington, conjured up by the scene with the military coat. Somewhere in the jungle of his consciousness a monster was stirring, and his soul fled in terror of its clutch. What was it—what was it that came tearing through the wilderness of his memories of two worlds? In vain he tried not to understand. The ghosts of forgotten impressions cackled in the wake of the pursuing monster, the breath of whose nostrils spread an odor of evil sophistries grafted on his boyish thoughts in a chimerical past.

His mind reeled in a whirlwind of recollection. Miss Ralston could not have understood some of the things David reviewed, even if he had tried to tell her. In that other life of his, in Russia, had been monstrous things, things that seemed unbelievable to David himself, after his short experience of America. He had suffered many wrongs,—yes, even as a little boy,—but he was not thinking of past grievances as he stood before Miss Ralston, seeing her as one sees a light through a fog. He was thinking of things harder to forget than injuries received from others. It was a sudden sense of his own sins that frightened David, and of one sin in particular, the origin of which was buried somewhere in the slime of the evil past. David was caught in the meshes of a complex inheritance; contradictory impulses tore at his heart. Fearfully he dived to the bottom of his consciousness, and brought up a bitter conviction: David Rudinsky, who called himself an American, who worshiped the names of the heroes, suddenly knew that he had sinned, sinned against his best friend, sinned even as he was planning to impersonate George Washington, the pattern of honor.

His white forehead glistened with the sweat of anguish. His eyes sickened. Miss Ralston caught him as he wavered and put him in the nearest seat.

"Why, David! what's the matter? Are you ill? Let me take this off—it's so heavy. There, that's better. Just rest your head on me, so."

This roused him. He wriggled away from her support, and put out a hand to keep her off.

"Why, David! what *is* the matter? Your hands are so cold—"

David's head felt heavy and wobbly, but he stood up and began to put on his coat again, which he had pulled off in order to try on the uniform. To Miss Ralston's anxious questions he answered not a syllable, neither did he look at her once. His teacher, thoroughly alarmed, hurriedly put on her street things, intending to take him home. They walked in silence through the empty corridors, down the stairs, and across the school yard. The teacher noticed with relief that the boy grew steadier with every step. She smiled at him encouragingly when he opened the gate for her, as she had taught him, but he did not meet her look.

At the corner where they usually parted David paused, steeling himself to take his teacher's hand; but to his surprise she kept right on, taking *his* crossing.

It was now that he spoke, and Miss Ralston was astonished at the alarm in his voice.

"Miss Ralston, where are you going? You don't go this way."

"I'm going to see you home, David," she replied firmly. "I can't let you go alone—like this."

"Oh, Teacher! don't, please don't. I'm all right—I'm not sick,— it's not far—Don't, Miss Ralston, *please*."

In the February dusk, Miss Ralston saw the tears rise to his eyes. Whatever was wrong with him, it was plain that her presence only made him suffer the more. Accordingly she yielded to his entreaty.

"I hope you'll be all right, David," she said, in a tone she might have used to a full-grown man. "Good-bye." And she turned the corner.

II

All the way home Miss Ralston debated the wisdom of allowing him to go alone, but as she recalled his look and his entreating voice she felt anew the compulsion that had made her yield. She attributed his sudden breakdown entirely to overwrought nerves, and remorsefully resolved not to subject him in the future to the strain of extra hours after school.

Her misgivings were revived the next morning, when David failed to appear with the ringing of the first gong, as was his habit. But before the children had taken their seats, David's younger brother, Bennie, brought her news of the missing boy.

"David's sick in bed," he announced in accents of extreme importance. "He did n't come home till awful late last night, and he was so frozen, his teeth knocked together. My mother says he burned like a fire all night, and she had to take little Harry in her bed, with her and papa, so's David could sleep all alone. We all went downstairs in our bare feet this morning, and dressed ourselves in the kitchen, so David could sleep."

"What is the matter with him? Did you have the doctor?"

"No, ma'am, not yet. The dispensary don't open till nine o'clock."

Miss Ralston begged him to report again in the afternoon, which he did, standing before her, cap in hand, his sense of importance still dominating over brotherly concern.

"He's sick, all right," Bennie reported. "He don't eat at all—just drinks and drinks. My mother says he cried the whole morning, when he woke up and found out he'd missed school. My mother says he tried to get up and dress himself, but he could n't anyhow. Too sick."

"Did you have the doctor?" interrupted Miss Ralston, suppressing her impatience.

"No, ma'am, not yet. My father went to the dispensary, but the doctor said he can't come till noon, but he did n't. Then I went to the dispensary, dinner time, but the doctor did n't yet come when we went back to school. My mother says you can die ten times before the dispensary doctor comes."

"What does your mother think it is?"

"Oh, she says it's a bad cold, but David is n't strong, you know, so she's scared. I guess if he gets worse I'll have to stay home from school to run for the medicines."

"I hope not, Bennie. Now you'd better run along, or you'll be late."

"Yes, ma'am. Good-bye."

"Will you come again in the morning and tell me about your brother?"

"Yes, ma'am. Good-bye.—Teacher."

"Yes, Bennie?"

"Do you think you can do something—something—about his *record?* David feels dreadful because he's broke his record. He never missed school before, you know. It's—it's too bad to see him cry. He's always so quiet, you know, kind of like grown people. He don't fight or tease or anything. Do you think you can, Teacher?"

Miss Ralston was touched by this tribute to her pupil, but she could not promise to mend the broken record.

"Tell David not to worry. He has the best record in the school, for attendance and everything. Tell him I said he must hurry and get well, as we must rehearse our pieces for Washington's Birthday."

The next morning Bennie reeled off a longer story than ever. He described the doctor's visit in great detail, and Miss Ralston was relieved to gather that David's ailment was nothing worse than grippe; unless, as the doctor warned, his run-down condition caused complications. He would be in bed a week or more, in any case, "and he ought to sleep most of the time, the doctor said."

"I guess the doctor don't know our David!" Bennie scoffed. "He never wants at all to go to sleep. He reads and reads when everybody goes to bed. One time he was reading all night, and the lamp went out, and he was afraid to go downstairs for oil, because he'd wake somebody, so he lighted matches and read little bits. There was a heap of burned matches in the morning."

"Dear me!" exclaimed Miss Ralston. "He ought not to do that. Your father ought not—Does your father allow him to stay up nights?"

"Sure. My father's proud because he's going to be a great man; a doctor, maybe." He shrugged his shoulders, as if to say, "What may not a David become?"

"David is funny, don't you think, Teacher?" the boy went on. "He asks such funny questions. What do you think he said to the doctor?"

"I can't imagine."

"Well, he pulled him by the sleeve when he took out the—the thing he puts in your mouth, and said kind of hoarse, 'Doctor, did you ever tell a lie?' Wasn't that funny?"

Miss Ralston did not answer. She was thinking that David must have been turning over some problem in his mind, to say so much to a stranger.

"Did you give him my message?" she asked finally.

"Yes 'm! I told him about rehearsing his piece for Washington's Birthday." Bennie paused.

"Well?"

"He acted so funny. He turned over to the wall, and cried and cried without any noise."

"The poor boy! He'll be dreadfully disappointed not to take his part in the exercises."

Bennie shook his head.

"That is n't for what he cries," he said oracularly.

Miss Ralston's attentive silence invited further revelations.

"He's *worrying* about something." Bennie brought out, rolling his head ominously.

"Why? How do you know?"

"The doctor said so. He told my father downstairs. He said, 'Make him tell, if you can, it may help to pull him off'—no, 'pull him up.' That's what the doctor said."

Miss Ralston's thoughts flew back to her last interview with David, two days before, when he had broken down so suddenly. Was there a mystery there? She was certain the boy was overwrought, and physically run down. Apparently, also, he had been exposed to the weather during the evening when he was taken ill; Bennie's chatter indicated that David had wandered in the streets for hours. These things would account for the grippe, and for the abnormal fever of which Bennie boasted. But what was David worrying about? She resolved to go and see the boy in a day or two, when he was reported to be more comfortable.

On his next visit Bennie brought a message from the patient himself.

"He said to give you this, Teacher," handing Miss Ralston a journal. "It's yours. It has the pieces in it for Washington's Birthday. He said you might need it, and the doctor did n't say when he could go again to school."

Miss Ralston laid the journal carelessly on a pile of other papers. Bennie balanced himself on one foot, looking as if his mission were not yet ended.

"Well, Bennie?" Miss Ralston encouraged him. She was beginning to understand his mysterious airs.

"David was awful careful about that book," the messenger said impressively. "He said over and over not to lose it, and not to give it to nobody only you."

III

It was not till the end of the day that Miss Ralston took up the journal Bennie had brought. She turned the leaves absently, thinking of

David. He would be so disappointed to miss the exercises! And to whom should she give the part of George Washington in the dialogue? She found the piece in the journal. A scrap of paper marked the place. A folded paper. Folded several times. Miss Ralston opened out the paper and found some writing.

> Dear Teacher Miss Ralston:
> I can't be George Washington any more because I have lied to you. I must not tell you about what, because you would blame somebody who did n't do wrong.
>
> > Your friend,
> > DAVID RUDINSKY.

Again and again Miss Ralston read the note, unable to understand it. David, her David, whose soul was a mirror for every noble idea, had lied to her! What could he mean? What had impelled him? *Somebody who did n't do wrong.* So it was not David alone; there was some complication with another person. She studied the note word for word, and her eyes slowly filled with tears. If the boy had really lied—if the whole thing were not a chimera of his fevered nights— then what must he have suffered of remorse and shame! Her heart went out to him even while her brain was busy with the mystery.

She made a swift resolution. She would go to David at once. She was sure he would tell her more than he had written, and it would relieve his mind. She did not dread the possible disclosures. Her knowledge of the boy made her certain that she would find nothing ignoble at the bottom of his mystery. He was only a child, after all—an overwrought, sensitive child. No doubt he exaggerated his sin, if sin there were. It was her duty to go and put him at rest.

She knew that David's father kept a candy shop in the basement of his tenement, and she had no trouble in finding the place. Half the children in the neighborhood escorted her to the door, attracted by the phenomenon of a Teacher loose on their streets.

The tinkle of the shop bell brought Mr. Rudinsky from the little kitchen in the rear.

"Well, well!" he exclaimed, shaking hands heartily. "This is a great honor—a great honor." He sounded the initial *h*. "I wish I had a palace for you to come in, ma'am. I don't think there was such company in this house since it was built."

His tone was one of genuine gratification. Ushering her into the kitchen, he set a chair for her, and himself sat down at a respectful distance.

"I'm sorry," he began, with a wave of his hand around the room. "Such company ought not to sit in the kitchen, but you see—"

He was interrupted by Bennie, who had clattered in at the visitor's heels, panting for recognition.

"Never mind, Teacher," the youngster spoke up, "we got a parlor upstairs, with a mantelpiece and everything, but David sleeps up there—the doctor said it's the most air—and you dass n't wake him up till he wakes himself."

Bennie's father frowned, but the visitor smiled a cordial smile.

"I like a friendly kitchen like this," she said quietly. "My mother did not keep any help when I was a little girl and I was a great deal in the kitchen."

Her host showed his appreciation of her tact by dropping the subject.

"I'm sure you came about David," he said.

"I did. How is he?"

"Pretty sick, ma'am. The doctor says it's not the sickness so much, but David is so weak and small. He says David studies too much altogether. Maybe he's right. What do you think, ma'am?"

Miss Ralston answered remorsefully.

"I agree with the doctor. I think we are all to blame. We push him too much when we ought to hold him back."

Here Bennie made another raid on the conversation.

"He's going to be a great man, a doctor maybe. My mother says—"

Mr. Rudinsky did not let him finish. He thought it time to insure the peace of so important an interview.

"Bennie," said he, "you will go mind the store, and keep the kitchen door shut."

Bennie's discomfiture was evident in his face. He obeyed, but not without a murmur.

"Let us make a covenant to take better care of David in the future."

Miss Ralston was speaking when Mrs. Rudinsky appeared in the doorway. She was flushed from the exertions of a hasty toilet, for which she had fled upstairs at the approach of "company." She came forward timidly, holding out a hand on which the scrubbing brush and the paring knife had left their respective marks.

"How do you do, ma'am?" she said, cordially, but shyly. "I'm glad to see you. I wish I can speak English better, I'd like to say how proud I am to see David's teacher in my haus."

"Why, you speak wonderfully!" Miss Ralston exclaimed, with genuine enthusiasm. "I don't understand how you pick up the language in such a short time. I could n't learn Russian so fast, I'm sure."

"My husband makes us speak English all the time," Mrs. Rudinsky replied. "From the fust day he said to speak English. He scolds the children if he hears they speak Jewish."

"Sure," put in her husband, "I don't want my family to be greenhorns."

Miss Ralston turned a glowing face to him.

"Mr. Rudinsky, I think you've done wonders for your family. If all immigrants were like you, we would n't need any restriction laws." She threw all possible emphasis into her cordial voice. "Why, you're a better American than some natives I know!"

Mrs. Rudinsky sent her husband a look of loving pride.

"He wants to be a Yankee," she said.

Her husband took up the cue in earnest.

"Yes, ma'am," he said. "That's my ambition. When I was a young man, in the old country, I wanted to be a scholar. But a Jew has no chance in the old country; perhaps you know how it is. It was n't the Hebrew books I wanted. I wanted to learn what the rest of the world learned, but a poor Jew had no chance in Russia. When I got to America, it was too late for me to go to school. It took me all my time and strength to make a living—I've never been much good in business, ma'am—and when I got my family over, I saw that it was the children would go to school for me. I'm glad to be a plain citizen, if my children will be educated Americans."

People with eyes and hands like Mr. Rudinsky's can say a great deal in a few words. Miss Ralston felt as if she had known him all his life, and followed his strivings in two worlds.

"I'm glad to know you, Mr. Rudinsky," she said in a low voice. "I wish more of my pupils had fathers like David's."

Her host changed the subject very neatly.

"And I wish the school children had more teachers like you. David likes you so much."

"Oh, he liked you!" the wife confirmed. "Please stay till he veks up. He'll be sorry to missed your vis*it*."

While his wife moved quietly around the stove, making tea, Mr. Rudinsky entertained their guest with anecdotes of David's Hebrew-school days, and of his vain efforts to get at secular books.

"He was just like me," he said. "He wanted to learn everything. I could n't afford a private teacher, and they would n't take him in the public school. He learned Russian all alone, and if he got a book from somewhere—a history or anything—he would n't eat or drink till he read it all."

Mrs. Rudinsky often glanced at David's teacher, to see how her husband's stories were impressing her. She was too shy with her English to say more than was required of her as hostess, but her face, aglow with motherly pride, showed how she participated in her husband's enthusiasm.

"You see yourself, ma'am, what he is," said David's father, "but what could I make of him in Russia? I was happy when he got here, only it was a little late. I wished he started in school younger."

"He has time enough," said Miss Ralston. "He'll get through grammar school before he's fourteen. He's twelve now, is n't he?"

"Yes, ma'am—no, ma'am! He's really fourteen now, but I made him out younger on purpose."

Miss Ralston looked puzzled. Mr. Rudinsky explained.

"You see, ma'am, he was twelve years when he came, and I wanted he should go to school as long as possible, so when I made his school certificate, I said he was only ten. I have seven children, and David is the oldest one, and I was afraid he'd have to go to work, if business was bad, or if I was sick. The state is a good father to the children in America, if the real fathers don't mix in. Why should my David lose his chance to get educated and be somebody, because I am a poor business man, and have too many children? So I made out that he had to go to school two years more."

He narrated this anecdote in the same simple manner in which he had told a dozen others. He seemed pleased to rehearse the little plot whereby he had insured his boy's education. As Miss Ralston did not make any comment immediately, he went on, as if sure of her sympathy.

"I told you I got my citizen papers right away when I came to America. I worked hard before I could bring my family—it took me four years to save the money—and they found a very poor home when they got here, but they were citizens right away. But it would n't do them much good, if they did n't get educated. I found out all about the compulsory education, and I said to myself that's the policeman that will keep me from robbing my David if I fail in business."

He did not overestimate his visitor's sympathy. Miss Ralston followed his story with quick appreciation of his ideals and motives, but in her ingenuous American mind one fact separated itself from the others: namely, that Mr. Rudinsky had falsified his boy's age, and had recorded the falsehood in a public document. Her recognition of the fact carried with it no criticism. She realized that Mr. Rudinsky's conscience was the product of an environment vastly different from hers. It was merely that to her mind the element of deceit was something to be accounted for, be it ever so charitably, whereas in Mr. Rudinsky's mind it evidently had no existence at all.

"So David is really fourteen years old?" she repeated incredulously. "Why, he seems too little even for twelve! Does he know?—Of course he would know! I wonder that he consented—"

She broke off, struck by a sudden thought. "Consented to tell a lie" she had meant to say, but the unspoken words diverted her mind from the conversation. It came upon her in a flash that she had found the key to David's mystery. His note was in her pocketbook, but she knew every word of it, and now everything was plain to her. The lie was this lie about his age, and the person he wanted to shield was his father. And for that he was suffering so!

She began to ask questions eagerly.

"Has David said anything about—about a little trouble he had in school the day he became ill?"

Both parents showed concern.

"Trouble? what trouble?"

"Oh, it was hardly trouble—at least, I could n't tell myself."

"David is so hard to understand sometimes," his father said.

"Oh, I don't think so!" the teacher cried. "Not when you make friends with him. He does n't say much, it's true, but his heart is like a crystal."

"He's too still," the mother insisted, shaking her head. "All the time he's sick, he don't say anything, only when we ask him something. The doctor thinks he's worrying about something, but he don't tell."

The mother sighed, but Miss Ralston cut short her reflections.

"Mrs. Rudinsky—Mr. Rudinsky," she began eagerly, "*I* can tell you what David's troubled about."

And she told them the story of her last talk with David, and finally read them his note.

"And this lie," she ended, "you know what it is, don't you? You've just told me yourself, Mr. Rudinsky."

She looked pleadingly at him, longing to have him understand David's mind as she understood it. But Mr. Rudinsky was very slow to grasp the point.

"You mean—about the certificate? Because I made out that he was younger?"

Miss Ralston nodded.

"You know David has such a sense of honor," she explained, speaking slowly, embarrassed by the effort of following Mr. Rudinsky's train of thought and her own at the same time. "You know how he questions everything—sooner or later he makes everything clear to himself—and something must have started him thinking of this old matter lately—Why, of course! I remember I asked him his age that day, when he tried on the costume, and he answered as usual, and then, I suppose, he suddenly *realized* what he was saying. I don't believe he ever *thought* about it since—since you arranged it so, and now, all of a sudden—"

She did not finish, because she saw that her listeners did not follow her. Both their faces expressed pain and perplexity. After a long silence, David's father spoke.

"And what do *you* think, ma'am?"

Miss Ralston was touched by the undertone of submission in his voice. Her swift sympathy had taken her far into his thoughts. She recognized in his story one of those ethical paradoxes which the helpless Jews of the Pale, in their search for a weapon that their oppressors could not confiscate, have evolved for their self-defense. She knew that to many honest Jewish minds a lie was not a lie when told to an official; and she divined that no ghost of a scruple had disturbed Mr. Rudinsky in his sense of triumph over circumstances, when he invented the lie that was to insure the education of his gifted child. With David, of course, the same philosophy had been valid. His father's plan for the protection of his future, hingeing on a too familiar sophistry, had dropped innocuous into his consciousness; until, in a moment of spiritual sensitiveness, it took on the visage of sin.

"And what do *you* think, ma'am?"

David's father did not have to wait a moment for her answer, so readily did her insight come to his defense. In a few eager sentences she made him feel that she understood him perfectly, and understood David perfectly.

"I respect you the more for that lie, Mr. Rudinsky. It was—a *noble* lie!" There was the least tremor in her voice. "And I love David for the way *he* sees it."

Mr. Rudinsky got up and paced slowly across the room. Then he stopped before Miss Ralston.

"You are very kind to talk like that, Miss Ralston," he said, with peculiar dignity. "You see the whole thing. In the old country we had to do such things so many times that we—got used to them. Here—here we don't have to." His voice took on a musing quality. "But we don't see it right away when we get here. I meant nothing, only just to keep my boy in school. It was not to cheat anybody. The state is willing to educate the children. I said to myself I will tie my own hands, so that I can't pull my child after me if I drown. I did want my David should have the best chance in America."

Miss Ralston was thrilled by the suppressed passion in his voice. She held out her hand to him, saying again, in the low tones that come from the heart, "I am glad I know you, Mr. Rudinsky."

There was unconscious chivalry in Mr. Rudinsky's next words. Stepping to his wife's side, he laid a gentle hand on her shoulder, and said quietly, "My wife has been my helper in everything."

Miss Ralston, as we know, was given to seeing things. She saw now, not a poor immigrant couple in the first stage of American respectability, which was all there was in the room to see, but a phantom procession of men with the faces of prophets, muffled in striped praying-shawls, and women radiant in the light of many candles, and youths and maidens with smouldering depths in their eyes, and silent children who pushed away joyous things for—for—

Dreams don't use up much time. Mr. Rudinsky was not aware that there had been a pause before he spoke again.

"You understand so well, Miss Ralston. But David"—he hesitated a moment, then finished quickly. "How can he respect me if he feels like that?"

His wife spoke tremulously from her corner.

"That's what I think."

"Oh, don't think that!" Miss Ralston cried. "He does respect you—he understands. Don't you see what he says: *I can't tell you—because you would blame somebody who did n't do wrong.* He does n't blame you. He only blames himself. He's afraid to tell me because he thinks *I* can't understand."

The teacher laughed a happy little laugh. In her eagerness to comfort David's parents, she said just the right things, and every word summed up an instantaneous discovery. One of her useful gifts was the ability to find out truths just when she desperately needed them. There are people like that, and some of them are school-teachers hired by the year. When David's father cried, "How can he respect me?" Miss Ralston's heart was frightened while it beat one beat. Only one. Then she knew all David's thoughts between the terrible, "I have lied," and the generous, "But my father did no wrong." She guessed what the struggle had cost to reconcile the contradictions; she imagined his bewilderment as he tried to rule himself by his new-found standards, while seeking excuses for his father in the one he cast away from him as unworthy of an American. Problems like David's are not very common, but then Miss Ralston was good at guessing.

"Don't worry, Mr. Rudinsky," she said, looking out of her glad eyes. "And you, Mrs. Rudinsky, don't think for a moment that David does n't understand. He's had a bad time, the poor boy, but I know—Oh, I must speak to him! Will he wake soon, do you think?"

Mr. Rudinsky left the room without a word.

"It's all right," said David's mother, in reply to an anxious look from Miss Ralston. "He sleeps already the whole afternoon."

It had grown almost dark while they talked. Mrs. Rudinsky now lighted the lamps, apologizing to her guest for not having done so sooner, and then she eased Bennie from his prolonged attendance in the store.

Bennie came into the kitchen chewing his reward, some very gummy confection. He was obliged to lock the pent-up things he wanted to say, until such time as he could clear his clogged talking-gear.

"Teacher," he began, before he had finished swallowing, "What for did you say—"

"Bennie!" his mother reproved him, "You must shame yourself to listen by the door."

"Well, there was n't any trade, ma," he defended himself, "only Bessie Katz, and she brought back the peppermints she bought this morning, to change them for taffy, but I did n't because they were all dirty, and one was broken—"

Bennie never had a chance to bring his speeches to a voluntary stop. Somebody always interrupted. This time it was his father, who came down the stairs, looking so grave that even Bennie was impressed.

"He's awake," said Mr. Rudinsky. "I lighted the lamp. Will you please come up, ma'am?"

He showed her to the room where David lay, and closed the door on them both. It was not he, but Miss Ralston, the American teacher, that his boy needed. He went softly down to the kitchen, where his wife smiled at him through unnecessary tears.

Miss Ralston never forgot the next hour, and David never forgot. The woman always remembered how the boy's eyes burned through the dusk of the shadowed corner where he lay. The boy remembered how his teacher's voice palpitated in his heart, how her cool hands rested on his, how the lamplight made a halo out of her hair. To each of them the dim room with its scant furnishings became a spiritual rendezvous.

What did the woman say, that drew the sting of remorse from the child's heart, without robbing him of the bloom of his idealism? What did she tell him that transmuted the offense of ages into the marrow and blood of persecuted virtue? How did she weld in the boy's consciousness the scraps of his mixed inheritance, so that he saw his whole experience as an unbroken thing at last? There was nobody to report how it was done. The woman did not know, nor the child. It was a secret born of the boy's need and the woman's longing to serve him; just as in nature every want creates its satisfaction.

When she was ready to leave him, Miss Ralston knelt for a moment at David's bedside, and once more took his small, hot hands in hers.

"And I have made a discovery, David," she said, smiling in a way of her own. "Talking with your parents downstairs I saw why it was that the Russian Jews are so soon at home here in our dear country. In the hearts of men like your father, dear, is the true America."

EXPLANATORY NOTES

Antin's Dedication

page

lix [JOSEPHINE LAZARUS] Lazarus (1846–1910) was an essayist, author of *Mystery, Prophecy, Service, Freedom* (1890) and *The Spirit of Judaism* (1895), and the sister of Emma Lazarus (1849–87), famous for the Statue of Liberty poem, "The New Colossus" (1883). Josephine Lazarus had reviewed Antin's first book, *From Plotzk* [the name of Antin's hometown Polotzk was misspelled] *to Boston* (1899), withholding her highest praise only in order not to "bring to self-consciousness a talent whose very charm lies in the absence of self-consciousness." Antin stated in the *New York Sun* (May 4, 1912): "my friend Miss Lazarus, to whom my book is dedicated, talked to me constantly about the autobiography I must some day write. . . . And she always believed that I would write it. For twelve years, from the time she first knew me until her death, she was always reminding me of this thing she wanted done." When Antin started to write, she sent the first chapters to Lazarus who "found in them what she had been waiting for. My one regret is that she did not live to see the completion."

Antin's Introduction

2 [my earlier self as a separate being] In a letter to her *Atlantic Monthly* editor, Ellery Sedgwick, Antin proposed giving the "heroine" a different name from the "author." She suggested "Esther Altmann," an adaptation of her mother's name "Weltman," and the two names together would suggest the meaning "human being from the Old World" (Alt-Weltman).

2 [One who has completed] In the 1910 manuscript of the autobiography, deposited by Antin in the Boston Public Library, the examples of Helen Keller and Booker T. Washington were given to illustrate these sentences.

3 [The Wandering Jew in me] In Eugène Sue's popular novel *Le juif errant* (1844–45), the titular figure—who has seven nails in his shoe that leave cross-shaped footprints—and his sister Herodias are quite marginal. Having met at the Bering Strait at the beginning, they can look forward to their deaths ("We are then forgiven") once the evil Jesuits and villains have been destroyed and working people can anticipate a happier life.

3 [I will write a bold "Finis" at the end] The 1910 manuscript did end with the word "FINIS."

Chapter I. Within the Pale (A version of this chapter appeared under same title in *Atlantic Monthly* in 1911)

5 [Pale] The area extending from Lithuania at the Baltic to the Black Sea of Bessarabia and the Crimea, and from the Russian-German border to a line west of Smolensk and Kharkov, in which Russian Jews were compelled to live by law from 1815 to 1917. See Martin Gilbert, *Russian History Atlas* (New York: Macmillan, 1972), 69–71.

5 [the world was divided into two parts] An allusion to the opening of Caesar, *De bello gallico* (The Gallic Wars).

5 [Polotzk] Antin's hometown, entered in her glossary, had approximately twenty thousand inhabitants at the time she emigrated, about half of them Jews. Mentioned for the first time in 862 as the center of Polochane, it became Lithuanian in the thirteenth century, was briefly conquered by Ivan the Terrible, but reverted to the Commonwealth of Poland and Lithuania. After the first Polish division of 1772, Polotzk became Russian.

10 ["pogrom"] Mob attacks took place in 1881, 1890, 1891, and, most notoriously, in 1903 (in Kishinev). Marshall Sklare, *American Jews: A Reader* (New York: Behrman House, 1983), 14, reports the work of scholars who have questioned the view that the pogroms were the central cause for Jewish mass emigration, pointing to the fact that probably the highest rate of emigration was seen in Galicia, a province that had no pogroms. Causes were in the fivefold expansion of the Jewish population in a weak economy, the development and availability of mass transportation, and the repressive Russian laws Antin reports that created a feeling of hopelessness.

12 [The white church] The St. Sophia Cathedral in Polotzk was built in the eleventh century and transformed into a three-nave basilica in the eighteenth century.

17 [large colored portrait] This passage invites comparison with the description of the portraits of George and Martha Washington, p. 175.

Chapter II. Children of the Law

27 [the Rav of Polotzk] Compare this passage with Antin's short story "Malinke's Atonement."

34 [burning bush] See Exodus 3: 2; see also chapter 18, pp. 251 ff.

Chapter III. Both Their Houses

38 [my grandmother herself carried the boy in her arms] Compare Antin's first day in the Chelsea school, p. 159, and her short story "The Lie."

41 [Prosperity is prosaic] An allusion to Edward Everett Hale; see note for p. 269.

45 [childlessness] Compare the short story "The Amulet."

Chapter IV. Daily Bread (Published in the *Atlantic Monthly* 1911 under title "The House of Bondage")

55 ["Zukrochene Flum"] "Slovenly" or "softhearted plum," or "plum gone to pieces."

57 [our father's strap] The effect of the description of corporal punishment of children (then very common) next to "My Father's Portrait" replicates

the two ways in which he was represented to the children. Antin's euphemistic and even mildly humorous description contrasts sharply with Henry Roth's account of the father's whip in *Call It Sleep* (1934).

Chapter V. I Remember

66 [if not revisited in later years] Here and elsewhere (e.g., p. 75), Antin strongly implies that she has not been back to Polotzk, perhaps because she may have finished the manuscript of her autobiography before taking the European trip in 1910 that brought her back to the scenes of her childhood. In the *New York Sun* (May 4, 1912) Antin was quoted as saying: "My husband was planning a European tour which included Stockholm. As we were studying the maps I suddenly realized how near this would bring me to Polotzk. From Stockholm there is a steamer to Riga and from Riga we could sail up the Dvina to Polotzk. On the map it was not more than a little excursion. I must go to Polotzk! But that idea opened the floodgates of memory. . . . I knew that the time to write had come. I should never be able to reproduce the old life if I let all the new impressions of Polotzk revisited—of the changes I might find—obscure my childish recollections."

68 [the burying-ground of Napoleonic soldiers] Polotzk was the site of two important battles in 1812, when the Napoleonic troops, led by Oudinot and Gouvion-Saint-Cyr, first managed to hold the town, but were ultimately forced to retreat across the Dvina by Wittgenstein's First Russian Corps. Interestingly, Antin does not respond to Napoleon in the way she would to Washington.

71 [Life Universal] The Emersonian side of Antin. Compare, for example, the first main section of Emerson's "Nature" (1836). Antin was exposed to Transcendentalism through Josephine Lazarus.

80 [Esau] Esau sold his birthright to his brother Jacob. See Genesis 26: 30–34.

85 [Froebel kindergarten] Named after Friedrich Froebel (1782–1852), who founded the first kindergarten in Thuringia in 1837.

Chapter VI. The Tree of Knowledge (In the 1910 manuscript, the equivalent chapter IV was entitled "With Rod and Rule")

107 [I used to lie] See Augustine's *Confessions* I. 19.

Chapter VII. The Boundaries Stretch (In the *Atlantic Monthly*, December 1911, under title "The Promised Land")

114 [And "America" became my dream] An early articulation of the notion of "the American dream."

Chapter VIII. The Exodus (The descriptive passages, based on *From Plotzk to Boston*, were inserted into this chapter at a later stage, after the 1910 manuscript).

134 [the epistle, in Yiddish] The letter (see Introduction, p. xxiii) is now at the Boston Public Library. It is identified as "Written and sent to Russia in 1894/ Brought back to America in 1910/ Put between covers for safekeeping in 1914/ by brother John F. Grabau." Antin's narrative that accompanies the Yiddish letter to her uncle Moshe Hayyim Weltman repeats the story of the lamp and the kerosene-soaked letter. But then the account, dated March 2, 1914, begins to vary:

> My father obliged me to make a fair copy to be sent to Polotzk, and the stained original he preserved. About two years later, he and Miss Dillingham between them persuaded me to translate the letter into English, and in 1899 the English version was published. . . . By the time I got to the English translation, I was tired of the whole thing, and I found my chief satisfaction in tearing up the oil-stained (Yiddish) original, a sheet at a time, as I was done with it. But the fair copy I had made so reluctantly turned up again, at a time when I was better able to appreciate it as a document.
>
> At the end of 1910, nearly seventeen years after it was written, I found it in the possession of my uncle, Berl Weltman, in Wilna, where I spent a few days on my way to revisit Polotzk. The letter had circulated widely in Polotzk, had been sent around to various branches of the family in different parts of Russia, finally winding up in Wilna. There it had been miraculously preserved during the revolutionary period of 1905, when everybody made it a point to destroy useless papers of every description, so as to have the fewer questions to answer when the police came to make domiciliary searches. (*Ms.Am.178, BPL)

136 [The Schidorsky brothers were Jews] In *From Plotzk to Boston* (1899), Antin writes somewhat differently: "I was aware of something like the sweet presence of angels in the persons of good Schidorsky and his family. I . . . said to myself, thinking of our benefactor, that he was a Jew, a true 'Son of Mercy.' " And in the 1910 manuscript, Mr. Schidorsky's ethnic background is not given at all.

141 [Our turn came at last] An interesting episode is omitted here. In *From Plotzk to Boston*, an old woman was desperately trying to find matzo, since there would be no kosher food on board. When the overseer tells her, "You can go and get your matzo, but the boat won't wait for you," everybody is in a dilemma: "She said she wasn't going to start on a dangerous journey with such a sin on her soul. Then the children decided. They understood the matter. They cried and begged to follow the party. And we did." Fortunately, just at that moment, the cook comes and brings matzo. "How relieved we were then!"

141 [a great big steamship] The Antins came on the *Polynesia* and landed in Boston on May 8, 1894.

Chapter IX. The Promised Land

152 [them in] The first edition had an error here and read "the min."

153 ["America is not Polotzk"] See also pp. 196 and 213.

158 [I wish, for my comfort] In the 1910 manuscript, the following episode, focusing on Antin's receiving preferential treatment over her sister, centers on the father's forging of Mashke/Mary's age. As a result of her father's ruse, Antin could go to school but had to pretend for many years to be two years younger than she actually was, whereas her sister Fetchke/Frieda had to start working. See p. xxvii of the Introduction, and compare the story "The Lie."

Chapter X. Initiation

165 [the Lord's Prayer] The 1910 manuscript reads "Our Father." Compare the title of chapter IV.

167 [SNOW] The somewhat different original text of this essay, entitled "The History of a Snow-Crystal," dated September 12, 1895, is preserved in the Boston Public Library.

Chapter XI. "My Country" ("The Making of a Citizen," *Atlantic Monthly*, February 1912, contains a version of this chapter starting from page 237)

176 [Even if I had never, never told a lie] This statement would have resonated with the confession about the age change in the 1910 manuscript. See the note for page 158.

186 [When the paper with my poem] I did not find the poem in the editions of the *Herald* surrounding Washington's birthday in 1895 or 1896.

Chapter XII. Miracles

197 [The heir of the ages] Antin had thought of calling the book "The Heir of the Ages" but had been told that this "has not a challenging sound." Ellery Sedgwick agreed, for he found that the phrase had "something of the taint of religiosity." It is biblically inspired (Paul's letters to the Hebrews 1: 2 and to the Romans 5: 13), and Antin may also have drawn it from John Fiske or Henry James.

Chapter XIII. A Child's Paradise

200 [a man who fills a chair at a great university] Probably an allusion to the paleontologist Amadeus William Grabau (1870–1946), whom Antin met at the Natural History Club, married in 1901, but never names in *The Promised Land*.

201 [the Rollo books] Jacob Abbott (1803–79) was the prolific author of numerous books featuring Rollo, such as *Rollo at School* (1839), *Rollo at Play* (1845), and *Rollo at Work* (1855).

Chapter XIV. Manna

207 [Wheeler Street] Sam Bass Warner, Jr., who identified the address as 11 Wheeler Street, also noted, that the street "no longer exists; its houses have been thrown down and its land incorporated into a housing project, Turnpike Towers, on a triangular plot bounded by Shawmut Avenue, Tremont Street, and Corning Street, next to the Massachusetts Turnpike."

213 [race suicide] The notion prevalent among eugenicists of the period was that the "superior stocks" had so low a birthrate that it might doom them to extinction if they did not procreate more or did not prohibit free immigration and curb the fertility of "inferior races." See Myre St. Wald Iseman, *Race Suicide* (New York: The Cosmopolitan Press, 1912).

Chapter XV. Tarnished Laurels

219 [Graduation Day] Antin graduated from the Winthrop School eighth grade in 1897.

Chapter XVI. Dover Street (See "A Kingdom in the Slums," *Atlantic Monthly*, March 1912)

224 [Dover Street] Now East Berkeley Street.
229 [Mr. Tetlow] Sedgwick identifies him as Mr. Tuttle.
230 [I entered the Latin School] According to Sam Bass Warner, Jr., Antin enrolled in the Boston Girls' Latin School, class of 1901, but never graduated, her class biography listing her merely under the category "attended."
233 [the dim tangle of railroad tracks below] The tracks leading toward South Station also provide a sense of connection between worlds. See, for example, pp. 5, 70, 121f., and 133–40.

Chapter XVIII. The Burning Bush

253 [Hale House] Now torn down and replaced by garages.

Chapter XIX. A Kingdom in the Slums (A version of this chapter appeared in the *Atlantic Monthly*, April 1912, under the title "The Immigrant's Portion")

265 [Public Library] Antin appreciates in the library, designed by McKim, Mead, & White and erected in 1888–95, what Henry James found missing, when he wrote in *The American Scene* (1907): "The Boston institution then is a great and complete institution, with this reserve of its striking the restored absentee as practically without *penetralia*. A library without *penetralia* may affect him but as a temple without altars; it will at any rate exemplify the distinction between a benefit given and a benefit taken, a borrowed, a lent, and an owned, an appropriated convenience."

269 [Edward Everett Hale] (1822–1909), a Boston clergyman, philanthropist, and writer who became best known as the author of the novella "The Man Without a Country" (1863), to the title of which Antin alludes (p. 178).

She also thought that the heading of the chapter "My Country"—which she considered as a possible title for the book as a whole—echoed Hale. Antin cites Hale's maxim, "Personal presence moves the world" (p. 183) and, in *They Who Knock at Our Gates* (1914), Antin invokes Hale's prayer, "Deliver us, O Lord! from our terrible prosperity." Hale's book *Ten Times One is Ten* (1870) inspired the founding of charitable societies under the motto "Lend a hand."

271 [Miss Hale] The painter Ellen Day Hale (1855–1940).

272 Bergland, 71–72, ponders the question whether Antin or Hale's daughter might be seen in the photograph of Hale's study on page 272. In the reproduction of this photograph in *The Bookman* (August 1912), included in the Antin scrapbook, the subtitle reads "Mary Antin in Edward Everett Hale's Library."

277 [pitch rubbish through their windows] Compare Antin's short story "First Aid to the Alien," in which a kind American professor teaches an immigrant child: "*Never* throw rubbish out of *any* window. That's not *American*."

Chapter XX. The Heritage

285 [I was in a dream] A 78 rpm recording was made of the page from here to the end of the book, omitting only the sentence starting with "I sank down. . . ." The record, Columbia label CO 29895, 36264, E 6-12, is preserved at the New York Public Library at Lincoln Center.

Appendix. How I Wrote *The Promised Land*

296 [The creator of Emmy Lou] See George Madden Martin (1866–1936), *Emmy Lou: Her Book & Heart* (New York: McClure, Phillips, 1902); Maggie Tulliver in George Eliot, *The Mill on the Floss* (1860); and Mark Twain, *The Adventures of Tom Sawyer* (1876).